"*This book is filled with useful tools, resources, and advice that will help business owners get affordable and flexible financing.*"
—Ken Yancey
Executive Director,
SCORE

"*I wish that entrepreneurs that pitch our 'business angels' would first listen to Asheesh Advani's commonsense advice about funding their businesses—great tips, documents and examples.*"
—John May,
Chair, Angel Capital Association

"*Unlike most writing about venture capital and small business financing, this book is simple and practical and full of solutions that will actually apply to real businesses in the real world.*"
—Tim Berry,
President of Palo Alto Software,
Author of *Business Plan Pro*

"*Loans from relatives and friends are a common form of small business finance, but this is the first book to address the topic comprehensively.*"
—Howard Stevenson, Professor,
Harvard Business School
Co-Author of *Winning Angels: The Seven Fundamentals of Early-Stage Investing*

"*This book is a must-read for entrepreneurs of all ages. Getting financing is difficult, but using the tools provided in this book will make it considerably easier.*"
—Steve Mariotti,
Founder and President, National Foundation for Teaching Entrepreneurship (NFTE)

"A vital resource for entrepreneurs seeking early-stage business financing. This books guides you every step of the way."

—David Verrill,
Managing Director,
Hub Angels Investment Group

"I highly recommend Asheesh Advani's well-written book to all entrepreneurs seeking private money for their businesses."

—William Bygrave,
Frederic C. Hamilton Professor for Free
Enterprise, Babson College
Co-Founder, Global Entrepreneurship
Monitor (GEM)

always up to date

The law changes, but Nolo is always on top of it! We offer several
ways to make sure you and your Nolo products are always up to date:

Nolo's Legal Updater

We'll send you an email whenever a new edition of your book
is published! Sign up at **www.nolo.com/legalupdater**.

Updates @ Nolo.com

Check **www.nolo.com/update** to find recent changes
in the law that affect the current edition of your book.

3

Nolo Customer Service

To make sure that this edition of the book is the most
recent one, call us at **800-728-3555** and ask one of
our friendly customer service representatives.
Or find out at **www.nolo.com**.

please note

Investors
in Your Backyard

How to Raise Business Capital
From the People You Know

By Asheesh Advani

NOLO

First Edition	FEBRUARY 2006
Editor	ILONA BRAY
Cover Design	TERRI HEARSH
Book Design	TERRI HEARSH
Proofreading	JOE SADUSKY
Index	BAYSIDE INDEXING SERVICE
Printing	CONSOLIDATED PRINTERS, INC.

Advani, Asheesh, 1971-.
  Investors in your backyard : how to raise business capital from people you know / by
Asheesh Advani
    p. cm.
  ISBN 1-4133-0420-6
  1. Small business--Finance. 2. Business enterprises--Finance. 3. Fund raising. 4.
Self-financing. 5. Commercial loans. I. Title

HG4027.7.A35 2005
658.15'8--dc22

2005051818

Quanity sales: For information on bulk purchases or corporate premium sales,
please contact the Special Sales Department. For academic sales or textbook
adoptions, ask for Academic Sales. 800-955-4775, Nolo, 950 Parker Street,
Berkeley, CA 94710.

Acknowledgments

I would like to express my gratitude to Helen Payne Watt, who served as the project manager for the research and writing of this book and enclosed CD. A book of this nature is drawn from the experiences and learning of several people. Helen was able to collect and synthesize the wisdom of many individuals, including a nationwide sampling of CircleLending's clients engaged in private loans. Thanks as well to the book's editor, Ilona Bray, whose vision of the final product guided this book from the start. Without Ilona's meticulous editing, this book would look more like a Ph.D. thesis than a reader-friendly resource. It is the yin and yang of Helen and Ilona that has contributed most to the quality of this book.

I would also like to thank the following individuals for generously contributing their time and professional wisdom to the project: Bob Baum, Grant Brown, Bill Bygrave, Charles Christman, Mike Dumbroski, Danvers Fleury, Jon Kasle, Meaghan Loughnane, Matt Maloney, Richard Mandel, Andrew Michel, Meara Murphy, Dan Narahara, David Richards, Jim Robichau, Jim Smith, Kevin Walker, and Bonnie Weinberg. I'm especially grateful for the expert contributions of Brett Magun, Shawn Megathlin, Eric Silverman, and Jeff Steele.

Finally, I would like to thank my wife who, with stunning patience and skill, balanced managing her own organization with being a new mother and miraculously ensured that our infant twin boys slept through the night for the duration of this project.

About the Author

Asheesh Advani is the founder and chief executive of CircleLending, a loan administration company based in Cambridge, Massachusetts. The company provides a full range of services for managing financial transactions between relatives, friends, and other private parties (see www.circlelending.com). Asheesh has worked with the World Bank in Washington, DC and written for Entrepreneur magazine.

Table of Contents

Getting the Most From This Book

A. Who Can Access This Kind of Financing 2

B. Deciding Which Parts of This Book to Read 4

1 Readying Your Business to Attract Private Financing

A. Financing Options for Your Start-Up Business 14

B. How Your Business's Legal Structure Can Advance— or Hold Back—Your Fundraising 27

2 What's in It for Both Entrepreneur and Investor?

A. What's in It for You, the Entrepreneur? 36

B. What's in It for Your Investor? 42

C. Mixing Money and Relationships Can Work 49

3 Your Financing Choices: Gifts, Loans, and Equity Investments

A. Basic Setup and Handling of a Gift 55

B. Basic Setup and Handling of a Loan 57

C. Basic Setup and Handling of an Equity Investment 61

D. Choosing Between Loan and Equity Capital 67

E. Tax Implications of Your Choice of Capital 67

4 Deciding Who to Ask for Money

A. Developing Your List of Prospects 78

B. Evaluating Each Prospect 89

5 Preparing Your Business Plan and Your Fundraising Request

A. Preparing Your Business Plan 100

B. Calculating the Amount of Your Request 107

C. Dividing Up Your Request Among Prospects 111

6 Developing Your Loan Request

A. Deciding Your Loan Terms 117

B. Drafting Your Loan Request Letter 136

7 Making the "Kitchen Table Pitch"

A. Planning How You'll Approach Your Prospective Lender 144

B. Making a Compelling Pitch 149

C. Handling Hesitancy and Concerns 156

D. After Your Prospect Says "Yes" (or "Maybe") 160

E. After Your Prospect Says "No" 167

8 Seeking Equity Capital

A. Where to Look for an Equity Investor 172

B. How to Ask for Equity Capital 184

C. Additional Steps That Professional Equity Investors May Request 199

9 The Final Agreement and Money Transfer

A. Why Documentation Is Important 216

B. Preparing a Gift Letter 223

C. Formalizing a Loan With a Promissory Note 225

D. Participating in the Preparation of the Stock Purchase Agreement 241

E. How to Close the Deal 257

10 Your Ongoing Relationship With the People Who Financed You

A. Communicating Your Progress 262

B. If You Received Loan Capital 270

C. If You Received Equity Investments 284

Appendixes

A How to Use the CD-ROM

A. Installing the Files Onto Your Computer 291

B. Using the Word Processing Files to Create Documents 291

C. Using the UCC Financing Statement 295

D. Accessing the Online Resources 297

B Forms and Worksheets

Best Bets List...300

Start-Up Costs Worksheet...301

Recurring Costs Worksheet...302

Collateral List 303

Loan Request Letter..304

Letter of Intent: Simple Version 306

Letter of Intent: Advanced Version...................................307

Gift Letter: Basic 308

Gift Letter: Loan Repayment Forgiveness..........................309

Promissory Note (for an amortized loan)...........................310

Promissory Note (for a graduated loan) 312

Promissory Note (for a seasonal loan)...............................315

Promissory Note (for an interest-only loan).......................318

Promissory Note Modifications for a Loan to a Business 320

Promissory Note Modifications for Signature by Notary Public 321

Security Agreement...322

UCC Financing Statement 325

Loan Log..327

C Online Small-Business Resources

A. Business Planning Resources..330

B. Loan Resources...334

C. Equity Resources 336

D Sample Equity Investing Documents

Term Sheet...340

Series A Preferred Stock Purchase Agreement.....................360

Index

Introduction

Getting the Most From This Book

A. Who Can Access This Kind of Financing 2

B. Deciding Which Parts of This Book to Read 4

Some people say that it's easiest to raise business capital if you don't really need it. However, if you're like most people who are starting or growing a business, you really do need capital—and you're well aware of the challenges of finding it. You can't very well buy equipment, hire people, pay for office space, and fund marketing without some capital.

But if you've already looked into bank loans and other commercial loans, you may have found that they're not designed for start-ups with unpredictable cash flows and will end up costing you a bundle in interest and fees. And if you've approached venture capital firms, you've probably already discovered that the odds of getting these big-leaguers to support a seed-stage company are worse than the odds of your becoming a professional athlete.

So, where do you go to find money that's available, flexible, and affordable? The answer is as close as your own backyard. Your relatives, friends, business associates, and other people you know are among the best sources of small business financing available.

A. Who Can Access This Kind of Financing

Is this book just for people with rich friends or incredibly sympathetic relatives? Not at all. Many more entrepreneurs than you might expect started their businesses with informal loans, investments, or even gifts. These are practical, time-tested financing sources. In fact, half of the CEOs asked in the 2004 Inc. 500 survey of the nation's fastest-growing private companies said that family was involved when they raised their start-up capital—as compared to a mere 7% who said they were funded by formal venture capital. (To see the survey, go to www.inc.com, then click on the Inc. 500 tab.)

Nor is it just a tiny handful of Americans who make informal investments. A total of 5% of Americans invested privately in someone else's business between 2000 and 2003. That's nearly 15 million Americans, and over half of those folks invested in the business of a relative or close friend. In dollar terms, these investments (most of which are loans) from friends, relatives, and associates add up to around $108 billion every year, or almost 1% of the nation's gross domestic product (GDP). Any way you slice it, millions of businesses benefit from informal investing. (Note: These statistics came from an annual worldwide study called the Global Entrepreneurship Monitor, found at www.gemconsortium.org, which evaluates the role of informal investments—their term for private loans and investments—in small business financing. We'll refer to this study elsewhere in this book as the "GEM Study," and you'll find a link to the 2003 U.S. Report in Appendix C.)

The real surprise shouldn't be that informal investing is so common; it's that one hears so little buzz about it on the street. Almost no in-depth, how-to articles or books had been written on the topic before this one, and believe me, we scoured the market. Perhaps the reason is that the very idea of borrowing from friends and family still inspires fear or misunderstanding. Entrepreneurs like you may wonder:

> ### UPS Began With a Loan From a Friend
>
> In 1907, Jim Casey borrowed $100 from a friend to start a bicycle messenger business in Seattle, Washington. In 1919, the business expanded from Seattle to Oakland and changed its name to United Parcel Service. Today, UPS is the world's largest package delivery company, with over $36 billion in sales. (See www.ups.com/content/us/en/about.)

- "Won't everyone say 'no'?"
- "If they do finance me, what happens if the business fails and I can't make good on the loan or investment?"
- "How will the money impact our personal relationship?"
- "Will my relatives and friends meddle in the business or bring up awkward questions at social events?"

Undeniably, there are emotional pitfalls to these transactions, along with financial risks and administrative requirements. But with preparation, understanding, and a few legal forms—all of which you'll find in this book—these pitfalls can, in most cases, be successfully overcome. I've already seen it happen in hundreds of cases. Five years ago, I started a business, CircleLending, Inc., that focuses on just this type of financing—we manage private loans between relatives, friends, and business associates. (In fact, many of the profiles in this book are of CircleLending clients, although in most cases their names and other identifying information have been changed.) The company now has clients in over 40 states and is the only business in the United States to set up and manage private loans.

In order to start CircleLending, I personally raised several million dollars from over 75 private investors, including many relatives, friends, and business associates. By now, I've got a good idea of how a wide variety of entrepreneurs can make informal financing work for them.

B. Deciding Which Parts of This Book to Read

The process of raising money from people you know has a natural beginning, middle, and end. You'll need to carefully consider whom to approach, prepare your request, approach your chosen prospects, draw up legal documents with those who've said "yes," and fulfill your obligations after the money has changed hands. To see the whole picture, I recommend that you read this book in its entirety.

But in case you're not the linear type or are already partway down the fundraising path, you might choose to drop into this book at the appropriate chapter, based on the snapshot descriptions below.

Chapter 1 provides a crash course in two small business basics you'll need to start raising funds for your business: the range of financing options available to you, and how the legal structure you've chosen or will choose for your business (sole proprietorship, partnership, corporation, or LLC) will affect your fundraising possibilities. Set the stage for raising money by knowing your financing options and by making sure

> ### Wal-Mart's Beginnings Included a Loan From Sam Walton's Father-in-Law
>
> The founder of Wal-Mart, Sam Walton, bought his first retail store in 1945 for $25,000 by borrowing $20,000 from his father-in-law, L.S. Robson, and using $5,000 of his own savings. Two and a half years later, Sam repaid his father-in-law. Today, Wal-Mart Stores, Inc. is the world's largest retailer, with around $300 billion in annual sales. (See Sam Walton's biography at http://en.wikipedia.org.)

your business is structured to properly handle the capital you raise.

Chapter 2 reveals how both you and your borrowers or investors have something to gain from your transaction, thus allowing you to feel less like a beggar and more like someone offering a financial opportunity. Because the prospect of mixing money and relationships nevertheless causes some folks discomfort, this chapter details exactly how you can structure the loan or investment to minimize real or imagined concerns.

Chapter 3 leads you into the gritty details of business finance, to help you decide what kind of money you

Subway Sandwich Chain Began With a Loan From a Family Friend

When Fred DeLuca graduated from high school in the summer of 1965, his family didn't even have enough money to pay for college tuition. At a reunion barbecue, he asked a visiting older family friend, Dr. Buck, for advice. Dr. Buck suggested Fred open a sandwich shop, and they talked over how such a business would work. Later, as he was leaving, Dr. Buck wrote Fred a check for $1,000. Today, Subway lays claim to being the world's largest submarine sandwich chain, with more than 21,000 restaurants in 75 countries. (See the company history at www.subway.com.)

want to raise for your business. Capital—the common term for money used to grow a business—can come to you in three forms, either as a loan, a gift, or an equity investment.

The vast majority of capital raised by small business owners from people they know comes in the form of a loan, where the lender expects repayment; therefore, this book will cover the topic of private borrowing in detail.

Some lucky entrepreneurs are able to raise gift capital from friends or family (with no expectation of repayment or other compensation) to launch their business. If that describes you, you'll find a section in Chapter 3 and references throughout the book on how to handle gifting and gift capital.

Finally, you may also be toying with the idea of raising equity capital from people you know. This means you would sell a stake—an ownership share in your business—to an outside investor. Instead of repayment, your investor would realize a return on his or her investment either or by receiving dividends, which are cash payments taken from company profits, or upon what is known as "exit" (usually when either the company or the investor's shares in it are sold). Equity capital is a hot topic in the universe of small business finance. Chapter 3 spells out some of the advantages and disadvantages of equity capital, and explains why so-called "business angels" are probably a better source of equity for you than venture capitalists, the more widely known option.

After these introductory chapters, we'll dive into the details of how to raise capital from people you know. In Chapter 4, you'll learn how to draw on your circle of contacts and create a list of people whom you might approach with your request. You'll learn who should go at the top of your list. We'll also help you start considering what might motivate your different prospects to agree to your proposal, and how to vary your approach accordingly.

Chapter 5 provides an introduction to two more essential tasks: writing a business plan and calculating the amount of your request.

Once these pieces are in place, if you've decided to raise loan capital, the next step is to prepare your loan request, as outlined in Chapter 6. If you've decided to raise equity capital, there's a bit more to learn about

---

Motown Records Began With a Loan From a Family Member

In 1959, the founder of Motown Records, Berry Gordy, Jr., was working on the Ford assembly line in Detroit and writing and producing songs on the side. He had an extraordinary eye for talent and decided to start his own record company, for which he borrowed $800 from his family. He called it "Tamla Records." Some minor and major hits followed. Gordy separately launched Motown records a few years later, and the company became not only a major label that created its own influential musical style, but one of the largest black-owned businesses in U.S. history.

the kind of folks who make equity investments. You should skip ahead momentarily to Chapter 8 to see who equity investors are, where to find them, and what to expect from setting up an equity investment.

After you've identified your prospects, it will be time to ask them for money. Chapter 7 is a step-by-step guide to making your loan request, and in Chapter 8 you'll find a similar section on how to make a request for an equity investment. Although I can't script your conversation for you, I will give you tips on making it comfortable for you and the other person and on handling the various responses you might encounter.

Once you and your lender or investor have shaken hands or otherwise agreed to a financial arrangement, the final step is to formalize the agreement with legally binding documents and to transfer the funds. Documenting the agreement is one of the most significant things you can do to mitigate the risks associated with a private loan or investment, and Chapter 9 provides the sample documents and other tools to achieve that.

> ### The Limited Began With a Loan From the Founder's Aunt
>
> Know the trendy clothing store called The Limited? In 1963, after a disagreement with his Russian immigrant father about how to run the family clothing shop, Leslie Wexner borrowed $5,000 from his aunt to open a small women's retail shop called Leslie's Limited. The Limited now operates around 5,600 U.S. stores and earns $10.1 billion in annual revenues. (See Wexner's biography at http://en.wikipedia.org)

The closing of the deal is also the opening of your new relationship with your lender or investor. Chapter 10 explains what your new legal obligations are, and suggests ways—above and beyond your legal obligations—to keep your lenders or investors happy.

Throughout the book, you'll find worksheets, sample forms, and letters as well as references to additional resources. The samples are gathered in the back of the book in Appendixes B and D, and the resource lists are gathered in Appendix C. In addition, enclosed on the back cover you'll find a CD-ROM containing electronic versions of the worksheets and sample forms and letters, as well as links to online loan calculators and additional state-by-state listings of resources.

Words You'll Need to Know

I've tried to keep the business jargon to a minimum in this book. However, for clarity's sake, I've chosen a few words to refer to some of the important people and concepts described here.

Investors. In its most technical meaning, this refers to equity investors, that is, people who buy shares in a business and thus become a co-owner. However, in this book, I'll use "investor" more broadly to refer to anyone who makes a loan, gift, or equity investment in support of your business. My reasoning is that people who provide money—regardless of the type—to the businesses of people they know tend to think of themselves as "investors." The word connotes the individual's personal as well as financial support for the business and the entrepreneur. (Nevertheless, in later chapters when we start discussing making and documenting your actual agreements with people, it will be necessary to distinguish among the three types of capital, and I'll refer separately to "borrowers," "lenders," "equity investors," and "gift givers," as separately defined below.)

Borrower. A person or organization (probably you, the entrepreneur, or your business) who receives money that you promise to repay.

Lender. A person (or organization) who loans you money expecting that you will repay it, over time, usually with interest.

Gift giver. Someone who gives you money with no legal strings attached. In fact, this category would hardly be worth discussing, if it weren't that the IRS can tax certain gifts.

Equity investor. A person or organization who buys shares in your business.

Informal loan, private loan, friends-and-family loan, interpersonal loan. All of these terms refer to a loan between private parties, as opposed to a loan from a bank, a company, or another organization. Be careful not to confuse these with "personal loans," which refer to a loan (from any type of lender) to be used for a personal purpose other than a business or a home—for example, for education, for a new vehicle, to pay down debts, or for an emergency.

Icons Used in This Book

 Warning. This icon cautions you to slow down and consider potential problems.

 See an expert. This icon lets you know when to seek the advice of a lawyer, accountant, or other expert.

 Fast track. This icon indicates that you may be able to skip certain material that may not be relevant to your situation.

 Recommended reading. This icon is used to make note of other books or resources for more information about a particular issue or topic.

 Tip. This icon signals a special suggestion that will help make your financing search go smoothly—or will assure that legal requirements are met.

Chapter 1

Readying Your Business to Attract Private Financing

A. Financing Options for Your Start-Up Business 14

   1. Minimizing the Amount You'll Need 15

   2. Using Your Own Money First 16

   3. Finding Cash in Existing Business Resources 18

   4. Asking Family and Friends for Money 19

   5. Visiting a Bank or Other Lender 20

   6. Seeking Out Business Angels, Not Venture Capital Investors 25

B. How Your Business's Legal Structure Can Advance—
or Hold Back—Your Fundraising 27

   1. Sole Proprietorship 28

   2. Partnership 29

   3. C Corporation 30

   4. S Corporation 31

   5. Limited Liability Company (LLC) 32

I f you were to ask random people on the street where they thought most small businesses got their start-up money, they'd probably answer, "From banks." They'd be wrong. Although banks might be eager to step in after your infant business has started to walk, they're likely to remain notably absent during its labor pains and birth. Most small businesses need to make creative use of personal resources, draw on their credit cards, and get financial help from friends, family, and associates in these early stages. And that's not necessarily a bad thing. This book was written to help you understand why money from people you know is the best financing option for many start-up businesses—and how to make it work for you.

If you do a little digging into business history, you'll find that borrowing money from family and friends is the stuff of entrepreneurial legend. But these success stories don't mean that you should just start ringing up wealthy relatives, or hitting up neighbors at the block party, without some preparation. Whether your business is at the dream stage, the planning stage, or actually up and running, you essentially won't know what to ask for until you:

- take stock of your options for start-up financing (see Section A, below), and
- understand the fundraising implications of your business's chosen legal structure (see Section B, below).

Small businesses in the United States represent 99.7% of all businesses and generate 60-80% of new jobs each year. (*Source:* Small Business Profiles for the States and Territories, 2005 Edition, U.S. Small Business Administration (SBA).)

Florist Uses Family Loan to Overcome Poor Credit Rating

When Jack Jones needed funds to open his flower shop (Jack's Flowers in Rockport, Massachusetts), he approached his sister for a loan. "To own my own business—a creative business—has been my dream from a fairly young age," said Jack. Unfortunately, though a master at dreaming, Jack wasn't always good at handling money. He'd racked up a history of not paying his bills on time, which had led to repossession of his car and a less-than-mediocre credit rating.

So, when Jack felt ready to raise funds for his flower business, he figured that going to a bank would involve "a lot of paperwork and possibly end in rejection."

But Jack believed that his older sister, Grace, would support his plans. To prove that he was serious about paying her back, Jack wrote up a formal loan request and proposed a repayment schedule that he knew he could meet. Grace agreed to the loan. "Where Jack is concerned, my head said, 'Uh-oh, don't do this,' but my heart said, 'He's my brother.' I ended up bridging the conflict between my heart and my mind by formalizing the loan with a promissory note," Grace says. She knows loaning her brother money is always a gamble, but she says he has a special kind of collateral. "I won't be happy if he defaults on the loan. I really don't expect it, but it's not like I will kick myself for loaning my brother money. I love him and was able to help him and it's all good karma."

The pair set up a $10,000 loan with 7.4% interest, to be repaid monthly for four years. Jack successfully repaid the entire loan. His reliable repayment record led his sister to make him a second loan a few years later, to open up a second shop in nearby Gloucester.

Jack's Flowers is now doing well and, most important, so is Jack and Grace's relationship. Of private lending, Jack says," I think it's a good way of borrowing money, of getting the capital you need to get past some sort of financial obstacle, without going through a bank."

A. Financing Options for Your Start-Up Business

Money from friends, relatives, and associates is only one of many sources that entrepreneurs like you might use to launch and grow a business. Let's take a closer look at all your possible sources, to see where this particular type of financing fits in.

The first table in this section lists sources of capital—loans or equity investments (purchases of ownership shares)—generally available to businesses. The second table matches each source of capital with the stage at which it becomes a realistic option for a growing business. You won't be surprised to see that most entrepreneurs use their personal savings, help from family and friends, and similar informal sources to get their business going.

The reason for this is that, put bluntly, most entrepreneurs don't have any other choice. Even if you're still wary of asking for money from people you know, they may be your most realistic option while your business is young and you have no or very few customers. Until your business begins generating significant revenue, you are only the tiniest dot on the radar screen of banks, venture capitalists, and other institutional investors. Research and common sense reveal that your best bet at this early stage is to seek the money you need from within your own resources, any business assets you've already put in place, and your circle of contacts.

Primary Sources of Financing for a Growing Business	
Source of Financing	**Description**
Entrepreneur's personal resources	Salary from current job, savings, home equity, retirement plan, credit cards
Relatives	A gift, a loan, or an equity investment
Friends, mentors, former employers, business associates	A gift, a loan, or an equity investment
Suppliers	Extension of trade credit
Business angels	Loan or equity investment
Banks and commercial lenders	Commercial loan
Venture capital	Equity investment

Typical Sources of Financing by Stage of Business

Stage	Research	Commitment to Start Business	Product Development	Launch	Early Growth	Growth Problems/Barriers	Mid-life Growth	Maturity
Level of revenue	0	0	Under $100K	Under $100K	Under $500K	$500K-$1M	Over $1M	Over $5M
Entrepreneur's personal resources	✓	✓	✓	✓				
Relatives		✓	✓	✓				
Friends, mentors, former employers, business associates			✓	✓	✓			
Suppliers			✓	✓	✓	✓	✓	✓
Business angels			✓	✓	✓	✓		
Banks and commercial lenders			✓	✓	✓	✓	✓	✓
Venture capital			✓	✓	✓	✓	✓	✓

1.   Minimizing the Amount You'll Need

Before you start planning to ask your Aunt Millie for a million dollars, think pragmatically about how much money you'll really need to launch your business. Experts recommend you start on a shoestring. Pouring too much money into a business at the beginning can be a mistake— and it's a mistake that many entrepreneurs make. A fair number of small businesses fail in their first year, so you're only asking for trouble if you raise and spend a lot of money, particularly for an untested business idea.

Starting on a shoestring means making the most of every dollar you have and not incurring costs that aren't absolutely necessary. For example, do you really need that corner office in the newly renovated industrial building downtown? Or can you get your enterprise going from your garage? Do you have to buy a new computer, or can you use the household computer after the kids' homework is done? Can you lease, rather than buy, space and equipment? Some say that a true entrepreneur sees an opportunity where others see a resource shortage. The more you can do with less, the further you'll be able to grow your business, and the better your prospects will look when you begin seeking external money.

Leasing rather than buying expensive equipment is one of the most cost-effective ways to avoid sinking too much money into an untested business. For example, your fine textiles business may depend on that 19th century, $45,000 loom you found; but until you're actually selling the $500 all-natural blankets it can produce, you might be better off leasing it (on a monthly basis) from the owner first. By lowering your monthly outlay, you also save your start-up cash for other items that you have no choice but to purchase with cash, such as printed materials and office supplies.

You may need less total start-up capital than you think. According to an Inc. 500 analysis of America's fastest-growing companies in 2000:
- 16% started with less than $1,000 in capital.
- 42% started with less than $10,000 in capital.
- 58% started with less than $20,000 in capital.

2. Using Your Own Money First

You probably already have first-hand experience digging into your own pocket to get your business going. Typically, at the earliest stages, entrepreneurs rely on personal resources, including savings and credit cards. See "Checking All Your Pockets for Cash," below, for some of the places you might go to scrounge up start-up money of your own.

Checking All Your Pockets for Cash

To make sure you haven't forgotten any possible sources of your own money, consider the options below:

- **Your salary.** Don't give up your day job! A steady income, even if you reduce from full time to part time as you get your business off the ground, can keep you solvent.
- **Personal savings.** You might use savings accumulated over the years, or a lump sum payment you've received, such as an inheritance or a severance package.
- **Equity in your home.** You can use the equity in your home—the difference between what the home is worth and the remainder due on the mortgage—to generate cash in a few different ways. You could refinance the home with a larger mortgage that pays off the old one and yields some extra cash for you. Or, you could get a line of credit, where the bank takes out a second mortgage on your home and gives you a checkbook allowing you to write checks up to the amount of your loan.
- **A loan from your retirement plan.** Check the terms of your plan carefully, but if loans are allowed for business purposes, this may be a good use of your own money. Plus, you'll be paying interest back to yourself. But be careful in borrowing from an IRA; it may be treated as a withdrawal and you'll have to pay a penalty tax to the IRS if you're not yet 59 ½ years old. For more information, see the article "Getting Your Retirement Money Early—Without Penalty" in the Property & Money section of Nolo's website at www.nolo.com.
- **Your credit cards.** Credit cards are a convenient, short-term way to finance your business. In fact, 68% of U.S. small business owners say they have relied on credit cards for business purposes at some point. Obviously, they're a terrible long-term method, since their interest rates can exceed 20% if you take a long time to pay.

For an expanded discussion of these points, see *Legal Guide for Starting & Running a Small Business*, by Fred S. Steingold (Nolo).

But do you have to dig into your own pockets? The short answer is "yes." No one else is going to believe in your business if you don't—and to prove your belief, you'll need to put your own "skin in the game," at least to the extent you can afford it. Some lenders or investors may want to see you exhaust your savings account, max out your credit cards, and borrow against any home equity, 401(k), or other retirement accounts before you begin reaching for their money.

Just how deeply you dip into your personal well will be used by some private investors as a criterion for getting involved. I've heard it referred to as a "straight-face" test: Can you honestly ask others to put their money at risk if you (and your family) have not done the same? Furthermore, lenders believe that you're less likely to walk away when the going gets rough if a sizable amount of your own money is at risk.

Of course, risking your own skin doesn't mean bleeding yourself dry. You'll need to establish a reasonable limit on the level of your personal investment and then stick to it. If you find yourself in discussion with prospective investors who are pushing you to overextend yourself by borrowing against a retirement plan or taking a second mortgage on your home, step back and reevaluate your plans.

Look before you leap into a new home mortgage to finance your business. This is your home that you're putting on the line—don't borrow so much that your very ability to make your monthly payments is put at risk. Your payments should remain low enough that even if your business is slow to get going, you'll be able to cover them. Also remember that every new mortgage comes with fees and closing costs. Make sure these don't add up to, say, several thousand dollars if your goal is to borrow only $5,000 to $10,000 for your business.

3.   Finding Cash in Existing Business Resources

You may not think you have much in the way of business resources, especially if you're operating on a shoestring out of your home, garage, or barn. But look around again, at the customers, suppliers, and equipment that you've accumulated so far, and you may be pleasantly surprised. A little creativity will lead you to ways to make the most of the business resources—the assets and the relationships—that you already have in place. Here are three suggestions.

Make good use of trade credit. Find out whether you can buy the goods or services you need on credit, meaning that the supplier won't require you to pay your bill for 30 or 60 days. This gives you some time to earn the income you'll need to pay back the supplier. If you're on good terms with your supplier, he or she may even allow you to spread your payments out across several months with no finance charges, as long as you keep up. Even if the supplier charges an interest rate, the rate may be considerably lower than you'd have to pay if you used your credit card to finance the purchase. Nearly two-thirds of U.S. small businesses reported in a recent study that they use trade credit as a form of business financing.

Explore the possibility of sale- or lease-backs. If you already own a piece of equipment or real estate, you can sell it to someone else, and then lease it back for your business use. Be cautious with these transactions, however. Make sure the fees are affordable, and look carefully at the fine print—some overly clever buyers put in a contract clause saying that you can lose the asset if you're late on a payment.

Enter the complex world of factoring your accounts receivable. If you already have customers, you may have accounts receivable—that is, a paper saying that someone else owes you money for a product or service you sold them. Accounts receivable is a business asset, because it represents money you are owed, and you may be able to sell this piece of paper to a factoring company. The factoring company then advances you 80-90% of the cash and collects on the account when it comes due. If you go this route, shop around for the company that will give you the best rate, and be careful of signing away a business asset as collateral.

4. Asking Family and Friends for Money

Asking family and friends for money—the main topic of this book—is often the next stage in your quest for start-up capital. A gift, a loan, or an equity investment from someone you know can fill a critical gap in the growth of your business. It allows you to lean on your friends' and family's trust and support to grow your business to the point where you've amassed the revenue, assets, and credit history usually required before banks or professional investors will invest.

Did you know? Private loans and investments are such a common source of small business financing that MBA students and finance professionals put a name to the practice. They use the phrase "the 4Fs" when referring to money loaned or invested in a new business by "founders, family, friends, and foolhardy strangers."

5.   Visiting a Bank or Other Lender

Although banks themselves can be found on virtually every street corner, bank money to launch your business can be harder to come by. Once you're up and running, bank financing is an important resource. But until your business has launched a product and has paying customers, your average bank or other traditional lender will probably view you as too great a risk for a commercial loan. Of course, if you're willing to put your personal credit rating at risk, you can go to a bank for a personal credit card, a personal loan, or a line of credit secured by the equity you have in your home or other collateral. Many entrepreneurs do this to get started, as described previously in Section 2.

If you're applying for a commercial loan with your business as the borrower, the bank will typically want to see that you've figured out how to make a profit and that you have the business assets to protect their loan. Many businesses don't reach that stage until as late as their third year of operation. When you get to this point, you're considered "bankable." It's getting to this point that can be a challenge. See "How Banks Choose Whom to Lend Money To," below, for the five hurdles institutional lenders tend to set for business loans. If you can't fly over the bars, you're out of the race, at least until your numbers improve.

How Banks Choose Whom to Lend Money To

Banks exist to make money. That means that, whatever their ads may promise, before a bank lends money it takes steps to ensure that it will be paid back. The criteria that banks use to evaluate applications are traditionally referred to as the "five C's" of credit.

You'll want to understand these criteria for two reasons: first, to appreciate how much more flexible private lenders will probably be, and second, as preparation. By mimicking the type of application you'd prepare for a bank when approaching friend-and-family lenders, you'll enhance your appearance of professionalism and be prepared to allay their possible concerns.

Capacity to repay is the most critical of the five factors. Any prospective lender, whether it's a bank or your Cousin Jane, will want to know exactly how and when you intend to repay the loan. To measure your capacity, banks will examine your business's expected cash flow, your intended schedule or timing for repayment, and your own personal trustworthiness when it comes to repaying loans. For that last piece of the analysis, the bank will look hard at your payment history on existing credit relationships—both personal and commercial.

Capital is the money you have personally invested in the business. Lenders will want to know how much you stand to lose should the business fail. Prospective lenders and investors will expect you to contribute your own assets and to undertake personal financial risk before asking for outside funding. It stands to reason that if you have a significant personal investment in the business, you're more likely to do everything in your power to make the business successful.

Collateral is an additional form of security you can provide the lender in case you can't repay on your own. "Collateral" means assets such as equipment, buildings, accounts receivable, and, in some cases, inventory that the bank can sell for cash. Most commercial lenders will require collateral on a risky start-up loan. Both business and personal assets can be used as collateral for a loan.

How Banks Choose Whom to Lend Money To (continued)

Conditions refers to the use of the loan money. Lenders understandably want to know how their money will be spent. Many banks prefer to know that the money will go directly toward making more money by building assets for your business, such as working capital, new equipment, and inventory. They are not as keen on paying for salaries, market research, or your overhead costs.

Character is the personal impression you make on the potential lender or investor. The lender decides subjectively whether or not you are sufficiently trustworthy to repay the loan or have sufficient business skills to generate a return on funds invested in your company. A bank will review your educational background and experience in business and in your industry. It will also judge the quality of your references and the background and experience of your employees.

Although traditional bank loans tend to be reserved for established businesses as described above, some banks and other financial institutions do offer small business loan programs, because they can get help from the federal government to lessen the risk you represent. Once you've hung out your shingle, take a trip to the bank (either the neighborhood or the mega-variety, in person or online) and ask whether it has a small business loan program.

Most small business loan programs are associated with the Small Business Administration (SBA), the federal agency charged with supporting U.S. small businesses. The SBA encourages banks, credit unions, and nonprofit financial intermediaries around the country to lend to small businesses.

One of the most popular ways the SBA does this is the 7(a) loan program. Here's how it works: You can receive up to $750,000 from your local 7(a) lender, with a partial guarantee from the SBA. The SBA doesn't actually lend you any money but provides backup to the bank or lender who does, to reduce the amount of risk that your lender takes on. For a state-by-state listing of the top small business bank lenders, go to the CD-ROM at the back of this book.

Around the country, various nonprofit organizations can also provide you with business capital and sometimes also free business assistance. Many of these organizations serve as financial intermediaries between the entrepreneur and both federal and state small business programs like the SBA. Most have a community improvement mission. But the fact that these are "do-good" nonprofits doesn't mean you should expect a handout. The interest rates they charge for a small business loan can be just as high as banks, and sometimes as high as credit card rates when they take a risk on a business that banks won't touch.

In other words, these organizations provide access to capital for individuals and business who might not otherwise be able to get it. Many serve the smallest businesses, known as "microenterprises" (see "Is Your Business Small Enough to Get Microenterprise Assistance?," below). Others aim to support medium-sized firms that achieve community development goals, like job creation or minority business ownership. Many of these organizations serve a particular region (like an urban neighborhood) or a particular group (like immigrant entrepreneurs). Whatever their mission, they have a common purpose: to "level the playing field" and encourage economic growth among entrepreneurs whom traditional lenders might not consider bankable. The CD-ROM at the back of this book contains a state-by-state listing of some of these nonprofit financial intermediaries.

Get to know a local banker. It's never too early to strike up a relationship with a local loan officer. He or she likely will have a good sense of the financing options available to you and can help you see the larger picture when it comes to the financial structure of your business. Your banker will also probably have experience helping other entrepreneurs in your community launch businesses and can recommend resources you should take advantage of. It's in the banker's interest that you successfully get your business off the ground and grow it until you run through your sources of informal capital—at which point you will presumably return to your friendly banker for bank capital.

Is Your Business Small Enough to Get Microenterprise Assistance?

A microenterprise is, as you might guess, a very small business. Specifically, it's a business with five or fewer employees that requires $35,000 or less in start-up capital and that lacks access to the traditional commercial banking sector. In addition, the term "microenterprise" tends to be used to describe businesses run by entrepreneurs who are low income or are struggling to make ends meet. There may be at least 20 million microenterprises in the United States, and possibly more.

The good part about being so small is that hundreds of nonprofit organizations around the United States are eager to provide a helping hand. Many of these are the lenders for the SBA MicroLoan Program, a start-up loan program to which even the newest businesses can apply. Although the maximum loan under this program is $35,000, the average loan is approximately $10,000. One catch is that MicroLoan borrowers typically have to enroll in technical assistance classes administered by the nonprofit intermediary making the loan. For some entrepreneurs, this is a great resource, providing cost-effective business training. For a state-by-state listing, see the CD-ROM at the back of the book.

To learn more about microenterprises, also see the report "Opening Opportunities, Building Ownership: Fulfilling the Promise of Microenterprise in the United States," available through the Aspen Institute in Washington, DC, at www.aspeninstitute.org.

Finding a Business Adviser or Mentor

Financing is just one of the many issues on your plate when starting a new business. Although this book will alert you to some of the other issues and suggest further resources to consult, there's no substitute for talking things over with an experienced, trusted adviser. To find a local mentor, ask for referrals from friends and colleagues, or look into mentoring programs offered by local industry groups.

You can also access free business advice through the SBA's national network of Small Business Development Centers (SBDCs). For example, SBDCs commonly offer free workshops and can arrange for a business counselor to meet with you to review your business plan (more on business planning in Chapter 5).

SCORE, the Service Corps of Retired Executives, is another nationally organized network that provides quality business advice to entrepreneurs. Better yet, their advisers will meet with you one on one, for free.

Both the SBA and SCORE have excellent websites worth a visit: www.sba.gov and www.score.org.

6. Seeking Out Business Angels, Not Venture Capital Investors

If equity capital is what you're after, you've probably heard stories from the once-promised land of professional equity investing: venture capital—million-dollar investments from high-rolling companies with endlessly deep pockets, and the like. Putting aside the hype, the basic idea is that, after an exhaustive review of your business opportunity, a venture capitalist gives you cash in exchange for shares in your business. If all goes well, the investor eventually exits the company by selling the shares to new investors, at many times the original price he or she paid you. If the ending is not so happy, venture capitalists get lower-than-expected returns (or no returns at all) and disappoint the people who invested in their venture capital firm.

The best part of equity investing from your perspective is that you get all the money up front, you don't have any payments along the way, and your investor gets money back only if your company does so well that all the owners are grinning. Sounds like a great deal, right? Well, hold on a minute. If you're contemplating sending your business plan to a list of venture capital firms you found on the Web, you may want to save your stamps.

The allure of venture capital beckons to most entrepreneurs, but in fact only a small group of companies with rapid growth potential actually get funded. In 2002, just $21 billion in venture capital was invested in about 2,500 companies. Though that may sound like a lot, it's a mere fifth of the $108 billion that gets distributed as informal loans and investments to millions of companies each year. Worse yet, only about 20% of the venture capital invested in 2002 went to start-up and early-stage businesses—increasingly, venture capitalists direct their investments toward established and expansion-stage companies that are already profitable.

However, this doesn't mean you should write off equity capital as a source of money to start or expand your business. Although venture capitalists are probably an unrealistic target for most start-up businesses, there are other people out there who may want to invest in, rather than lend money to, your young business. You may be lucky and have some wealthy friends and family who can make an equity investment in your business. Even if you're not, you have another excellent option.

"Business angels" are affluent individuals, often successful entrepreneurs themselves, who invest in up-and-coming entrepreneurs like you. The trick is that business angels don't go around advertising free money. These are private individuals, often with other jobs; some operate alone and some as part of a network or a structured group. The challenge is to find these potential equity investors among your friends, family, and other business contacts. (You'll learn how to find these folks and ask them for money in Chapters 3 and 8.)

B. How Your Business's Legal Structure Can Advance—or Hold Back—Your Fundraising

If you're still deciding on a legal structure for your business—that is, choosing whether to operate as a sole proprietorship, partnership, corporation, or LLC—you're probably weighing the advantages and disadvantages when it comes to ease of setup, degree of personal liability, tax advantages, and the like. Let me, however, add one more consideration to the mix: your fundraising possibilities.

An entrepreneur running a solo, unincorporated Web design shop out of his or her barn will have different fundraising options from the founders of an incorporated Web design company. The solo entrepreneur can't, for example, raise equity capital, because selling equity shares means dividing up ownership, and it's impossible to have more than one owner in a so-called "sole" proprietorship.

Even if the solo entrepreneur brought in a second person and started a partnership, he or she would have trouble raising equity capital, because as co-owners, the investors would be just as liable for the company's debts and liabilities as the owner would. These limitations on fundraising by sole proprietorships and partnerships are perhaps the most important issues to understand, but there are other layers to the analysis, as covered below.

Your main choices of business structure are:

- sole proprietorship (see Section 1, below)
- partnership (see Section 2, below)
- C corporation (see Section 3, below)
- S corporation (see Section 4, below), and
- limited liability company or "LLC" (see Section 5, below).

Picking the right legal structure can be a complicated decision, because you need to be able to look into your crystal ball and project how big you want to get and what type of capital you'll need in order to get there. The subsections below give you a primer on balancing fundraising and other considerations. Also see "Ways to Organize Your Business," below, summarizing the key advantages and drawbacks to these five legal structures.

Your legal structure is not set in stone. Make the most informed choice possible now, to save on setup costs and paperwork. But remember that you can always change the legal structure later, to fit the needs of your growing business.

1.   Sole Proprietorship

Most small businesses are organized as sole proprietorships, at least at the beginning. This is by far the cheapest and easiest way to set up a business—with a single owner, who receives and reports all the profits and is responsible for any debts or liabilities. Establishing a sole proprietorship requires almost no formalities, and you'll personally own your business assets.

The main drawback to sole proprietorships is that personal liability means personal risk—the owner could literally lose his or her shirt because of unexpected losses or lawsuits. Even if the situation doesn't become so dire, one slow month may be all it takes to eat up your family's vacation savings, for example, in paying your employees' salaries.

In addition, as mentioned earlier in this section, a sole proprietorship can have, by definition, only one owner. So if you want to raise capital by selling shares in your business, you'll need to find a legal structure that can accommodate multiple owners.

> **EXAMPLE:** Jamie, who has always loved kayaking, starts a small one-person business renting three kayaks for either personal use or guided tours. After a glowing write-up in a popular sporting magazine, he is flooded with customers. Jamie decides to raise capital to grow Jamie's Kayaks into Jamie's Outdoor Play, a year-round multisport expedition and outdoor gear company.
>
> Jamie's first loan, of $10,000, is from his friend Josh, a fellow boating enthusiast. Jamie knows that, as the sole owner, he will be personally liable for that loan. Jamie next approaches his father-in-law—who is interested in the business but turns out to be a business angel who would rather make a $50,000 investment and become a co-owner. If Jamie wants this investment, he will need to

change the legal structure to one that offers his father-in-law both a share of the company in exchange for his investment and protection from the company's liabilities (a protection nearly all investors expect).

2. Partnership

A partnership is a relatively simple and inexpensive way to organize a business that has more than one owner. In a general partnership, you and your partners jointly own your business's assets and liabilities, usually based on how much each partner brings to the table. Small groups of people who want to pool some resources for a business or real estate project tend to use the partnership structure to do it. Again, however, personal liability is an issue—both you and your partners will be personally liable for the debts of the partnership.

One way to get around the liability problem of a general partnership is to invite certain partners—in particular, your investors—to join as "limited partners." As long as these new partners remain "passive investors," meaning they take no role in running the business, they are protected by "limited personal liability." That means they are liable only up to the amount that they contributed to the business. Another advantage to limited partnerships is that they allow you to invite investors in without dealing with the complexities of selling ownership shares and managing equity investors. (Limited partnerships are most often used in real estate, so that one or more general partners can buy and sell properties while the limited partners provide the capital.)

Jamie, in the kayak example above, could invite his father-in-law to invest as a limited partner. If his father-in-law agreed to this, he'd have the semi-comfort of knowing that limited partners are liable only to the extent of the investment they made in the business, and not for any business debts or liabilities that arise out of the negligence of another partner or manager. For example, if a customer drowned on a business-led outing and the customer's family sued the business for $5 million, a limited partner would not be liable.

However, if Jamie achieves the growth he projects in his business plan, Jamie's Outdoor Play will be on track to being a very profitable business, and his father-in-law might prefer to have an actual ownership stake through a corporate or LLC structure. As a limited partner in the growing business, Jamie's father-in-law would be entitled only to those profits that are passed through to the limited partners as designated by the partnership agreement.

Plan on repaying your debts, no matter what business structure you choose. I'm not counseling you to find a structure that allows you to wriggle out of your obligations. I assume that your intentions are to make responsible use of your family's and friends' money—and that you'll try to repay them regardless of whether your corporate structure allows otherwise.

3. C Corporation

If you set up your business as a C corporation (the standard, most commonly used corporate structure), it becomes its own legal entity. The corporation, not its owners, will own your business's assets and liabilities. This ingenious structure acts as a buffer, since neither you nor your investors are personally liable for unpaid debts of the business. In fact, if you plan on selling any shares in your business to investors (in the form of stock), or if you dream of one day "going public," forming a corporation (or an LLC, as described in the next section) is an obvious choice for you.

If, in the earlier example, Jamie's friend Josh had made his $10,000 loan to "Jamie's Outdoor Play, Inc.," rather than to Jamie himself, he'd have to sue the corporate entity if Jamie failed to repay—and would have no recourse against Jamie himself (unless Josh had gotten Jamie to personally guarantee the loan, which many lenders understandably do). If Jamie's corporation went bankrupt before repaying, Josh, as a lender, would be among the first in line for repayment—but he would have to hope that the company had enough assets to repay him, because he couldn't get the money directly from Jamie (again, unless he'd had Jamie personally guarantee the loan).

During your efforts to raise loan capital, you may well find that, especially in the early days, lenders want reassurance that someone will be responsible for the corporation's debts. That someone will most likely be you. You may well be asked to personally guarantee loans, meaning you pledge your personal assets as a backup if the business's assets are insufficient to pay off the debt. In fact, the SBA requires that all owners with more than 20% equity in a business provide a personal guaranty before they receive an SBA-backed loan, so that if the business fails, the lender has recourse against you personally. Still, this doesn't cancel out the benefits of incorporating—it's the unexpected liabilities you should be most worried about.

4. S Corporation

More and more entrepreneurs are taking advantage of an IRS tax status for corporations called "subchapter S tax status." While regular, C corporations pay corporate federal income tax, an S corporation does not. Instead, the S corporation's tax obligations are passed through to and paid by its owners, on their personal tax returns. This avoids the problem of "double taxation," the bane of investors in C corporations.

It's called double taxation because the C corporation must pay taxes on any profits it makes before it distributes profits to shareholders, yet the shareholders must also pay taxes after they receive these distributions (in the form of dividends or other gains). The net result to shareholders in a C corporation is that there's less money to be shared after the IRS has taken its cut, making an S corporation structure tempting to potential investors.

Also, even if your S corporation loses money, there's some good news for your equity investors. An S corporation passes both gains *and* losses through to its shareholders, who must then report both on their personal income taxes. They can use these pass-through losses to offset their other sources of personal income, potentially lowering their overall tax bill.

Before you leap at S corporation status, however, realize that it's really designed for smaller companies sharing ownership between the founder and a few investors. In fact, to be eligible for subchapter S tax status, your corporation must have 75 or fewer stockholders, all of whom are resident aliens or citizens, and you must issue only one class of stock. In addition, no other corporations may be investors in your company, only individuals.

5.   Limited Liability Company (LLC)

The LLC structure is a relatively new and increasingly popular legal structure for growing small businesses. It is distinct from any of the three structures listed previously yet offers a combination of their advantages. Structuring your business as an LLC offers you (and your equity investors) both the limited personal liability of a corporation and the pass-through tax advantages of a partnership or S corporation. For example, LLCs usually have a clause in their operating agreement detailing the formula used to determine the annual profits each member will receive. The most common formula is the member's share of profits times his or her tax rate.

Even better, LLCs are fairly simple to set up. Given the choice between an LLC and a corporation, experts agree that most small business owners would be better off forming an LLC.

Want more detailed information on setting up your LLC? Take a look at *Form Your Own Limited Liability Company*, by Anthony Mancuso (Nolo), which provides forms, step-by-step instructions, and guidance on when you do and don't need an attorney.

Ways to Organize Your Business		
Type of Entity	**Main Advantages**	**Main Drawbacks**
Sole Proprietorship	Simple and inexpensive to create and operate Owner reports profit or loss on his or her personal tax return	Owner personally liable for business debts
General Partnership	Simple and inexpensive to create and operate Owners (partners) report their share of profit or loss on their personal tax returns	Owners (partners) personally liable for business debts

Ways to Organize Your Business (continued)		
Type of Entity	**Main Advantages**	**Main Drawbacks**
Limited Partnership	Limited partners have limited personal liability for business debts as long as they don't participate in management General partners can raise cash without involving outside investors in management of business	General partners personally liable for business debts More expensive to create than general partnership Suitable mainly for companies that invest in real estate
Regular Corporation	Owners have limited personal liability for business debts Fringe benefits can be deducted as business expense Owners can split corporate profit among owners and corporation, paying lower overall tax rate	More expensive to create than partnership or sole proprietorship Paperwork can seem burdensome to some owners Separate taxable entity
S Corporation	Owners have limited personal liability for business debts Owners report their share of corporate profit or loss on their personal tax returns Owners can use corporate loss to offset income from other sources	More paperwork than for a limited liability company, which offers similar advantages Income must be allocated to owners according to their ownership interests Fringe benefits limited for owners who own more than 2% of shares
Limited Liability Company	Owners have limited personal liability for business debts even if they participate in management Profit and loss can be allocated differently than ownership interests IRS rules allow LLCs to choose between being taxed as partnership or corporation	More expensive to create than partnership or sole proprietorship State laws for creating LLCs may not reflect latest federal tax changes

Want more information on choosing an appropriate business structure? See the following resources:

Legal Guide for Starting & Running a Small Business, by Fred S. Steingold (Nolo), which includes detailed analysis of the tax burdens, personal liability, ease of setup, and other features of each small business structure, and

The Small Business Start-Up Kit for California by Peri Pakroo, (Nolo), particularly Chapter 2, "Choosing a Legal Structure." Pakroo discusses each of the six options described in Section B, above, and includes material that is relevant across all 50 states.

■

Chapter 2

What's in It for Both Entrepreneur and Investor?

A. What's in It for You, the Entrepreneur? 36

   1. Private Money May Be Available When Other Money Is Not 37

   2. Private Money Could Be Cheaper 38

   3. Private Loans Offer Flexibility 38

   4. Private Money Represents Validation From Key Supporters 41

   5. Private Investments Require Less Work Than Other Sources of
      Equity Capital 42

B. What's in It for Your Investor? 42

   1. Making a Private Investment May Satisfy Altruistic Motives 43

   2. Making a Private Investment May Satisfy Self-Interested Motives 44

   3. Making a Private Investment Often Serves a Mixture of Motives 47

C. Mixing Money and Relationships Can Work 49

One of the biggest myths about private lending and investing is that entrepreneurs like yourself are essentially preying on the charitable instincts of your friends and family—using your desperation as a way to extract money, all the time knowing that they may never see that money again. The truth is much different.

Yes, there are risks involved for people who make investments in a start-up business, even if those people are related to the founder. But taking risks is a fact of life for any investor in the U.S. economy—it's difficult to gain significant rewards without first taking major risks. By accepting the risk that your business may fail, your lenders and investors stand to gain financial as well as emotional rewards if it succeeds. The lenders may earn higher interest rates than they could have gained elsewhere, and the equity investors may profit from their shares in a successful business.

Also, as a backup, you can take various steps to protect both your lenders and your investors from the risks involved.

This chapter will take an honest, detailed look at what each side has to gain from this financial relationship; starting with you, the entrepreneur (see Section A, below), moving on to your investors (see Section B, below), and concluding with some thoughts on how to successfully mix money and relationships (see Section C, below).

A. What's in It for You, the Entrepreneur?

Let's start with the easier question: What advantages do private loans or investments offer you and your business, especially as compared to other financing alternatives? The four most important advantages are that private money:

- may be available when other money is not
- could be cheaper (though not always)
- offers great flexibility, and
- represents validation from your key supporters.

1.   Private Money May Be Available When Other Money Is Not

If you've already maxed out your personal sources of cash, but don't yet have the collateral or revenue to attract bank or professional equity financing, the advantage of private money is obvious: It's your best, and sometimes only, source of start-up capital. You're not alone in this situation—many entrepreneurs face a capital gap at this most-critical stage in their new venture.

Most banks will deem a start-up too risky for a loan, once they've compared you against the five Cs checklist described in Chapter 1. That takes you right back to your friends and family, to whom you are a known quantity. They know your strengths and weaknesses. They probably won't do a five Cs evaluation of your loan request, or even a credit check (though you might impress some by offering to provide one). Your friends' and family members' belief in you is an intangible personal asset that you can use to your advantage—and turn into a tangible business asset.

If you're trying to raise equity capital, launching right into the big leagues of professional venture capital is likely to be a waste of your time. But that doesn't mean there's no one willing to take a gamble on you and your business idea. Better to start close to home and look to the people who already know and trust you, who might also be willing to put some money behind you. Chances are you'll be able to find friends and family and even a few business angels to take a chance and invest when you need it most. Later on, you can worry about attracting the attention of the heavy hitters.

Has a bank rejected your loan application? If you're raising private money from people you know because you have, in fact, been rejected by a bank or other lender, make sure that you understand and address whatever concerns led to the refusal—before you ask anyone else for money. It's worth taking the time to fix any problems, whether the problems relate to your business plan or to your personal financial situation. If you don't do this vital repair work, you may end up subjecting your friends and family to risks that professionals spotted and you knew of but did nothing about.

2. Private Money Could Be Cheaper

Where loans are concerned, even if you could get a bank loan, the high fees and interest rates might make it an overly risky choice for your fledgling business. Banks, credit card companies, or other financial institutions will charge you market-rate fees and interest, and possibly high penalties if you are slow to repay. Your interest rate will be inversely linked to your credit score; in other words, the lower your credit score, the higher your interest rate. Even a small-business banker or a microlender is likely to charge 10% interest or more. From their standpoint, they're gambling on an unknown quantity and want to be assured of some reward to cover their risk. For you, however, that could mean some expensive monthly payments.

By contrast, family, friends, and other private lenders tend to be focused on helping you. You'll find that most of them simply hope that you will succeed and that they will get their money back. They may protest at the very idea of your paying interest, assuring you that a rate of 0% is just fine. In other words, they're typically not out to make money off the deal. This doesn't mean you should take full advantage of their generosity—as you'll see in Chapters 3 and 5, which discuss how to pick an interest rate, there are many reasons to pay a rate closer to market rates. Nonetheless, even if you go as high as 6-9%, which is currently typical for private business loans, you will still come out ahead in today's market. A bank or a credit card company would charge you a lot more for high-risk start-up capital.

For example, the SBA 7(a) loans mentioned in Chapter 1 can currently cost as much as 11%, as shown in "Interest Rates Under the Popular SBA 7(a) Loan Program," below. If you're borrowing from a lender without the benefit of an SBA loan program (which provides a government guaranty for the loan as long as the interest rate charged is below certain limits), your rate may be even higher.

3. Private Loans Offer Flexibility

Loans from banks and other institutional lenders are nearly always standardized so that the lenders can manage them in a cost-effective manner. By contrast, one of the joys of private lending is its flexibility.

Interest Rates Under the Popular SBA 7(a) Loan Program

The interest rate charged on a 7(a) loan is decided between the borrower and the lender but is subject to SBA maximum levels. These limits are determined by adding a set number to the prime rate, that is, the rate at which banks lend to their most creditworthy customers. In other words, the SBA allows lenders to charge you any rate as long as it doesn't exceed the limits they set, which vary with the prime rate. Over the last ten years the prime rate has ranged from a low of 4% to a high of 9.5%. At the time this book was published, it stood at 6.25%; you can look it up by doing an Internet search on the phrase "prime rate."

To determine the maximum interest rate you could be charged for an SBA 7(a) loan, you need to know three things:

- the current prime rate
- how much money you need (less than $25,000; between $25,000 and $50,000; or more than $50,000), and
- how long it will take you to repay it (less than or more than seven years). The first table below shows you how much to add to the prime rate given the amount and the term of your request.

SBA 7(a) Loan Program Maximum Addition to Prime Rate

Loan Term	Loan Amount		
	<$25,000	$25,000-$50,000	>$50,000
Less than 7-year term	+4.25%	+3.25%	+2.25%
Greater than 7-year term	+4.75%	+3.75%	+2.75%

The second table uses the current prime rate to show you what late-2005 interest rates for these types of loans look like. For example, according to the second table, a loan for $40,000 with a term of less than seven years could have cost you as much as 9.5% in late 2005.

Maximum Interest Rate Charged If Prime Rate Is 6.25%

Loan Term	Loan Amount		
	<$25,000	$25,000-$50,000	>$50,000
Less than 7-year term	10.5%	9.5%	8.5%
Greater than 7-year term	11%	10%	9%

You can learn more about SBA loan programs at www.sba.gov/financing/index.html.

This comes in handy at two important junctures: first, when you set up your repayment plan, and second, if and when you need to make changes to that repayment plan. You're not up against an institution that preprints thousands of standard form loan contracts and would be horrified at your suggestion that it alter a single clause. Instead, you're borrowing from someone who is just as interested in a feasible repayment plan as you are.

When you sit down to create a schedule for your repayments, you should think first about what you can afford, and then create a schedule that makes keeping up with your payments possible. Don't assume that you have to follow the typical bank model, in which small business loans are "amortized"—meaning that repayment is scheduled to begin immediately, at a set amount for every installment. With your private loan, you have the option of designing a repayment plan that more closely matches your business's expected schedule for turning a profit. For example, your schedule could start with a six-month grace period (where you don't make any payments), then switch to interest-only payments for the next 12 months, then move to a graduated (gently increasing) payment schedule for 36 months. (You'll see in Chapter 6 how to design a repayment plan to fit your situation.)

Profit predictions being uncertain, however, your well-laid repayment plans may turn out to be impossible, or nearly so. This is the second time when your friends' and family members' understanding and flexibility can literally save your business, by allowing you to make adjustments to your repayment plan.

> **EXAMPLE:** Runako starts a catering company with a loan from his mother, set up as a month-to-month repayment plan. While Runako's food suppliers demand immediate payment, his customers are less attentive to the calendar. One month, after catering two large weddings, Runako realizes that his payment to his mother is due the next day, while the brides and grooms who owe him money have seemingly left on long honeymoons. Fortunately, with a simple call to his mother, Runako is able to delay that month's payment—without the penalties that a bank might have charged.

As long as you communicate with your lenders early and clearly, temporary adjustments to your repayment plan may allow you to recover from the many bumps that you will probably encounter on the road to success. You can call this "patient capital"—financing that is flexible and allows you to repay as you are able.

Private loans can also help you build your credit rating. Historically, one of the downfalls of private lending has been that when borrowers did a good job making payments, only they and their lenders knew about it. Now, loan-servicing companies like CircleLending provide borrowers with optional credit reporting services, so that repayment performance is reported directly to the national credit reporting companies. In this way, the on-time payments on your private loan from relatives or friends can help establish or improve your business's credit rating, which makes your business look like a better credit risk if and when you go to the bank for subsequent financing.

4. Private Money Represents Validation From Key Supporters

The advantages of having your earliest investors include people you know may be personal as well as financial. Entrepreneurs report that the validation they feel from receiving the financial support of family and friends can be a big boost. The start-up phase is usually a very difficult time in the life of both the entrepreneur and the business. Money is tight, both personally and in the business, and even the most minor decisions count.

You may be exhausted after launching your computer consulting business, staying up late at night after coming home from your "real job" and skipping weekend social events to meet a code deadline for your first customer. Or you may be learning painful lessons about how a rainy holiday weekend can wreak havoc on your gourmet beachside ice cream shop. Your family and particularly your spouse may be feeling the stress of your single-minded focus on the new business, at the expense of personal priorities. At times like these, having someone you know express his or her belief in you and your idea by writing a check can mean a lot.

Russell Simmons, a leader in the music recording industry, openly admits how much it meant to him to have his mother's support when he was starting out. In Lemonade Stories, an award-winning film about famous entrepreneurs and their mothers (www.lemonadestories.com), he describes his early days, when he would occasionally lose money on his hip-hop events. After promoting a party in Harlem that no one attended, Russell found himself completely broke. "I remember sitting outside and my mother coming out. She gave me money … and it was enough to start me over again and give me another opportunity. It was a tremendous push, because it wasn't the money, it was the investment in me. It was the belief in my future."

5. Private Investments Require Less Work Than Other Sources of Equity Capital

Raising and managing investments from professional equity investors can be a painful and exhausting activity. By raising your first few equity investments from friends and family, however, you give yourself a lower-effort dry run for the business angels you'll approach next and any professional venture capitalists you may chose to deal with after that.

Here's one reason that equity deals take a lot of work: You will need to convince investors that you are the right person, with the right idea, at the right time. Friend and family investors will normally require less "selling" on your part, because they know and trust you. They are predisposed to like what you have to say and to believe that you are going to succeed. Equity investors with whom you don't already have such a cozy relationship will be a lot more neutral and will require a lot more time and information before they're comfortable enough to invest, as you'll see in Chapter 8.

B. What's in It for Your Investor?

The more you hear about the benefits that loans and equity investments from friends and family offer you—low interest rates, the possibility of putting off repayments in a pinch, and emotional support during rough times—the worse a deal they might sound like for your investors. Yet seen from your friends and relatives' point of view, the reasons to make a private investment are actually quite rational and solid. These include:

- altruism, or an unselfish concern for your welfare
- self-interest, in cases where the lender or investor might benefit financially from the loan or investment, and
- a recognition that by combining your resources, both you and your lender or investor can come out ahead.

1. Making a Private Investment May Satisfy Altruistic Motives

Some people, particularly those closest to you, may be motivated to lend you money out of an unselfish desire to support you. Their sense of personal commitment is so strong that it outweighs any considerations of financial gain or loss. For example, your parents are practically hardwired to want to see you succeed. It's not a far step from the pride they gain from seeing an A+ on your report card or watching you hit a home run—particularly if they can tell their friends about it.

Or perhaps you have a best friend who's always thought of you as the sibling he or she never had, and who has supported you every time you've asked. That person is likely to want to invest in your business for altruistic reasons. Altruistic lenders help out because they can, and in some cases also to try to provide you a developmental opportunity and to nudge you towards independence.

The mother of Richard Branson, founder of the Virgin Group (Virgin Records, Virgin Music, Virgin Airlines, and so on.), is a good example of an altruist who knew when a financial boost would help ensure her children's independence. When Branson was 17, he started a national student magazine, with his mother's financial help. Not long after, Branson convinced his parents to let him quit school to run the magazine full time. Branson got the bright idea of advertising and selling discounted records through the newspaper. From those humble beginnings, Virgin Records was born; without his family's support, Branson says, he would have gone out of business altogether. (See www.lemonadestories.com, www.virgin.com.)

Ironically, entrepreneurs are often most hesitant about taking money from people who those to whom they feel the closest, out of concern that the lender or investor will be disappointed if the business fails. However, it's usually only when entrepreneurs actually deceive others about their business's prospects that true disappointment sets in. No one wants to find out that their nearest and dearest has conned them. If you are doing your best at running your business, and are openly communicating about your business's financial situation, your family and friend investors are likely to be unusually patient and forgiving about the business's fits, starts, and even failures. (Indeed, their very patience can be the key to your business's eventual success.)

2. Making a Private Investment May Satisfy Self-Interested Motives

Although altruism runs deep in the human psyche, people must consider their own interests, too. In fact, experts researching intrafamily lending have found that self-interest is the main reason that most family members agree to finance a business start-up. That's good news for you: You don't have to feel like a beggar, and you don't have to limit your requests to your most saintly friends and relatives. There's a certain comfort in knowing that an investor acting out of self-interest is also an investor who has evaluated the options and believes that the opportunity you are offering is a good one.

Watch out for investors with hidden agendas. There's a difference between self-interest and utter selfishness, and you'll need to distinguish between the two. For example, a private investor may be lending you money so that later he or she can later call in the favor and ask you to do more than you'd ever bargained for. You'll learn more in Chapter 4 about how to sort through your circle of contacts and identify your "best bet" prospective investors.

a.   Private Investments Can Make Money for the Investor

A private investment is, at its most basic, a financial transaction. Any private investor who is not operating out of pure altruism will approach the deal with an eye toward the market. The person will probably compare the terms of the loan or investment you're offering with what he or she could get (or is getting) by putting the same amount of money in a savings account, CD, or other investment. If you can offer a better return with acceptable risk, the prospective investor may well take you up on it.

I once made the mistake of asking a private investor why he was considering an investment in my company. He contorted his face, implying it was a silly question. Obviously, his motivation was to make money. Because I had been raising money primarily from close friends, work colleagues, and relatives up to that point, I had forgotten that most investors are simply motivated by financial returns—and I realized that no one is going to protest if their investment makes them money, not even your grandmother.

> **EXAMPLE:** Sumalee wants to start a shop in Los Angeles selling Thai desserts. She approaches her tax accountant about a loan of $4,000, offering to repay the principal (original loan amount) plus 8% over the course of three years. The accountant is financially savvy enough to know that he could never earn that kind of return on a three-year CD. Of course, Sumalee's offer presents many risks—retail shops are expensive to set up and operate, and Thai desserts are not yet well known in the United States. What's more, the FDIC won't come along and bail Sumalee's lenders out if her venture fails, as they would if an FDIC-insured bank failed. Nevertheless, the accountant knows that Sumalee has a good head for business and likes the idea of an 8% return on a short-term loan, so he lends her the $4,000. The 8% rate she offered was enough to overcome her accountant's concern about the risk normally associated with a small start-up retail shop.

If you will be proposing not only loans but also equity investments in your business, the gamble could pay off even bigger for your investors.

An equity investor gains an ownership stake in a growing company—a company that might eventually be sold for a heap of money, far beyond the initial investment. At that point, the investor would be entitled to a proportional share of the proceeds.

Whether you offer loans or investments, these are financial opportunities that your friends, your family, and even other people to whom you're not as close might evaluate and rationally choose to take advantage of. As long as you provide accurate information about your business's prospects, it's ultimately up to them to decide whether your offer has a chance of providing a greater return than other uses of their money.

b.　Private Investors Like Getting Involved With a Successful Business

Some entrepreneurs enjoy helping others get a start, by providing financial support and cheerleading in the early stages. They are likely to value your entrepreneurial spirit and feel good when they can use their knowledge and experience to foster that spirit. In fact, studies show that most business angel investors are themselves successful entrepreneurs. In addition to the lucrative returns they hope for in their equity investments, many of them simply enjoy the thrill of joining in at the ground floor of an exciting new business. They did it themselves and are eager to be a part of it all over again. The most successful of these actually do angel investing for a living. Some investors also get a thrill from being "in the know" about a potential moneymaker that is not open to the general public.

> **EXAMPLE:** Jennie is both an entrepreneur and an experienced business lender. The owner of a successful women's fitness business, Jennie currently has nine outstanding loans to friends and colleagues ranging from $8,000 to $35,000. In each case, someone she knew came to her with a business idea that was related to her area of expertise and caught her imagination. She made one loan to a feminist ethnographer, one to a water-birth center, and one to a maker of women's workout gear. Jennie made sure that all the loans were formalized with the proper documentation and serviced

through a loan servicing company so that Jennie doesn't have to spend her valuable time watching the calendar for late payments. Although some of the borrowers are doing well and others are struggling, Jennie gets satisfaction from her involvement and support in each of the nine businesses.

3.   Making a Private Investment Often Serves a Mixture of Motives

Behavioral experts say that few private investors are motivated solely by altruism or self-interest. Most often, their decision making is driven by a combination of the two. This makes particular sense when you realize that the boundaries between altruism and self-interest aren't always clear—for example, when a grandparent glows with joy at your success, is that altruistic sentiment or self-interested pride at the accomplishments of his or her gene pool?

We'll leave the distinctions to the academics—your investor will probably catch onto the "win-win" aspects of your proposal pretty quickly. And nowhere is this simultaneous mix of interests clearer than in the family setting, where private loans or investments can help maximize overall wealth and serve the elder family members' estate planning goals.

For example, in some families, private investments between parents and children or other younger generations serve as a form of intergenerational wealth transfer. Parents or other relatives who were already planning to leave you money can transfer it to you now, when you really need it to launch your business, and potentially avoid taxes by doing so. For a description of how this works, see "Using Private Loans to Maximize Gift Tax Exemptions," below. You can learn more about the tax implications of gifting, loaning, or investing money in Chapter 3.

Even if your lenders prefer not to make the transfer an outright gift, but to style it as a loan, the net result is beneficial. That's because, if you view the family as one unit, the unit as a whole comes out ahead financially—why should you pay interest to a bank, rather than to your family (who may eventually gift or leave the money to you, anyway)?

Or why should some anonymous investor reap huge rewards because you had the skills and determination to make your business a roaring success, when you have friends and family able to play the same role?

Early asset transfers, such as private loans and investments, are particularly beneficial for wealthy families. Under current tax laws, estates worth over $2 million are heavily taxed when the person dies. Reducing the estate value to less than that amount through early transfers of money is beneficial for everyone.

Using Private Loans to Maximize Gift Tax Exemptions

Under current federal tax rules, someone who gives away more than $12,000 per year to any one person will be assessed a federal "gift tax" at the same rate as the estate tax. (It's the IRS's way of making sure people don't use gifts to avoid later estate tax payments.) However, there are two ways you and your giver can avoid the gift tax.

The first is for your giver to make sure he or she doesn't go over the $12,000 per year tax-free limit (or "exclusion"). Thus your parents (two people) can gift you up to $24,000 a year or even gift you and your spouse or partner up to $48,000 (up to $12,000 from each individual to each individual).

The second way is for your giver to structure the gift as a private loan to you that lasts several years, being sure to document this with a legal agreement and a repayment plan. The trick will be to pick financial terms that result in no more than $12,000 in payments due over the course of any one year. Then, each year, your lender must send you a letter stating that all payments scheduled for that year are forgiven. Your attorneys may, however, advise you, the borrower, to make a few payments each year, so as to create a repayment paper trail.

There's no doubt about it, raising money from people you know can feel like asking for a favor. But, if you get into this mindset, you'll compromise your very effectiveness. Think about it this way: You are offering someone the opportunity to get involved in an exciting business venture, to play a role in your success, and even to earn a little profit.

C. Mixing Money and Relationships Can Work

At this point, you may be thinking, "Okay, I see the benefits, but doesn't someone often get hurt when you mix money and relationships?" After all, even William Shakespeare advises us: "Neither a borrower nor a lender be; For loan oft loseth both itself and friend, and borrowing dulls the edge of husbandry" (Lord Polonius in *Hamlet*). A badly handled loan or investment could probably do a lot more damage than dulling the so-called edge of husbandry. Indeed, numerous current-day commentators will tell you to steer clear of relationship loans altogether. Maybe you've seen cautionary news headlines such as these:

- "Funding and family: Mix with care."
- "It's all relative: A family loan can be a recipe for disaster ... it doesn't have to be."
- "Are intra-family loans hazardous to your financial health?"
- "Preparation vital before seeking friends & family loan."
- "Banking close to home: Starting a business with help from friends and family doesn't have to mean making enemies."

Despite all these prophecies of doom, the simple truth is that most of the relationship-bruising that happens around loans or investments occurs because the transactions were handled badly in the first place. That's where this book comes in—it will help you make the loan or investment relationship clear and legal at the outset, to avoid miscommunications, misunderstandings, and basic mistakes. With a little planning, you can structure the deal in a way that protects relationships and allows both parties to achieve their goals.

> ## One Loan That Actually Improved a Relationship …
>
> Jason approached his father for help in launching a business importing Shona sculptures from Africa. In the past, Jason's ever-helpful father had made several supposed "loans" to support his son's wild ideas—but ended up writing them off as gifts when the ventures fizzled.
>
> This time, however, Jason's father had a feeling that his son was better able to take responsibility for his own business affairs. For one thing, Jason had prepared the terms of the loan in advance and shown his father a draft of the legal document representing his promise to repay his father. The pair set up a $9,000 loan.
>
> Two years later, Jason paid back the loan in full, with interest. Better yet, he and his father both say that the loan improved their relationship. Jason had never managed to pay back any money before, in part because he hadn't taken the loans seriously. By acting in a businesslike manner, Jason was able to justify his father's faith in him.

Still, you may have more-specific concerns about mixing business with friendships and other relationships. Below are some of the leading concerns I've heard from borrowers as they consider asking for private loans or investments, combined with a preview of the best practical means to forestall these concerns. (We'll get into the practical details in later chapters.)

If you're worried that: "I don't want to disappoint my lender if I'm unable to keep up with the payments I promised."

Be sure to: Carefully watch your cash flow situation, and communicate problems to your lenders as soon as you're aware of them. Generally, when you borrow from friends and family, they aren't fixated on receiving your payments by each deadline and will be flexible if they think it will help you succeed in the long term. If you're having difficulty making payments, be up front with your lender about your situation, and suggest an alternative repayment plan that works for both of you. In most cases, your lender will appreciate your proactive response and accommodate your request—which should ultimately allow you to get your business back on its feet.

If you're worried that: "My investor will constantly be anxious about the possibility of my business failing—and hate me forever if it does."

Be sure to: Realize that yes, investors may worry, and business failure at this early stage is a risk you are responsible for making clear to them. If a particular lender ranks high on the worried scale, but might be more willing to make the loan with some protection against the risk, you can offer to secure the loan with collateral (as explained in Chapter 5). Collateral significantly reduces your lender's risk because, if you default on the loan, your lender will be entitled to receive and sell the item of collateral (such as a vehicle or office equipment) in lieu of being repaid. If you do have troubles, but you are honest and open about the situation, your lenders are highly unlikely to hate you.

With family and friend equity investors, it is your responsibility at the outset to explicitly outline the risks involved and make sure that each investor can tolerate the risk; in other words, is willing to lose the investment. You shouldn't take an equity investment from someone who cannot afford to lose the money.

If you're worried that: "Even after I pay my lender back, the lender may still feel as though he or she did me a favor, and that I owe something."

Be sure to: Pay your lender a fair interest rate from the get-go. Even better, pay the lender more than he or she would have earned putting the money in a similar investment. If yours is a three-year loan, make sure to pay more than a three-year CD would earn. When you set up the loan, point out the market factors based upon which you picked the rate. That should help satisfy the lender that you owe him or her nothing after the loan has been repaid. Also, by using a formal loan request to ask for the money, and then a legally binding promissory note (your promise to repay the loan) to formalize the deal, you help make clear that this is a business transaction, not a favor.

If you're worried that: "My investors will meddle in how I run my business."

Be sure to: Realize first that, unlike a lender, an equity investor is entitled to a certain amount of information about your business, because he or she is a co-owner. Professional equity investors in particular will require regular updates and are entitled to a certain amount of say in how you run the business.

If you want someone who made you a simple loan to keep a distance, formalize the loan with proper documentation, to make clear that this is indeed a loan, not a case of your leaning on the person for aid. Seeing that you are serious about treating the loan in a businesslike manner should help your lender understand that his or her role doesn't extend beyond that of a lender.

If you're worried that: "My lender or investor will scrutinize everything I spend money on that isn't related to my business. What if I buy a new coat or take a vacation—will the person wonder whether I'm doing it with his or her money?"

Be sure to: For a lender, set up a mutually agreed upon repayment plan, so that your lender will always know that you were current on your obligations to him or her before you spent anything on yourself. Of course, if your business is hobbling along on other people's money, it's not wise financially or personally to make extravagant purchases. Your lender does have a right to know how his or her money is being used, especially if you are missing payments. The best way to keep your lenders out of your business is to sign a repayment plan and stick to it.

For equity investors, you're just going to have to grin and bear it. If you're doing well, the investor probably won't be paying as much attention to your new clothes or vacation destinations. If you're struggling to keep up with your quarterly revenue projections, however, you can bet that the investor will be looking over your shoulder as you write checks. In particular, the investor will want to make sure that nothing extra is headed to you personally.

■

Your Financing Choices: Gifts, Loans, and Equity Investments

A. Basic Setup and Handling of a Gift 55

B. Basic Setup and Handling of a Loan.. 57

    1. Loans Should Be Formalized in Writing.. 57

    2. Most Loans Require You to Pay Interest 58

    3. You May Also Need to Offer Collateral 60

    4. Loans Require Ongoing Management 61

C. Basic Setup and Handling of an Equity Investment 61

    1. Equity Investors Expect Compensation for Their Risk........................... 62

    2. Equity Investments Mean Dealing With Shared Ownership 65

    3. Equity Investments Require Compliance With Securities Laws 65

    4. An Attorney Must Formally Document an Equity Investment 66

D. Choosing Between Loan and Equity Capital.. 67

E. Tax Implications of Your Choice of Capital 67

    1. Dealing With IRS Limits on Gift Amounts... 69

    2. When Loans May Lead to Tax Liability 70

    3. When Loans May Lead to Tax Deductions... 72

    4. How Your Business's Legal Structure Affects Taxation
       of Its Profits.. 75

A n elderly gentleman I once knew, when asked how he liked his steak, liked to answer, "On the plate." You may feel similarly about your business capital—in your bank account would be just fine. You do, however, have a few options: You can raise the money you need in the form of a gift (no repayment expected), a loan (repayment expected), or an equity investment (in return for shared ownership in your business).

Even if you think you already know which you'd prefer, take a look at your other options, so that you won't be caught off guard if your prospective investor suggests or would prefer one of them. Understanding the boundary lines between the different options will also help you be crystal clear about both the investor's and your expectations of the deal, thus avoiding miscommunications and misunderstandings.

This chapter will discuss:

- basic requirements for setting up and handling a gift (see Section A, below)
- basic requirements for setting up and handling a loan (see Section B, below)

Key Features of Gifts, Loans, and Equity Investments			
	Repayment expected?	Type of repayment	Necessary documentation
Gift	No	None	A letter documenting the amount of the gift and noting that the giver does not expect repayment.
Loan	Yes, and normally with interest.	Repayment of principal and interest at specified intervals for a set amount of time.	For an unsecured loan, a promissory note. For a secured loan, a promissory note, security agreement, and UCC filing.
Equity Investment	Yes, but not at a set amount.	An ownership interest in your company.	A stock purchase agreement detailing the price of the shares, the number of shares, and the rights and responsibilities of both the business and the investor.

- basic requirements for setting up and handling an equity investment (see Section C, below)
- the comparative advantages and drawbacks of loans and equity investments (see Section D, below), and
- how your choice of financing type will be treated by the IRS (see Section E, below).

Remember, this chapter won't give you full instructions on any of these subjects—just enough information to know what to expect and start planning for.

A. Basic Setup and Handling of a Gift

Gifts of business capital, like other gifts, may come to you unexpectedly. You might be casually talking to someone you know about launching your new business, only to have the person offer a gift of money to help you get started. If this hasn't yet happened to you, it may still be worth asking more directly for such a gift. In polite society, asking someone for a gift of money doesn't normally look too good—but when you're starting a business, it can make sense. Of course, you probably would only approach people whom you knew were already thinking of making you a gift, such as a grandparent or other well-off relative.

A gift is the simplest form of capital you can receive. It implies no ongoing obligation to the giver, other than your personal ethical obligation to thank the person and maintain good relations (as discussed in Chapter 10). Of course, you'll want to make sure that the amount of the gift falls within IRS limits for gifting, as explained in Section E of this chapter.

As for documentation, all that's necessary is a letter explaining that the money is a gift, mostly for the giver's files (though you should carefully keep your own copy, as well). The giver needs to keep a copy for tax purposes, to assure the IRS that this transfer wasn't in reality an interest-free loan. (You'll find sample letters in Chapter 9.) Once that formality is taken care of, you're good to go.

Make Sure Your Family Means "Gift" When They Say "Gift"

You'd think it would be easy to communicate what is a loan and what is a gift. But when you look at how real families operate, the lines are often surprisingly blurry. Take the case of Ernie, whose parents had been giving him a so-called "gift" of around $20,000 annually (depending on the then-current gift-tax exclusion) since he was a teenager. This money was kept in a separate bank account in Ernie's name, but here's the catch: It was not to be touched by Ernie without his parents' permission. When Ernie entered business school, they mutually agreed that Ernie could use the money for school expenses, but that Ernie would have to pay back to the account anything he withdrew.

Just a few years later, Ernie had graduated from business school, owed about $70,000 to the account, and was planning a wedding with his fiancée, herself recently out of grad school. Neither had enough money saved up for the dream wedding both wanted (which would cost about $18,000). Ernie by now had developed a sense of entitlement to the money, legally in his name. He did intend to repay the education loan to the account but also wanted to use some to fund the wedding.

However, Ernie's parents remained firm that the money could be used only for education, real estate, or other asset-building opportunities. After months of tension, the family compromised. They decided that Ernie could withdraw up to $10,000 of the remaining funds in the account for the wedding, as an out-and-out gift. But if Ernie wanted to use any more for the wedding, or as living expenses until the pair settled into new jobs, it would have be as a loan, to be repaid to the account.

B.   Basic Setup and Handling of a Loan

Chances are, most of the informal financing you arrange will come in the form of a loan. Most family members and friends want to see their money back at some point, and very few of them are ready for the gamble of equity investing. In fact, nearly half of informal investors in the United States expect repayment within two years, and only 20% of people who loan or invest money informally expect *never* to be repaid. (*Source:* 2003 GEM study.)

Don't get bogged down in the vocabulary. The terms loan, loan capital, debt, debt capital, loan financing, and debt financing all mean just about the same thing, namely money borrowed with an expectation of repayment.

As you know, a loan is based on a simple idea: Someone gives you money and you promise to pay it back, usually with interest, over a set time period and in accordance with certain terms. It's so simple and familiar that you can borrow money on a handshake—but I don't recommend that approach, for reasons laid out in Section 1, below.

The main question for you at this point is, what tasks and obligations do you take on when you agree to a loan? Your four main obligations include:

- documenting the transaction in writing
- paying interest to your lender
- in some cases, setting aside collateral to help guarantee your repayment, and
- keeping up with your ongoing repayment obligations.

1.   Loans Should Be Formalized in Writing

For your sake and the sake of your lenders, it's best to set up every loan similar to the way a bank would, with a signed agreement and a repayment schedule. Even before a prospective lender has agreed to make you a loan, you'll increase his or her confidence by explaining that you'll be following these business standards. He or she is probably familiar with the basic principles of lending, so the more you shape your request to match something he or she recognizes, the better. Also, using a traditional banking document like a promissory note sets a formal, businesslike tone to the exchange, encouraging both parties to take the agreement seriously.

After the loan has been made, the fact that you put your agreement into writing actually increases the chances that you'll successfully repay it and thus protect your relationship with your lender. The written documents will spell out in detail when and how you're expected to repay—including what to do if you realize you're going to be late. Once your business gets underway, you'll have plenty of other issues to think about, and trying to remember what you and your lender informally agreed to over lunch should not be one of them.

The name of the legal document that a bank would use to formalize a loan, and that you should use, too, is a "promissory note." This is a piece of paper that says, in effect, "In return for giving me $X, I promise to pay you $Y plus interest of Z%." Once you've signed the promissory note, it's legally binding. That doesn't, however, mean that preparing one requires a team of lawyers or pages of fine print. Your promissory note can be as brief as one page, as long as it covers the material detailed in Chapter 9.

2.   Most Loans Require You to Pay Interest

When you borrow, you're using the lender's money—money that he or she could be using elsewhere—and in most cases, you'll need to pay for the privilege. If you've ever taken out a car or home loan, you're probably used to the way interest rates are set, as a fixed or variable percentage of the total amount of the loan. Monthly payments are ordinarily calculated to include a portion of the loan, called the "principal," plus interest.

Friends and family who lend you money are often willing to do so at below-market interest rates. Chances are they're more interested in supporting your efforts than in turning a profit, and some might even insist on earning no interest at all.

As you prepare to approach prospective lenders, however, you should plan on paying interest, for several reasons. Most important, you need to ensure that you meet IRS guidelines for private lending (more on this in

Saved by Promissory Notes: Renaldo's Restaurant

After two years in the restaurant business, Renaldo felt that success was on the way, but he still wasn't making enough money for a bank to take his loan request seriously. Yet Renaldo needed a significant sum in order to purchase new refrigeration equipment. Fortunately, Renaldo had the respect of his colleagues in the food industry, two of whom independently decided to lend him the needed money. At different times, over a beer at Renaldo's bar, each agreed to a three-year loan—and sealed the deal with nothing more than a handshake.

Renaldo had every intention of repaying his lenders and assumed he would pay each in one lump sum at the end of the three years. His colleagues, however, assumed differently. One expected regular monthly payments; the other expected monthly interest-only payments with a lump sum payment at the end. Sure enough, the conflicting assumptions quickly rose to the fore. Thrust into financially insecure positions, the lenders started mistrusting Renaldo, who became distressed at the deterioration of his relationships and the looming, unanticipated monthly payment obligations.

Renaldo finally realized he needed to formalize each loan. Through brief phone calls, he clarified what each lender expected and drafted two promissory notes. He created custom payment schedules that were appropriate to each of his two lender's wishes, but also long enough that he would be able to afford the regular payments. Renaldo thus saved both his relationships and his affordable and flexible source of business capital.

Section E, below). Also, just because Aunt Jean adores you doesn't mean she doesn't deserve to earn interest on her loan. A respectable interest rate, something like what she'd earn on a savings account or CD, may make her feel happier about the whole arrangement. And for prospective lenders who aren't that close to you, offering an interest rate that exceeds what they'd earn elsewhere is a great way to attract their attention.

Choosing the right interest rate is an important part of preparing your loan request. You'll learn more about how to choose the right rate in Chapter 6.

3. You May Also Need to Offer Collateral

When banks decide whether to make loans, especially to new businesses, they carefully scrutinize the creditworthiness of the borrower. But even that isn't usually enough for them. To make double sure that you will actually pay them back, banks often insist that you "secure" their loan by naming a piece of property that they can sell if you don't make your loan payments. This property is known as "collateral" or "security." Your promise of the collateral must be recorded both in the promissory note and in a security agreement.

The most familiar example of a secured loan is a home mortgage, in which the home itself serves as security, which the bank can sell, or "foreclose" on, if you fail to make the mortgage payments. Business loans tend to be secured by business assets, such as machinery or real estate, or the owner's personal assets, such as your home or car.

It's unlikely that the people with whom you're close will ask you to provide collateral for your loan. Unlike bank loans, most private loans, especially between relatives, are "unsecured." Private lenders usually like to have a promissory note, but no more. For most of them, your word is good enough when it comes to your intention of making good on the promissory note.

Just because a loan is unsecured doesn't mean that the lender has no recourse if you fail to repay it. Your lender is legally entitled to sue you for repayment, which may ultimately give the lender access to some of your assets.

Regardless of whether your friends and family lenders are likely to insist on it, there may be a good reason to offer some of them a secured loan. Telling someone that you are willing to put your home or equipment on the line says a lot. Also, it may be a key protection for lenders who later need that money for some other purpose, such as retirement or their children's education. Just don't forget that you risk losing the asset—such as an important piece of business equipment or your home—if you can't pay back the loan.

4. Loans Require Ongoing Management

Assuming you negotiate a traditional loan arrangement, you'll probably have to make monthly payments to your lender, by a certain date each month. If you're the sort who sometimes forgets to pay the credit card bill on time, you may find that this requires developing new habits and organizational skills.

In addition, committing to a loan repayment plan assumes that your business really will make money—which no one can guarantee. At least you'll have the advantage of working with a private lender, who is likely to be flexible when you can't meet your repayment obligations—but you nevertheless need to seriously consider whether you and your business can handle these monthly payments before signing onto a loan.

C. Basic Setup and Handling of an Equity Investment

There's a third way to raise the business capital you need: You can sell shares in your business to an "equity investor." Equity investors can range in experience and sophistication, from a family member who knows nothing about business or investing to a professional equity investor who buys shares in promising young businesses for a living.

Even if no one in your current circle is a likely equity investor, keep this type of financing in mind. If your business does well, it may not be long before you begin generating the revenue and showing the profit potential to attract professional equity capital.

Raising money for your business through equity investments is very different from raising it through borrowing money. You'll need to:

- compensate your investors for the risk they've agreed to take on
- share ownership in the business
- comply with securities laws, and
- hire an attorney to put all these agreements into a legal document unique to your financing situation.

1. Equity Investors Expect Compensation for Their Risk

Equity investors tend to invest anywhere from $50,000 on up and don't expect monthly payments in the mailbox. (Although some may require dividends, these are nearly always reinvested in the business, and never actually paid out in cash.) This is great for your month-to-month cash flow. Instead of always having to worry about how you'll make the next payment, you can use your cash to build your business.

Unlike a loan, if your business loses money or goes broke, part of the bargain is that you don't have to repay your investors their initial investment. Your investors are clearly taking on a high level of risk; they should understand and accept that they are not guaranteed to get their money back. To compensate for this risk, equity investors usually require:

- an attractive reward if you succeed, and
- acceptable protection if you fail.

a. Rewarding Equity Investors When You Succeed

Equity investors get into this game primarily because if the business succeeds, they win big. If your business grows very fast, investors stand to earn a lot more than they would have by merely making you a loan and collecting interest. In some ways, the potentially high returns are only fair—the investor is not receiving regular payments of principal and interest, or any rights to collateral, and is taking a huge risk on your doing what you say you're going to do. In return, you have to compensate the investor with a bigger potential payoff.

Equity investors measure what they earn (or hope to earn) from your business in terms of their so-called "return on investment" (ROI). ROI is an annual percentage that an investor earns upon exiting the deal.

Why an Equity Investment Can Be More Lucrative Than a Loan

If your mother-in-law makes you a loan of $10,000 and you repay it with 6% interest over the course of two years, the total amount repaid to her at the end of the two years will be $10,637. Once you have repaid her, the deal is done, regardless of how well your business is doing.

But if instead your mother-in-law buys shares in your business, and you do well, she stands to make much, much more. If, for example, your business is valued at $100,000, then her $10,000 buys her 10% of your company. (The actual price of each share depends on how much the entrepreneur and the investor agreed the business was worth—known as valuation—at the time the investment was made).

Next, let's imagine that, thanks to your mother-in-law's investments and the investments of a few other folks, you manage to grow the business until it's worth $500,000. Now her 10% is worth $50,000, a lot more than the $10,637 she would have gotten back for her loan. Of course, she can't just sell her shares (called an "exit") whenever she feels like it—there is no market for shares in privately held businesses. She has to wait for another investor (an individual or a business) to come along, decide that the opportunity is still a good one, and pay for her shares.

There's a reason that not everyone chooses equity investing, however. By deciding to make an equity investment instead of a loan, your mother-in-law would take on the risk that your business may fail entirely. In that case, people who made simple loans will get to stand in line ahead of the investors to get paid back out of whatever is left from your business. The investors divide up the remaining assets according to their stake in the business. Sometimes, there's nothing left to divide up.

But, you get the idea: Equity investors who make an investment in a business that grows to the point where other investors want to buy it are rewarded with a big payoff. The game for the investors is to find the business that will make this a journey to success while they go along for the ride.

In other words, it answers the investor's question, "By what percentage did the money I put into this deal increase each year by the time I got it back?" Professional investors such as venture capitalists like to see the value of their stake in the company grow at a rate of greater than 20% per year.

Did you mean IRR or ROI? You might also hear or see investors use the phrase "internal rate of return" (IRR). This is a percentage very similar to ROI, which investors use to determine whether the opportunity you're offering meets their objectives for the money they expect to earn on their investments. Specifically, the IRR is the rate investors feel they'd have to earn on an investment to make it worth the risk they perceive in the deal.

Equity investors tend to expect that they'll have to stick around for a few years for you to achieve your growth—but not much longer. Three to seven years is the average time that an equity investor expects to pass before he or she exits the deal. By that time, the investor figures that you will have sold the business, bought back his or her shares, or taken the company public on the stock market.

b.   Protecting Equity Investors From Possible Failure

When equity investors give you their money, they hope for high returns. But they also protect themselves from the chance that you could fail as spectacularly as they hope to see you succeed. The investors do this in two ways. First, they make sure that they stand a better chance than any other investor of getting their money back if the business goes belly up. They draw up long, complicated, legal documents with terms like "liquidation preference" and "dilution protection." These ensure that the investor will be able to collect a return, sometimes at two or three times the initial investment, leaving other less-privileged company co-owners (like you) with nothing.

Equity investors also protect themselves by being informed and involved in your business and any relevant decision making. They might take a seat on your board of directors, obtain special voting rights on critical matters, and require reports on both financial and operations matters. The benefit of this is that most professional investors are extremely knowledgeable and can provide you excellent guidance and advice. The downside is that you'll find yourself spending a lot of time and effort just keeping your investors up to date on everything they want to know.

2.   Equity Investments Mean Dealing With Shared Ownership

While monthly loan payments can be a burden, at least you remain in complete control of your company. If you decide to raise equity capital, you'll have to give up some of that control.

Recall from Chapter 1 that if you want raise money by selling shares, you'll need a legal structure that can accommodate carving up the business among co-owners.

Sharing ownership means sharing decision making. Your investors will have some say in the way you run your company. Some investors will want to know about your choices at every step of the way. One entrepreneur I know hit a stretch where one of his investors became preoccupied with the business's finances and requested *weekly* financial reports for several months. As you can imagine, those weekly reports quickly became a burden.

This isn't to say that you should avoid equity investors, just that you should know what you're getting into. If the time seems right, don't be scared off. Equity investors can provide exactly the combination of cash and management advice that you need to grow your business to the next level.

3.   Equity Investments Require Compliance With Securities Laws

Depending on how many investors you take in and how much money you raise, you may also need to comply with federal and state securities laws. The law calls corporate shares and (usually) LLC membership interests "securities." Federal and state securities laws regulate the offering of these securities to investors. This means that before you sell an investor a share in your business, you'll need to hire an attorney who can ensure that your offering complies with the law.

As your attorney will undoubtedly tell you, selling securities creates a lot of paperwork, starting with registering your sale with the Securities and Exchange Commission (SEC) as well as with whichever agency handles securities in your state. Fortunately, not all offerings of securities must be registered. Generous exemptions are provided, which normally allow a small business to dole out shares to a limited number of investors without complicated paperwork. For example, the following sales of shares are exempted:

- private offerings to a limited number of persons or institutions
- offerings of limited size, and
- intrastate offerings.

Determining precisely which exemptions apply to your offering is your attorney's job. You can do some background reading yourself, though. Start with two of Nolo's free online articles, "Corporations FAQ" and "Limited Liability Company FAQ," at www.nolo.com.

4. An Attorney Must Formally Document an Equity Investment

In addition to advising you on how to comply with securities law, you'll need an attorney to create the documents that formalize an equity investment. There's too much at stake (such as ownership and control of your business, not to mention a lot of money), and too much that's unique to your financing situation to just use a boilerplate form. I've never heard of any credible business owner who tried to sell shares in a company without the help of an attorney.

The key document you'll need in order to sell shares in your business is typically a stock purchase agreement, whose main elements include:

- the basic terms of the purchase and sale of stock (such as the purchase price, closing date, and conditions on closing)
- representations and warranties by the business and by the investors (statements that each party agrees are true), and
- identification of any other documents that may need to be produced for the closing, such as a certificate of incorporation, a list of the investors purchasing stock, and a list of disclosures by the company.

Fortunately, you don't need to pay an attorney to start from scratch. You'll find a sample stock purchase agreement discussed in Chapter 9 and available on the enclosed CD-ROM. Although the document needs to be tailored to your specific requirements, it's an excellent starting point, and you can familiarize yourself with its contents and start gathering information before meeting with the attorney.

D. Choosing Between Loan and Equity Capital

What's the bottom line here—is loan capital or equity capital better for your business? Unfortunately, there's no clear answer to that question. Even the experts don't agree when it comes to judging these two vastly different finance animals. The first is tame and predictable and hopefully uneventful. The second is extreme and unpredictable and could result in either huge gains or huge losses for your investors. To help compare the two, see "Advantages and Disadvantages of Loan and Equity Capital," below (reprinted from the article "Raising Money for Your Small Business: Loans vs. Equity Investments," online at www.nolo.com).

E. Tax Implications of Your Choice of Capital

No introduction to raising gift, loan, and equity capital would be complete without a discussion of the tax implications of each financing method. I've heard from reliable sources that transactions within a family group come under special IRS scrutiny. The IRS simply presumes that any transfer between family members is a gift, unless it sees proof to the contrary.

You'll see in this section how the IRS will view gifts, loans, or investments in your business. Your goal is to minimize your tax liability, as well as the liability of your lender or investor.

Create a paper trail of your financing activities. Now's the time to get organized about documenting and filing the records that prove your version of where the money came from and where it has gone. Whether you receive financing in the form of a gift, loan, or equity investment, make sure you have the proper letters and agreements for you and your lender or investor to share with the IRS.

Advantages and Disadvantages of Loan and Equity Capital

	Loan Capital	Equity Capital
Advantages	The lender has no management say or direct entitlement to profits in your business.	Investors are sometimes partners or board members and often offer valuable advice and assistance.
	Your only obligation to the lender is to repay the loan on time. Loans from close relatives can have flexible repayment terms.	You can be flexible about repayment requirements.
	Interest payments (but not principal payments) are a deductible business expense.	If your business loses money or goes broke, you probably won't have to repay your investors.
Disadvantages	You may have to make loan repayments when your need for cash is greatest, such as during your business's start-up or expansion.	Equity investors require a greater share of your profits than interest on a loan.
	You may have to assign a security interest in your property to obtain a loan, which may place your personal assets at risk.	Your investors have a legal right to be informed about all significant business events and a right to ethical management.
	Under most circumstances, you can be sued personally for any unpaid balance of the loan, even if it's unsecured.	Your investors can sue you if they feel their rights are being compromised.

1. Dealing With IRS Limits on Gift Amounts

You may receive up to $12,000 each year from any one person as a tax-free gift. This means that if you receive less than $12,000 from someone, no one needs to report anything. If you receive more than $12,000, the giver should file a gift tax return (IRS Form 709, *U.S. Gift Tax Return*) for the amount given over $12,000. Although the giver probably won't have to pay any tax for that particular year, the IRS will be keeping tabs on the giver's lifetime giving—the maximum is $1 million before taxes are owed. Even so, the giver's tax liability won't be settled until he or she dies and estate taxes are calculated.

Looking for details on the annual gift tax exclusion? See the IRS website at www.irs.gov, in particular Publication 950, *Introduction to Estate and Gift Taxes.*

If someone wants to give you more than $12,000 in a single year without using up any of his or her lifetime exclusion, there is a way to achieve that within the business-financing context. Simply structure the transfer as a loan, with repayments due periodically over a number of years. Your "lender" then has the option to receive or forgive payments as they come due. If your lender wants to turn your scheduled loan repayment into a gift, he or she can do so by writing you a "loan forgiveness letter" before the payment is due. Your attorney may also recommend that if you set up a private loan but expect to receive most or all of the repayments as gifts, you make a few payments (either at the beginning of the loan, or each year) to show the IRS some proof beyond the promissory note that the gift is a loan.

EXAMPLE: Emil's best friend Juan, who happens to be a millionaire, gives Emil $30,000 with which to start a printing and engraving business. However, Juan wishes to both make a gift and avoid exceeding his annual gift tax liability. After consulting with his accountant, Juan asks Emil to write a promissory note saying that he'll repay the loan with a repayment plan that includes quarterly payments each year for three years.

Each year, Emil makes his first quarterly payment, but then, before the 2nd, 3rd, and 4th quarter payments come due, Juan sends him letters declaring that the next payment is to be forgiven. In this way, Emil gets a substantial gift from Juan, and Juan does not exceed his annual gifting exemption with the IRS.

To benefit from the gift tax exemption, a gift must be made to you as an individual, since no exemption exists for business entities. Even if the gift is set up to be made to the business, the IRS will simply attribute it to the owner of the company. For example, if your uncle gives you $10,000 for a car and then another $10,000 for your new coffee shop in the same tax year, he will have made, in effect, a $20,000 gift to you. Since he has exceeded the annual gift tax exclusion, he will have to file a gift tax return so that the IRS can record the $8,000 against his lifetime exclusion from estate taxes.

2. When Loans May Lead to Tax Liability

Your private loan is not as private as you might think. For one thing, if the IRS sees the funds in your bank account and you can't prove they're from a loan, the IRS may treat the transfer as a gift. (See Section a, below.) For another, if you don't pay interest at the minimum IRS-approved rate, the IRS will view your lender as if he or she had in fact received the extra interest and then gifted it back to you. (See Section b, below.)

a. Tax Liability for Disguised Gifts

If you don't create documents showing that this money transfer was a loan, the folks at the IRS might suspect that it was actually a gift. The IRS pays particular attention to intrafamily loans and assumes that there may be a gift hidden in them that should be taxed. Especially if you're planning to borrow from a relative, the most effective way to protect everyone involved is to use a detailed promissory note specifying your intent to repay the money, the time frame in which the loan will be repaid, and the amount of interest charged. (All these clauses are included in the sample promissory note discussed in Chapter 9.)

If the loan is very large and you want to be extra safe, some family attorneys recommend that you also create proof that repayments are being made, such as a loan log or copies of deposited checks. If you are in fact planning to spread a large loan across several years and then receive periodic gifts of your repayments from your lender (as described in "Using Private Loans to Maximize Gift Tax Exemptions," in Chapter 2, Section B), consider making occasional payments. That will create a paper trail in case the IRS comes sniffing around. Be cautious: No one wants to have their "loan" assessed as a "gift," especially if it causes the lender/giver to exceed the gifting limit. If you have any concerns, consult with your accountant or a tax attorney.

b.   Tax Liability If You Pay Too Little Interest

In the IRS's unending search for taxable income, it keeps an eye out for cases where lenders receive less interest than they should. As for how low the IRS thinks an interest rate should go, it publishes this monthly, as the so-called Applicable Federal Rate (AFR). If you pay less than the AFR on a private loan of more than $10,000 (there is no such requirement for loans less than $10,000), the IRS will apply the AFR and calculate what you should have been paying. This is called "imputing interest."

The IRS will then treat the difference between what your lender actually received from you and what he or she should have received (namely, the AFR) as a gift. If that makes the gifts from your lender to you exceed $12,000, then your lender will have to file a gift tax return for the amount over $12,000.

Although filing the return is a pain, the lender's overall gift tax liability may not actually increase by much. You'd need to have a huge loan for the imputed interest in one year to exceed $12,000. (For example, if you're paying 1% on a loan on which the IRS says you should be paying 4%, the loan would have to be $3.3 million before the imputed interest exceeded the $12,000 annual gift exclusion!)

The upshot is that, for any loan over $10,000, the IRS will be expecting the borrower to pay at least the AFR. If you pay less than that, you can assume that the IRS will start imputing interest and will keep tabs on the amount as it relates to the lender's total gift tax liability.

Don't feel bound to the AFR. If you think your lender is willing to charge you a very low interest rate, don't be afraid to save money by selecting an interest rate below the AFR. Even if your lender charges you 1%, chances are the amount of interest the IRS imputes will not exceed the $12,000 gift exclusion for each year.

Below is a sample AFR table, from just before this book was printed. However, these numbers change monthly, so when you're ready to sign a promissory note, check the latest AFR on the IRS website. (Go to www .irs.gov and search for "AFR." The first document that comes up should be the "Index of Applicable Federal Rates." Click that link and you'll be taken to a list, arranged in date order—download the most recent table.) Alternatively, you can find a current AFR table at the CircleLending website at www.circlelending.com/afr.

To use the AFR table, match the term of your loan with the frequency of payments that you promise to make. For example, using the table below, a four-year loan to be repaid monthly should be paying at least 4.01% in interest.

Sample AFR Table				
February 2006	**Period for Compounding**			
Loan Term	**Annually**	**Semi-Annually**	**Quarterly**	**Monthly**
Short Term (<3 yrs)	4.39%	4.34%	4.32%	4.30%
Mid Term (3-9 yrs)	4.40%	4.35%	4.33%	4.31%
Long Term (>9 yrs)	4.61%	4.56%	4.53%	4.52%

3. When Loans May Lead to Tax Deductions

There are a few benefits to the IRS learning about your loan: You may be able to deduct your loan setup costs as well as your interest payments. (See Section a, below.) As you probably know, deductions are subtracted from your taxable income, thereby indirectly reducing your overall tax bill. Also, if all else fails and you default on the loan, your lender might be able to claim a tax deduction. (See Section b, below.)

a.   Tax Deductions Based on Setup and Interest Costs

The two most relevant tax deductions for a new small business owner based on your loan are:

- the costs of setting up the loan, and
- your interest payments.

You are allowed to deduct (as a business expense) any business start-up costs, up to a maximum dollar amount set by the IRS each tax year. For the 2004 tax year that figure was $5,000. The costs of setting up and managing your private loan—for example, photocopying your loan proposal, paying for your lender's lunch, hiring an accountant or attorney to help, and the like—are all deductible under this provision.

Second, you can deduct as a business expense all interest that you pay or accrue during the tax year on debts related to your business, so long as all of the following are true:

- You are legally liable for the debt.
- Both you and the lender intend that the debt be repaid.
- You and the lender have a true debtor-creditor relationship.

Formalizing your private loan with a promissory note (which you'll learn to create in Chapter 9) will help you meet these requirements.

 The following resources provide more details on the tax implications of borrowing business capital:

- To learn more about deductions for your private loan, see IRS Publication 535, *Business Expenses*.
- For more tips on tax deductions from which you might benefit, see "Deductions Your Small Business Shouldn't Miss" and "Small Business Taxes FAQ," in the Business & Property section of Nolo's website at www.nolo.com.

b.   Bad-Debt Tax Deductions for Your Lender

If your worst-case scenario occurs and you default on your loan, your lender will probably want to claim a bad-debt deduction. The least you can do is to help the person claim this deduction successfully. As mentioned earlier, the IRS assumes that intrafamily transfers of money are a gift, so if your lender tries to claim a bad-debt deduction when you can't repay, expect the IRS to scrutinize the whole affair.

One attorney describes a situation where a mother wrote her son a check for over $100,000 towards his farming operation. Their agreement was informal. For the first few years the operation did well, and the son made regular payments to the mother. But then came a drought, and before long, not only had the son's payments dried up, but the mother ended up having to pay off a bank loan her son had taken out while trying to keep the ill-fated operation afloat. That tax year she took a tax deduction of nearly the whole amount, but the IRS rebuffed her, saying that no evidence existed to show that she'd expected repayment from her son. She appealed to a judge, but he agreed with the IRS, noting that neither mother nor son had treated the transaction as an enforceable loan. (Find this and other real-life stories at www.taxfables.com.)

To avoid a situation ending like the one described above, your lender must prove two things: that he or she indeed loaned you the money, and that he or she took the necessary steps to try and collect upon the loan. Here's what you can do to help your lender make the case for a bad debt deduction:

- **Make sure your lender has a copy of the promissory note**. If for some reason your lender has lost the original, make him or her a copy of yours. (If you have to go through this, you and your lender will both be relieved that you properly formalized the loan with a promissory note.)

- **Provide dated copies of evidence that the lender tried to get his or her money back from you**. Reminder emails and letters, for example, are good forms of evidence. If you and your lender are managing the loan yourselves, you'll have to assemble these from your records, and hopefully you'll have kept them all carefully filed away. If you're using a third party to service your loan, the company or professional should be able to provide these records for you. The IRS will expect to see that your lender behaved like any normal lender would when you refused to pay and wrote you serious letters or hired a collection agency to attempt to recover the funds.

- **Write a letter to your lender.** The letter should acknowledge that the lender made many attempts to collect upon the loan and that you are unable to pay. Provide a personal financial statement, if possible, showing that you are unable to pay.

Your loan default falls into a category generically known as short-term capital losses, which your lender must report on a tax form called Schedule D, *Capital Gains and Losses.* The Schedule D must then be included with the lender's individual 1040 tax form. (All of these items are available at the IRS website at www.irs.gov.)

4.   How Your Business's Legal Structure Affects Taxation of Its Profits

Your decision process regarding the best legal structure for your business (discussed in Chapter 1) comes back into play in this section. Your business's legal structure determines the rate at which any profits your business earns will be taxed. While lenders won't care about how much you're taxed (because it's irrelevant to their loan payments), if you have equity investors, both you and they will care a lot.

For example, if you're operating a sole proprietorship, any profits you earn will be taxed at your individual tax rate. The same holds true for partnerships, in which the partners, both general and limited, are taxed at their individual tax rates.

If your business is organized as a corporation, you'll encounter the double taxation mentioned in Chapter 1—any profit you make will be taxed first at the corporate rate. Then, if you distribute any of these profits to your shareholders in the form of dividends, each will have to pay taxes on those "gains" at their individual rate. In the accounting lingo of the IRS, the opposite of "gains" is "losses." Although losses hurt when they happen, at tax time losses can be handy for reducing your overall tax burden. Unfortunately, while gains are taxed at both the corporate and individual levels, losses are not similarly shared. The corporation can deduct losses, but shareholders may not.

However, if your corporation elected subchapter S status (or was formed as an LLC), shareholders *can* in some cases deduct their share of corporate losses on their own individual taxes. This can mean a great deal to your investors. When an investor has multiple sources of investment income, up to $3,000 in losses can be used to offset capital gains, reducing the overall tax burden. Please consult your tax adviser for a full discussion of these complex issues—the tax implications for each situation can be unique.

LLCs—an increasingly popular legal structure for small businesses with individual equity investors—need to file a form with the IRS electing whether to be taxed as a corporation, a partnership, or other entity. (You actually get to tell the IRS how you want to be treated, instead of the other way around!) Whichever structure you choose will, however, mean a different form of taxation for your investors. For example, a partnership does not pay tax on its income but "passes through" any profits or losses to its partners, as described above. Therefore, if your business is structured as an LLC that is reporting as a partnership, the investors (known as "partners" by the IRS in this scenario) will have to include these "pass-through" items on their individual tax returns.

Most entrepreneurs will select pass-through status, but you should evaluate your unique situation with an accountant or attorney to make the right decision for you and your investors. A good resource to draw on is *Form Your Own Limited Liability Company,* by Anthony Mancuso (Nolo).

■

Deciding Who to Ask for Money

A. Developing Your List of Prospects 78

   1. Brainstorming a List of People 80

   2. Narrowing Your List 81

   3. Creating Your Best Bets List 87

B. Evaluating Each Prospect 89

   1. The Two Cards Prospects Bring to the Table 89

   2. How Your Prospect's Business Experience and
      Personality Combine 91

If your face was on the ten o'clock news, how many people would look up and say, "I know that person!"? The list is probably longer than you'd think—and includes more prospective investors than you'd imagine. They need not be millionaires, and they need not be loyal relatives.

> **EXAMPLE:** Ahmet Ertegun grew up in a musical home and by the age of five had fallen in love with jazz. After graduate school, he and his friend Herb Aramson started a record label. When the first few albums didn't do well, they decided to sell the company and start over. They were unable to convince any of Ahmet's father's friends to invest, so they turned to Dr. Vahdi Sabit, the family dentist. Sabit put up $10,000 by mortgaging his house. Atlantic Records became one of the great soul labels in U.S. history and survives today as part of Time-Warner. (See www.history-of-rock.com/atlantic_records.htm and www.bsnpubs.com/atlantic/atlanticstory.html.)

This chapter will help you brainstorm a list of potential investors and sift through their names to decide which ones to ask for money. You'll learn how to:

- identify the people you plan to approach, and narrow that list to your "best bets" (see Section A, below), and
- evaluate the mix of business experience and personality that each prospect would bring to your business (see Section B, below).

A. Developing Your List of Prospects

If you're like many small business owners, your first reaction to this book's topic may be, "But I don't know enough people with money, much less people I'd feel comfortable asking for money." Don't let that initial reaction stop you. Asking people you know to pitch in on financing a new or growing business is anything but a radical idea. Before anyone had ever heard of banks, informal, person-to-person loans were the way many businesses got started—and the way many investors made money.

Although modern banks have reduced the need for private financing, they haven't supplanted it. With approximately five out of every 100 adults in the United States having invested privately in someone else's business within the last three years, it's clear that private financing remains alive and well. It is, however, often hidden behind the doors of the family home. A whopping 42% of private investors are close family members, such as a spouse, sibling, child, parent, or grandparent. (*Source:* 2003 GEM study.) If you add in the 10% of investors who fall within the "other relative" category, that's more than half of all private investing coming from someone related to the entrepreneur.

Who Makes Private Investments	
Relationship of investor to entrepreneur	Percentage of private investments
Close family	42%
Other relative	10%
Work colleague	6%
Friend or neighbor	29%
Stranger	9%
Other	4%
Total	100%

But let's not overlook the fact that nearly half of private loans and investments come from people who are *not* related to the entrepreneur (29% friends and neighbors, and another 19% who are work colleagues, strangers, and others). Clearly, you should cast your mental net widely when thinking about your circle of contacts.

Chances are that you, like many entrepreneurs before you, will need to piece together business capital from several small investments. Finding one person who can provide all the financing you need is unlikely and could be overly time consuming. To assemble your capital, you may need to both rekindle old relationships and start new ones. "Many of the most successful entrepreneurial ventures—those that create jobs, wealth, innovation, and economic growth—got off the ground because of the founder's ability to tap into his or her personal network for capital," says Carl J. Schramm, a leader in the field of entrepreneurship.

The three main steps toward tapping your network are to:

1. brainstorm a list of the people you know
2. narrow your list based on trust, money, experience, and lack of emotional baggage, and
3. create a summary, "best bets" list.

1. Brainstorming a List of People

Your first step is simply to draw up a huge list of names, including your family, friends, and beyond. You are in search of people with whom you already have, or can establish, a trusting relationship. You also want to identify people who are interested in seeing you succeed, either for personal or for business reasons.

Proper brainstorming involves not rejecting anyone who pops into your mind. Now is not the time to think about how remote your relationship to a particular person is, or how unlikely he or she is to invest in your business—it's just time to make a list.

To make the process of thinking up names somewhat systematic, visualize the people you know as occupying three concentric circles. All three circles are in orbit around you, at the center of this mini-universe. (Just don't tell people that you think of them this way!) The innermost circle includes your nearest and dearest, the middle circle includes your other current relationships, and the outermost circle includes people with whom you aren't in direct, regular, or current contact.

It will be easiest to start your list with the people in your inner circle—those with whom you have the closest relationships. The obvious suspects include parents, grandparents, siblings, aunts, uncles, cousins, and in-laws, as well as close friends and neighbors. Go through your brain for people whose names, phone numbers, and email addresses are already there. Then check on who is programmed into your cell phone or written on the babysitter's emergency contact list. And don't forget the relatives you rarely contact because you know you'll see them every year at Thanksgiving or at the beach.

The middle circle includes people with whom you are a bit more distant relationship-wise, but with whom you currently and regularly associate, particularly in the course of your professional life. These should be folks who think well of you because of what you do and how you do it. Think about business associates; fellow volunteers; members of your church, temple, or mosque; people with whom you've worked in current or past jobs; and supervisors or employers in those workplaces. If you're in business right now, consider which of your customers or suppliers really like what you do. Also think about any potential business mentors or entrepreneurs—people who may have good knowledge and information about the kind of business you're in, and whom you either know already or could get to know. Most of the contact information for people in this circle will likely be in your address book or computer.

Finally, the outermost circle reaches to folks with whom you've had contact in the past, friends or acquaintances you rarely see, and people you know only through someone else. These people should either know your name or recognize and think highly of a mutual acquaintance. Beyond your business experience, think back to teachers, college friends, mentors, professors, coaches, and others who might have an interest in seeing you succeed. If you happen to know any business angel investors—affluent individuals with experience and an interest in helping new businesses get started—add their names, too, if you haven't already.

To come up with some names for this circle, skim through your address book, email database, holiday greeting card list, old school yearbooks, alumni directories, employee rosters from old jobs, and even party invitation lists.

If your brainstormed list feels short, you might ask a trusted friend or colleague to help out. He or she may know of local people who have invested in other businesses or simply remember a mutual contact that you'd forgotten.

2.   Narrowing Your List

To turn your long list of contacts into a short list of prospects, evaluate each person in terms of the following four characteristics. Circle the names of people who possess *at least two* of these characteristics:

- trust in you
- ability to afford the investment
- business experience, and
- lack of emotional baggage.

⚠️ **Don't choose a lender out of desperation**. Although you need the money, don't go so far as to take it from people you don't trust or like. As entrepreneur Andrea Lang of the AromaDough Café says, "I avoid people who only seem interested in the money part, and not in what it takes to grow the business; people who say they can't wait to tell 'their people' about the deal, or people who are pushy. It's a gut feeling ..."

a.   Trust in You

Identify those people who know your character or abilities and trust that your deeds will match your words. Family and friends with whom you have good relationships, and people with whom you've worked, especially your supervisors or employers, may fall into this category. Someone who is a "control freak" probably does not trust you, or his or her trust may come with a high price tag. (See "Avoiding the Control Freaks," below.)

Avoiding the Control Freaks

Some investors are the very opposite of self-sacrificing—their loans will come with strings attached. For example, they may want to have a say in running your business, or they may enjoy the power associated with having you become reliant on them. Even some parents and grandparents fall prey to this, perhaps as the natural result of paying for your diapers and food since day one. For other relatives, friends, and business associates, lending you money creates an opportunity to exert control over your life, your business, and your interactions with them.

You may remember an episode of the classic TV show M*A*S*H, where the crusty, elitist Dr. Charles Winchester acts according to character when paychecks for his fellow doctors are delayed. He becomes a de facto loan shark, fronting his friends some cash but expecting that each perform favors for him until he is repaid. If you know your prospects' personalities, you can probably predict which ones are the Dr. Winchesters and decide how to proceed accordingly. It's quite possible that you should not proceed with some of them at all.

Of course, not every investor who wants to be involved in your business is a true control freak. In particular, if you attract money from business angels, you should expect that they will exert a degree of financial control. It's part of their way of doing business—they make the risky investment, you give them the power to protect their investment. These investors will expect to be notified of progress with your business and may want to exercise control either formally, via a seat on the board of directors, or informally, via company visits. (See Chapter 8 for more detail on the types of involvement that equity investors may want.)

b.   Ability to Afford the Investment

The higher a person's net income, the more likely he or she is to agree to an informal investment. While it's great to have a long list of people who trust and adore you, the ones who can't spare the cash—or can't spare enough to make a difference—should simply be crossed off your list.

How do you figure out whether a person can afford a private investment in your business? You may know that the person already makes private loans or investments, through gossip by family members or word of mouth among friends or colleagues. If you know a "cashed-out dot-commer," that is, someone who made a lot of money during the Internet bubble of the late '90s, he or she probably has money to invest.

Observing the cars that people drive or the vacations they take can alert you to some who have money. (But watch out for the people who simply spend every dime of their income.) Other people are less showy in their behavior, and you may need to spend some time building the relationship to get a sense of their financial situation.

For each prospect on your list, ask yourself: "Can he or she afford to lose the investment?" For equity investors, this is a real risk, and for each one, you should be able to answer "yes." For lenders, the risk is a bit lower, especially if you secure the loan with your business or personal assets. However, even lenders should still be able to say that losing the money wouldn't sink them financially. Andrea Lang, who has been raising money from over 20 people to start her café, says that she has never and will never ask for money from someone she knows can't afford to lose it. It's simply one of the fundraising principles she's set for herself.

Finally, finding people who can provide larger amounts means less work for you overall. If you can, for example, raise $50,000 in two $25,000 loans, it will require a lot less effort (both before and during the loan) than raising $50,000 through ten $5,000 loans.

> ⚠ **Don't even think of borrowing from someone who relies on a limited fixed income, such as Social Security.** No matter how optimistic you feel about your business's chances for success, the risks aren't worth it—their income is too precious.

c.   Business Experience

People who are themselves entrepreneurs are the most likely to invest in other businesses. Perhaps the reason is that, as said in the GEM report, "they understand the entrepreneurial process; they are able to evaluate the prospects of another entrepreneur's venture; and they like to support other entrepreneurs with both money and advice." Pundits say that the average successful entrepreneur has private investments in three other businesses, and the average successful senior-level corporate executive has investments in five other private ventures. So if you think that people who own their own business have their hands too full to invest in yours, think again. Your business may be just the extracurricular activity they're looking for.

Business experience is not a necessary characteristic for a lender. After all, the lender's level of involvement in your business is totally up to you. But business experience is an important characteristic to have in an equity investor. While you may get some "love money," that is, an equity investment from a relative who doesn't really know or care about the business, most equity investors won't invest until they've carefully analyzed the opportunity. They are likely to take their role as shareholder seriously, requesting information and calling to get business updates. Finding knowledgeable investors who can advise you based on their experience will prove invaluable.

Surveys Say That Your Best Bet Is ...

The most promising prospect for an informal investment is an older male relative, himself an entrepreneur, with high income and high net worth. Sounds stereotypical, and it may change in the future, but that's what the numbers currently show. Of course, your circle may not include anyone who fits this profile, and you may do just fine raising money from all types of people. But if you have anyone in your circle who matches the description above, definitely put him at the top of your list.

d.   No Emotional Baggage

Emotional baggage is the stuff that weighs people down. Review your list to make sure there are no people with whom, in your gut, you feel nervous about entering a financial relationship. If you find any, cross them off.

Past conflict between you and the other person is the biggest red flag, especially if it remains unresolved. For example, if just last year you didn't speak to your brother for six months due to a misunderstood remark to his girlfriend, and your relationship is still a bit shaky, you should probably not consider him a prospect—not even if he has the money and related business experience to make him a good prospect. Similarly, you should not ask a person for money if you aren't on good terms with his or her spouse or partner. A private loan or investment can be a great source of friction within the home if the couple does not see eye to eye on it.

If asking your parent or parents for money could cause tension in the family, avoid that as well. Many families do quite well at sharing their resources between generations; see "The Family Bank," below. But you know your family best. If you believe that the loan or investment would only cause tension with your siblings and anxiety on the part of your parents, crossing them off your list at the beginning might be best.

The Family Bank

If your parents or other elders are well off, you're probably not the only one in your generation hoping for a loan or other money transfer. Some families deal with the competing requests by adopting a "family bank" approach, in which the parents make loans available to all their children, on condition that the children agree to certain preset standards.

Family banks and similar concepts are not new ideas. They've been in use for many generations in some wealthy families. The family bank was particularly common before institutional lending and credit cards became prevalent. The point is to leverage the family's financial resources in a win-win transaction between family members—the children gain the use of the parents' money, and the interest payments stay within the family. The family bank can be a great source of help, but also a great source of friction if not properly managed.

To make family banks work for multiple loans within the same family, the lender should take the following steps:

- Treat each loan request with the same respect and analysis, by focusing on its financial merits.
- Keep everything in writing, as if the borrower and lender were strangers. Relying on people to remember the exact terms of their loan is a recipe for trouble.
- Establish some standards to which all loans must adhere, such as a minimum interest rate, a maximum loan amount, and required documentation.
- Keep each borrower's loan terms and status private. If the borrowers want to share information, that is their prerogative.
- Communicate to everyone involved the benefits that accrue to borrowers in good standing, such as lower interest rates and better repayment terms.
- Communicate to everyone the events that would trigger the "bank" to stop making loans in general, or to one person in particular.
- Consult with a family accountant or attorney on a regular basis to handle the tax implications of the family bank in general, and of each loan in particular.

Of course, very few relationships are perfect, and people can change. In some cases, a successful investment experience may represent a big step forward for a relationship.

> **EXAMPLE:** Cal was a recent college graduate with no savings or credit to speak of. His parents offered him the money he needed to launch his business, but he wanted to demonstrate his independence and refused to take the money as a gift. Instead, they agreed to formalize it as a loan, with a generous repayment structure. Cal borrowed $9,000, which for him was a lot of money. He made his payments on time even during the many months when he was cutting it close. For Cal, showing his parents he could be financially independent and responsible was just as important to him as getting the money he needed to launch his business.

Whatever you do, don't ignore relationship issues when considering whom to ask for money, particularly when it comes to family members. If the business fails, people will take sides, and things could get very uncomfortable. Be honest with yourself about whether the personal relationship can handle the financial risk of a private loan or investment.

3. Creating Your Best Bets List

Now let's take the remaining names on your list and create something more organized. Draw up a table that lists "Best Bets"—that is, people with at least two of the characteristics described in the previous section. (You'll find a worksheet for this in Appendix B and on the CD-ROM at the back of this book.) Include columns for each person's name, a brief description of why the person appears to be a good prospect, and the best way to contact the prospect.

Even after you've created your table of best prospects, don't discard any of your draft lists. Remember, this is just the first phase of a long process. You'll probably need to come back to your old drafts for more ideas later; see "Expanding Your Circle," below. Even the most distant contact that you wrote off during the first round could lead you to your next source of capital.

Best Bets List

Prospect Name	Prospect Description	Contact Information
Jane Smith	Mother, has money, trusts me, and we have a good, open relationship.	Use home phone: 111-222-3333
Joe Thompson	Uncle who started, managed, and sold his business; I think he might have invested in some other businesses of his golf buddies.	Use email or cell phone: 111-333-4444
Pete Williams	Friend from college; reconnected at reunion, turns out he's been very successful in the same industry that I'm trying to enter.	Dig up his business card from desk drawer: ____-__-____

Expanding Your Circle

When I started raising money for CircleLending, I tapped out my list of best prospects pretty quickly. My business needed additional money to grow, and I had to both revisit my brainstorming list and come up with some new names. I asked people in my inner circle (both my investors and others I'd never even approached) whether they would each mind sharing the names of three contacts—relatives, friends, or business associates—whom they thought might be business angel investors.

A number of people agreed to think it over. By now, they'd heard me talking a lot about my new business and were happy to be asked for such an easy (and cheap!) way to participate. Nevertheless, getting back to me obviously wasn't the first thing on their minds, and I had to follow up in many cases. Within the next two years my circle of new investor contacts grew considerably using this technique.

My former boss at a consulting company was just one of the people who helped in this effort. He had already made a small equity investment in my new business. Then, after I asked for his list of three, he introduced me to two of his associates, each of whom soon invested in the business as well. Later, as I built relationships with the two new investors and they grew to trust me and the business, each introduced me to new associates of theirs, prospects who amazingly led to even larger investments. All this from asking my former boss for a few names!

B. Evaluating Each Prospect

At this point, you should have a good idea of whom you're going to approach about financing. However, before asking them for money, you've got one last bit of background work to do: gathering your thoughts and knowledge about each prospect. Once you understand what makes each of them tick, you'll be better able to craft an appropriate loan or investment proposal (using the instructions in upcoming chapters).

1. The Two Cards Prospects Bring to the Table

You may recall that people invest in their entrepreneurial pals and relations for a variety of reasons, ranging from altruism to self-interest— and usually involving a complex mix of the two. You may know exactly why your prospect would invest in you, or you may have only a hunch. However, the most successful requests are usually the ones that cater to the prospects' experiences in two areas critical to successful lending and equity investing: experience with business investing, and comfort with the idea of mixing money and relationships.

a. Experience With Business Investing

If your prospect has previously made other private loans or investments, great. He or she is likely to understand key issues such as why your business seems to need a lot of money up front, why you may not be making much of a profit at the beginning, and how to improve your marketing plan. Other relevant experience includes having started a small business, worked in a senior position at a small business, or invested in the stock market. If your prospect has any of this in his or her background, consider him or her savvy. Savvy prospects may be open to either a loan or an equity investment.

A less-savvy or inexperienced prospect may not have the skills to really evaluate and fully understand your request. The result is that you'll have to explain it clearly and help educate the person (especially when it comes to the risk of losing the investment). This doesn't mean you should take this prospect off your list, especially if he or she has always supported your endeavors and is likely to do so again. It just means this prospect is probably better suited to a loan request, not an equity investment, and that in making the request, you shouldn't muddy the waters with a lot of business details.

b.   Comfort Mixing Money and Relationships

The second area to consider is your prospect's past experience—and comfort level—with mixing money and relationships. Is your prospect someone who would think of an investment as a business transaction, or would he or she consider the agreement part and parcel of your personal relationship? If at all possible, find out whether your prospect has done any of informal, private investing before, and how it turned out. Someone who had a positive experience—namely who worked with an honest, preferably successful businessperson whose profits paid the investor back and then some—is obviously more likely to invest again than someone who got taken for a ride.

If your prospect doesn't appear worried by mixing money and relationships (whatever his or her past level of experience with such transactions), consider him or her to be analytical. If the prospect's relationship with you isn't particularly close, he or she is especially likely to take an Analytical approach to the transaction. For example, your golf partner probably won't obsess over the possibility that loaning you money will make the two of you less likely to have deep and open conversations.

Even with some closer relationships, like family or good friends, you'll find some prospects who can compartmentalize (separate their emotions from the facts). If, for example, you know that certain family members always play fair in an argument (without manipulating or saying "you must not love me"), it's a fair bet that they treat other transactions analytically as well.

A worried prospect is someone who fears that providing money for your venture could damage your relationship or his or her relationships with others if and when they find out. (See "The Family Bank" in Section A, above.) For example, a person known as a "worrywart," one who hates uncertainty, or a parent concerned about creating sibling rivalry or jealousy is likely to fall into the "worried" category.

2. How Your Prospect's Business Experience and Personality Combine

To get a full picture of how your prospect will react to your request and behave as an investor, consider the interplay between his or her business experience and comfort level mixing money and relationships. For example, a prospect with no business experience who also thinks it's a social faux pas to mention the word "money" may be hopeless, while one with no business experience but a cool-headed approach to unusual financial or other opportunities might be a good prospect.

Fortunately, you don't have to reinvent the wheel in terms of analyzing these various combinations. The four possibilities are shown on the Prospect Tyall into identifiable behavior patterns. After matching one of your prospects to a square on this matrix, see the corresponding subsection below for more details about what you can anticipate from this person.

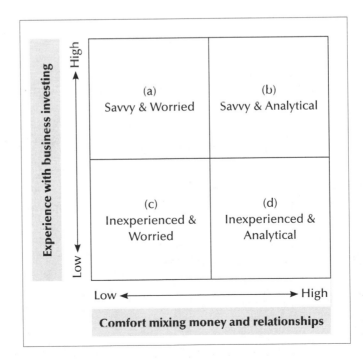

a.   The Savvy and Worried Prospect

A savvy and worried prospect has experience with business investing but also harbors concerns about mixing money and relationships. For example, your mother, who successfully invested in her colleague's business five years ago, may have the experience to make informal investing work, but might also worry that an intrafamily loan could be less smooth. Her imagination may bring up scenarios in which you take it personally if she refuses to forgive a series of late payments. She may fear awkward conversations about your lifestyle choices while you have her money. As if that weren't enough, she may also fear that your struggling younger brother will cry foul and want an equivalent amount of money.

Your main job with these savvy and worried prospects will be to alleviate their sense of emotional risk. For example, if you ask the person for a loan, you'd be wise to carefully explain your plan for repaying it, including your month-by-month obligations and how you would handle any missing or late payments. This will help move the transaction from the personal to the business realm. The prospect is then reassured that he or she isn't signing up for a future of painful conversations with you.

You could also offer to share the details of the loan with other family members. Once they know the details, and have had a chance to ask you questions ("do you really plan to pay it back?"), you'll hopefully be able to forestall any jealousy or misconceptions.

If these measures don't help remove the person's sense of emotional risk, getting money from this prospect may be more trouble than it's worth. But for most prospects, setting out your expectations up front prevents awkward interactions down the road, and allows you to get on with business.

b.   The Savvy and Analytical Prospect

The savvy and analytical prospect has experience with private business investing and is able to treat the deal analytically. This person is not daunted by mixing money and relationships. As you might guess, savvy and Analytical prospects are the ideal combination. Some of them may already be angel investors.

For example, perhaps your optometrist dabbles in business investing, has known you since you were a kid, and likes your idea. As long as you can make a professional pitch and offer a respectable hope of return (a competitive interest rate on a loan or a high chance of success with an equity investment), your optometrist will probably be comfortable with making an investment and not think twice about any relationship risk.

Savvy prospects are, for the most part, motivated to invest because they've done it before and probably like it. That's why a high percentage of informal investors are successful entrepreneurs. These are people with business experience and a belief that the agreement can be handled in a way that doesn't hurt the personal relationship. These prospects tend to be found in the outer circles of your contacts list (not many people are related to angel investors).

Your main job in making an appeal to this kind of prospect is to present your request with the utmost professionalism. You'll want to include a detailed explanation of how the investment will play out, whether it's a loan or equity investment, and what kind of return you are offering. At the same time, you'll want to make the investment process easy. A savvy and analytical prospect is probably juggling several balls at once, and the easier you make it to invest in you, by providing the necessary paperwork and information in an organized fashion, the more positively the prospect will respond.

c.   The Inexperienced and Worried Prospect

Now for the prospect with the furrowed brow. An inexperienced and worried prospect is someone who has limited experience with this kind of business investing *and* is nervous about emotional risk to your relationship. Despite all this, however, he or she may still be supportive of you or your business idea. For example, even though your older brother has kids entering college and limited cash on hand, he may be the type who would give you his left kidney. The problem may be, he has gotten into trouble before, lending money to a college buddy. (And his wife, who is your sister-in-law, never lets him forget it.) You know he'll be reluctant to introduce that tension into your relationship.

Prospects who are inexperienced and worried may be the most trouble. If you have any of these on your final list, think very carefully about whether it's even possible to alleviate the risks from this prospect's perspective. If not, you may want to cross the person off your list. For example, make sure you are confident that your request is within the prospect's financial means. If you ask for too much from someone who cares deeply for you or feels responsible for helping you out, the refusal will likely be painful for you both.

Let's say, however, that you decide it's worth approaching a certain inexperienced and worried prospect for a loan. You're likely to find that this person would prefer to seal the deal with a handshake, because in his or her mind, the loan is more about trust in you than a belief in the business. You'll want to respond by explaining that the best way to protect your personal relationship is to make the agreement almost as if you were strangers—that is, to set it up and manage it in a businesslike fashion, with signed, legal documents and a repayment schedule. Explain the terms in the documents and how they translate into a schedule of repayments that you'll be able to afford. Also explain what your plan is in the event that you run into financial trouble.

d. The Inexperienced and Analytical Prospect

The inexperienced and analytical prospect has limited business experience but is comfortable mixing money with your relationship, perhaps because your relationship wasn't that close in the first place. This might appear an unlikely combination—why would someone without much business experience and without close ties to you want to make an investment in your business? Such investments are less common than others, but they do occur.

> **EXAMPLE:** Leo's neighbor, Lydia, is a woman of modest means who loves his business idea and thinks he's great at getting things done. Lydia knows that Leo has done wonders turning the annual block party from a gathering of a few lawn chairs into a neighborhood event complete with charity fundraisers and water games for the kids. As a disability rights activist, Lydia's business investing experience is minimal, but she's not the type to intrude.

Leo suspects she'd keep the neighborly relations separate from the business agreement. Such a person might make an excellent candidate for a loan or investment.

Don't worry if your prospect doesn't seem to fit neatly into one of these boxes. Just picking one of the four characteristics described above will help you ask for money in a way that's both attractive to your prospect and helps him or her feel comfortable with the level of risk being assumed.

Chapter 5

Preparing Your Business Plan and Your Fundraising Request

A. Preparing Your Business Plan 100

    1. Drafting the Narrative Description 101

    2. Preparing the Financial Description 103

    3. Supplying Supporting Documents 106

    4. Drafting an Executive Summary 107

    5. Adding a Cover Letter 107

B. Calculating the Amount of Your Request 107

C. Dividing Up Your Request Among Prospects 111

    1. Asking for All the Money From One Person.....................112

    2. Asking for the Same Amount From Each Person 112

    3. Asking for Different Amounts From Different People........112

The most effective way to ask for money for your business is to pitch—or sell—your idea, as you'll learn how to do in Chapter 7. But you can't sell someone on an idea that you haven't fully developed—and the established method for developing a business idea is to write a business plan. Even the amount you ask people for will depend in part on the analysis within your plan.

If you were to apply for a bank loan, the loan officer would almost certainly ask to see your business plan. Even when it comes to private lenders, there's a very good chance that one of their first questions in response to your overtures will be, "Sounds interesting, can I see a copy of your business plan?" Needless to say, having your plan ready and waiting is a sign that you literally mean business.

Don't make the mistake of thinking that a business plan is just a hoop through which you must jump to gain access to the business capital you need. It just so happens that a well-thought-out business plan is one of the best predictors of small-business success—not because there's any magic in the paperwork itself, but because of the thinking and research that you will pour into it.

The exercise of plotting out your business's immediate future in detail, and backing up your projections with researched facts and figures, will be an illuminating and at times shocking journey. It may help convince you that your idea is right on—or it may persuade you not to give up your day job. It will also help you figure out exactly how much money you need to raise.

So, where do you begin? Section A, below, will highlight the important subjects for you to research and think through. In Section B, below, you'll learn how to extract key financial information from your business plan in order to determine how much you'll need to fundraise. Then, in Section C, below, you'll take the table of best bet prospects you developed in the last chapter and estimate how much to request of each person listed.

There isn't space in this book to provide a complete discussion of how to write a business plan. For that, you should turn to the wealth of business plan preparation resources available to entrepreneurs, including books, software, and online resources, such as those listed below.

The Perils of Jumping Without Looking

Faced with losing his job when his employer, the Common Ground Diner, announced its closing, Marty Erkin figured it was time to start his own business. Loyal customers were sad to see the diner go, and Marty felt that, as the accountant and host for the past two years, he had the experience to make a new restaurant work. He and several other former employees found a property just a mile away and pooled their resources. One suggested they draw up a business plan, but Marty figured they would just pick up where the Common Ground Diner had left off. They were just $10,000 short of what they needed when Marty came up with the idea of asking some of the diner's most loyal customers to pitch in.

Marty remembered that a couple named Allen had been teary-eyed at their final meal at the Common Ground Diner. He invited the Allens for a coffee at the new property, energetically described his vision for a new place, and asked if they would be willing to help. The couple got back to Marty a week later. Their offer was by no means a sweet deal— $10,000 at 15% interest, to be repaid in 12 monthly payments. Marty balked at the size of the monthlypayments. Realizing, however, that the cash would allow Marty's Place to open in time for tourist season, he accepted the deal and signed the promissory note.

Marty's Place opened as scheduled. But between rainy weekends and a road construction project around the corner, it just couldn't draw enough customers. The Allens began calling regularly, asking whether they were making any money yet. Marty made his first two payments but then was unable to keep up, which only increased the pace of the calls and began a series of tense and emotional drop-in visits.

As the weather turned colder, Marty's colleagues jumped ship. Marty, now unemployed, was left to liquidate the business's assets and pay off its debts as best he could. His father ended up bailing him out and paying off the loan to the Allens.

Without a business plan, Marty had gotten in over his head. Had he spent some time planning his business and working more in the restaurant industry, his venture might have had a different outcome. The Allens, too, were left with a bitter first experience with informal investing.

High-quality business planning resources include:
- The U.S. Small Business Administration (SBA), at www.sba.gov. Further described in Chapter 1 and in Appendix C, the SBA is the federal agency charged with supporting small businesses in the United States. In addition to providing numerous free resources on its website, the SBA funds small business loan and guarantee programs nationwide and funds free business counseling through local university extension programs and community development agencies.
- Bplans, created by Palo Alto Software Inc., at www.bplans.com. The website contains hundreds of sample business plans.
- Nolo, the nation's premier legal self-help publishing company, at www.nolo.com. Check out the small-business portion of its website for free articles on start-up and legal issues for entrepreneurs. Nolo also sells the book *How to Write a Business Plan*, by Mike McKeever.
- The SCORE Association, also described in Chapter 1 and in Appendix C, provides tools for entrepreneurial education leading to the formation, growth, and success of small businesses, at www.score.org.

A. Preparing Your Business Plan

There is no one way to write a business plan, nor any one format to put it in. Focus on putting together the most effective business plan for your needs in a way that is, paradoxically, both thorough and concise. Typical plans range from a few pages to over a hundred pages.

To get ideas, look at sample business plans for existing businesses in your industry (for example, on the www.bplans.com website). Draft your plan based on what you feel is effective—or flawed—in what you see. After creating a first draft, look to free small business counselors like the ones at your local SBA or SCORE office to review and provide comments on your plan.

Already have a business plan you feel confident about? Skip ahead to Section B to calculate your fundraising request.

Nearly all the business plan advisers out there recommend that the main body of your plan include:

- a narrative (written) description of the business
- a financial description of the business, and
- supporting documents.

Once you've developed these sections, you'll also want to write an executive summary and a cover letter for your plan. Although these are the last things you'll prepare, they are the first and most important sections any prospect will look at.

1. Drafting the Narrative Description

In the narrative section of your business plan, communicate the opportunity you see and the business you plan to build in response. At a minimum, include descriptions of the opportunity, the product or service, the market, the competition, and the people who will make it all happen.

Business opportunity. Try beginning with a problem statement and then presenting your business as a solution. For example, you might explain that a local airport lacks shuttle service, and how you will fill this gap. If you have already started your business, cite any of its accomplishments to date, such as the number of customers served, products sold, or contracts received. These show that you have gained some traction (momentum) in solving the problem. Investors are particularly interested in knowing that you have real, live customers; how many you have; how much they pay you; and how you'll get more.

Operating plan. Provide a simple overview of how your business operates. If you will make a product, describe the process through which you will acquire your materials and create the product. If you will sell a service, describe your activities behind the scenes and in dealing with customers. For example, if you plan to analyze data freely available from the U.S. government and then sell your analysis, describe how you will get the raw data, what the analysis will include, what you will produce, and how you will package and deliver it (perhaps as a printed report, CD-ROM, or downloadable file) to your customers.

Pay attention to the implication of your operating plan on your cash flow. Make sure that you've thought through the timing of when you will receive payments (cash inflow) and when you will need to pay for things (cash outflow). Making sure you have enough cash on hand when the bills come due is one of the biggest challenges many entrepreneurs face.

Market analysis. Do your best to quantify the opportunity you have identified. Estimate the size of your market in numbers and dollar figures. Show who the customers are by giving some demographic information (see "Compiling Demographic Information," below) and describing how you plan to reach them. Also describe why you think these customers will buy from you.

Compiling Demographic Information

Knowing who your customers are and what motivates them to pick your product or service over a competitor's is an important part of your business plan. Do your best to describe the people most likely to patronize your business. Do they fall into a certain age group, geographic pattern, gender, interest group, or ethnic group? For example, if you believe that your product will appeal most to older, female, churchgoers in your region, then you can tailor your marketing strategy accordingly. (You will probably need to find methods of communication that reach that group, such as particular newsletters, radio shows, or events you can sponsor.)

Test your demographic theories by talking to owners of similar businesses in similar geographic areas, by observing their customers, and by talking to or surveying your existing customers if you've already floated a start-up or test version of your business. Then, collect information on how many people fit that description, with help from your local reference librarian and the U.S. Census Bureau (www.census.gov).

Competition. Don't kid yourself; someone else out there is probably already doing what you want to do. Identify who they are, then figure out why your product or service is better. Companies compete primarily on two fronts: cost (who charges the least) and quality (whose product or service is the best.) Be honest about whom you are up against, and state clearly why you will be the one to win the customers.

Personnel. Provide brief biographies of yourself and any key employees. Include your education and work experience. Highlight any training and professional experience specific to your industry or to starting and running a business.

2. Preparing the Financial Description

Like it or not, you will need to understand and present your business in financial terms to be successful. This section provides only a summary of the financial terms and statements that are critical for entrepreneurs to understand and use. If these are not yet familiar to you, consult additional resources and get advice from a business counselor or adviser. While you can hire a good accountant to help you get started, that doesn't let you off the hook completely. You personally will need to be able to tell the story of your business idea with numbers—and to make sure that the numbers tell as compelling a story as your narrative does.

Start with a Sources & Use of Funds Table as described in Subsection a, below. Next, if you're already earning some money by selling your product or service, you (or your accountant) should add the three standard financial statements described in Subsection b, below. Then use the spreadsheets described in Subsection c to show how your business will grow. These tables and spreadsheets deal in projected, not actual, figures but are a critical piece of the planning puzzle for anyone considering investing in you.

Look for a good, local accountant. He or she should be able to help you set up effective financial and management systems and even get you going on the right software package. Being able to generate accurate and timely records will be crucial to your ability to understand your business, make mid-course corrections, and generate the reports and records investors might require. At this early stage you don't need an expensive accounting firm; you need someone who is affordable and who has experience helping businesses get off the ground.

a. Putting Your Request Into Numbers

At the beginning of your business plan's financial description, you should include what's known as a "Sources & Use of Funds Table." The purpose of this table is to let your prospect know exactly how much you are raising overall, whom you are raising it from, and what the money will be spent on. See the sample below, for a fictional company called "ABC Business."

The "Uses of Funds" portion of the table will show how much business capital you are attempting to raise, by detailing what you need it for and how much each item costs. The "Sources of Funds" portion of the table shows where you plan to raise the capital from and how much will come from each source. Make sure the total "Uses of Funds" figure matches the total "Sources of Funds" figure.

Sample Sources & Use of Funds Table: ABC Business

Uses of Funds:

Two trucks @ $12,000	$24,000
Recurring costs for six months @ $500/month	3,000
Total	$27,000

Sources of Funds:

Personal savings	$ 5,000
Personal line of credit	12,000
To be raised from private investors	10,000
Total	$27,000

---

b. Portraying Existing Business Activities Numerically

As a business owner, you must become familiar with the three standard financial statements that show what's going on with your business: the balance sheet, income statement, and cash flow statement. All existing businesses generate these three financial statements on a quarterly basis and at the end of each fiscal year (annually). Some also do it monthly. You can find templates—spreadsheets you can fill out with your own figures—on the SBA website. (Click "Financing," then look under the "Basic Financing Topics" heading and click "Understanding Financial Statements.")

Balance sheet. This financial statement shows a summary of your business's assets (what you own) and liabilities (what you owe). It's a snapshot in time. In other words, the statement is used to communicate the financial condition of a business at any one point, for example, at the end of a quarter or the end of a fiscal year.

Income statement. This monthly or quarterly statement shows how much your business actually earned after your expenses were all paid out that period.

Cash flow statement. This monthly or quarterly statement shows where your business's cash came from and where it went during the period.

c.   Projecting Future Business Plans Numerically

Even existing businesses include projections in their business plans. Investors are even more interested in the future of the business than they are in its past and want to see what story the numbers tell about the future growth you have in mind. The bulk of the financial description of your business plan will be financial projections.

Financial projections are spreadsheets that show projections—in other words, your best guesstimates—of the finances of your business anywhere from a few months to several years into the future. The two most common types of projections to include in your business plan are a break-even analysis and pro forma financials.

Break-even analysis. A break-even analysis shows how much income you'll need to earn to cover your expenses. After that point, your income will presumably increase faster than your expenses, and your business will begin turning a profit. If you don't have a break-even analysis already, you can create one for your business online, at the SCORE website. (From the Business Toolbox, go to the template gallery. When you click on "Break Even Analysis," you'll be presented with a worksheet that you can fill in and adjust to match your own business situation.)

Pro forma financials. These are simply any of the three standard financial statements, projected into the future. The figures that appear in pro formas are projections of how the business *thinks* it will perform on each item. These projections usually extend out for three years. They force you to detail the economics of your business and how events like an increase in the cost of a raw material or a lowering of tax rates will affect your bottom line. Experienced investors may review your pro formas to see whether you understand the economics of your own business and whether you've been realistic in projecting its future. Several templates are available at the SCORE website mentioned above. The "12-Month Profit and Loss Projection" is a particularly common one to include in a start-up business plan.

3. Supplying Supporting Documents

Because most of the material presented in your plan reflects your subjective opinion of your business, it's important to provide some objective backup. Helpful supporting documents usually include, but are not limited to:

- tax returns
- copies of any contracts, leases, licenses, or letters of intent, and
- your résumé and the resumes of your key employees.

If you're just getting started, you obviously won't have tax returns. And if you're starting on a small scale, you may not have signed any contracts or leases. Do your best to think of equivalent items that will show that you're serious about starting this business, or that others have expressed an interest in participating or buying from you. For example, if you have a prospective customer who could be a significant buyer, such as another business, you could try to get the customer to put into writing his or her interest in buying a certain amount of your product at a certain price. This isn't a legal agreement, simply a letter of interest you can show to investors.

4. Drafting an Executive Summary

A good plan includes an executive summary, usually no longer than one page, capturing the highlights of the plan. While it's easiest to wait until *after* you've drafted your business plan to create your executive summary, it should be positioned *before* the plan when you package it up for others to see. In some circumstances, the executive summary can serve as a standalone document, such as when you need something short and sweet to share with a prospect.

To draft the executive summary, refer back to the narrative description of your business, and pull the strongest points from each section. Use the same headings, but use just the few sentences or one paragraph that conveys the most important information from that section. Extract financial highlights that best illustrate the opportunity, such as a projected profit margin or a pending contract. If you have a particularly powerful table, logo, or graphic, use it. The bplans.com website has executive plans you can review to get a sense of how to write your own.

Make your executive summary an attention grabber. Investors will always read the summary first, because it's the shortest description of the business. They will continue to the details only if they find the summary compelling.

5. Adding a Cover Letter

When you share your plan with others, always include a cover letter prepared for the person and the occasion. Include your contact information on the letter and an encouragement that readers contact you with any questions.

B. Calculating the Amount of Your Request

Don't make the mistake that many entrepreneurs do, and simply raise as much—or as little—as you think your lenders can part with. Another common mistake is to think that if you can just raise enough for that one piece of equipment and your first month of lease payments, and that the rest will take care of itself. Instead, you'll need to figure out exactly how much money you'll need to start or expand your business and to keep it running for as many months as it takes until you find customers and get established. You can calculate this amount in three easy steps:

Step 1: Identify and total your predicted start-up (or expansion) costs.

Step 2: Identify and total your predicted recurring costs.

Step 3: Total the two figures from steps one and two.

The three sections below will guide you through these steps. You'll also find copies of the relevant worksheets in Appendix B and on the CD-ROM. In addition, you can find an online calculator for estimating start-up costs at the SBA website, under the financing section at www .sba.gov/financing/basics/estimating.html. Most entrepreneurs will be able to estimate their start-up costs on their own, using one of these tools. However, if you are already in business, or you have a complex array of income and expenses to estimate, you may need some help from a small business adviser or accountant.

You'll probably need more money than you think. Many entrepreneurs underestimate how much money they'll need to get their new business off the ground. Take the time to understand how your business will both earn and use cash. When you make projections (in your business plan and in the worksheet on this page), be conservative. Pay particular attention to the ability of your business to make a profit—that's where most entrepreneurs go wrong, by being overly optimistic. Consider creating three sets of projections: "best case," for how you hope things will work out; "base case," for how you can confidently predict things will progress based on current information; and "worst case," assuming 50% or less of your base case scenario.

Step 1: Estimating Your Start-Up Costs

Estimate the start-up (or expansion) costs you will incur prior to your first day of business. These include one-time expenses you will have to pay before you can open your doors. The list in the table below will give you an idea of what to include. Use the "other" line for items unique to your situation. Calculate a total at the bottom.

Startup-Up Costs Worksheet

Description	Estimated cost
Legal fees	$
Rent (include deposit and 1st month)	$
Office equipment	$
Insurance (initial premium)	$
Business license	$
Stationery, logos, letterhead	$
Initial advertising	$
Other	$
Total start-up/expansion costs	$

Step 2: Estimating Your Recurring Costs

Estimate the costs you will incur on a regular (usually monthly) basis regardless of what happens with your business. For example, you'll have to pay your monthly rent no matter how many widgets you create to fill your orders, or how much income your business generates.

Describe the basis for the cost in the description column. For monthly costs, record the dollar amount in the second column. For costs that occur less regularly—for example, quarterly insurance payments or annual trade association dues—divide the cost up into a monthly amount, and include that as well. Total all the rows in the second column to find out your total recurring monthly costs.

Recurring Costs Worksheet

Description	Estimated monthly cost
Monthly rent	$
Payroll	$
Utilities	$
Insurance	$
Ongoing advertising	$
Association and other memberships	$
Other	$
Total monthly recurring costs	**$**

Step 3: Calculating Total Funds Needed

The last step is to combine the start-up costs (step one) and the recurring costs (step two) to get the total amount you'll need to raise for your business. But before you can do this, you need to determine how many months of recurring costs to add.

Figure out how many months it will take you to find customers and get established. Some entrepreneurs will want to plan their finances all the way to the month when they expect to break even (where income meets expenses). If you created a break-even analysis as part of your business plan, refer back to it for this figure. Some entrepreneurs pick an arbitrary number like three, six, or 12 months, knowing they may need to raise additional capital down the road. Think carefully about how many months of costs you will incur before you can earn enough revenue that you don't need outside money to make ends meet.

Total Funds Worksheet

Total of your start-up/expansion costs (from Step 1): $ _____

  Recurring costs (from Step 2) $ _____

  Number of months   X _____

Total recurring costs   =   + $ _____

Total funds needed $ _____

Once you have calculated the total amount needed to launch your business, subtract from it any funds you have already raised. For example, if you plan to use a line of credit you have with a bank, decide how much you can use from that source. If you're planning on using money from your personal savings, subtract that amount as well. The amount you're left with is the amount you'll need to raise from your prospects.

C. Dividing Up Your Request Among Prospects

Now you know how much money you want to raise in total. The next step is to divide up that amount into smaller parts and write down a likely dollar figure, or a range, next to each name on your prospects list. Don't worry about being too exact—these numbers will probably change as you discuss the request with each prospect. The point here is to get to an amount that you can use when you first approach a prospect; an amount you've picked for good reason, not pulled from thin air. Pick one of the following three ways to divide up the total:

- Ask for all the money from one person.
- Ask for the same amount from several people.
- Ask for different amounts from different people.

If, no matter which way you slice it, the total amount you think you can request from your prospects falls short of what you'll need for your business, go back and reconsider the people you crossed off your brainstorming list.

1.   Asking for All the Money From One Person

The first possibility, asking for all the money from one person, has both pros and cons. The pro is that it makes your life a lot easier if you have to manage a financial relationship with only one person. The con is that, from the investor's perspective, it might feel risky to be the sole person providing cash for your venture. Spreading the request out among several people reduces the burden on each one. In the early stage, it also gives you alternatives in case you get turned down.

2.   Asking for the Same Amount From Each Person

You might ask for the same amount from each prospect if you really don't know much about individual financial situations. Rather than spending time trying to guess or ask around about your prospects, it might be simpler and easier to ask for the same amount from each, especially if it's just a few thousand dollars.

An advantage of this option is that it can make your life easy. For example, if you need to borrow only $6,000 and you have three well-off prospects, asking for $2,000 from each allows you to use the same loan request letter, and possibly even the same loan terms. For those who say yes, it will be easy to prepare promissory notes, because they'll be virtually the same.

If you're raising money from several people, don't promise to pay them all on the same day each month. It's smarter to space out the payments to come due at different times of the month, so you don't set yourself up to have everything due at once. The exception would be if you're confident that the payments are small enough that dealing with them simultaneously won't be a problem.

3.   Asking for Different Amounts From Different People

The obvious disadvantage to the second option is that it doesn't take into account what you know about your prospects' individual financial situations. If your uncle could spare $5,000 and your book club pal would be more comfortable with $1,000, why ask both for $3,000? It doesn't take a lot of work to divide your total into differing amounts based on what you know about each individual prospect.

Selecting a range of possible loan amounts (for example, between $1,000 and $4,000) is fine as well. When the time comes to make the request, such an approach allows you to suggest the range and let the prospect pick the actual amount.

It's often best to let the prospect pick the final amount. Instead of guessing that your grandmother could lend you $8,000, put her on your list for $5,000 to $10,000. Then let her nail down the exact dollar figure. To some prospects it just plain feels better to suggest the amount of the investment, instead of just saying yes to an amount that has been decided for them in advance.

Now add a fourth column to the "Best Bets" table you created in Chapter 4. Using the strategies described above, enter the amount of money you believe you can realistically ask of each person.

Chapter 6

Developing Your Loan Request

A. Deciding Your Loan Terms..117

   1. Will You Offer Collateral?... 118

   2. How Much Interest Are You Willing to Pay? 123

   3. When and How Do You Want to Repay?.............................. 126

B. Drafting Your Loan Request Letter... 136

   1. Reviewing the Sample Request Letter.................................. 137

   2. Using the Sample Loan Request Letter as Your Guide 140

Reprinted with permission of Dave Swann and the Honolulu Star-Bullet.

I f you're a "let's get this over with" type, you might—now that you've got
your business plan and know the amount you need to raise and whom
you're most likely to raise it from—be tempted to just pick up the phone.
Don't. You risk sounding only slightly more professional than the fellow in the
cartoon above if you approach your prospect before you've thought through
key elements of your loan request and are ready to both answer questions and
offer written materials spelling out the details.

➡ **This chapter is focused on requesting financing in the form of a loan.** If
you're planning to raise your money in the form of a gift, skip ahead to the
gift section of Chapter 9. If you plan to raise only equity investments, skip ahead
to Chapter 8.

The good news is that you don't need an M.B.A. to do this final prep work.
This chapter will show you how to:
- decide on your proposed loan terms, such as your interest rate and
repayment schedule (see Section A, below), and
- prepare a written loan request letter, which you'll later give to your
prospective lender (see Section B, below).

Eventually, I'll let you call your prospect. It's not that phone calls are taboo. In fact, after you've done the homework described in this chapter, a simple phone call, or other quick contact, may be just the ticket to opening communication channels between you and your prospective lender. However, flat out asking for the money now—without having done some important background work—practically guarantees that you will be turned down.

A. Deciding Your Loan Terms

In the world of banks and other institutional lenders, your loan options would mostly be limited to particular interest rates, repayment plans, and the like—take 'em or leave 'em. With a private loan, however, you have the opportunity to custom design a loan that works for you. But you must also take into account what your lender may want from the deal, particularly if your lender isn't entirely comfortable making the loan. For example, your nearest and dearest may be eager to loan you money for no collateral and at zero interest. More-distant lenders, however, may not agree to a loan until you offer better-than-market-rate interest and a piece of business equipment as collateral.

By the way, we're not yet talking about creating any written materials to show a prospective lender—that will come in Section B, although you should keep some fairly detailed notes for later use. The idea now is that either when you first approach a prospective lender, or during the discussions that follow soon thereafter, you'll be ready to tell the person.

- whether or not the loan will be secured with collateral
- what interest rate or range of rates you can offer, and
- how you will repay the loan.

Start by envisioning your ideal or typical loan—you can customize it to individual lenders later. You might even use this section to draft alternate sets of loan terms, which you'll ultimately choose between or offer as options to lenders. The important thing is that you run the numbers and figure out your own needs and limits now, before a lender asks you any probing questions.

Different Terms for Different Lenders

When Soo-Kiat needed $10,000 to start a technology business in his university's business incubator, he first turned to his uncle. His uncle generously proposed a $5,000 interest-free loan, to be paid back over the course of three years. Soo-Kiat accepted. However, he still needed another $5,000.

Soo-Kiat's list of best prospects included several business school professors and a former employer. To make his loan request tempting to these savvy and analytical investors, Soo-Kiat put together a package with three loan options: 1) a 10% interest rate on a 12-month loan of $2,500; 2) a 12% interest rate on an 18-month loan of $2,500; and 3) a 15% interest rate on a 12-month loan of $5,000.

Notice that all three options had short repayment periods and high interest rates. This was intended as compensation for the fact that Soo-Kiat had no assets with which to secure the loan. He knew the prospects wouldn't operate based on the same altruistic motives as his uncle.

Soo-Kiat's strategy worked. Two prospects from his list agreed; one chose the first option, the other chose the second. Over the next three years, his business earned enough to keep up with each of his three repayment plans (from his uncle and the two other lenders) and to pay himself a respectable salary.

1. Will You Offer Collateral?

Here's another reason not to mourn if a bank or other traditional lender turns down your application for a loan. You can practically count on banks requiring you to secure their interests by providing collateral (property that the bank could sell if you failed to make your payments). The only form in which such traditional lenders might make an unsecured loan to a new business is by offering you a high-interest credit card. By contrast, as you'll see below, the vast majority of interpersonal loans are unsecured.

a.   Why Most Private Loans Are Unsecured

Friends and relatives tend to accept unsecured loans because they know your character and trust you to follow through on your promises. In fact, some private lenders would actually prefer that you not provide any collateral. They reason that your relationship will suffer if, for example, you offer up your home as collateral and then default on your loan. That would put your lender in the awful position of deciding whether to sell your home out from under you in order to collect.

Not sure whether collateral will reassure or alarm your family member? When planning to request a loan from a family member, start by assuming that an unsecured loan will satisfy his or her needs. The trust level between you and your relative is likely high enough that you won't need to put your personal or business assets at risk. You can always mention the possibility of attaching security to the loan later, if it seems appropriate after the two of you talk things over.

Even Family Might Require Collateral

After being turned away by several banks, Bill asked his father to lend him money to launch Neighborhood Transmission Services, a Los Angeles-based AAMCO franchise that provides automotive parts, transmission services, and general repairs. "The banks were reluctant to even consider my proposal," said Bill, and "the third-party financing I did manage to find carried exorbitant rates."

Bill's father agreed to a $20,000 loan with a two-year term, but on the condition that it be secured by the new company's assets. "I love him, but this is a business deal," said the father. He took a security interest in most of the shop equipment, including the most valuable part, the shop's new hydraulic lift.

"Private lending was a unique fit for what we needed," added Bill. "We were able to set up a quarterly payment structure, with an interest rate that was workable both for my father and my company." The loan is still in active repayment and the security provision has not needed to be exercised. Both parties hope it never needs to be.

Of course, I've recommended that you cast your net widely when looking for potential lenders, and some of your prospects may be less interested in preserving your relationship than in protecting their money with a security interest. If that's at all foreseeable, your next task is to decide what you will offer as collateral.

b.   What to Offer as Collateral

If you plan to offer a secured loan to your prospective lenders, you'll need to come up with a list of the property you are willing to give up if you can't repay. I've known entrepreneurs to offer up everything from manufacturing equipment to their inventory of variety store goods.

Creating this list isn't exactly fun: It means considering the failure of your business and your default on the private loan. However, as an entrepreneur, you've hopefully either learned to live with risk, or you feel certain that you'll find a way to repay the loan whether or not your business is a roaring success.

And you can take some comfort from the fact that, even if you do agree to a secured loan and you ultimately can't pay it, your friends and family probably won't resort to selling off your collateral. Although I've seen many cases of secured loans made between family members, including a fair number in which the borrower later had trouble repaying, I can think of only a handful in which the family members went so far as to exercise their security interest and liquidate the borrower's assets. More typically, if the borrower is teetering towards default, the family member will agree to restructure the payment schedule or accept deferred payments.

Nevertheless, you'll want to choose your collateral carefully, just in case a distant friend or a Scrooge-like family member exercises the option to foreclose. The following types of business assets are commonly used as collateral to secure a business loan:

- office equipment, such as computers, printers, copiers, phones, faxes, and furniture
- business equipment, such as manufacturing equipment, machinery, and tools
- vehicles, such as trucks, bulldozers, and forklifts
- real estate
- contracts, such as government orders for goods or services

- inventory, such as raw materials or in-process or finished goods
- accounts receivable, that is, records of people who owe money to your business
- investments owned by your business, such as marketable securities, CDs, bonds, and T-bills, and
- purchase orders.

If you don't have any—or enough—of these available to you, you may still find creative ways to use other, less-tangible types of business assets. For example, you could offer to assign the remainder of your prepaid lease to your lender. Similarly, you could assign a line of credit, patents, or name recognition and brand loyalty to your lender. Although these are hard to value, they do represent a source of economic value to your business.

Will you be offering any items of collateral that will depreciate in value as they age? If so, your lender may want you to factor this into your agreement. Most computers, for example, are now considered old after 18 to 24 months, so they should be used only for loans of a shorter length. If your lender chooses, you may need to develop a schedule documenting how much the computer will be worth for each year that it is being used to secure the loan. In addition, some lenders will want a provision put into the agreement allowing them to ask that new collateral be put up partway through the life of the loan if the original asset becomes worth less than the remainder of the loan.

If your business assets are insufficient to provide adequate collateral, you can also turn to your personal assets, such as:

- real estate, such as a home or land
- bank accounts
- investments, such as marketable securities, CDs, bonds, and T-bills, and
- vehicles.

Other personal assets you might put to work as collateral include your share of a family-owned piece of property. Or you might assign your rental deposit (held by your landlord) or some other type of deposit held by an unrelated third party. I probably don't have to remind you of the risks of putting your personal assets on the line—on the other hand, enduring some personal risk is often a necessary part of the entrepreneurial life.

Once you have a good idea of the business or personal items that might work as collateral, draw up a list containing a description and the approximate value of each, like the sample below (also available as a blank template in Appendix B and on the CD-ROM at the back of this book). Make your best guess at the value of your assets; you shouldn't need to actually have them appraised unless your lender asks you to.

Sample Collateral List

Item Description	Approximate Value
Business Assets	
Machinery	$12,000
Van	10,000
Accounts Receivable	1,200
Personal Assets	
Home equity	$45,000
Car	15,000

Next, identify which of these assets you are willing to offer as collateral for a secured loan. Traditionally, the borrower offers a menu of assets for collateral, and the lender gets to decide which ones are sufficient to secure the loan. Your lender may pick just one asset, as token collateral to keep you on your toes, or may "over-collateralize" the loan, asking for a security interest in assets whose value adds up to more than the loan itself. While this may not seem fair, it's up to your lender to decide how much collateral he or she needs in order to feel that the loan is secure, or safe. Then, it's up to you to decide how much you need the person's money, given the strings the lender has attached.

⚠ Using collateral will require extra paperwork. Much later, after you've agreed to a loan and are drawing up the documents for it, your "promissory note" will need to discuss and describe any collateral you've promised, in what's called a "secured interest provision." You'll also need to prepare and sign a document called a "security agreement." Finally, you'll need to file documents to publicly record the security interest, with a state or county office. (More information on all these steps is provided in Chapter 9.)

2.   How Much Interest Are You Willing to Pay?

To the inexperienced borrower, arriving at an interest rate may feel like pulling a number out of a hat. However, the process can be approached more scientifically.

Start with the Applicable Federal Rate (AFR) as your base. This is the rate set by the IRS as a minimum for private loans—use anything less and the IRS will consider the difference between your rate and the AFR to be a gift and will impute interest on it, putting your lender at risk of gift tax liability. (Refer back to Chapter 3 for this discussion.)

The AFR changes monthly, but not drastically. To give you an idea, between mid-2004 and mid-2005 the AFR ranged between approximately 2% and 5%. To see the latest rate, visit the IRS website at www.irs.gov and search for "AFR." Then, using the drop-down index, select the current month and year.

Offering to pay someone the relatively low AFR probably isn't going to make the person leap from his or her chair. To figure out how high above the AFR you should go, consider the alternatives available to both you and your lender. What interest rate would you have to pay to get money from another source? On the other side of the negotiating table, what return could your lender be earning elsewhere? You want to arrive at a number that lets both you and your lender feel like you're getting a good deal.

Most of the business borrowers I've worked with lately end up paying around 8%, although some have gone as low as the AFR and others as high as 20%. But before you choose, let's look at both your and your lender's competing alternatives in more detail.

a.   Researching the Interest Rate You'd Pay Elsewhere

On the open market you're likely to pay interest at one of the following three rates.

Your credit card rate. Over two-thirds of U.S. small businesses use a credit card for business purchases. The interest rate you'd pay to do this depends entirely on your personal and business credit. Look for the Annual Percentage Rate (APR) noted on your personal or business card monthly statement to find out how much you'd pay if you used that card for your business's start-up expenses. Introductory rates can be 0% or very low, but watch out; those are usually just bait to reel you in. After the first six months, credit card rates often skyrocket to 20% or more (and higher if you include fees). (However, if you can pay off the debt within the six-month period, you've beat the credit card company at its own game.)

Your local bank rates. Over half of all U.S. small businesses use commercial loans, lines of credit, or other financial services from banks. Small businesses that borrow from banks currently pay, on average, a 9.4% interest rate. But remember, banks rely heavily on your personal and business credit rating, as well as the financial performance of your business, to determine the interest rate they'll offer you. The weaker your credit or business performance, the higher your interest rate.

If you want to know exactly how much a bank loan will cost you, submit an application. You can do so either online to a lender like Bank of America (the top small business lender in the country), or in person, at your local bank. Any of these lenders will probably start discussing one of the SBA programs described back in Chapter 2.

For example, under the SBA 7(a) program, bank lenders pick the rate to offer borrowers, but it cannot exceed the prime rate plus 4.75% (currently equaling 11%; see the table in Chapter 2, Section A) for a loan less than $25,000.

An alternative financial intermediary, such as a nonprofit lender or credit union. These sources of capital are willing to take on more risk, for example, by lending to borrowers who've been turned down by traditional banks due to a spotty credit history. They are also willing to lend smaller amounts than banks. However, they charge commensurately higher interest rates, to compensate for this added risk and flexibility. One nonprofit I know of charged interest rates between 10% and 15%. Although this might sound exorbitant, the group was quite successful in helping many small businesses get off the ground—businesses that might otherwise not have started or grown, because others weren't willing to take a chance lending to them.

b. Researching the Interest Rate Your Prospects Could Get Elsewhere

If you're going to wow your prospective lenders with your professionalism, you'll need to show them that you're aware of the competition for their money and can preferably meet or exceed the going rates. These rates all change daily. The best way to find them easily and for free is at www.bankrate.com. However, I've included the rates from around the time this book was published, below. Use these as ballpark figures and to get an idea of the categories that you'll eventually need to look up.

Your various sources of competition for your prospect's money include:

- **Money market accounts.** These earned about 2.5% in late 2005.
- **CDs (certificates of deposit).** Look for the CD with the term (length) that matches the term you plan to offer in your loan request. A one-year CD was earning 3.4%, and a five-year CD was earning 4% in late 2005.
- **An account at ING** (a Web-based firm offering some of the most competitive rates available) was earning 3% in late 2005 (www .ingdirect.com).

It's not too hard to offer better-than-market rates if your loan is short term (less than three years.) For example, the above short-term investment options currently are paying at or below the AFR, so by simply meeting the present IRS minimum you would beat them. But for prospects to be attracted to your risky proposition, particularly without taking a security interest in your assets, you may need to offer a significantly higher return on their money, something more in the 5% to 12% range.

c. Researching Your State's Limits on Interest Rates

Even if you're feeling wildly generous and want to pay your lenders interest rates in the 20%-and-up range, your state's usury laws may forbid it. Most states exclude loans for business purposes from the reach of these laws, but some don't. Usury laws were enacted to protect borrowers from exorbitantly high interest rates, on the assumption that the lenders hold all the cards. If a situation arises where your lender is found to be charging you a usurious rate (even if you suggested it), your lender could be forced to repay any excess monies they received, lower the interest rate to the highest rate allowed by state law for any future payments, and pay additional civil penalties for violating your state's usury laws.

If your lender is someone you know, he or she probably won't try to charge you an absurdly high interest rate, and I doubt you'll suggest it yourself. In any case, as a general rule of thumb, most states allow lenders to charge you up to 15% interest per year without running afoul of the usury law. Still, the usury limit varies widely from state to state, and different rules usually apply to commercial lenders and private lenders. Check your state's laws to be sure; look under "interest" or "usury" in your state's statutes, which are accessible through the Nolo website at www.nolo.com/statute/state.cfm.

d. Arriving at an Interest Rate That Satisfies Both Borrower and Lender

Once you've done your research, it shouldn't be hard to settle on a range of interest rates that will satisfy both you and your lender—for example, between 4% and 9%. Rates in this range could realistically be lower than you'd be able to get for a small business loan from traditional sources, yet higher than your lender would be able to earn for a short-term cash investment with a commercial entity like a bank. Settling on a range like this is as far as you need to go for now. You and your lender can decide on the exact interest rate later.

3. When and How Do You Want to Repay?

Although I've been talking up the flexibility of friends and family when it comes to making loans, the bottom line is that most lenders expect to be repaid—and sooner than you might think. In fact, nearly half of private investors expect repayment within two years, and almost three-quarters expect to be repaid within five years. In preparation for approaching your lender, you'll need to design a repayment plan that covers:

- **payment frequency**—how often you'll make payments
- **alternatives to scheduling identical monthly payments**—whether all your payments will be of the same amount and at the same time,

Keeping Interest Payments in the Family

Dale Stoddard needed three new trucks for his fast-growing kitchen remodeling business in Sacramento. He found a dealer with the trucks he wanted, at the price he wanted. Based on Dale's established business, solid revenue, and good credit, the dealer's financing program offered him a rate of 7.2% for a $66,000 loan, to be secured by the new trucks.

Dale could afford the loan—7.2% wasn't at all unreasonable. But he got to thinking about how much he would pay the company in interest on top of the price tag for the three new trucks and wondered whether there were any alternatives.

A few days later, Dale visited his mother, who happened to mention that her CD investments were earning barely 4%. She asked whether Dale knew of any investments that would be secure but would earn her a higher return.

That night, Dale drew up two loan request letters, one to his mother and one to his grandmother (Dale knew that she, too, had a considerable portion of her retirement assets in low-interest CDs). Dale prepared the requests so that they offered the same terms as the dealer-financing program had offered him: 7.2% interest for a secured loan of $33,000. Dale's main goal was to make the loans safe. He felt confident with the course his business was taking, and in case of problems, his family would gain the right to sell his trucks.

Dale's mother and grandmother were both delighted by his offer. He also told each up front that he'd already been approved for financing at the same rate by the dealer, so that they wouldn't feel under any pressure to say yes—he had, after all, other options. Dale offered to retain CircleLending to service the loan, "so we wouldn't have to talk about the loans over the supper table."

Both loans are currently in active repayment. "There's just no sense in paying 7.2% to the dealer when I could be paying it to my family," Dale notes.

or whether you'll choose an alternate arrangement with variable payment rates or times

- **payment amount**—how much you'll pay per installment
- **payment logistics**—whether you or a hired third party will be the one handling the payments and associated paperwork.

You don't need to write up your repayment plan yet. For now, simply consider your options and take notes for your own use. Later, after you've begun discussions with your prospective lender, you'll look back at these notes, make adjustments according to your discussions, and then write up a more formal plan that meets both your needs.

a. Payment Frequency

You can schedule your loan payments to come due monthly, quarterly, semiannually (twice a year), or annually. Or, if you and your lender prefer not to deal with a long string of small payments, you can simply agree that you'll repay the entire amount (with interest) as a lump sum on a certain date.

I recommend you stick with a traditional monthly loan commitment. Monthly payments are habit-forming—the good kind of habit. By forcing yourself to start making monthly payments as soon as possible, you will build your lender's confidence in you, develop financial practices that will be crucial to your success, and may even boost your credit score.

What if you're pretty sure you won't be able to make your payments right away? You can structure your loan agreement to account for this, for example, by commencing your repayment schedule after a few months or quarters or by starting out making interest-only payments. After the start-up phase, your agreement should shift into a regular repayment schedule. Subsection b, just below, further explains some of your options.

b. Alternatives to Scheduling Identical Monthly Payments

The standard, easy way to pay back a loan is for every payment to include the same amount of principal and interest, and for payments to be made on a regular schedule, month by month or period by period. (This is called an "amortized loan.") However, as the field of financing has become more sophisticated, a number of new options have opened up. The ones you're most likely to find useful include not only the traditional amortized loan, but what are called "graduated," "interest-only," and "seasonal" loans.

You might also make your life easier by adding special provisions to your agreement allowing for deferred payments and a grace period for your regular payments. (To determine how much each payment will be, you'll need to use a loan calculator, as described in the next section and available via the enclosed CD-ROM.)

Amortized loan. Let's start with the easy case, a perfectly viable choice. In an amortized loan, each payment consists of a combination of principal (the actual amount you owe) and interest (the extra amount you pay for use of the lender's money). You've probably dealt with an amortized repayment schedule before, when paying off a car loan or a mortgage. You must pay the exact same amount in monthly or other periodic installments over the term of the loan, as illustrated in the graphic below. You should select an amortized repayment plan only if you're reasonably certain you'll have an adequate cash flow from early on, as well as consistently throughout your business cycle.

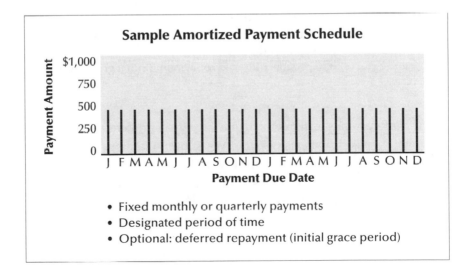

Sample Amortized Payment Schedule

- Fixed monthly or quarterly payments
- Designated period of time
- Optional: deferred repayment (initial grace period)

Graduated loan (also called a start-up loan). Similar to an amortized loan, a graduated loan would require you to make regular payments consisting of a combination of principal and interest. However, the amount you'd pay each time would vary, as you can see in the sample below. You'd start off making reasonably low payments, and later increase these by a scheduled percentage before leveling off to a fixed amount for the remaining loan term. These increases are called "steps," and loan calculators allow you to select how many steps you will have in your graduated loan. This is an excellent repayment choice for most new businesses. Loan calculators can also help you consider how your payments on a graduated loan would change over time.

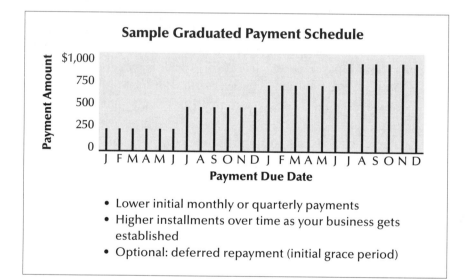

Sample Graduated Payment Schedule

- Lower initial monthly or quarterly payments
- Higher installments over time as your business gets established
- Optional: deferred repayment (initial grace period)

Interest-only loan. As the name suggests, an interest-only loan allows you to make payments of pure interest over a number of months or years. Most interest-only loans end with a final payment that includes the last bit of interest owed plus the entire amount of the principal (called a "balloon payment"). See the sample below for how the numbers play out. On the one hand, this plan keeps your monthly payments very low. On the other hand, by not repaying any of the principal along the way, you will find yourself well into the loan without having reduced the total amount you owe by even a penny. And unless you are well prepared, the balloon payment can be very difficult to make.

Balloon payments can blow up on you. Putting off making a large, lump sum payment until the end of your loan term carries obvious risks. What if your business hasn't gone well, or for other reasons you haven't saved enough to basically repay the entire loan at once? By now, your lender's enthusiasm for your business idea may have faded, and he or she may be reluctant to renegotiate the loan. Unfortunately, you wouldn't be the first entrepreneur to regret having entered into this tempting loan arrangement—it's one of the main reasons that the default rate for private loans is higher than that for bank loans.

A less risky approach is to periodically make balloon payments throughout the life of the loan. And you can deflate the balloon payment by remembering that you aren't stuck in this arrangement—if you someday find yourself in the happy situation of having extra cash, you can usually prepay portions of or the entire principal. But over the long term, you'll probably end up paying more interest than with an amortized loan. That's because you're taking longer to pay off the principal.

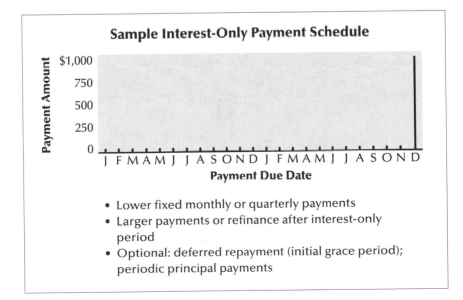

Sample Interest-Only Payment Schedule

- Lower fixed monthly or quarterly payments
- Larger payments or refinance after interest-only period
- Optional: deferred repayment (initial grace period); periodic principal payments

Seasonal. Some businesses live and die with the seasons, meaning that they earn significant revenue only during certain months of the year. Usually tourism and holiday-related business have considerable fluctuations in their annual cash flow. For example, although Mack & Manco's Pizza on the Ocean City boardwalk in New Jersey is a year-round business, its pizza sales soar in June, July, and August, when all the visitors come to town. If your business is seasonal, you might consider a repayment plan that allows you to make lower payments during the off-season months and higher payments during the high-season months, as illustrated in the sample schedule below.

One of CircleLending's earliest clients was a thriving Halloween products business. Despite its success, August, September, and October were the only months during which it drew in any significant revenue. On top of this concern, the business needed cash early in the year, in order to make purchases from overseas suppliers. To accommodate these unusual needs, the owner and his lender customized a payment plan allowing him to make interest-only payments in the off-season months, and larger payments, which included a portion of the principal, during the Halloween-season months. I've never heard of a bank extending this kind of repayment plan.

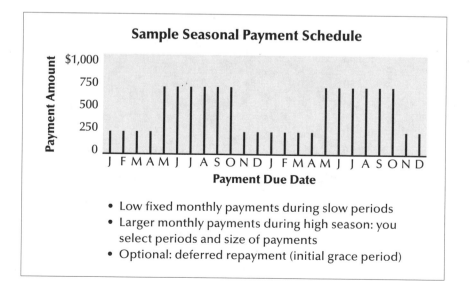

💡 **You can design a one-of-a-kind repayment plan.** While the repayment plan types described above are the easiest and most commonly used, you're not limited to these. I've known creative entrepreneurs who combined two or more of the standard repayment plans to fit the expected cash flow of the business at different points over the life of the loan. It's all up to your ability to anticipate your needs and your lender's willingness to be flexible.

c. Payment Amount

How much you'll pay per installment is a simple matter of mathematical calculation, after you've determined the total loan amount, the interest rate, the term of the loan—that is, the length of time until it's paid off—and the schedule or type of repayment plan. The CD-ROM included with this book will help you with this calculation, by linking you to online loan calculators at the CircleLending website. After you've entered the appropriate information, the calculator for the type of loan you pick will generate a schedule of payments.

Try a variety of combinations until you find a schedule that works for you. If the term of the loan and the interest rate you imagined leave you with monthly payments that aren't affordable for your business, try a longer term or a lower interest rate.

Let's follow the thinking and calculation process used by Bill (whom you read about in Section A, above), when he borrowed $20,000 from his father to start Neighborhood Transmission Services. In planning his repayment schedule, Bill used a loan calculator to compare two options: amortized and interest-only loans.

First, Bill plugged in the terms for an amortized loan, which Bill found would require him to make quarterly payments of $2,730, for a total interest payment of $1,842. He kept a copy of that table:

Amortized Payment Schedule
$20,000 loan, 8% interest, quarterly payments for two years

Due date	Principal	Interest	Total
11/1/2005	$2,330.20	$400.00	$2,730.20
2/1/2006	2,376.80	353.40	2,730.20
5/1/2006	2,424.34	305.86	2,730.20
8/1/2006	2,472.83	257.37	2,730.20
11/1/2006	2,522.28	207.92	2,730.20
2/1/2007	2,572.73	157.47	2,730.20
5/1/2007	2,624.18	106.02	2,730.20
8/1/2007	2,676.64	53.53	2,730.17
Total:	**$20,000.00**	**$1,841.57**	**$21,841.57**

Then, Bill plugged in the same terms but changed one, the payment schedule, to make it an interest-only loan (see below). Bill was stunned to see that, although he'd have payments of only $400 each quarter, overall they'd add up to $3,200 in interest—for the same-sized loan! Plus, on one day two years from the start date, he'd get slammed with a $20,400 payment. That was a day Bill decided he'd avoid entirely—he went with the amortized loan.

Interest-Only Payment Schedule
$20,000 loan, 8% interest, quarterly payments for two years

Due date	Principal	Interest	Total
11/1/2005	$0.00	$400.00	$400.00
2/1/2006	0.00	400.00	400.00
5/1/2006	0.00	400.00	400.00
8/1/2006	0.00	400.00	400.00
11/1/2006	0.00	400.00	400.00
2/1/2007	0.00	400.00	400.00
5/1/2007	0.00	400.00	400.00
8/1/2007	$20,000.00	$400.00	$20,400.00
Total:	**$20,000.00**	**$3,200.00**	**$23,200.00**

One of the first questions I ask someone who's entering into a friends-or-family loan is, "How much can you afford to pay each period?" (whether monthly, quarterly, or on some alternate schedule). Before you answer this question, look at the financial projections in your business plan—in particular, at the cash flow you've predicted during the months or years you'll be paying off your proposed loan.

Obviously, you shouldn't promise to pay back amounts that will eat up much or all of your projected income. Determine a range of how much you can afford to pay each period, and decide whether that should be a fixed amount over the life of the loan, or whether you can realistically expect to increase your payments after your business gets underway. Plan carefully for a repayment schedule where your payments will always be less than your income projections.

d.   Payment Logistics

The final thing to consider is what you'll tell your lender about the logistics of repayment—literally, who will take care of sending your checks on time. Whomever you choose will also need to deal appropriately with any late or missed payments. In addition, your business will need to file end-of-year reporting and tax statements, which you may need to send copies of for use by your lender (or your lender's accountant) in preparing his or her own tax returns. You have two main options for who handles all this.

Do It yourself. You can send a check every period by the due date specified in your promissory note. If you choose this route, you'll also need to keep a loan log (see how to do so in Chapter 9) and will probably want to hire an accountant to prepare a year-end report of the loan for the lender's taxes.

The benefit of this route is that it keeps the relationship informal and costs less out of pocket. The challenge is that it's one more piece of paperwork you need to worry about and spend your valuable time on. Additionally, both you and your lender may actually prefer that the relationship be a formal one, handled by someone else. If you think this is the case, consider the next option.

Hire a neutral third party to manage repayment. Consider hiring an accountant, financial adviser, attorney, or other third party (such as a company like CircleLending) to manage your private loan. The benefit is that makes the relationship more formal, like a business transaction, not a personal contact. It creates a buffer so that if there is a problem, someone else will sort it out and you and your lender will hardly need to discuss it.

You can expect to pay $100-$150 per hour to hire an accountant to administer your loan. It may take no more than an hour per month to administer (including reminding you to pay, receiving the payment and depositing into your lender's account, and following up for late or missing payments). On the other hand, if you're making monthly payments, this bill can add up. In addition, your accountant will need to provide an end-of-the-year tax report to both you and your lender, which may take one to three hours to prepare and send. If there are any complications in the records, like a few missed payments or changes in the payment schedule, or if the person creating the report is different from the one managing payments, preparation of year-end reports can certainly take longer.

If you were to hire CircleLending to set up your loan, you'd pay $199 for a custom promissory note and servicing setup, then $9 per month for ongoing service, including year-end tax reporting.

B. Drafting Your Loan Request Letter

Although we're still in the realm of background work, the final step in this work is to collect your thoughts into a draft loan request letter. Don't send the letter yet; as you'll see in Chapter 7, it's best to make personal contact with your prospect first, to talk about your idea. But as soon as your prospect either invites you to send some information or actually agrees verbally to the idea of a loan, you'll want to have your draft letter all-but-ready to send.

Unlike the lengthy loan applications that banks and institutional lenders demand, loan request letters to private friend and family lenders have no standard format or required elements. Most can take the form of a one- or two-page letter from you to your potential lender.

The sample letter outlined here is just that: a sample. Don't use it word for word, but do feel free to adapt it to your needs. If you use it more than once, adapt it each time so each prospect receives a personalized request. (Family members, in particular, are likely to compare letters.)

By the time your prospect finishes reading this letter, he or she should know that you are asking for a loan for your business, how much money you need, what interest rate you are offering, and when he or she can expect to be repaid. Here are the elements to include in a loan request letter:

- **An opening.** State your purpose for writing, namely to raise a stated amount of money for a particular business. Specify the amount or the range you're asking of this prospect.
- **A progress report.** Mention how much money you've already raised, if relevant. This helps the lender understand that you're serious, and that other people are convinced that your business is worth lending money to.
- **A description of the business or product.** Describe what you do, the need it fills, and the expected market for it.
- **A description of who will manage the business.** Say why you and any cofounders are well suited to running this business, including your relevant skills and experience.
- **A summary of your proposed loan terms.** Draw on the background work and loan calculations you did in Section B, above, to summarize the loan terms you're offering. You can either do this right in the letter or attach additional sheets summarizing the loan options.
- **Your loan servicing plan.** Indicate who will set up and handle loan payments and related paperwork.
- **A respectful and enthusiastic closing.** This is a personal letter, not a legal document. Sign off in a way that reminds the person of any previous conversations you've had and sets the stage for future conversations.

1. Reviewing the Sample Request Letter

The sample shown is an actual letter I created for a CircleLending client, whom I'll call Esmeralda. At the time we drafted this letter, Esme (her nickname) needed $15,000 to open her downtown bakery and had

Sample Loan Proposal Letter: Esme's Cafe

Dear Friend and Supporter,

I am excited to tell you about a way for you to support Esme's Café and earn an attractive return. Esme's Café is raising $15,000 from relatives, friends, and business associates, and I thought you might be interested in participating. Attached to this letter are three loan options for you to consider; the loan amount and interest rate varies with each. I've already raised $10,000 from family members and from a first-place award in a local business plan competition. I thought you might be interested in providing a loan for the remaining $5,000.

Esme's Café is located at the heart of a thriving residential and business neighborhood, close to high-profile city landmarks like the train station and the university. Esme's Café will tap into this bustling market by providing specialty coffee, baked goods, wrapped sandwiches, and cold drinks. In addition to the high visibility and foot traffic of the location, two new government offices across the street employ together about 1,800 people, ensuring a steady stream of customers.

Based on my 20+ years of experience in the restaurant industry, and in sales and marketing in our area, I truly believe that this café in this location is a winning combination. In case you are interested in additional business and financial information, I have also included my business plan for your review.

I offer you this opportunity because I believe it is good for my business and good for you. For me, it allows me to raise the money I need to grow my business from people I trust, and at an affordable rate. For you, the 10%, 12%, and 15% interest rates I'm offering provide a competitive short-term return on your money. If you choose to make the loan, after a six-month grace period you will receive monthly installments for 18 months.

In addition, my proposal offers you the protection of a legally binding loan agreement and the convenience of a third party to manage the repayment. I have retained CircleLending, a firm that specializes in the administration of private loans between relatives, friends, and business associates, to handle our loan. CircleLending has created a promissory note for us and will manage the repayment of the loan. My repayments to you will be preauthorized to come out of the Esme's Café corporate account electronically, and the funds will be deposited into a bank account that you designate. CircleLending will also provide us real-time access (both online and toll-free) to payment status and history, will maintain records, and will provide year-end tax summary reports.

I hope that you will consider this mutually beneficial opportunity. I truly believe that Esme's Café is poised for success and I look forward to your support in growing the business. Thank you for your consideration; I look forward to discussing this opportunity with you further.

Sincerely,

Esmerelda Sanchez

Esmerelda Sanchez
Esme's Cafe

already raised $10,000. She'd decided to offer anywhere from 10% to 15% to entice her prospects, but was still unsure of which combination of amounts and interest rates would move them to sign on the dotted line. The two prospects she'd already contacted about her business idea were colleagues of an acquaintance, so they were fairly distant to her, but both were successful women known for their private support of female entrepreneurs throughout the city. Both women had, over the phone, invited Esme to send more materials for their consideration.

Esme polished up her business plan with a local business counselor. After that, the two of us designed a menu of three loan options from which her savvy and analytical lenders could choose. All three were for an amortized two-year loan with a six-month deferment period. However, the amounts and interest rates were different. The prospect could choose between making a loan of $2,500 at an interest rate of 10%; $3,000 at an interest rate of 12%; or $5,000 at an interest rate of 15%.

2. Using the Sample Loan Request Letter as Your Guide

Let me point out some features of this letter that you might adapt for your own use, or change entirely. (The basic letter is included in Appendix B and on the CD-ROM accompanying this book.)

Paragraph 1. Remember, Esme had only spoken with her prospects by phone; she'd never actually met them. When we drafted the letter, we made it somewhat formal, to reflect both the distance in the relationship and the fact that both prospects were savvy and analytical. However, if you're preparing your letter for a prospect with whom you have an informal, friendly relationship, you'll want to make the tone a bit less formal. Just don't go too far. Even the closest family and friends feel most confident when their private business loan is treated as a business deal instead of an off-the-cuff favor.

You'll also notice that this borrower chose to give the reader various loan amount options, for the business reasons described earlier. Of course, you don't have to offer your lender such options—you can just state in this opening section how much you're asking of this particular lender, or state a range of loan amounts, and leave it at that.

Paragraph 2. Notice that the letter mentions funds that had already been raised. If you can do the same, such information will greatly boost the credibility of your loan proposal. The psychology is simple: "If so-and-so thinks this is a sound business idea, why shouldn't I participate, too?" If you use this approach, be sure to say exactly how much you've already raised towards your goal, and how much remains.

Paragraph 3. Fortunately, Esme had already prepared a solid business plan, from which it was easy to glean information about the business, the product, the opportunity, and the market. Beyond the basics, don't spend too much time on business details. The purpose of the proposal letter is not to sell your business—but to sell the idea of a loan to your business. If the prospect wants more information about the business, you'll be able to attach a copy of your executive summary or your full business plan (which is just what we did).

Paragraph 4. It's always important to announce why you are the right person for the job, even if your background is far different from the one described in this sample. No matter what, try to communicate your unique passion and expertise. If you have cofounders, certainly identify them, and if one or more brings something compelling to the business, state it. Be brief, though; this is not the place to sketch out your current or dream organizational chart.

Paragraph 5. In spelling out more of the terms of the loan request, notice that we opened with a statement about how a private loan is mutually beneficial. Although some lenders are in it for the money, many are also in it to help you out, and it's smart to recognize that intention in your letter. If you don't attach options as separate sheets, or if you want to offer only one, you could adapt the paragraph like this:

> For you, the 10% interest rate I'm offering provides a competitive short-term return on your money. If you choose to make a $5,000 loan, after a six-month grace period you will receive monthly installments of $238 for 24 months, resulting in a total repayment of $5,724.

Paragraph 6. Obviously, because I drafted this sample for a CircleLending client, it names CircleLending to manage repayment. If you'll be handling repayment on your own, however, you could say something like the following:

In addition, my proposal offers you the protection of a legally binding loan agreement. If you agree to the loan terms set forth in this letter, I'll prepare a promissory note reflecting my promise to repay the loan at these terms. The loan will start on the day we transfer the funds, and monthly payments will begin six months later, on the first of each month. I'll send a check from my business account to the address you specify, will maintain a loan log of my payments, and will have my accountant provide you year-end tax summary reports.

Paragraph 6. The formality of your closing will depend a great deal on your relationship with your lender. This letter takes a businesslike tone because it was to be used with acquaintances, not family members. Your own letter might sound much more conversational—for example, you might say, "I hope that you've gotten a better idea of my plans by seeing them in writing. Of course, we'll want to talk this over more in person, perhaps after next week's picnic."

Chapter 7

Making the "Kitchen Table Pitch"

A. Planning How You'll Approach Your Prospective Lender 144

    1. Casual Conversation or Informal Meeting? 145

    2. Where's the Best Place to Meet? 146

    3. What Can You Bring to Illustrate Your Plans? 148

B. Making a Compelling Pitch 149

    1. Creating Excitement Around Your Business Idea 150

    2. Easing Into Your Request 151

    3. Wrapping Up the First Conversation 152

C. Handling Hesitancy and Concerns 156

    1 Concerns About the Prospect's Own Financial Limitations 156

    2. Concerns About the Viability of Your Business 157

    3. Concerns About the Impact on Your Relationship 159

    4. Concerns About What Others May Think 159

D. After Your Prospect Says "Yes" (or "Maybe") 160

    1. Appeal to Your Lender's Personality Type 161

    2. Offer Various Loan Options 163

    3. Offer Special Incentives 163

    4. Offer More-Generous Terms to Less-Willing Lenders 165

E. After Your Prospect Says "No" 167

    1. When to Move On 168

    2. When to Ask Again 168

A ctually asking for the loan or investment is, for many entrepreneurs, the most fear-inducing part of this process. Our job in this chapter is to help you make me ask and a way that feels natural to both you and your prospect. To do so, you'll want to prepare what we call the "kitchen table pitch."

You may have heard of the "elevator pitch" entrepreneurs use when raising money from venture capital investors. They script and practice a slick sales pitch for use when they have a potential investor cornered and only one to three minutes to make a lasting impression.

Your friends, family and others probably don't want to hear a slick sales pitch, but they certainly do want to look you in the eye and hear a straight-forward account of your plans. In contrast to the anonymous and often aggressive approach embodied in the elevator pitch, your approach should be warm, informal, and in keeping with the relationship that you've already built with the person. At the same time, a "pitch" is, by nature, short and snappy.

This chapter will show you how to make a kitchen table pitch, specifically how to:

- plan where and how you'll make your pitch, and what to bring along (see Section A, below)
- make a compelling pitch (see Section B, below)
- handle hesitancy and concerns (see Section C, below)
- follow up after the prospect says "yes" or "maybe" (see Section D, below), and
- follow up if your prospect says "no." (see Section E, below).

Will you be approaching potential equity investors as well as lenders? If so, most of the advice in this chapter will apply to you, too, but also look closely at Section B of the next chapter. Equity investors tend to be a more savvy and analytic bunch than family and friend lenders, and they'll probably expect a more sophisticated approach from you.

A. Planning How You'll Approach Your Prospective Lender

Asking for money is not as big a deal as you might imagine. Your friends and family won't gasp or faint at your suggestion—they're more likely to be intrigued by your business plans, or even flattered that you've thought to involve them.

Some people may actually jump at your request. Remember our example of Dale Stoddard (Chapter 6), who offered his mother and grandmother a loan arrangement at an interest rate that was nearly double what they were earning on their CD investments? They couldn't wait to invest—the decision was an obvious and easy one. But make no mistake; they wouldn't have been half as eager if Dale hadn't done his homework. He'd researched his and his lenders' alternatives and had made the investment safe by securing the loan and setting up a repayment plan he could easily meet. He was able to offer the loan as a win-win situation so that, according to Dale, the actual ask wasn't hard at all.

Every private loan request will be different, and there's no predicting how yours will unfold. But especially if you don't have an offer that's as cut and dried as Dale's, you'll do best by planning the actual request in advance. Here's what works:

1. Decide whether it's better to bring your request up in casual conversation or at an informal meeting.
2. Pick a setting that's suited to your relationship.
3. If you'll be holding a meeting, bring a few well-chosen illustrative materials.

1. Casual Conversation or Informal Meeting?

The first decision is just how casual you should make your first approach. For some people, it might be appropriate to bring up the request in casual conversation, while for others, you'll be better off scheduling an informal meeting.

If your prospect is someone you see regularly, in settings where you have the time and privacy to chat about your personal and professional life, then bringing up your request in casual conversation is probably the right choice. Most entrepreneurs requesting private loans from family members do so during a discussion about what's going on in their life, something family members naturally want to hear about.

If you decide to ask for money in casual conversation, the idea is to let it come up when the conversation turns to you and your work. Instead of directly asking the listener for money, you'll phrase it more generally, saying that you need to raise some money for your business and you're trying to figure out how to do it and whom to ask. You'll learn more about this gentle approach in Section B2, below. People like to be asked for advice, and that can often lead to financial support.

If you're asking for money from someone whom you don't see every day, or for whom a more business-like setting seems appropriate, then you're better off scheduling an actual meeting. Call or email the person and say that you would like to get his or her input on your business idea, then set a time and place to meet. There's no need to deceive your prospect about the purpose of the meeting, but you also don't want the meeting to sound like a sales pitch before it even starts. Keep your meeting request friendly and show your genuine excitement at sharing your business idea and hearing the other person's thoughts.

One person I approached using an informal meeting was a long-time friend from high school who was married to an investment banker. The couple had made some other informal investments. I set up a meeting over a weekend lunch, after explaining that I needed their advice. After some genuine small talk, I started to tell them about my business idea and asked for guidance on fundraising. Soon they were on my side, brainstorming people whom I should contact. Before they knew it, they were suggesting making an investment to help me get started.

2. Where's the Best Place to Meet?

An actual kitchen table is, of course, not crucial to your "kitchen table pitch." However, whether you elect to schedule a meeting in advance or not, you should choose a setting that is similarly comfortable and informal. The closer the relationship, the more informal the setting should ordinarily be. For example, when I first approached my aunt about a business loan, I opted for a "home theater pitch"—in the basement of her home, where our families had watched many movies together. There was no need to schedule this one ahead of time: I simply brought up the topic of my new business on one of my regular visits, when we were discussing family news.

The more distant the relationship, the more formal the setting might be—for example, at the person's office, a restaurant, or on other neutral ground. When I was ready to raise money from some business associates, I sent an email inviting them to join me over lunch in a conference room we used regularly for business meetings. I billed it as a brainstorming meeting for my new business concept, and they were eager to give me their ideas. Though a conference room may sound somewhat formal, it put us all at ease because we had spent much time together there. We all felt like we were in our "comfort zone" in those swivel chairs overlooking the Charles River.

A restaurant or café is a good location for meeting someone with whom you're not especially close. It's a common location for mixing business and pleasure, and one where neither of you enjoys a home turf advantage. With the waitstaff taking care of details like refilling the coffee cups, you're free to concentrate on your conversation. And most towns offer a wide variety of restaurants, so that you can find a cuisine and ambience that both of you will enjoy.

However, restaurants have some disadvantages as meeting places, too. The main one is that someone has to pay the bill—and there's no obvious answer as to who should do so. If you pick up the tab, the potential lender may feel that you're too loose with money or don't need his or her help. If you don't pay the bill, the lender may feel insulted—here you've gone and suggested the meeting, asked for money, and now you want to be treated to a free meal as well? There's no way to know which reaction you'll get. Some entrepreneurs go so far as to say that you should never meet at restaurants at all.

I suggest a more moderate approach: If you feel that a restaurant setting suits you and your potential lender, choose an inexpensive restaurant (preferably one that's a cut above greasy spoon or fast food) and pick up the tab. That way you can assume the role of host and prove your thriftiness all at once.

Are you on a strictly fast food budget? If so, opt for a meeting in an upscale coffee house instead of a fast food chain restaurant. A gourmet cup of coffee makes a better business impression than a burger and fries served at a plastic table.

In the end, your instincts will be the best guide to a location that will put your potential lender at ease and in good spirits. Draw on your past together and your relationship to think up the right place.

3. What Can You Bring to Illustrate Your Plans?

Your casual conversation is not the time to bring along notebooks full of business plans and promissory notes—particularly if you plan to "just happen" to run into your relative while he or she is walking the dog. But if you decide to use an informal meeting to first bring up your request, bring something tangible to show the person. A brochure, a sample product, a website, or an article in the newspaper would all serve to explain your business and give it credibility. Pick something you can slip into your purse, pocket, or backpack and that doesn't require a carrying case or overhead projector.

Also make sure that whatever you bring makes your idea come to life. Photos or drawings of your product or planned site are particularly good, since visuals attract people's attention and take your description out of the realm of the imagination. If you plan to open a bakery, bring sample cookies. If you happen to be near a computer, your newly launched website can be effective for show and tell.

If you don't have any such materials on hand, it's okay to create something just for the meeting. Even something as simple as a printout of a color logo and tagline can help others get a more tangible sense of your business idea.

At one of my informal meetings in a shared conference room, I was surprised at how much my prospects liked some presentation boards I assembled. They contained graphics describing my first product, called Handshake Plus, a private loan setup and management service. I paid a graphic designer for a few hours of work to design the boards, which included my business logo, bullet point highlights of the product (how it would work, the price), and a picture I'd found on the Web of two people shaking hands.

A business logo always makes a good impression. Try to have yours ready for any important prospect meeting, especially if it's with an equity investor. Feature your logo on your product brochure or website, a presentation board, or even your business card, and bring these to your informal meeting. If you don't have a logo already, visit www.logoyes.com where, for a reasonable fee, they can help you create one.

Letting the Oven Timer Do the Talking

When Andrea Lang, who is opening a café in Washington, DC, feels ready to ask a prospect for money, she invites the person to the café site for the meeting. Often, she plans the visit for a time and a day when at least two things will happen: First, she schedules the delivery van to arrive at that time to pick up the flowers that she arranges and places for several offices weekly (an existing side business that will help support the café in its early stages).

Second, she arranges for the baked goods and coffee that she provides as a catering service (another side business that generates cash for, and word-of-mouth interest in, her café) to be ready. There's nothing better than a timer going off during a meeting indicating that a freshly baked batch of carrot bread or other specialty baked good is ready to be pulled from the oven. One prospect was so pleased by the fresh coffee and carrot bread that he brought his wife back just a few days later to try them for herself. Andrea says, "I like my prospects to see how busy I am; and they are always impressed to see that I'm already in business even though my doors aren't even open."

B.   Making a Compelling Pitch

I can't script your pitch conversation for you—the one where you actually ask for money. Your words and manner will depend on whom you're approaching and how well you know him or her. It will also be affected by where you've chosen to approach the person. If you've agreed to meet for lunch or coffee, for example, the person will expect a fairly leisurely conversation lasting a good hour or so. The opposite will be true if you plan to simply chat with a family member over the appetizer table at your annual New Year's party.

No matter where you plan to speak with your prospective lender, however, following a few basic principles will give you your best shot at getting an enthusiastic response:

1. Start with your business idea.
2. Ease into the loan request.
3. Keep any agreement verbal.

Don't change the way you behave when you ask for money. Be yourself. This even includes dressing like yourself: Showing up in a suit for a restaurant lunch with your mother will probably put her on her guard (unless that's normally how you visit with her).

1. Creating Excitement Around Your Business Idea

After some small talk, start telling the story of your business plans—whatever part of them you think will most interest your prospective lender. Your job is to spark your prospect's imagination. Describe the great product or service you are developing and why you think it will sell, using any of the materials you've brought along to illustrate your description. (Also, any time that it seems appropriate, you can offer to send a complete copy of your business plan after you get back to your desk.) List several specific business goals you have for the upcoming months, such as trade shows to attend, sales goals to achieve, and new product versions to design. Explain why you think now is the right place and the right time to launch your business—and why you are the right person to do it.

Don't forget, however, that you billed this meeting as a conversation to enlist your prospect's input. Before you've delivered a feature-length monologue about the merits of your idea, ask your prospective lender some genuine questions. Tailor your questions to your prospect's interests or experience—everyone probably knows something relevant to your business, whether from being a fellow business owner, a marketing or communications expert, or simply a choosy consumer. You could ask for ideas on how to make your plan work, or ask what would make this person buy the product or service.

Listen closely to the answers; you may glean useful information, and the answers will give you clues as to where your prospect's true interests lie. The more you leave room for genuine give-and-take, the greater the chances your prospect will suggest participating of his or her own accord.

Express confidence. Confidence in yourself and in your business idea are critical messages to communicate during this pitch conversation. Of course, that doesn't mean hiding the challenges that you'll face. By showing that you've thought these through and are ready to face up to them, you will only enhance your appearance of readiness.

2.   Easing Into Your Request

Many fundraising advisers suggest that you "be direct" in making your request for a loan. Unfortunately, some people take that to mean you should hit lenders with your request before they've even had a chance to open their lunch menu. In my experience with family and friends, it is actually more effective to be comparatively indirect. Yes, you've been waiting a long time and may be eager to just blurt out your question and get it over with. But hold off until you've reached a point in your conversation where the question seems to arise naturally.

Be sure that your prospect is engaged in your idea before you bring up your request for money—that is, if the person hasn't already offered to help. In some cases, you may need only to start talking about what you want to do before your prospect starts volunteering to help make it happen.

> **EXAMPLE:** When Jay needed $45,000 to launch his general contracting business, he went to a favorite uncle and aunt. The couple already knew he'd been unhappy working for his past employer and planning to start his own company. At a regularly scheduled visit to his uncle and aunt's home, Jay told them he had put together his business plan and was ready to get started. When his aunt asked, "How can we help?," Jay replied that he "needed a lot of money." He asked whether they had any suggestions as to where he should begin looking. To Jay's utter amazement, his uncle asked, "How much is a lot of money?" and proceeded to finance the entire loan.

If you need to make your request more explicitly, use, in the lingo of fundraising, a "soft ask". After some conversation about your business plans, you might say, "I need to raise about X dollars to get started, and I thought you might be interested in participating."

If the person looks at all uncertain at this point, you might acknowledge any tensions that have entered the room with a comment like, "No pressure, of course." Next, explain why you thought of this person; something like, "I thought it might appeal to you because I know you started your own Web design business a few years ago," or "I thought of you because I know you have a background in business." But there's no need to be apologetic or back down—your manner should continue to show your confidence that you've offered your prospect a reasonable investment opportunity.

3. Wrapping Up the First Conversation

Think of your kitchen table pitch as the mere opening to a longer conversation. Your main goal for the moment is for your prospective lender to say "yes" to the idea of a loan—not to sign on the dotted line. But regardless of whether your prospective lender reacts positively during your pitch, it's best to leave this initial conversation or meeting open-ended. Allow some matters to remain unresolved until after the person has had a chance to think things over. This way, you can keep your potential lender at ease and demonstrate that you, the person the lender knows and trusts, haven't suddenly transformed into an aggressive salesperson.

a. If the Conversation Goes Well

Let's say the conversation is going well. If you get a "yes," you've crossed into the land of working out the details—details that can just as well be left for later, as described in Section D, below. Explain that you'll send your lender a letter detailing the loan terms and next steps. If your lender is nevertheless so gung-ho that he or she can't resist asking a few more questions, there's no need to act coy.

If, for example, your prospect wants to talk about exactly how much you need to borrow, start by offering a range, such as "between $10,000 and $30,000." (The amounts you choose will depend upon the amount you figured out in Chapter 5.) This helps the lender feel like he or she is not rushing into anything and can go home, perhaps contact an accountant, and think about how much he or she can offer.

Cultivating a Prospect Over Several Months

One of Andrea Lang's best loan prospects (for her Washington, DC café, described earlier) is someone she has never met. The prospect is a friend of a close colleague of Andrea's from her days in hotel food service. When the former colleague heard about Andrea's business plans, he didn't have the money to spare but gave her the number of his friend, a successful doctor.

Andrea didn't know the doctor personally but had seen her at a recent social event. The first time she called, she introduced herself by mentioning the event, using the name of the mutual friend, and saying that her friend indicated the doctor might be looking for local investment opportunities. But Andrea knew it was important to build a relationship with the doctor and spent at least three months building "rapport" before presenting her actual loan request. This included conversation about Andrea's own heart surgery, the doctor's business dreams, and Andrea's business plans. The doctor, a traveling cardiologist, was rarely in town to meet in person, so all these discussions took place by phone. The doctor even introduced Andrea to an independent coffee supplier, so now her café can carry its own line of coffee beans. Andrea also discovered that this would be the doctor's first private loan and that the doctor hoped to make other loans and one day start her own business.

"The doctor just believes in helping people advance," Andrea notes. Finally Andrea sent the doctor her loan request, packaged with three loan option sheets and a copy of her business plan. The doctor called back, right away, and confirmed, "I want to do it." But that wasn't the end, because the check is not yet in the mail. "I don't want to be pushy," says Andrea, "and I know she means what she says, she's just very hard to pin down."

Repayment is another issue you might touch upon during your conversation but should try to avoid entangling yourself in deep discussions over. Drawing on your draft loan proposal (which you will soon customize and send to your lender), simply describe how and when you'll pay the money back. For example, you might say, "I'm anticipating a repayment schedule of five years, with interest of course." Most lenders, however, will be glad to have a chance to sit with what they've heard so far and wait to receive your request in writing.

In any case, once your prospect has heard enough to agree to the idea of an investment, it's time to wrap up your pitch conversation. Explain what the next steps will be. Say that you will shortly be sending your business plan and a loan request letter, after which the two of you can hammer out the details of the investment before signing the final agreement. The final step will be what's called the "closing," described at the end of Chapter 9, where you will sign the promissory note and the lender will give you the funds.

I specifically advise against giving the lender a copy of your loan request letter or business plan during this initial conversation or meeting. You should have them virtually ready to send as soon as you get home, but for now, preserve the informality of the meeting and the comfort of the personal relationship by sticking with purely verbal discussions and agreements.

b. If the Conversation Doesn't Go Well

Now let's imagine that the conversation hasn't gone so swimmingly, and your prospect is uncomfortable or unwilling to agree to a loan. If possible, don't let him or her actually say the word "no." If you sense that the person is trying to find a way to decline, help out by saying something like, "I can tell that you're not comfortable with this yet—can I contact you again in six months to show you my progress?" This lets both of you off the hook for now and gives you a reason to call back six months later.

Don't worry; very few people make their financial decisions quickly, let alone on the spot. In fact, entrepreneurs often receive a lukewarm reception long before they get an eventual yes. This is because even your strongest supporter will likely have some questions he or she needs answered before making an investment in your business.

In fact, expect most prospects to go home and review your request and maybe your business plan. Some will want to consult others—probably a spouse or partner, and maybe a professional adviser like an attorney or accountant. It will be up to you to follow up through email, phone, or additional meetings, if these are what the prospect needs to get to yes.

Following Up After Six Months

If you do put your conversation on hold for six months or some other period of time, be sure not to drop the ball after that time has passed. One of the most valuable things you can take away from a meeting that didn't go well is an agreement to follow up. This gives you the reason, and the excuse, to call again on this prospect. Even if you choose not to renew your request for a loan, it's only fair to follow up, so that you don't leave the matter hanging between you.

When the agreed-upon period of time has passed, contact the prospect and ask if you can meet again to share the progress your business has made. If the person agrees to a follow-up meeting, that's an excellent sign—it would have been all too easy to just say "no" to your meeting request.

Prepare for the meeting by creating a visual representation of what you achieved in the intervening months. A table, a bar chart, or slides where you spell out milestones accomplished and those yet to come will be useful. You could even just prepare a checklist of "items accomplished" and "items to do." If you've had any favorable press coverage or customer feedback, those can be very effective at bringing life to your tables and charts.

When you go to the follow-up meeting, bring these materials with you. Your goal is to communicate the progress you've made since you last met. You may even want to make checks on the checklist or use a marker to fill in a bar on a bar chart to illustrate your growth. By showing that you can do what you say you will do, you may cause the person to happily agree to the loan.

C. Handling Hesitancy and Concerns

Many of the questions you'll hear from prospects will be centered around the loan itself, such as how much money you're asking for, how you'll use the money, and when and how you'll repay it. You'll already know the answers from having drafted your loan request letter or business plan.

However, some investors may also raise more general concerns, most commonly over their own finances, the viability of your business, the impact on your relationship, and what others might think.

1   Concerns About the Prospect's Own Financial Limitations

Prospects concerned about their finances may tell you that they don't have the money, it's not handy, or they already have a plan for it. Here are some ways you can respond to their concerns.

"I don't have the money to give you." Suggest a lower amount. Ask whether the person can think of someone else you might contact.

"I have other plans for that money." Politely ask about the plans. It may be that you can make the term of your loan short enough to repay your lender in time for the other needs. For example, if a relative has moved children's college savings into a money market account while the kids are still in high school, you could structure your repayment to be completed before college tuition payments begin. In this case, you may want to offer collateral, to offset any risk to the hard-saved education dollars.

"I can't access the money. It's tied up in an investment/retirement plan/ annuity." Encourage your lender to contact his or her financial adviser or accountant to find out whether the money can be moved, without penalty, to an account that allows private investing. For example, a self-directed IRA is a retirement account that allows the account owner to make investments for tax-free retirement investing in private businesses like yours. (See "What to Tell Your Prospect About Self-Directed IRAs," below.)

What to Tell Your Prospect About Self-Directed IRAs

Most folks with IRAs (individual retirement accounts) don't look beyond the standard menu of mutual funds or stocks offered by the financial institution managing the account. They may not realize that a few institutions also allow account holders to invest the money in private business or real estate investment opportunities of the person's own choosing. That gives the investor the tax advantages of retirement investing while hand picking their investments.

Only a handful of companies offer a self-directed IRA product, although these are rapidly gaining in popularity. Your prospect should check with a financial adviser about his or her current IRA and whether there are any self-directed IRA products, but chances are he or she will need to set up a new account with one of the few companies that offers them. At this point, the most well-known company and the one with the most experience is Pensco. Materials about self-directed IRAs are available on its website, www.pensco. com.

Suggesting that your lender set up a self-directed IRA to make you a loan may be the type of smart advice that will make your lender consider your proposal from a tax-efficiency point of view.

2.   Concerns About the Viability of Your Business

Your prospect's impression of your business plan will have an inevitable impact on his or her willingness to make the loan. The prospect may be justifiably dubious about how you're going to sell your wacky widgets or may just be expressing a lack of knowledge about your business or the whole world of business. Remember, you've been living with this idea for months—its brilliance may not be so patently obvious to someone who's hearing it for the first time.

Explaining not only the potential for success, but also the risks associated with an investment in your business, is an important part of your job. Take the time to show why you think you can do what you say you can. (If you ever make a request to a professional investor for equity capital, you will be put through a particularly painful process called "due diligence," in which the investor sends you pages of questions to answer about how your business works, in addition to doing his or her own analysis of its potential.)

"I don't believe your business will succeed." Offer a loan secured by collateral so that the lender will know that, even if your business goes belly up and you don't have a dime, the lender can sell the collateral to cover your debt. Once the prospect believes that the money is safe, you can also explain why you think your business will in fact succeed. Send both the executive summary and the complete version of your business plan. Offer to present your plan to your prospect in person and to answer any questions. If you have other investors, you could ask one to provide a reference.

You can also take steps to show your prospect that you take personal responsibility for the debt—in other words, that he or she will get paid no matter what. If your business is a sole proprietorship, or if you plan to sign the promissory note so the loan is to you instead of to your business, you become personally liable for the debt. If the loan will be to your incorporated business, you can still assume personal liability if you think it would make the difference for your prospect. To do this, add yourself as a coborrower on the promissory note, so that both the business and the individual can be held liable if the loan doesn't get paid.

"I don't think you have the skills to run your business." Emphasize your experience. Talk to your prospect about former jobs you've held that relate to your business. Mention small business trainings, classes, or workshops you have taken; business counselors you have met with; and people you plan to hire.

If you feel that your responses still don't adequately alleviate the prospect's concerns, and if you respect his or her business experience, take the objections to heart. Ask whether the person has any advice for resolving the problems, and heed the advice whether or not you take this person's money.

3. Concerns About the Impact on Your Relationship

The prospect may naturally be worried about how lending you money will impact his or her relationships, either with you or with others. To reduce the person's sense of relationship risk, reassure him or her that the loan or investment will be kept as businesslike as possible, as follows.

"What if we disagree over the terms of the deal?" Emphasize the flexibility inherent in a private loan (or investment) like the one you're proposing—there are a multitude of ways to structure the deal, so you're bound to find one that meets both your and your lender's needs. Also explain that the two of you will discuss the terms of your agreement and put them in writing, so that both of you can refer back as needed during the life of the arrangement. Let the prospect know that you're planning on drawing up legally binding agreements and will keep detailed records of payments for accounting and tax purposes. Explain that since this is a private deal, the two of you can always make changes to handle unexpected circumstances. (In fact, loans between family and friends end up being restructured quite often.)

"I'm afraid that our relationship will suffer if there's a problem paying back the loan." You must respect and acknowledge this fear. Clearly, you don't want your relationship to be damaged, either. Show how you can prevent problems with the loan from turning into problems in the relationship. Point out that the promissory note will include actions to be taken in the case of late payments, missed payments, and default. Also point out that if the two of you decide to use a third party to administer the loan, the third party can advise you on how to handle and resolve problems before they hurt your relationship. Sometimes it helps to know that there will be a buffer between you and your lender.

4. Concerns About What Others May Think

Even if you think your request is only between you and your lender, be aware that the lender may be thinking about what other people will either say about this loan or have said about private lending in general. You can't directly control such external factors, and the opinions or feelings of other people tend to be a common source of lender concern.

Further complicating the picture is that hesitant lenders often point to a third party when they can't bring themselves to say "no" in their own voice. That means they could be expressing real concerns based on outside pressure, or simply using these concerns to mask something that they don't want to tell you. Here are some ways you can respond to such concerns.

"My spouse (or partner) won't like the idea of my lending you the money." Offer to review your loan proposal with your lender's spouse or partner. Reassure your lender that you don't need a decision on the spot—this is a business matter, not a case where you've run out of cash and need a quick handout. Explain how you plan to make it a business transaction by signing a promissory note that obligates you to repay. (Your lender's spouse or partner might be comforted by knowing that the promissory note provides solid grounds upon which to sue you if you still don't come through.)

"I have a friend who lent someone money and never got a dime back." Emphasize that if the loan is set up and managed correctly, the likelihood of successful repayment is much higher. Explain what consequences you would face, under the written agreement you plan to sign, if you made a late payment, missed a payment, or defaulted. Also stress why you will be a good borrower—for example, your manic attention to monthly budgets or your track record of paying your credit card bill in full every month. You might even offer to share a copy of your credit report to prove your loan-worthiness. (Copies of your credit report can be obtained once a year for free from a centralized source mandated by the federal government—go to www.annualcreditreport.com, or call 877-322-8228 for more information or to place a request.)

D. After Your Prospect Says "Yes" (or "Maybe")

Now let's say that your prospect has either verbally agreed to invest in your business, or at least promised to think it over after looking at your written loan proposal. Here's where you'll be happy to have done your background work. When you get back to your desk or computer, revisit the loan request you developed in Chapter 5, in order to make additions or changes based on your conversation. Three of the best ways to polish up your written request so as to clinch your lender's interest are to:

- appeal to your lender's personality type
- offer options, including different loan amounts or terms, and
- offer special incentives.

Does the Loan Request Letter Just Seem Wrong for This Lender?

While the one- to two-page loan request letter described in Chapter 5 works well for most lenders, it's not your only option. Here are two other ways to present the information; but you can prepare anything you think will suit your lender.

A slideshow. Some people, especially those with business experience, might respond well to a few PowerPoint slides or a complete slideshow. Especially if you are adept at using charts, graphs, and pictures to tell your story, a slideshow makes a nice focal point for a follow-up meeting.

A concept paper. This is something longer than a letter but shorter than a business plan. You might describe your idea, the need for it, and how it would work. You need not include all the business details like how you're financing the business, how the economics will work, who you intend to do the work, and so on. This presentation works well for supportive lenders who are eager for details but prefer reading a short paper to a complete business plan.

---

1. Appeal to Your Lender's Personality Type

You may recall the four lender personality types described earlier (in Chapter 4): savvy, inexperienced, worried, and analytic. Depending on which type best describes your lender, you can vary the loan terms as well as the language in your loan request letter. As you look at your letter, ask yourself: How well does it address this particular potential lender's motives and concerns? Are there subtle ways in which you can alter the proposal itself, or your wording, to make it feel right to the potential lender?

If your lender is savvy. A savvy lender will be attracted to a competitive interest rate, so offer as much as you think you can afford. Use the loan calculators included on the CD-ROM at the back of this book to determine exactly how different interest rates affect your regular payments and total repayment. Your letter might also mention key financial information about your business, such as an impressive growth in revenue or a great profit margin. Be businesslike and succinct in your communications.

If your lender is inexperienced. An inexperienced lender probably agreed to the loan because he or she wants to support you, so it's important to acknowledge the importance of the relationship.

But if your lender is inexperienced, it's also your job to make sure he or she understands the risks. Although you don't need to spell out any gruesome worst-case scenarios in your loan request letter, make sure that this person recognizes that if your business doesn't grow the way you plan for it to, you may be at risk of not being able to make your payments and going into default. Even an inexperienced lender should be able to afford to lose the investment. If talk of risk worries your lender, consider securing the loan with collateral or not taking money from this prospect at all.

If your lender is worried. A worried lender needs assurances. Your letter should mention how and when you will pay back the loan, and how you will handle a cash crunch if it occurs. Lenders worried about emotional risk want to feel that the deal is separate from your relationship. If you decide to hire someone else to manage the loan, explain how this approach can keep the lines of separation clear. If you think the lender is also worried about the loan's impact on other friendships or relationships, offer to share the basics of your loan request with the others so that there are no secrets. (See "The Family Bank" in Chapter 4.)

If your lender is analytic. An analytic lender wants a hassle-free loan. This means you should have your paperwork in order and make it easy for the lender to be hands-off. In the loan request letter, spell out the details of how the repayment will work. Analytic lenders tend to appreciate the conveniences of loan servicing by third parties, as well as special services such as automatic debiting and crediting of bank accounts. The easier you make it, the better.

Also, don't worry this person with a lot of informal communications. There's no need to call and ask details about his or her weekend camping trip if all you need is to ask at which address the lender would like to receive your draft promissory note for review.

2.   Offer Various Loan Options

There's no need to give your family and friend lenders a take-it-or-leave-it proposition. You can demonstrate your flexibility by offering several loan options, each containing a different loan amount and interest rate. For example, you might let your prospects chose between a high-interest loan that lasts several years and a shorter-term loan with a lower interest rate. Protect your own interests by suggesting a repayment schedule that suits the unique needs of your business, such as an interest-only loan, a graduated repayment loan, or a seasonal loan.

The sample letter requesting loans for Esme's Café (in Chapter 6) offered three options. (Esmeralda didn't lay these out in the letter, but in a separate attachment—you can format your request either way.) She intentionally matched the higher loan amounts with higher interest rates, in the hopes that a higher rate would motivate a lender to select a larger loan amount. This approach worked, and she actually received a bit more than she needed to launch the café. That allowed her to buy an additional piece of equipment that had been on her radar screen but that she hadn't yet figured how to finance.

3.   Offer Special Incentives

If you feel that your potential lender needs a little extra convincing, you might adjust your proposal to add some special incentives, such as the following.

Offer a demand option. If your prospective lender appears to be reluctant only because he or she may need the money back before you're done with it, you can offer to include a "demand option" in your loan agreement. This provision says that at any point during the life of the contract, the lender has the right to demand full repayment. Offering a demand option can be just the tool you'll need to get a hesitant lender on board. Of course, such a provision comes with obvious risks—you need to be prepared for the possibility that the lender could demand payment at any time, and you'll still need to convince your lender that you're capable of repaying the entire loan at a moment's notice. If you want to offer your lender a demand option, but know that you couldn't pay on demand until your business has been up and running for a while, say the first year, one solution might be to offer the demand option but delay the effectiveness of the demand until one year into the term of the note.

Offer an adjustable interest rate. If you're offering any long-term loans—perhaps of three or more years—realize that some of your investors, especially the savvy ones, may be unwilling to let you lock in an interest rate for that length of time. If rates go up, the lender is going to be looking longingly at other investments with higher returns. Of course, no one can predict how far interest rates might rise or fall during the course of your loan. But the savvy investor may want to protect against being stuck with an interest rate that turns out to be on the low side.

To satisfy the lender's interests, you could, for example, structure your loan so that you pay a fixed rate for a year (allowing you to predict your monthly expenses in the early stages of your business), after which the rate becomes adjustable, fluctuating every year. You would probably tie the interest rate to the prime lending rate, perhaps adding a percentage point or two to further attract the lender. This tool may not make a huge difference in your payments but may give the savvy investor some security.

Offer to make a bonus payment. Identify a specific business milestone, such as a level of revenue or a number of customers served. Propose to your lender that, upon reaching that milestone, you'll make a predetermined bonus payment of, for example, $3,000. (This payment would be on top of your regular payments.) Offering such a bonus shows your lender that you are committed to succeeding in your business and helps him or her feel a stake in that success. Of course, it's best to choose milestones that really do reflect success—if, for example, you simply offered a bonus after one year, you'd have no way of predicting your ability to pay it.

Offer an ownership stake in your company. Even if you initially approached your lender about a standard loan, there's nothing to stop you from incorporating elements of equity investment into your proposal. (For more information on equity investing, see Chapter 8.) You'd basically be creating a hybrid, combining the relative safety of a loan with the ownership benefits of an equity investment. Some ways to structure this include:

- As a convertible note, which starts out like a loan and then, at a specified conversion date, gives the lender the option to either continue repaying the loan or to convert the principal into an equity position, meaning that the lender now becomes an owner in the company (an investor).
- As a revenue-linked loan (also known as "royalty-based financing") in which, in exchange for the investment, you pay a set percentage of your revenue each month to the investor until a predetermined period of time or repayment amount has been met. The investor thus receives regular payments that grow (or decline) as your business grows (or declines). This type of financing is sometimes preferred by businesses that don't want to lose ownership control but need larger investments. It's also sometimes preferred by investors who prefer regular payments over time to one big payoff event in the form of a sale of the business or an initial public offering.

4.   Offer More-Generous Terms to Less-Willing Lenders

If you'll be approaching multiple lenders, try to enter into agreements with your most likely supporters first. These will probably be your closest family members, who may be not only willing, but eager to agree to loans that offer you maximum flexibility at minimum interest. With these loans in hand, you're now free to offer more-secure loan proposals to your less-convinced lenders.

EXAMPLE: Lina wants to buy into a health food store franchise but will need $50,000 to do it. She explores several different funding sources, including a bank loan and the franchiser's financing program, but eventually turns to her circle of friends and family.

After presenting her idea, Lina receives generous promises of support, in the form of a $20,000 loan from her mother and a $5,000 loan from her sister. They agree to structure each of their loans the same way: with a ten-year term, to start with deferred repayment for one year, turning into an interest-only loan over the following three years (thus keeping Cynthia's payments as low as possible), then becoming a standard amortized loan for the remaining seven years.

However, their offers leave $25,000 to be raised. Cynthia has also identified a number of other prospects, including a distant cousin, a former employer, and an associate from a prior job. Because she has been out of touch which these prospects for a while, she wants to impress them with her professional approach to her private fundraising and to set the stage for a business relationship.

Knowing that her first two loans won't require any payments for a year, Cynthia can approach these prospects with more standard loan offers. Her former boss and associate each end up agreeing to a standard amortized six-year loan beginning after a six-month deferment period. Unfortunately, Cynthia's cousin decides she is not in a position to invest. The terms of all these loans are detailed in the table below.

Note that, although the various loans in the above table are structured very differently, the amount repaid ends up being about the same. With some similarly careful calculating, you can set up loans that feel unique to each lender but that result in monthly payments and an overall total that you can afford.

⚠️ **Don't forget to calculate your monthly payments under every loan scenario you offer.** For example, when Esmeralda offered interest rates of 10%, 12%, and 15%, she accepted the possibility that she might end up paying anywhere between $115, $142, and $242 per loan per month. Make sure the timing and the amount of all the loan repayments are manageable. Consider their impact on your business finances as a whole; don't just consider them one by one. Until the promissory notes are signed, nothing is set in stone. Adjust your requests as your fundraising moves forward to keep your repayment obligations in line with what you can afford.

Summary of Loans Obtained by Cynthia

Loan Terms	Mother and Sister	Former Boss and Associate
Loan amount	$25,000	$25,000
Repayment plan	Deferred/Interest-only/ Amortized	Amortized
Interest rate	5%	7%
Principal to be repaid	$25,000	$25,000
Interest to be repaid	$3,750 + 4,681.22 = $8,431.22	$6,694.45
Total to be repaid	$33,431.22	$31,694.45
Schedule	One-year grace period; interest-only payment for 3 years ($104.17 each); reverts to amortized loan for 7 years ($353.35 monthly payments)	Six-month grace period; 72 monthly payments of $377.32

E. After Your Prospect Says "No"

What if, even after you try to address your prospective lender's concerns, or the person agrees to review your customized loan request, he or she nevertheless turns you down? Your first task is to listen carefully to the person's reasons. If he or she expresses concerns that ring true, or if you hear a similar message from several people, you'll learn important lessons for the future. You'll also be able to decide whether to move on, or whether the prospect left some room open for future discussion.

Don't push so hard that you endanger the underlying personal relationship. There's no point in arguing with someone who truly doesn't want to loan you money. Some people may not even tell you the real reason for their hesitation. However, for those who openly express a concern that you can allay by providing more information, there's no harm in following up accordingly.

1.   When to Move On

There are two circumstances in which you need to take "no" as the lender's final answer. The first is if your lender has given you a clear and firm refusal and you accept that his or her concerns or objections are valid. Perhaps your proposal is just not a good fit, in which case it's time to focus your fundraising energy elsewhere.

Second, move on if your lender has given you a muddled refusal that seems to be masking some concern that he or she is unwilling to communicate. If some gentle nudging doesn't bring the issue to the surface, you probably want to let sleeping dogs lie. Besides, do you really want to get into a business transaction with someone who won't say what's on his or her mind from the beginning? You'll be much happier dealing with a lender who gives you clear signals and allows you to address real concerns.

2.   When to Ask Again

Just as with your initial pitch, it's worth keeping certain prospects on your list for future contact—especially those who were at least interested enough to review your loan request letter. Keep track of prospects that you sensed had a favorable opinion of you and your business idea but weren't fully convinced for some reason or other. Here are some logical times to return to those people.

When the agreed-upon amount of time has passed since your initial meeting. If your prospect declines for now but welcomes you to call back in six months, do it. In Section B, above, you'll find a discussion about how to handle a follow-up meeting.

When you've got a more-convincing presentation. As you gain experience in fundraising, you may realize that your early presentation wouldn't have convinced you, either. When you've had more practice and have a more-professional proposal to make, contact a reluctant prospect again. However, it's probably wise to let at least a month or two pass, so your prospect doesn't just roll his or her eyes at seeing you back so soon.

When your business has gained a major new customer or supporter. Being able to show that your business model works, and that you are attracting customers and generating revenue, sends a very positive signal to savvy investors. Some lenders and investors don't like to be the first to jump. But if you go back and tell them about the others who have already put their money into the mix, they may want to do the same.

When your potential lender's circumstances have changed. Maybe your prospect has sold some land or stock, received an inheritance, or taken a great new job. And even if your prospect's financial circumstances haven't changed radically, his or her outlook may have changed due to personal circumstances—for example, your prospect may have a new sense of confidence after surviving a difficult divorce and entering a new relationship. Any of these situations might create an opening for you to return with an update on your business progress and a new loan proposal.

Chapter 8

Seeking Equity Capital

A. Where to Look for an Equity Investor 172

   1. Family and Friend Investors 174

   2. Business Angels 177

   3. Venture Capital Funds 182

B. How to Ask for Equity Capital 184

   1. Establishing a Relationship 184

   2. Making Your Pitch 189

   3. Seeking a Nonbinding Agreement 193

C. Additional Steps That Professional Equity Investors May Request 199

   1. Drafting Your Offer: The Investment Proposal 201

   2. Understanding The Investor's Offer: The Term Sheet 203

From a business owner's standpoint, the great thing about equity capital is that you don't have to pay it back—at least not anytime soon. If all goes well, your equity investors' gamble will pay off either when you sell the business or buy them out, or—in the rarest of success stories—your company makes an initial public offering (IPO) and your investors sell their shares on the stock market. In fact, even investors who require you to pay dividends rarely require they be paid in cash, only that the money be reinvested into new shares for the investor. That all translates to no liability and no monthly payments.

Not surprisingly given the higher stakes for the investors, equity capital can be harder to obtain than loan capital. There is no security or collateral available for early-stage equity investors. Nevertheless, you may have already decided that seeking equity capital is worth your while (based on the introductory discussion in Chapter 3). Or, maybe you've already made a kitchen table pitch to a family member requesting a loan, but he or she in turn suggested an equity investment. In either case, read portions of or this entire chapter to learn:

- where to look for equity investors if you don't already have them (see Section A, below)
- how to ask for equity capital and reach an initial agreement to invest (see Section B, below), and
- what additional steps professional equity investors may require before finalizing their agreement (see Section C, below).

Only a corporation or an LLC can sell an ownership interest. If your business is set up as a sole proprietorship or a partnership, you'll need to change your legal structure before you can raise money through equity investments. Refer back to the discussion of legal structures in Chapter 1.

A. Where to Look for an Equity Investor

There are more equity investors out there than you might realize—but they won't be wearing name badges. Being an equity investor is not necessarily a profession (though it can be for some), and you can't ordinarily just look up an investor in the Yellow Pages. Possible sources

Get Legal Help Complying With Securities Laws

Although this chapter covers a lot of equity fundraising activities that you can do on your own, you'll also need to involve an attorney experienced in securities law. The attorney can help you plan your offering and draft the stock purchase agreement (the document that sells shares in your company to an investor). The attorney can also help you cope with the overarching presence of the federal Securities and Exchange Commission (SEC) and affiliated state securities regulators.

Federal and state laws require that every offering of securities (that is, every sale of shares in your business to someone else) be either registered or exempted from registration. The accounting and paperwork preparation costs to register an offering are substantial (sometimes upwards of $800,000). Fortunately for entrepreneurs like you and me, several exemptions are available that should help you raise equity capital from friends and family, business angels, and venture capital investors without meeting onerous registration requirements.

The most commonly used exemption is known as "Regulation D" of the federal Securities Law of 1933. Regulation D exempts you from registering your offer if it's 1) a small offering (less than $5,000,000 worth) or 2) an offering of any size that involves only wealthy and sophisticated investors.

This book isn't big enough to help you understand all of the conditions and restrictions involved in complying with both the federal and state securities laws (yes, there are state laws as well, and they vary state by state, another reason you'll need an attorney). Even if you're pretty sure you'll be exempt, engage an attorney before embarking on the path of raising money by selling your company's stock. Choose an attorney who has specific experience with securities law, so that your offering will fully comply (in the cheapest manner, of course) with the relevant laws and regulations— it's no fun tangling with the SEC if you get it wrong.

of equity investment for your small, early-stage business include the following, in order of their likeliness to invest in you:

- family and friends with both money and appropriate business experience (see Section 1, below)
- other individual investors known as "business angels" (see Section 2, below), and
- professional investors such as venture capital funds (see Section 3, below).

⚠️ **Not all equity investors behave true to their category.** For example, a family member who happens to be experienced in business might invest in ways that make him or her seem more like a business angel. Business angels with a lot of experience and money often form groups that act like venture capital funds. As you read the following sections, just remember that in real life, the lines get blurry and the descriptions in this chapter are your guideposts, not a definitive street map.

1. Family and Friend Investors

Equity investors can be found among your family and friends in two ways: Either they sniff you out, or you find them. If you're lucky, a family member or friend might hear of your business efforts and express some interest. Based on what you know about the person, talk informally to get a sense of where the person's interests lie and to decide whether to make a loan request (as described in Chapters 6 and 7) or an investment proposal (as described later in this chapter).

Another way an equity investment might unfold is that you begin with a loan request but find that your listener is more interested in an investment. If so, consider whether he or she matches the characteristics laid out in this section.

To decide which people on your best prospects list (from Chapter 4) may be good candidates for an equity investment, consider whether each has:

- money to invest
- experience with business or investments, or
- a suitable temperament to join you in your business venture.

Your prospective investor doesn't need to have all three of these characteristics, although you won't get very far if he or she doesn't have the first one, money to invest. If your prospect does in fact have all three, he or she fits the definition of a business angel, described in Section 2, below.

a.   Does Your Prospective Investor Have Money?

The ideal equity investor has money—and enough of it that if your business goes belly-up, he or she could stand to lose every penny. Now, if you'll be asking for a $6,000 investment in order to buy an espresso machine for your café, you might know a number of people who could handle this risk. But if you'll be asking for $100,000 to get your dream restaurant off the ground, then you'll need to choose your investors with extra care. When taking money from people who trust you, you also take on a particular responsibility to protect their interests. Make sure you don't lure them into financial waters over their heads.

In fact, your ideal equity investor has not only enough money to spare for your venture, but enough so that the federal laws essentially say, "That's a wealthy, sophisticated investor; he or she doesn't need the protection of the securities laws, so you don't need to register your offering to this person." Put another way, the easiest way to exempt yourself from the registration requirements of federal and state securities laws (with the help of your attorney) is to limit your investors to either:

- "accredited investors" (a securities law concept meaning individual investors who either have a net worth of at least $1,000,000 or who have earned over $200,000 per year for at least the last two years; see Chapter 9 for a fuller definition), or
- other companies or legal entities with at least $5,000,000 in assets.

Although some exemptions allow for limited participation by non-accredited investors, they tend to impose so many other conditions on the business owner—like having to file the offering materials in advance and make various specific disclosures—that reaching out to nonaccredited investors becomes prohibitively expensive and time consuming. Your efforts are probably better spent offering equity securities to people with enough money to qualify as accredited investors—and no one else.

b.   Does Your Prospective Investor Have Business or Investing Experience?

Look for equity investors who have either experience at owning or running a business, particularly one similar or relevant to your business, or experience investing in other small businesses. Ask yourself these questions:

- Has this person "been there" before—in other words, will the two of you quickly reach common and familiar ground when discussing your business or the person's investment in it?
- Does this person know things that you need to know in order to achieve success?
- Has this person achieved his or her own success in a line of business related to yours?
- Has this person invested in, mentored, or otherwise been supportive of a business similar to yours?

If you can answer yes to any of these questions, this person probably will be worth approaching with an investment proposal. If you can answer yes to more than one of the questions, even better—your ideal equity investor has two sets of experience: business experience to draw upon in advising you at critical junctures in your growth, and financing or investing experience with which to make an informed decision about buying a stake in your business.

c.   Does Your Prospective Investor Have the Right Temperament?

Look for an investor who likes and is supportive of you, and with whom you are comfortable communicating. The relationship between you and the equity investor needs to be considerably more aligned than the relationship between you and your lenders. This is because investors are legally co-owners, with every right to get involved in the business and be informed of its progress. Before you rush to accept the person's money, remember that you'll be spending a lot of future time explaining what you're doing with it.

d.   The Ethics of Working With Family and Friend Investors

After you've considered whether your prospective equity investors have one or more of the three characteristics described above, think again about whether you can ethically request each person's help. Equity investing is highly risky. You are taking the investors' money and promising to pay it back only if your company succeeds. Even if your business does avoid bankruptcy, years may pass before it generates enough cash to actually pay people for their participation in the company. When you approach your family and friends, make sure they understand the risks and aren't just blinded by their desire to support you and your business endeavor.

If you have a friend or family member who doesn't really meet the qualifications listed above, or whom you feel uncomfortable having as an investor, suggest a traditional loan or a gift instead. You could even customize a loan agreement, giving the person the option to convert the loan into stock at a predetermined future date. This is known as convertible debt, discussed previously in Chapter 7.

⚠ Separately agreeing to pay back your equity investors if the business fails probably won't work. I've known and heard stories of entrepreneurs who raised equity from people they knew by selling shares in their business, with the verbal promise to repay the original amount if the business ever failed. Though this might sound like an ingenious way to protect both your and the Investors' interests, it's just the opposite. Investors must stand in line behind debtors to be repaid if the company fails. In addition, it is unethical and potentially illegal to make verbal promises that you cannot necessarily keep. You may also land in trouble if you need to disclose such verbal agreements to future investors or institutional lenders.

2.   Business Angels

If a person outside your circle of friends and family offered to invest a large amount of money in your business, and said that he or she didn't need any repayment until you sold the company or his or her share of it, that would sound like a deal made in heaven, right? A few wealthy individuals out there are willing to do just that sort of deal—and they're commonly called business angels. The prototypical angel is very wealthy, usually with experience in both running a business and in financing risky start-ups. He or she is probably willing to privately invest anywhere from $50,000 to $1 million and will do so with little fanfare.

Business angels tend to be former entrepreneurs who, either on the side or full time, have segued into making highly risky investments on a private basis. Angels typically invest in promising businesses where the business owner has maxed out his or her personal financial resources as well as the amount he or she can request from friends and family but can't yet attract investments from professional venture capital firms. Often the angel is making one of the earliest, if not the very first, equity investment in the business.

Although business angels are often hard to find, because they invest privately and often individually with only the help of an attorney, they are a much more likely source of money for you than venture capitalists. The latest estimates (from the Center for Venture Research, 2003) show that angels provided $18.1 billion in start-up financing to early-stage companies, while venture capitalists provided just over $300 million to the same type of start-up companies in the same year.

If you don't already know any business angels, but are pretty sure that you want to sell shares in your business, get started looking now. It can take at least six months, and probably more like a year, to find a business angel and build the relationship to the point where the person actually invests in your business. Don't wait until you're desperate for a cash influx!

a. Where to Look for a Business Angel

It may be that you have a relative, friend, or associate who, you now realize, could be or become a business angel. But you can also look for local angels outside that circle, with whom you've had no previous contact. The best way to find business angels is through their "gatekeepers." Talk to your attorney, banker, and accountant. Ask whether they know any business angels themselves, or whether they have any colleagues who know of local business angels. Ask around at local chamber meetings, business conferences, or other get-togethers within your industry.

Heard on the Street

In their own voices, here's the advice several experienced entrepreneurs and angels give to entrepreneurs like you:

- "No matter what you think, it always takes twice as long and costs twice as much."
- "Most entrepreneurs fail to realize the best source of financing and the cheapest is customers."
- "The challenge is to get angels excited about the business concept, which is hard since they might look at hundreds of possible deals."
- "Get a seasoned lawyer who has been through capital equity financing. The closing stages of raising money are a legal process, and a bad deal in earlier stages can affect your attractiveness to investors in later rounds."
- "As a woman entrepreneur, I found little discrimination in the world of angel investing. Having a good business plan is more important than gender."
- "Ask for help, even if you have to hire someone to make some introductions. Angel investors are a small club and entrepreneurs need an introduction to get a deal done."
- "Use informal networks to be referred to angels … it vastly increases the chance that your business plan will be reviewed."
- "Only 1-2% of business plans to angels or VCs ever receive funding. Read the right books, learn the financings concepts, and be fully prepared to present the concept well. Incomplete business plans are unacceptable in today's competitive environment."

To learn more about how angels think and how to attract them to your business, see the profiles of over 20 angel investors and read articles written by angels on the Angel Investor News website at www.angel-investor-news.com.

You don't need to conduct a nationwide search. Business angels prefer to invest in markets and technologies that they know. They also like to invest close to home, both because they know the area and because it makes it easier to stop in and check on your progress.

Studies show that the typical equity investor is an older, white male. But don't let that stop you from approaching people of all types—there are plenty of atypical investors to be found, and money and experience tend to be their main indicators. A successful entrepreneur with money and experience has probably invested informally in about three businesses, two of which have failed. A successful corporative executive with money and experience has probably invested in five businesses, three of which have failed. Both may be eager to improve their record and are just waiting for the right opportunity to come knocking.

The best place to expand your search for angels beyond those you know or know of personally is to go to the Internet. In some parts of the country, organizations exist that connect entrepreneurs and angels in a particular region. For example, an organization called C-Cap is dedicated to connecting local entrepreneurs with angels in the Cincinnati area. Entrepreneurs submit a business summary online according to the instructions on the website, and C-Cap makes the connection. For more information, see www.c-cap.net.

You'll find a list of over 200 structured angel groups nationwide in Appendix C and can link directly to each one's website from the CD-ROM included with this book. Also check out the website of the Angel Capital Association (www.angelcapitalassociation.org). For a listing of venture fairs, see the website for the popular book *Every Business Needs an Angel*, http://everybusinessneedsanangel.com/resources. Finally, you can find links to websites and articles about angel investing at a website called Angel Investor News, designed for both entrepreneurs and investors (www.angel-investor-news.com.)

b.   The Trend Toward Structured Angel Groups

To avoid being mobbed by entrepreneurs pitching the latest, greatest business ideas, business angels have traditionally kept a low profile. In recent years, however, many business angels have started hanging out with one another to share stories, learn new investing practices, and talk about entrepreneurs and business opportunities. Nationwide, many are beginning to form angel groups structured as informal networks, informal funds of accredited investors, or formal funds set up as an LLC (sometimes called dinner clubs).

If you still feel like you're looking for a small fish in a big pond, take heart: Many of these newly formed business angel groups have websites with contact information for local angels, and some even meet regularly to hear pitches from entrepreneurs like you. If you've made the connection and attracted the interest of a group of business angels, you and a few other entrepreneurs may be invited to their monthly event to make your pitch.

One outgrowth of business angels' newfound talkativeness is that your reputation as an entrepreneur will quickly spread among members of the group. Members particularly enjoy singing the praises of an entrepreneur they've discovered and selected for funding. As one observer of this secretive industry says, "Find an individual business angel, and you've found a choir." The more formal groups also like to pool their funds, voting on each deal and giving the entrepreneurs the chance of winning an investment of $250,000 to $500,000 from one group.

The downside of angel groups is that they tend toward more-professional investing behaviors than shown by individual investors, and many are moving "up market," away from the youngest businesses and riskiest deals. In short, they're behaving more and more like venture capital funds, requiring extensive due diligence (a formal investigation into your business's potential) and insisting on greater rights and privileges in return for their purchase of shares in your company. Such demands put a burden on you that family, friend, or solo angel investors rarely do.

Some entrepreneurs with whom I've spoken even feel that the more-organized business angels are becoming more like vultures than angels. As they begin to compete with venture capital funds to make investments in the most promising companies, they have to be quick and smart to find the best deals before the VCs do. One way they've been known to do this is to hover, wait for you to show weakness or a slowing in growth of revenue, and then swoop in and offer their equity investment, but at a lower price (dollars per share) than you expected.

But business angels, especially the solo and informally organized ones described above, remain your best bet for equity capital once you've exhausted your circle of friends, family, and business associates. This is particularly true if you're not yet ready to attract the attention of professional venture capital funds. Angels can also be great mentors and trusted advisers as you grow your business.

3. Venture Capital Funds

Securing an equity investment from a venture capital fund is a huge undertaking that only a very few entrepreneurs ever achieve. I'm amazed at how the mythology of venture capitalists throwing around money has nevertheless lingered from the late 1990s—and lured many entrepreneurs to waste time and money chasing after them. Your time would be far better spent seeking a business angel. But just in case you still believe venture capital is in your future, or you just want to know what all the hubbub is about, let's briefly look into it.

Venture capital funds are professional firms that raise money from wealthy people and invest it in risky, young companies that project high revenue growth within a few years. Although some venture funds may invest as little as $250,000 in a firm, those investments are typically part of a round (a group of investments that occur at the same time, allowing the business to meet its total need from several sources). These rounds are rarely under $1 million. The preferred practice of venture capital firms is to make initial investments of $2-$10 million, in businesses whose revenue is expected to reach $50 million or more. They also often invest with the understanding that they'll invest additional funds in later rounds.

Venture capital investors generally won't part with their money until they feel fairly certain that when they exit the deal (sell their shares) in three to seven years, they'll realize returns exceeding 20% per year. It's not unusual for venture-backed firms to achieve growth rates of 25-40% per quarter in their earliest years, and that's the pace the venture capitalists want to see. Unless you have such a business, you are not likely to be a candidate for a venture capital investment.

Until recently, venture capitalists were recognized as a good source of money for promising start-up businesses. As late as 1999 to 2001, venture capital investors as a group took some huge risks betting on sexy, young technology companies. Stories of business plans sketched out on bar napkins over drinks abounded—and many of those funds got burned when the companies failed to translate their big Internet dreams into tangible profits. Now, venture funds have for the most part become quite conservative—they've retreated to safer, later-stage investments. Angel groups have taken their place as the main source of seed capital investment for entrepreneurs.

Venture capital funds are also heavily concentrated in just a few cities around the country, and they mostly make their investments in these areas. The largest concentrations are in California's Silicon Valley, Boston, and New York City. Smaller clusters of venture capital firms also exist in Southern California, Seattle, Austin, the Raleigh-Durham area, and the Chicago-Detroit area. A few firms (like one called Village Ventures) are trying to create a nationwide presence, but the bulk of investors simply like to stay in cities with high concentrations of economic and entrepreneurial activity.

Look Into Nonprofits That Make Small, "Micro-Equity" Investments

Microenterprise organizations—that is, nonprofit groups that provide technical support and loans to disadvantaged entrepreneurs—have found that for many cash-strapped start-up businesses, monthly payments on a loan are an impossibility. Yet the businesses are typically too small and too risky to attract the interest of angels or traditional venture capitalists.

In response to this problem, these nonprofits have developed a tool called "micro-equity" investing, in which they kick in up to $35,000 and take a direct ownership position in the business. Their equity position gives them a certain level of control, for example, allowing them to hold a portion of stock or serve on the company's board of directors. Like the businesses that venture capitalists invest in, businesses hoping to earn a micro-equity investment must clearly show immediate capital needs and have a strong plan for long-term growth. Only a few groups make these kinds of investments, but to find out whether one exists in your area, call the Association for Enterprise Opportunity, www.microenterpriseworks.org.

B. How to Ask for Equity Capital

When raising business capital from equity investors, you can expect events to follow a logical sequence, not unlike the one for raising money from friend and family lenders. You'll need to:

- establish a relationship (see Section 1, below)
- make your pitch (see Section 2, below), and
- seek a nonbinding commitment (see Section 3, below).

You'll follow more or less the same sequence whether or not you approach friends, family, colleagues, or business angels. (Since so few young businesses actually receive traditional venture capital, we're going to leave the subject of how to ask for it to the many books already out there on that topic.) Once you have a nonbinding commitment, you'll look at Chapter 9 for instructions on formalizing the deal.

Don't fret if the sequence gets out of order. When raising money from people who are themselves successful entrepreneurs or experienced investors, you sometimes have to let them take the driver's seat. Your prospect may be thrilled at your idea during your informal meeting one morning over coffee and sketch out the terms of the deal on a café napkin. Go with the flow. Have your attorney create the stock purchase agreement based on the napkin-inked terms, and forward it to the investor for review.

1. Establishing a Relationship

Equity investing is fundamentally about relationships. When someone makes an equity investment, he or she is making a large bet, and the bet is on you. The investor is gambling that you can and will do what you say you're going to, both in terms of growing your company and earning a handsome return for your investors. Obviously, no investor is going to make such a bet on someone who hasn't earned his or her trust, either through a long-term relationship or some persuasive interactions.

a.   Choosing a Mix of Investors

Even if you know a bunch of people who are equity investors, that doesn't mean you'd want all of them simultaneously involved in your business. In particular, ask yourself how many actively involved investors you can cope with at once. People who buy shares in your business have a right to get involved in internal matters, and they usually do—perhaps by serving on your board of directors, acting as advisers, or otherwise lending their ear—and their opinions.

Some investors, particularly the sophisticated angel investors, may want to be paid for their advice and involvement. When or whether it's appropriate to compensate investors outside of the investment agreement (for example, as consultants or advisers) is a very grey area. Traditionally, compensation agreements are made privately between you, the investor, and your attorney, and no one else hears about it. See "Dealing With Investors Who Want to Be Paid," below, for more on this. Thankfully, not all investors want to be so actively involved. A reasonable number prefer to be more passive and simply receive regular updates and remain uninvolved beyond their investment.

You should aim to gather a mix of passive and active investors, so that you know whom to call for advice and support but aren't constantly barraged with either requests for information or unsolicited advice. The table below summarizes how active, semi-active, and passive investors are most likely to participate in your business.

Dealing With Investors Who Want to Be Paid

Occasionally, an investor will deem him- or herself so vital to your success that the investor will want to be paid for his or her time. Investors have usually been around the block a few times and can be extremely helpful when it comes to plotting business strategy; signing deals with critical business partners; and networking to meet new suppliers, customers, or investors. But try not to agree to anything until *after* the investor has made the investment, or you'll find yourself essentially buying the investment that the person is dangling in front of you.

You can compensate investors outside of the stock purchase agreement in various ways, the most common being through consulting arrangements and stock options. Hiring the investor as a consultant requires only a simple consulting agreement, similar to the one you'd use with your graphic design or technology consultants. If your company offers stock options, you can issue an appropriate amount to the investor—the exact number will depend on the size of your stock option plan or budget, the value of the introductions that the investor makes on your behalf, and the size of the investor's purchase of shares. A good limit here is to keep the investor's compensation to between 5% and 15% of the value of his or her investment. Setting up a stock option plan and compensating investors with stock options will require an attorney, because it's a fairly complex agreement.

Again, compensating investors is a private matter that should be dealt with tactfully, though not kept hidden. If you have 60 investors and have entered into compensation agreements with three of them, there's no need to tell the other 57 about it. However, if you have four investors, and have entered into compensation agreements with three out of the four, it makes sense to disclose those agreements to the one who's being left out.

Investor Participation Levels		
Level of involvement	Type of involvement	Implications for you
Passive	• Attending board meetings as an observer. • Receiving financial reports, news clippings.	• Invite the investors, but don't expect active involvement. • No need to pay.
Semi-Active	• Don't like attending meetings, but want tasks to do in an advisory role. • Helpful with interviewing job candidates. • Helpful making introductions to other funding sources and business contacts.	• You may need to compensate with either cash or stock options.
Active	• Acting as a consultant for any and all aspects of the business; want tasks with deadlines.	• You probably need to compensate with either cash or stock options.

Wondering how much contact your equity investors will regularly want from you? For a full discussion of what to expect and how to provide meaningful and interesting oral and written communications for your equity investors, look ahead to Chapter 10.

b. Cautions When Accepting Investments From Family and Friends

Although you may find it easiest to approach people you already know for an investment, be sure you think through the implications of having each particular person involved in your business. Some say that taking on an investor is like getting married. You will need investors with the skills and temperament either to stay out of your way or to help you solve problems when the going gets rough. You specifically don't want investors who will become a problem or drain your energy with their own anxieties.

Luckily, you probably know your friends and family well enough to make a sensible decision about whom to steer clear of. (Although people you don't know well can certainly surprise you with their problems, they probably won't push your buttons as quickly as a family member might!)

c.   Business Angels Take Time to Get to Know You

Business angels don't just descend from heaven without preliminaries. They usually already know or have built a relationship with the entrepreneur. This is partly because they need to feel confidence and trust in you before taking a risk on you and your business. It's also because they simply like hanging out with entrepreneurs. Business angels tend to enjoy the role of mentor and get a kick out of living the entrepreneurial life vicariously.

If your prospect is a business angel, there's no need to beat around the bush—the investor probably knows exactly why you're trying to get to know him or her. Especially if you met the investor after your stunning three-minute pitch at his or her angel network monthly meeting, both of you know that you need money and that the investor has it. But he or she probably won't offer it to you before getting to know you and your business a little better, so you may need to make contact and have several conversations to achieve a comfortable and trusting relationship. Remember, although you need money, you also need to make a wise choice about whom you're bringing on board.

During your early conversations with a prospective business angel, you may be struck by the degree of interest this person shows in you personally, not just in what your business does or sells. This isn't merely your imagination at work. Business angels take a keen interest in who you are—what your skills, weaknesses, and quirks are, and more.

Business angels will ask around about you behind your back. They will check out what kind of car you drive and be curious about whether and where you take vacations. Their impression of you, as well as your business experience and your management skills, are all critical to their decision to invest. They will also talk to each other about you, and rely on what they hear from the people they know and trust.

Finally, business angels are interested not only in you; they also want to know about the other people who'll be involved in your business. At a meeting (though probably not the first), it's a good idea to introduce your cofounders and any key employees. Prospective investors will hope to find that you've gathered an experienced and innovative management team to help you grow the business.

2.   Making Your Pitch

The principles outlined in the kitchen table pitch in Chapter 7 mostly apply here as well; they just need to be adjusted in two ways. First, prospects for an equity investment probably want more business and financial information than most lenders. Second, your pitch will probably come as no surprise to them. Although a relative, friend, or colleague may need to be brought up to speed on your business, anyone with business experience, or who is a business angel, will know exactly why you've approached him or her. That means there's no need to ease up to anything, only to do it well, at the point when you:

- present your business idea (see Subsection a, below)
- supply the details (see Subsection b, below), and
- ask for an investment (see Subsection c, below).

Given how important it is to make a good impression with a prospective investor, there are also a few things you could say that would indeed make a bad impression; these are spelled out in Subsection d, below.

a.   Presenting Your Business Idea

As described in the previous chapter, you'll need to decide when and how to meet with your investor. Once you're in the meeting, your job is to get your prospect as excited about your idea and the opportunity as you are. Don't be afraid to tap into the passion you have for your idea when you explain why, how, and when it's going to work. Enthusiasm is contagious, especially if the story you are telling makes sense and the prospect agrees that the pieces come together.

A good way to engage your prospect regarding your idea is to focus on the parts of your business that you think are most compelling to that particular investor (just as you would when approaching a potential lender, as discussed in Chapter 7). For example, if your prospect is an expert about the type of product you're producing, talk a lot about why yours will be unusually high in quality or easy to produce. If your prospect is an expert in marketing, focus on what's innovative about your marketing plan.

b. Supplying Details About Your Business Plan

Before your equity investor agrees to commit a dime, he or she will want to know enough about your business plan to think that it's both a great idea and one that you and your team will be able to execute successfully. A savvy investor will nearly always ask to see a copy of your business plan, probably before the meeting, to decide whether the meeting is worth his or her time. But if the investor doesn't ask for the plan in advance, then he or she certainly will ask for it afterwards. Even friends and family members who don't ask for your plan (and this would be rare) will appreciate being offered a copy.

Now is when it's crucial to have created a well-thought-out, articulate, written business plan (as described in Chapter 5). You'll need to be able to talk about your business in a coherent way and answer questions. About the only way to do this effectively is to have gone through the process of preparing the actual business plan.

Share the plan before the meeting if you have a chance, and do bring the full plan to the meeting. Use it only for your own reference, however. You should be able to answer basic questions without referring to it, but it's okay to have it in your hand to look up a specific market estimate or revenue figure. If you hand it over to the investor, chances are you'll get bogged down in details related to the presentation of the plan or the many tidbits of information within it. Besides, telling your investors you'll send a copy after the meeting is a great excuse for following up. The experienced fundraiser always creates a reason to contact the investor after the meeting.

Questions Likely to Arise During Your Pitch Meeting

Don't walk into your meeting until you can answer the following questions.

What are you selling? The investor will want to hear you describe your product or service.

Who are you selling it to? The investor wants to hear how big your market is, along with a description of your potential customers.

Who else does this? What makes it unique? The investor will try to understand your market and why you may (or may not) have a unique competitive advantage. The investor will also test your knowledge of where you stand in relation to your competitors.

Why now? The investor is concerned with your timing, to understand why now and not next year—or last year, for that matter—is the right time to launch your business.

How much will you sell it for? What are your costs? While family and friend investors may not be deeply interested in your business's finances, business angels will be. They will want to understand the economics of your business, in order to assess whether your projections are sound. For example, the angel will want to know how much your customers will be paying, how much it will cost you to get the product to the customer, and what kind of a profit margin you can generate.

Who is the team? Business angels in particular want to know not just about you, but also the names, education, and experiences of the people you have collected around your idea. Early-stage investors truly believe that a great management team can make a bad business idea work, and that a bad management team can bring down even a great business idea.

c.   Asking for an Investment

The directness of your "ask" should be adjusted to the person you're approaching. I tend to use a "soft ask" with family, friend, and colleague investors, and a "hard ask" with nonfamily, business angel investors. A soft ask, as you may remember from Chapter 7, involves leading up to the topic of money gradually, focusing mainly on your business plans and your reliance on the other person as an information resource. A hard ask involves not only presenting your business idea, but openly soliciting the other person's financial participation.

I used the soft ask approach with the business associates whom I met over lunch in the company conference room, as described in Chapter 7. I had scheduled the meeting via email and shared an agenda that included items like "Sizing the Opportunity" and "Meeting a Need." I billed it as a "brainstorming meeting"—which it legitimately was, because I valued the opinions of this group. I told them about my idea and the work I had done to support it, let them get as excited about it as I was, and then started talking about the money I would need.

Your meeting with a business angel investor should be more direct. Even when you set it up to "get some advice about your business plan," the experienced angel knows what's coming. During the meeting, you should present your business idea and ask for the investor's input, but also be ready, at some point, to ask "Can I count on you for support?"

d.   How to Avoid Turning Off a Potential Investor

Talking to your potential equity investors can at times be nerve-wracking—you have to convey a lot of information convincingly and correctly. It's a good thing that you and your investor already have a level of trust established. Nevertheless, you should choose your words carefully. Even if you're not a trained orator, you can significantly help your cause just by avoiding saying the following three things to your investor.

"I have big plans for the future!" "Big plans"—for example, to turn your start-up chocolate pretzel store into the next big franchise—may appear vague or overly ambitious. Your investor expects you to be visionary, but also expects you to achieve the short-term financial projections that will move the business from a concept to a profitable venture.

"I'm doing this so I can spend more time at home with my kids." Investors don't risk their cash on "lifestyle businesses" that are run second fiddle to the entrepreneur's personal life. They invest in businesses that are likely to grow quickly and make a profit, so the investor can exit and realize a big fat return. Investors usually enjoy the ride as well, but most are primarily in it for the money. If you're starting a business to spend more time with your family instead of at the office, think hard about raising equity capital. The truth is that investors will choose the entrepreneur who puts the success of the business ahead of all else and will expect you to be the one turning out the lights at the end of a long day.

"I've got customers knocking down my doors to buy this product!" Honesty is the most important value that investors can find in an entrepreneur, and your investor will be trying to assess your degree of honesty from day one. Avoid the temptation to puff up your market figures, your projected profits, or your colleagues' resumes beyond the bounds of reality.

3.   Seeking a Nonbinding Agreement

Just because you've done your part pitching your idea and asking for money doesn't mean that the money—or even a reply—is forthcoming. Here are two tips for increasing your chances of bringing your investor on board: First, be ready for the process to take time. Even with a prospect who seems to be interested, you'll find yourself leaving messages, sending emails, and generally tracking folks down to get an answer or close a deal. Second, get an initial commitment in writing. Even though it's nonbinding, a letter of intent is a great tool for turning a committed prospect into an investor.

a.   Give It Time

Understand that the process of raising equity capital simply takes time: time to get to know each other; time for the prospect to hear your pitch; and time for the prospect to review your plan, research your business, come back to you with questions, and consult with his or her own advisers. And all these steps take place even before the prospect agrees to invest. Once the prospect finally says "yes," you'll still need to sort out details such as the actual dollar amount and the wording of the legal documents.

Just how much time all this takes depends, of course, on the personalities and schedules of your investors. When raising money from relatives, friends, and angels, it could take as little as three months to close a round (get the total needed amount) from five to six investors. For raising a larger round from ten to 15 investors, you could easily spend well over six months.

Why does this process take so long? Part of the reason is that you yourself probably can't commit all your time to fundraising—you're busy setting up and running your business. Your investors, too, have other pressing matters vying for their attention. Setting up and holding meetings between the two of you, leaving phone messages, coordinating schedules, drafting documents; all of these take time. Most important, getting to know each other will require a series of both social and business interactions. Be patient; rushing a relationship is virtually impossible and won't help you in the long run.

Before you start asking for money, make sure you know how much you'll need and when you'll need it by. A simple method for figuring out your total cash needs is available in Chapter 5, but setting the timing is a harder task. Plan for the fact that not all the money will come your way immediately. With equity fundraising, many months may go by before you get what you need. That means you'll need to understand your cash flow well enough to plan—sometimes as much as a year in advance—how much you will need, and by when.

In addition to the time required by the investment process itself, other timing issues may come into play. For example, any major life events that you know about for your family and friend prospects, like a move, a marriage, or a new baby, are distracting enough that you probably shouldn't ask the person going through them for money. (The exception would be if the person already knows why you're hanging around and invites a request.)

b.   Get It in Writing

When your prospect finally says something along the lines of, "Yes, I'm interested in investing," you've achieved the verbal agreement, but it's not a done deal yet. It will be a done deal when the investor signs the stock purchase agreement described in the next section and the next chapter—but that's a highly complex document that will need attorney help and extensive review.

The trick is to navigate your way between these two points, the verbal agreement and the written contract, without losing the investor's interest and commitment. Getting something in writing, even if it's not legally binding, is a useful interim task to help keep the process on track. Indeed, the most experienced or proactive investors will suggest or require certain written documents, as described in Section C below. However, for the slightly less sophisticated investors, or even the sophisticated ones who are a little hard to pin down, you can try using what's known as a "letter of intent" (LOI).

An LOI is a simple letter that you prepare in advance, addressed to yourself, with a space for your investor to sign. It's very short (see the samples below) and simply says that the investor is "considering an investment." Because of its simplicity, the investor shouldn't have to think twice before signing it—but psychologically, he or she will be much more likely to proceed with the deal after having signed it. Also, once the investor signs the LOI, it's your go ahead to having your attorney customize the draft stock purchase agreement for this particular investor. Once it's drafted, your attorney can send the stock purchase agreement to the investor for his or her review and, ultimately, signature.

You can certainly go without an LOI if it seems appropriate, but after you've been around this block a few times, you'll find that angel investors in particular can be notoriously difficult to pin down. They'll agree to the investment verbally but then neglect to return calls and seemingly forget what they said to you.

Your LOI request won't come as a surprise to any experienced angel investor; it's a typical step in the process. A signed LOI is also useful in that it allows you to nudge other investors by letting them know that you've already received other monetary commitments—even though you don't have the legal agreements signed.

With most family and friend investors, you can skip the letter of intent. Once the investor has agreed verbally, get an idea of the range of how much the investor will kick in (such as "I could do between

$25,000 and $50,000"). Then you can have your attorney prepare the stock purchase agreement. Explain to the investor that you will send "the paperwork" within the next few days. All that's left is to follow up by forwarding the draft stock purchase agreement for review and signature, as described in the next chapter.

Of the sample letters of intent below, use the simple version when you haven't yet discussed the terms of the investment with the investor, but you've simply agreed on an amount and the investor's general willingness to invest. The advanced version is more suited to when you're in the midst of a fundraising round, where you have a set of terms that you're offering to a whole group of angel investors. You'll notice that the samples contain blanks to be filled in—it's fine to fill these in by hand at the meeting, before the investor signs. These sample letters are also available in Appendix B and on the CD-ROM at the back of this book.

Sample Letter of Intent: Simple Version

A letter of intent can be as simple as a few lines on your letterhead that read:

> I am considering an investment of $_____ in the business known as _____ .
> This is a letter of intent to invest, but it does not reflect a binding obligation.
>
> _____
> Signature [*investor's signature*]
>
> _____
> Name and address. [*investor's name and address*]
>
> _____
>
> _____
> Date [*date of signature*]

Sample Letter of Intent: Advanced Version

If you're raising a round of equity capital—offering the same terms to a whole group of investors—your letter of intent should reflect these details, as in the following:

I am considering a purchase of Series A Preferred Shares in the amount of _____ units. I understand that each unit comprises _____ Preferred Shares (a $ _____ investment at $ _____ per share). Please forward investment documentation to me at the address below. This is a letter of intent to invest, but it does not reflect a binding obligation.

_____

Signature [*investor's signature*]

_____

Name and address. [*investor's name and address*]

_____

_____

Date [*date of signature*]

Pinning Down an Indecisive Investor

Stan, I'll call him, was a senior-level partner in the firm I worked at prior to launching CircleLending. As a colleague, I knew he had both money and a wealth of business experience. I guessed that he had either already done some angel investing or would be an excellent candidate for doing so. I also learned two other important pieces of information about Stan:

1. When he did invest, he was particularly focused on the economics of the business. That suggested to me that he would

Pinning Down an Indecisive Investor (continued)

need a detailed explanation of how I would achieve the growth rates reported in my financial projections.

2. He was notoriously hard to pin down, both for a meeting and for the actual investment, so I would have to work extra hard at getting a commitment from him.

Stan knew that I was starting my own business. I told him I was forming a board of advisers and asked for a meeting to get his input. After describing my business idea, I showed Stan several slides with financial information, including quarterly revenue growth over the previous year and the number of new clients each quarter. I also had a few slides with quotes from recent press we had received and one with a pie chart detailing where I felt different types of clients could be found. (Note: These "slides" were created as part of a business presentation package, for which I printed out color copies so I could lay them on the table in front of us.) Slides provide a chance to graphically illustrate key points without pulling out the business plan.

When I felt Stan was really getting excited, I said, "I'm not sure if you have the appetite for angel investing" and he bit: "Yes, of course, I've done a bit of that." (There is a sort of prestige in entrepreneurial and investing circles for having the guts and the money to be a business angel.)

Stan said he'd be willing to invest $25,000. But I didn't let the conversation stop there. I said, "I'm thrilled you are considering an investment. I brought with me a basic letter of intent; tell me how much of this round you want me to reserve for you." Stan did balk at being asked to commit, but I knew that if I didn't pin him down at the meeting, I was not likely to get a second chance. We closed the deal two weeks later, when Stan signed the stock purchase agreement my attorney had prepared.

Keeping in Touch With Reluctant Investors Pays Off

Catherine launched an innovative Web design service company in 2001. One of her first employees introduced her to his close friend—a young, moderately wealthy entrepreneur named Aaron. Aaron was impressed at the initial growth of Catherine's business, particularly as it followed so closely on the stock market crash of 2000, when very few entrepreneurs were able to raise money for new businesses. But Aaron said he was not making investments at that time, because of the state of his investments in the stock market.

During the course of the first six months, Catherine focused on keeping Aaron updated on the business and finding excuses to build rapport with him. For example, she sent him monthly updates on the business's activities. In their first meeting, she had given him a list of ten activities that needed to get done to grow the business—with the first three already checked off. When Catherine met with Aaron three months later, she produced the same list, which by now had seven of the ten items checked off.

By the time six months had passed, Aaron was willing to make a $15,000 investment. In the years since, he has invested another $100,000 in the form of loans, equity, and even a gift or two. He remains one of Catherine's company's most active backers.

C. Additional Steps That Professional Equity Investors May Request

As mentioned previously, the end point of your negotiations with any equity investors will be a legally binding stock purchase agreement. But if you're dealing with a professional equity investor—like a structured angel group—you're not there yet. At issue now is that some investors are likely to require additional steps along the way, before they feel ready to invest.

If your business is garnering attention from a structured angel group, the investment process will begin to look more like that shown in the chart below—which resembles the steps taken in arranging a traditional venture capital investment. Although a full explanation of this process is outside the scope of this book, this section will help get you started and prepare you to work intelligently with an attorney.

Professional equity investors typically prefer a few steps between when you make your pitch and when they agree to invest. Most often these include a written proposal by you, often called an investment proposal, and a written offer from them, best known as a term sheet.

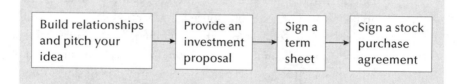

As the chart above shows, after the first stage of connecting with a professional investor and pitching your idea (described in the previous section), you'll usually be asked to provide the highlights of the deal in a written investment proposal (see Section 1, below), which is often a lot like a business plan summary.

After several conversations and meetings, the investor may determine that he or she wants to invest in your business, at which point he or she will present you with a term sheet. (See Section 2, below.) A term sheet, like an LOI, is the first written hint that an investment agreement is in the offing, although, also like the LOI, it's not legally binding.

Once both of you have agreed on the terms in the term sheet, an attorney (usually the investor's) will prepare the stock purchase agreement, by which you actually sell shares in your company to the investor.

The phrase "term sheet" may mean different things to different investors. Usually, "term sheet" refers to the investor's offer to the entrepreneur of the terms at which he or she is willing to invest. But the occasional investor may ask *you* for a term sheet. This is most likely to happen in the midst of a fundraising round, which the investor has learned about. The investor may call or email you and ask for a term sheet, meaning a summary of the terms of your round. Check with your attorney if you need help understanding exactly what type of document the investor needs.

1. Drafting Your Offer: The Investment Proposal

An investment proposal is a combination of highlights from your business plan and highlights of the investment opportunity. This is not a legal document, and nobody signs it; it's your business plan and fundraising request rolled into one.

If you find a website that can connect you with business angels in your local area, you'll probably be asked to submit an investment proposal online, and the website will give you very precise instructions on how to prepare it. If you get the attention of a structured angel group, they, too, will probably have a format in which they'd like to see your plan submitted. Every entrepreneur—and every investor—has his or her own idea of the best way to present and organize this information. But typically, an investment proposal will at least include the following sections, summarized from your business plan:

- **Company name and address.** Don't forget to include these basics; you'd be surprised at how many do.
- **Contact person.** Identify the person to contact, whether it's you or someone else; don't make your investors guess from the names found elsewhere in your summary.
- **Type of business.** Describe just enough about what your business makes and does to help the investor zero in the on the industry, as well as the growth stage your business has reached. Equity investors are savvy and will get it quickly.
- **Company summary.** In less than half a page, get the investor interested and get him or her hooked. Because these are experienced folks, you can, if you're ready, bring in sophisticated analyses of profit margins, market size, and the like (so long as it really makes your case—don't just throw this stuff out to impress the reader, or it might backfire).

- **Management.** List your top two or three people and give a sentence or two describing each person's background. Focus on your managers' experience in your industry and in running a business.
- **Product or service and competition.** Give a brief description of what you are selling. Describe who else is selling the same thing, and indicate why your product or service is unique. Discuss your competitive advantage, and explain why customers will come to you and not your competitor.

The last four sections make up the investment request. These are:

- **Funds requested.** Indicate how much you plan to raise in equity capital during this round. Some entrepreneurs describe previous successful fundraising efforts.
- **Use of proceeds.** Be brief but specific about how you'll use the money you're raising. Reassure investors that the money will be spent growing the business—purchasing new equipment, hiring new salespeople—not growing your own salary.
- **Financial projections.** Using a spreadsheet like the ones described in Chapter 5, attempt to project income and expenses out over several years. Some investors like to see projections that extend out five years, even if common sense tells you that this is wildly speculative. Everyone knows these are only projections, but you do need to show specifically what you will be spending and how much you expect to earn.
- **Exit.** Most investors will want to know how, in three to seven years, they'll be able to get their money out of the company. Tell them your plan. Options include a buyout by a larger company, an initial public offering (IPO), or your coming up with enough cash to buy their shares back.

Once you've drafted your proposal, try to look at it through the eyes of an investor who is interested in finding a real opportunity, a smart plan for meeting it, and a leader who can see it through. See "How Angel Investors Judge Investment Proposals," below, for an example of how one angel investor analyzes the requests put before him.

How Angel Investors Judge Investment Proposals

A very successful business angel investor I know has developed a "mental model" to review the many investment proposals that come his way. He grades each in three areas: the people, the timing, and the investment case.

- **The people.** The investor asks, "Who are they?" and "How do they work together?" In his experience, bigger management teams are better. Bigger teams bring both broader and differentiated views to a business, and more resources to deal with the excitement and vicissitudes of running it.

- **The timing.** The investor asks, "When is the right time to do this?" and "Where is this business in its life cycle?" Good timing is a matter of both luck and planning. He makes an assessment of whether the timing is too early, too late, or on time for the particular idea. While too early may be acceptable in some cases, too late is rarely rewarded.

- **The investment case.** The proposal needs to make a compelling case for the business opportunity. He asks, "What is the business summary saying?" and "Why should I, as a potential investor, adviser, customer, or employee, choose to follow the vision of the founders?"

2.   Understanding The Investor's Offer: The Term Sheet

If an equity investor likes your investment proposal, he or she will likely want to learn more and will begin a process of inquiry about your business called "due diligence." This involves the investor examining your company's management, finances, and market prospects. While a more-extensive due diligence process will come after the term sheet is signed, early inquiries (sometimes in the form of meetings with you, simple requests for more information than is available in your business plan, or requests for business and personal references) are common as the investor tries to understand the opportunity and your business.

After these initial inquiries, if an investor still wants to proceed, he or she will prepare a term sheet (also called an investment memo or a commitment letter) and send it to you. The term sheet, which is somewhat analogous to the LOI discussed earlier, means the investor is prepared to make an investment according to the terms spelled out in the document. Unlike the LOI, the term sheet represents an actual offer from the investor, and both parties can sign. It's written in sufficient detail so that every necessary aspect of the agreement is spelled out and put on the table for discussion. Technically speaking, you have still not reached a legally binding contract, but it's a sign of serious planning toward that end.

You need to decide whether you want to accept the offer spelled out in the term sheet—including any strings attached. Review the document with your attorney and decide whether you either agree or disagree with each and every item. You'll soon reach the critical juncture where you agree to the terms and you either sign the memo (but see "How Binding is a Term Sheet,?" below), or you realize that this relationship isn't going to work out.

For a sample term sheet, see Appendix D. The term sheet provided is one of a series of model legal documents provided by the National Venture Capital Association (www.nvca.org). It was created by a coalition of attorneys who specialize in venture capital financings. Even if you're not approaching any true venture capitalists, you'll find that some angel investors use similar term sheets. This document should be tailored to each specific situation but provides an excellent starting point.

Professional investors tend to prepare their term sheets using language from traditional corporate financing documents. To decipher them, you have little choice but to learn some of the legal jargon used to describe each of your rights and responsibilities. To make things more complicated, every equity investor has his or her own preferred term sheet format. I can't walk you through every possible combination of words and format, but you can probably expect to see the following sections or areas of discussion:

- type of stock
- amount of the investment

- rights, preferences, privileges, and restrictions on the stock
- items for the stock purchase agreement
- right of first refusal, and
- other items.

How Binding Is a Term Sheet?

Despite the level of detail, a term sheet is not a legally binding document. In other words, you can still back out and not face a lawsuit. Most term sheets will have a clause that explains this, such as:

This Term Sheet does not reflect any binding commitment or agreement, and unless and until a binding Note Purchase Agreement and Note are executed, no party shall have any obligation or liability.

Once you and your investor both sign the document, however, it is considered ethically binding. In some cases, your investor may require a provision that you pay a specified "break-up fee" if you fail to close the deal. In addition, if you back out of the deal after signing, word will likely get around. Remember, business angels talk to each other. If you fail to close on a signed term sheet, don't be surprised if you have trouble finding another willing equity investor in your area.

a.   Type of Stock

You'll find the type of stock the investor wants to purchase in your business named right on the title of the document. For example, the term sheet in Appendix D is titled:

Term Sheet for Series A Preferred Stock Financing of ABC, Inc.
Typically, early-stage investors purchase common stock, preferred stock, or convertible preferred stock. As you progress to later rounds of fundraising, you should also learn about warrants, options, debt securities, partnership interests, and equity hybrids, which combine features of different securities.

The term "Series A" you see in the sample title indicates which fundraising round this term sheet is for; the letters progress sequentially

(The first time you raise money from several equity investors at once—a financing round—it's called "Series A"; the second time, the documents refer to "Series B"; and so forth.)

Common stock refers to the most basic form of ownership in a company, and the one that founding members, managers, and employees normally receive for their role in launching the enterprise. It comes with a few basic rights, like the right to vote in shareholder issues and to attend meetings. But common stock offers fewer rights than any other form of security. For example, if the business fails and has to be liquidated, common stockholders don't receive anything in return for their shares until lenders and preferred stockholders have been paid off. If the money runs out in the course of these payments, the common stockholders are out of luck. (Historically, business angels bought common stock, but they are increasingly holding out for preferred stock.)

Preferred stock is similar to common stock, except that it is given repayment priority if the company fails and its assets must be sold. Preferred stockholders are also usually entitled to dividends at a specified rate (if and when dividends are declared by the board of directors and before payment of a dividend on the common stock, which rarely happens). Preferred stock is a way of granting a superior level of influence and rights to selected investors. It is the usual choice of professional angel and venture investors, because it gives them a promise of some return on their investment and some control over internal decision making. They feel justified in demanding this return because they pay cash for their shares, while most common stockholders in private companies were granted shares in return for helping found the company or as part of a compensation package. However, it's only fair to offer preferred stock to your friends and family members, as well.

Convertible stock is a variation on preferred stock, and the first choice of most professional investors. Its distinguishing feature is that it offers its holders the right to convert to shares of common stock if the company performs well.

Following the title there may be a short paragraph like the one in the sample that states the purpose of the document and establishes a few other rights and responsibilities that are considered good investment etiquette. For example, term sheets often include a "no-shop provision," asking that the business promise not to "shop"—that is, offer additional shares in the business—to other potential investors behind the scenes (presumably trying to get a better deal). The no-shop provision can appear twice, both in the opening and in more detail as its own clause in a final section titled "Other Matters" or something similar. Often, the "no-shop provision" is combined with a confidentiality provision, which serves to protect the privacy of the business information you've shared with the investor.

Are you giving investors confidential business information? Make sure your confidentiality is protected. Insist that the term sheet contain a confidentiality provision, either as part of the no-shop provision or as a stand-alone term. This way, the investor will agree to keep a lid on your business information in the course of the negotiations and due diligence. Such a promise is clearly to your benefit.

Term sheets also often include language, either in this opening or at the end of the "Other Matters" section, saying that the agreement is conditional on satisfactory completion of "due diligence, legal review, and documentation." (For more information on due diligence, see "Investors Poking Around Your Business: Due Diligence," below.) This language basically means that the term sheet will go into effect only if additional research and review of your investment opportunity show that you are in fact what you say you are.

Trying to figure out what to do about a no-shop clause in your term sheet? It's worth agreeing not to shop around, as a demonstration of your good faith in dealing with the investor—but limit such a no-shop clause to a reasonable period of time, like 45 to 90 days, depending on your reasonable expectations of when the deal will close.

Investors Poking Around Your Business: Due Diligence

Any professional investor will insist on conducting what's called "due diligence." The purpose is to determine whether everything you've said in person and in your business plan about your business and its prospects are true, at least as far as you can be expected to know. If the investor's resulting report doesn't reflect favorably on your company, the investor can pull out of the deal. (The investor's right to pull out is stated right in the term sheet.)

You'll probably have to supply customer lists, marketing materials, organizational charts, business strategy reports, and financial projections. The investor may place calls to your larger customers, confirming that you do business with them and inquiring about the quality, timeliness, and cost of your product or service as compared to your competitors'. While venture capital firms tend to do the most extensive due diligence, one entrepreneur told me that the most rigorous due diligence process he'd ever endured was actually for a structured angel group.

For your part, you should require a signed term sheet from the investor before allowing inquiry of a more sensitive nature, such as customer calls. In any event, be sure to have the investor sign a well-prepared confidentiality agreement before you give him or her access to any confidential, proprietary, or otherwise-sensitive information.

b.   Amount of the Investment

The first few terms of the term sheet will ordinarily refer to the basics of the proposed investment and are sometimes called the "Offering Terms." A "closing by" date is usually specified up front, meaning the date by which the stock purchase agreement is signed and the money changes hands. This Offering section will include the name of your investor, the dollar amount of the investment, and usually the resulting percentage of ownership that the investor will gain in your business.

One of the most important terms to appear in the term sheet also occurs in this Offering section and is called the "pre-money valuation." For someone to be able to buy a portion of your business, he or she will need to know how much the entire business is worth. In other words, you can't sell a piece of the pie until you've established, by an objective measurement, how much the whole pie would go for. This business value is calculated by taking the value of the current assets of the business and adding the potential reflected in the financial projections. Other items might be included in the calculation as well. For example, if the company owns some sort of intellectual property or pending patents, these might also be attributed a value.

Settling on the pre-money valuation can be one of the biggest sticking points in the whole process. If you were to agree, for example, that your fresh-baked pie was worth $5, then someone who wanted to buy 10% of it would have to pay you 50 cents. However, if you agreed that the pie was worth $9, then an investor would have to pay you 90 cents to get the same 10%. Of course, the investor wants as many shares as he or she can get for the money, while you want to give away as little ownership as possible for the amount you need to raise.

Once you've agreed on the pre-money valuation, the investor will usually also calculate a post-money valuation and include it in the memo. The post-money valuation is simply the pre-money amount plus the amount invested, which makes the company worth more overall.

Sometimes instead of (or in addition to) a pre-money valuation, the term sheet will include a capitalization table. This table will show how ownership in your business is distributed (type of security, number of shares, percent of company) among existing owners, both before and after the new investment. For a sample capitalization table, see the sample term sheet in Appendix D.

c.   Rights, Preferences, Privileges, and Restrictions of the Stock

In the section of the term sheet that usually comes next (often called the "Charter"), the investor will lay out the rights, preferences, privileges, and restrictions on the stock or "security."

The term sheet will spell out the special protections and privileges that your investor requires. At a minimum, he or she will likely ask for certain rights at liquidation, plus rights to be paid regular dividends. Rarely, however, do investors ask that the dividends be paid in cash.

In order to gain influence over decision making at your company, the investor may also ask for voting rights, representation on the board of directors, and information rights. And for further protection, the investor may insert special rights that he or she will gain if the company issues a new round of securities, such as antidilution provisions.

Antidilution provisions are meant to ensure that an investor's shares are never worth less than they were when they were acquired. Typically, inexperienced early-stage investors do not require "antidilution provisions," which would protect their initial investment. But later investors do, often at the expense of the earliest investors. For example, shareholders of preferred stock can use a "full ratchet" in their dilution provision, which means that even if the value of the company decreases in the next round, they will continue to own enough shares to give them the same percentage ownership as they purchased when they initially invested. (This decrease in a company's valuation can happen if new investors decide the company was overvalued and agree to invest only if the valuation is lowered.)

Comb through these conditions with your attorney to make sure you understand the implications of each and every right your investor is requesting and that you aren't giving away too much.

You're not just protecting yourself; you're protecting your other, common-stock investors. If you agree to a liquidation preference for your professional investors, it may have devastating consequences for your early-stage family and friend investors, who may have bought common stock with no such protection.

d. Items for the Stock Purchase Agreement

The next section in the sample term sheet includes just a few items that are summarized in the term sheet but will likely be spelled out in further detail in the final, legally binding stock purchase agreement. The most important one is the representations and warranties section.

Representations and warranties are where the investor sets forth the important highlights of your business presentation—those that he or she believes to be true and that influenced his or her decision to make an investment. This section will state that the offer is based on several assumptions, for example the assumptions that:

- You are not the subject of any pending legal claims.
- Agreements are in place that bind some of your key employees to you.
- You agree to take out "key man insurance" to safeguard the company against the possibility of your death.

Offers to technology companies also usually require some proof that the intellectual property that gives the company its competitive edge, like an invention or a new process, is protected by a patent (whether pending or existing). Investors naturally want to make sure that other companies can't take advantage of the discovery.

⚠️ **You'll probably have to make more representations and warranties before the deal is done.** While just a few basic representations and warranties are typically included in a term sheet, the stock purchase agreement often contains a longer list.

Although not included in the sample term sheet, a list of affirmative and negative covenants may also be included in this section. These are promises that you will do certain things (affirmative covenants) or will not do certain things (negative covenants). For example, an affirmative covenant might promise that your company will provide the investor with specified financial statements and other materials, such as notices on any pending government actions or loan defaults. A negative covenant might contain your promise to limit your company's expenditures in certain areas, such as capital improvements. Another common negative covenant prevents your business from loaning or advancing money to any employee or other company, or from selling any company assets, outside the regular course of business.

e.   Right of First Refusal

Investors want to be given first dibs when new shares in the company become available. To secure this right, the investor includes a "right of refusal" in the term sheet, giving him or her the right to buy new shares in the company as they are made available.

The right of refusal provision is decidedly to the advantage of the investor, because it gives him or her the option of buying additional shares and thus owning a greater percentage of the company every time a new round of financing occurs. It can be a hassle for you, because it means each investor with a right of first refusal must sign off on the sale of new shares, saying that he or she refuses the offer to buy the new shares. This adds one more administrative task to your already time-consuming fundraising work.

But if your investor won't sign the agreement unless it's got a right of refusal provision, including one is not the end of the world. For one thing, each time you need to raise more money, you'll probably want to go back to your earliest investors, anyway.

To minimize the busywork, draft the right of refusal provision to make your logistical obligations as informal as possible. For example, what you don't want is a provision (not uncommon in term sheets) stating that you have to present each investor with a signed letter of intent from any prospective investors, after which the investors have 60 days to get back to you. This could make your life difficult as you try to juggle attracting new investors and communicating with existing investors. Instead, push for a provision stating that you will email existing investors if and when a prospective investor makes an offer, after which the investors have ten days to get back to you.

In addition, you could tweak this clause to make it more friendly to your interests, by having it state that only an investor with at least a certain percentage of ownership in the company (for example, 25%) has the right to purchase these additional shares. This way the right applies to only the very few largest owners of the company.

f.   Other Items

Refer to the remainder of the sample term sheet in Appendix D to preview additional provisions and terms you might find in a term sheet. These include matters to do with the board of directors, fees, the registration of shares for sale, and types of insurance.

Who pays the lawyer's fees? The investors nearly always insist that you pay their legal expenses out of the money they will be giving you. Unfortunately, you don't have much negotiating power here; it's the industry standard. If at all possible, try to get the investor to agree to a cap on these fees, or to agree that you will each pay your own bills (in effect cutting the total fee amount in half).

Chapter 9

The Final Agreement and Money Transfer

A. Why Documentation Is Important...216

   1. How Documentation Sets Expectations..217

   2. Why You Want These Expectations in Writing....................................218

   3. How Documentation Helps Professionals and
      Others Understand Your Agreement..221

B. Preparing a Gift Letter...223

   1. Creating a Basic Gift Letter..223

   2. Creating a Loan Repayment Forgiveness Letter.................................224

C. Formalizing a Loan With a Promissory Note..225

D. Participating in the Preparation of the Stock Purchase Agreement.....241

   1. Understanding Your Disclosure Obligations.......................................242

   2. Meeting Your Disclosure Obligation..243

   3. Reviewing the Stock Purchase Agreement...246

   4. Protecting Your Family-and-Friend Investors' Interests....................255

E. How to Close the Deal...257

   1. Closing a Private Business Loan...257

   2. Closing an Equity Investment...258

Believe it or not, the hardest part of your work is done. You've asked people for money to grow your business, and some have said yes, they're willing. Now you just need to document each agreement and receive the actual funds. To help you carry out these steps, this chapter will:

- review why documentation is so important (Section A, below)
- help you prepare the documents themselves, including:
  - a gift letter if it's a gift (see Section B, below)
  - a promissory note if it's a loan (see Section C, below), or
  - a stock purchase agreement if it's an equity investment (see Section D, below), and
- guide you through receiving the funds and closing the deal (see Section E, below).

A. Why Documentation Is Important

You've heard me talk before about the importance of documentation. But let's give this topic some final attention, lest you be tempted to skip this step and just reach for the check. The most important thing you can do when you receive a private investment is to commit the agreement to writing. Handshakes and oral agreements have been known to work, but they're basically a gamble that everything will go right in the months and years to come—including events outside anyone's control, like deaths in the family.

Writing down the agreement is just plain smart for the following reasons:

- **It sets expectations.** The simple act of talking through the terms of the deal when the agreement is made ensures that both parties have the same understanding of how it will play out.
- **It puts those expectations into writing.** Having your responsibilities in print and available to both parties also ensures a mutual understanding of how and when your obligation will be met and helps assure your investor that he or she can enforce the promises you've made.
- **It makes the agreement available to others.** Documenting the agreement formalizes it in the eyes of important players in your financial life such as the IRS, your attorney, your accountant or

other professional advisers, or even your or your investor's family members (particularly important in the event that your investor dies).

1.   How Documentation Sets Expectations

Although the outlines of your agreement may have seemed clear when you shook hands on it, you'll probably be surprised, when walking through the process of formalizing the agreement, at all the unforeseen questions that arise.

Some of the most basic questions include: Is the money a gift? A personal loan? A business loan? An equity investment? Even if you think these issues were covered in your conversation, you may have heard your uncle saying, "I'll put $20,000 into your business" to mean an equity investment, when he meant it as a loan—or vice versa. Either way, the two of you now have conflicting expectations about the nature and timing of repaying the money. If you don't sort out what you each expect will happen next, your relationship will inevitably sour as your uncle waits for repayment to begin while you go about growing your business without a thought to loan payments.

Less-obvious questions about the details of your agreement also need to be dealt with: How will the interest rate be set? What if you don't repay on time? What type of communications will your equity investor expect to receive from you? How often? It's no fun going back to someone months later to negotiate such issues. Far better to take the time to talk through the terms and document the agreement at the outset, when everyone is feeling optimistic.

> **EXAMPLE:** Theresa accepts a $20,000 informal loan from her aunt and uncle in order to start a health-care consulting business. They discuss the loan at a family barbecue, where everyone is in good spirits, and they decide not to bother signing any formal paperwork. A few days later, Theresa's aunt and uncle do their part and send her the check. Theresa launches her business and, through many long nights of hard work, pushes it to the break-even point a year later. She then decides to take her spouse and children on a much-needed Disneyland vacation—before repaying a penny of her aunt and uncle's loan.

When Theresa's aunt and uncle hear about the vacation, they're shocked. They view it as a frivolous expense and can't believe that Theresa would have been setting aside vacation money without first repaying them. The subsequent family reunion turns into a tense affair, with Theresa's aunt and uncle asking pointed questions about her airfare and hotel expenses.

If Theresa, in the example above, had simply documented the loan—say, with a promissory note detailing a repayment plan beginning after a 12-month deferment period, maybe with interest accruing during the deferment—her aunt and uncle would not have had any reason to expect repayment yet. Under that agreed-upon schedule, she would not have even missed a payment. In fact, when Theresa's payments began arriving on time, her aunt and uncle might have marveled at her ability to manage the obligations of a new business and a young family at the same time. Instead, both parties had to suffer through hard feelings and misunderstandings—and ultimately draft a promissory note to redeem the situation.

Private lenders report greater confidence in the borrower when they've signed a promissory note. Even those who started out saying, "C'mon, I trust you, let's not waste time writing this down," often end up glad to have been talked into documenting the transaction. It saves them from any guilty feelings about looking over your shoulder. When the business is going well, they get paid. When the business has hit a rocky spot, the fact that you've missed one of your regularly scheduled payments means that they're among the first to know.

2.   Why You Want These Expectations in Writing

With everything you have to deal with in running your business, the last thing you need is a cloud of unclear or shifting expectations hanging over your head. Each month when you do the books, you'll be plenty clear on how much you owe to your landlord, your suppliers, and your advertisers. But what about your mother? If she gave you $8,000 to get started, would you know or remember exactly when and how she wanted it back? Having a written document to refer to is the cleanest way to run your business.

Your lender or investor will also appreciate the legally binding nature of a written agreement. Part of your job in persuading someone to make a loan or investment is assuring the person that he or she will have recourse beyond just chasing you down to fulfill your half of the deal. That recourse may include going to court. Courts are far more easily persuaded by signed documents than by oral so-called promises. And if it ever comes to a court battle, you, too, will probably appreciate that the judge won't be choosing between your word and the investor's. (Fortunately, lawsuits rarely happen in private financing situations.)

The writing you'll need to prepare should be either:

- a letter from the person who made the gift, if it's a gift
- a promissory note from you if it's a loan, or
- a stock purchase agreement drafted by your attorney (or your investor's attorney), to be signed by both you and your investor.

Written agreements create a framework, not a cage. While your promissory note makes your debt to your lender binding, the way in which you repay the debt can be adjusted along the way to accommodate changing circumstances. Neither you nor your lender need worry that you'll feel constrained by the agreement—but you'll probably be happy to have it as a starting point.

Perhaps more than any other type of cash injection, loans (as opposed to gifts or equity investments) can give rise to all manner of later misunderstandings if undocumented or poorly documented. For example, a loan with a monthly repayment plan gives you twelve times a year when something can go wrong—maybe because you didn't pay, didn't pay enough, paid late, and so on. But a promissory note will include repayment terms from which you can find out exactly how much is due and on what dates. If you can't make a payment, the plan itself will tell you how to proceed.

What If Your Lender Just Hates Signing Anything?

Even though it's in the lender's best interest to document the loan, family and friends themselves are often the ones to insist that they don't need a bunch of documents to give you money. That can make you feel awkward about turning your supposedly easygoing conversations into a "big deal." But the discomfort you might feel now is nothing compared to the difficulties that might arise later if you don't formalize the loan agreement.

Some lenders aren't merely being polite—they are really, truly uncomfortable about signing formal agreements with a friend or family member. The sight of legal language may make them nervous, even when you've taken pains to make its meaning clear. And some people might even feel that it's offensive or inappropriate for you to ask for formal documentation—like you're turning a friendship into a business transaction. If you meet with this level of resistance, don't be shy about trying to change your lender's mind—again, he or she is likely to appreciate it later. You can tactfully try any or all of the following approaches:

- Explain that your accountant (or attorney) needs a complete and legally binding document before you can begin using the money for your business needs.
- Explain that you need to have the documents in place for the IRS, to show that the money is in fact a loan, not a gift.
- Explain that you have read many articles in the media about how undocumented loans have a higher failure rate and can jeopardize personal relationships.
- Recount a specific case you've heard of where confusion over loan terms and repayment of an undocumented loan ended badly for the borrower and lender. Here's one: When Jay needed capital to build an ice rink, he convinced his dad that the idea would be a success. His dad informally gave him $40,000 over the course of three years. The rink was built but never came anywhere close to turning a profit. Jay had to declare bankruptcy, and his dad turned to his accountant to help write off the bad debt. Unfortunately, there was no loan agreement, and no documentation of any attempts at repayment, and ultimately the IRS wouldn't accept the claim that it was a loss. Not only did Jay's father lose the $40,000 and the chance to write it off, the whole affair created a rift between the two that took years to heal.

> ## Equity Investments *Require* a Written Stock Purchase Agreement
>
> No equity investor worth his or her salt would ever settle for an agreement penned onto a napkin. The investor will want a legally binding stock purchase agreement, prepared by an attorney and signed by both parties.
>
> There are several fairly obvious reasons for this. First, there's usually a lot of money at stake with an equity investment, and the investor will want as much certainty as possible about what's going to happen with that money. Second, an equity investor is buying something with his or her money—namely a share in your business. The only solid way to prove that this exchange took place is to put it in writing, with attention to various legal niceties. Third, the equity investor is probably not a member of your family, so he or she has every reason to expect that the deal will be handled in a businesslike fashion.
>
> If, despite our predictions, someone tells you that he or she wants to make an investment but without a stock purchase agreement, it's possible the person is thinking about a gift or loan instead. Inquire about what the person wants in return for his or her "investment." There is no way for the investor to become a legal owner of your business without a stock purchase agreement.

3. How Documentation Helps Professionals and Others Understand Your Agreement

You and your lenders or investors aren't the only people who might take an interest in your financial agreement. Accountants, attorneys, personal financial advisers, and other professionals may need to see a written contract explaining the terms of the agreement. They too need to know what is expected of each party when they review or advise you on your financial situation.

What's more, the documentation may be needed at some point to explain your transaction to the IRS or other oversight agencies. For example, if the IRS or other tax authority were to question whether the arrangement was really a loan, one of its first requests would be for a copy of the promissory note. Or, if a you were to default on the loan and be unable to ever repay it, one of the few consolations available to your lender would be a bad debt deduction on his or her taxes. But without a promissory note, the IRS might deny the deduction and call the transfer a gift.

In an equity investment situation, your documentation will serve to explain the nature of the transaction not only to professionals and to federal oversight agencies, but also to other investors who may join your enterprise in the future. These future prospective investors will take a careful look at the existing stock purchase agreements to find out what rights and responsibilities your current investors enjoy. What they see will influence the term sheets they draft and present to you.

And let's not forget how written documents can avert the family misunderstandings that commonly arise due to undocumented or even poorly documented financing arrangements. For example, let's say you or the person who transferred you money dies, leaving behind an outstanding, undocumented gift or loan. During the probate process, the executor of the estate will need proof of the gift or loan in order to allocate money in the proper direction. It's not unusual for other relatives to assume that a money transfer was a loan instead of a gift, especially if they didn't hear about the transfer or didn't receive similar treatment themselves.

> **EXAMPLE:** Serena's grandfather gave her $10,000 one year in order to start a yoga studio. He told her, "No need to repay it, I don't need the money, and I'll get more enjoyment out of watching you fulfill your dreams." Unfortunately, no one overheard this conversation, and the grandfather didn't create a gift letter. He died a few years later. Serena's sisters and brothers got wind of the gift and assumed it to be a loan, since none of them had received a similar gift. If Serena wasn't going to repay it, they wanted to subtract $10,000 from her share of their grandfather's estate. It was Serena's word against theirs. The money was finally treated as a gift, but the conflict left lingering resentments.

B.   Preparing a Gift Letter

For tax and other reasons, even an outright gift needs to be supported by some written documentation. Gift letters typically take two forms, either:

- a basic letter documenting a one-time gift to the individual, or
- a loan repayment forgiveness letter, documenting that a certain payment or group of payments once due to a lender under a loan agreement is now to be considered a gift.

1.   Creating a Basic Gift Letter

When someone intends to transfer money as a gift, not a loan or investment, he or she needs to write a letter to the recipient explaining this. The letter should explicitly say that the money is meant as a gift and that the giver does not expect to be repaid. This is a very simple letter that you or the giver can draft at home. It doesn't need to be notarized to be valid.

Below is a sample letter that Kalah Brown drafted for her grandfather to sign when he gave her $9,000 to help launch her children's bookstore, Hobby Horse Books.

Basic Gift Letter

Kalah Brown
123 Main St.
Princeton, NJ 08540

To Kalah:

By my signature below, I hereby gift $9,000 to my granddaughter Kalah Brown to use as she wishes. I expect no repayment or services in return for this gift.

Marcus Brown
Marcus Brown

Date: January 1, 2006

2. Creating a Loan Repayment Forgiveness Letter

Even if a money transfer starts out as a loan, a generous lender can easily turn part or all of it into a gift, simply by saying, "No need to repay it after all." Of course, you'll want to get this in writing, for tax and other financial reasons.

The appropriate documentation for such decisions is commonly called a loan repayment forgiveness letter. The "forgiver" should send this to the borrower before the payment being forgiven comes due. The letter can be short, simply identifying the loan and stating the originally agreed-upon repayment amount and due date, then expressing the lender's forgiveness of that repayment. (See the sample below.) The lender must sign the letter and give it to the borrower, keeping a copy for his or her own records. The lender will also need to include a copy with his or her annual tax paperwork.

If you enter into a loan agreement knowing that your lender will probably forgive some or all of the payments (for tax reasons, some lenders may prefer structuring the initial transfer of funds as a loan), it makes sense to set up the loan with annual or quarterly payments. This saves the lender from sending monthly loan forgiveness letters—a task that might make any lender feel a lot less forgiving. Remember, if the amount the lender wants to forgive each year is higher than $12,000, the lender may exceed his or her annual gift tax exemption. Have your lender consult with his or her tax adviser about any concerns regarding how the IRS may perceive your particular arrangement.

For example, if Kalah's grandfather had wanted to provide $30,000 to help launch the bookstore, but wanted to do it without exceeding his annual gift tax exemption, the pair could have set up a loan for three years with annual payments of $12,000 or less. Then, each year, Kalah's grandfather could have sent her a letter like the one below, forgiving the payments when they came due.

Sample Loan Repayment Forgiveness Letter

Kalah Brown

123 Main St.

Princeton, NJ 08540

To Kalah:

I made you a loan of $30,000 to you on July 1, 2005. This loan has an annual payment due to me on July 1, 2006 in the amount of $10,000 ("Annual Payment").

By my signature below, I hereby forgive all of this Annual Payment.

By signing this notice, I understand that I do not waive the right to choose to receive any subsequent Annual Payments under the Promissory Note you signed on July 1, 2005.

Marcus Brown

Marcus Brown

Date: January 1, 2006

C. Formalizing a Loan With a Promissory Note

The only legal document you'll need in order to formalize a loan is a promissory note—a written promise to pay the amount you specify, within a period of time you indicate, at a rate of interest you specify. The most basic promissory note could be executed in one sentence—an IOU that could fit on the back of a napkin:

> *Dear Aunt Hilda, I owe you $5,000.*
> *Signed, Your Nephew, Ben*

However, legal and business realities have stretched the standard promissory note well beyond napkin size. A good promissory note will:

- identify both the borrower and lender by name
- state that the lender has given the borrower sum of money
- set out the repayment terms of the loan, such as the amount and the due dates
- spell out the consequences of late payments, missed payments, and default, and
- contain your (the borrower's) signature.

Still, it's possible to draft your own promissory note without a lawyer, by following the instructions below.

Handling your loan professionally now will make it easier to obtain and handle bank loans later. Getting familiar with promissory notes is great practice for the future, when you may want to ask banks and other institutional lenders for new funding. Sticking to a payment schedule—or understanding your cash flow well enough to anticipate problems and make arrangements for meeting your obligations—gets easier over time. And it's a practice that will come in handy when you're accountable to institutional lenders.

Start your drafting efforts with a quick read-through of the sample promissory note for an amortized business loan, below. Although promissory notes vary in content and length, the sample is in a widely accepted format and is relatively easy to follow. For more detailed, clause-by-clause explanations, see the sections that follow.

If you're planning to arrange something other than an amortized loan, keep reading this section nonetheless. Much of the language used is common to any kind of promissory note, and I'll discuss adaptations you can make for other types of loans.

Looking for the right sample promissory note? In addition to the sample promissory note provided below, you'll find a blank template for an amortized loan, as well as three others for graduated, interest-only, and seasonal loans, in Appendix B and on the CD-ROM in the back of this book.

Sample Promissory Note for a
$10,000 Amortized Loan to a Business

Promissory Note

1. **For Value Received,** Margaret Hollis ("Borrower") promises to pay to the order of Emily Hollis, of Chevy Chase, Maryland ("Lender"), the sum, in United States dollars, of ten thousand and 00/100 ($10,000.00) dollars, plus interest accruing at an annual rate of twelve percent (12%) on the unpaid principal amount beginning on April 1, 2005 (the "Debt").

2. **Transferability.** Borrower understands that the Lender may transfer this Note. The Lender or anyone who takes this Note by Transfer and who is entitled to receive payments under this Note is called the "Note Holder" and will have the same rights and remedies as the Lender under this Note.

3. **Monthly Installments.** Payment of the Debt shall be made in monthly installments, which include principal and interest, as follows:

   Beginning on October 1, 2005 and continuing monthly on the first of each month (the "Due Date") until September 1, 2008 (the "Final Due Date"), Borrower shall pay to the Lender or Note Holder the sum of $332.14 each month (the "Monthly Payment"). On the Final Due Date, Borrower shall pay all amounts remaining due under the terms of this Note.

4. **Grace Period and Late Fee.** If the Borrower fails to make any payment in the full amount and within ten (10) calendar days (the "Grace Period") after the date it is due, Borrower agrees to pay a late charge to the Lender or Note Holder in the amount of $25.00 (the "Late Fee"). Borrower will pay this Late Fee promptly but only once on each late payment.

5. **Security.** [choose one]

   ☐ This is an unsecured note.

   ☐ Borrower agrees that until this Note is paid in full (including principal and interest, if any), this Note will be secured by a separate security agreement and, if applicable, a Uniform Commercial Code financing statement, giving Lender a security interest in the following property: [describe asset] _____

   _____

6. **Default and Acceleration.** If any installment payment due under this Note is not received by Lender within the Grace Period, the note will be in default and the entire amount of unpaid principal will become immediately due and payable at the option of Lender without prior notice of default to Borrower.

7. **Prepayment.** This Note may be prepaid in full at any time without cost or penalty to the Borrower.

8. **Attorneys' Fees.** If Lender prevails in a lawsuit to collect on this note, Borrower agrees to pay Lender's attorneys' fees in an amount the court finds to be just and reasonable.

9. **Waiver.** The undersigned and all other parties to this Note waive the following requirements:

   • presentment of the Note for payment by Lender

   • refusal of payment by Borrower after presentment of the Note by Lender, otherwise known as dishonor, and

   • Lender's notification to Borrower of Borrower's refusal to pay.

10. **Lender's Rights.** Lender's decision not to exercise a right or remedy under this Note at a given time does not waive the Lender's ability to exercise that right or remedy at a later date.

11. **Liability of Individual Borrowers.** The term "Borrower" may refer to one or more borrowers. If there is more than one borrower, they agree to be jointly and severally liable.

12. **Governing Law.** This agreement will be governed by and construed in accordance with the laws of the state of _____ .

Borrower's signature: _____

Print name: _____

Date: _____

What's with all the capital letters? You might notice that the sample promissory note contains many capitalized words in parentheses and quotation marks, such as "Emily Hollis, of Chevy Chase, Maryland ("Lender")." This allows "Lender" to be used as shorthand for Emily throughout the note. Capitalizing the term is a legal custom, telling the reader that this term has been defined earlier and has the same meaning throughout the document.

a.   Establishing the Debt, the Borrower, and the Lender

The sample promissory note starts off with some old-time legalese—"for value received." This phrase merely refers to the money or other assets the lender has already given you. It shows that you aren't just out-of-the-blue promising to send your lender monthly payments but are doing so in return for money that the lender gave you first.

From the opening paragraph of the sample note, you learn that Margaret Hollis has received $10,000 from Emily Hollis of Chevy Chase, Maryland. For simplicity's sake, the note refers to Margaret from now on as "Borrower." You also learn that Margaret promises to repay Emily the principal amount plus 12% interest that begins accruing on April 1, 2005. The date people insert here is usually either the loan start date (the date the note starts, as specified here) or the repayment start date (the date the first payment comes due). (You'll see these two accrual starting date options when you use the loan calculators on the included CD ROM.)

If you want the loan to be to your business, whether a corporation, a partnership, or an LLC, you do this by naming the business as the borrower in this opening paragraph, and by signing on its behalf. Insert the following as the first line:

> **For Value Received**, [*name of your business*], a [*the U.S. state where your business was formed*] corporation/partnership/LLC with its principal place of business in [*city, state of business*] ("Borrower"), promises to pay ....

This language is separately included in Appendix B and on the CD-ROM—look for "Promissory Note Modifications for a Loan to a Business."

Name your business as the borrower whenever possible. You'll waste any personal protection from liability that you've achieved if you are the borrower.

Paragraph two of the sample contains what's called the "transfer provision." This allows the lender to sell the note and give the new holder the same rights as the original lender. While, technically, the new note holder could claim these rights anyway, this clause lets everyone know about this possibility in advance.

b. Detailing Your Repayment Obligations (Amortized Loan)

The next paragraphs of the promissory note (3 and 4) provide more detail regarding the borrower's payment terms and schedule. The sample note tells us that from October 1, 2005 to September 1, 2008 (after a six-month deferment of the loan repayment that began in April of 2005), the borrower needs to make monthly payments of $332.14, due on the first of each month. On the final day, the note says, any outstanding amounts come due as well.

When creating your own promissory note, you don't necessarily have to choose the first of the month as your repayment date. The 15th is another common choice. While some people prefer the 1st, in order to coincide with other bill paying (such as rent, utilities, and other monthly business expenses), others prefer the 15th specifically so as to gain a breather after paying all these other bills.

The repayment paragraphs contain two more facts both you and your lender need to know. First, the grace period is the number of days you have after the due date to make your payment without being considered late. Second, if you do send a payment but it's beyond your grace period, you must include the stated late fee. The sample note is gentle on the borrower, by allowing a ten-day grace period after the payment was initially due (but note that it's ten calendar days, not business days—weekends and holidays count). Most people negotiate a grace period of between seven and 15 days and a late fee charge of $25. Since this is a private loan, however, you and your lender can choose any grace period or fee you mutually think appropriate, or none at all.

> **EXAMPLE:** Nicole knows she has a tendency to pay bills a few days late. After her brother said he'd lend her $4,000 to start her graphic design business, she asked that the promissory note contain a 15-day grace period. Her brother, however, didn't want to spend a whole 15 days wondering whether she was ever going to pay and suggested a seven-day grace period. To reach a compromise, they agreed to a ten-day grace period but with a $75 late fee. That way, Nicole has the flexibility she wants, while the late payment penalty increases her brother's chances of getting paid in a timely fashion.

⚠️ **One day after the payment due date, you're late.** Inexperienced entrepreneurs have been known to drop the check in the mail on the due date, which means that by the time the check arrives, late fees may already be due (unless there's a grace period). Don't make this mistake—mail your payments several days before they're due, at the latest. If you think you'll have trouble managing this, hire a third party to arrange a direct transfer from your to your lender's account, with reminders sent to you in time to reschedule or delay a payment if your budget requires it.

c. How to Adjust the Repayment Language for Other Types of Loans

If you and your lender agree to a repayment schedule other than an amortized one, such as a graduated, seasonal, or interest-only schedule, replace the amortized language in the sample above with the appropriate language from the options below (also available in Appendix B and on the CD-ROM at the back of this book). You'll need to have a copy of your repayment schedule handy, preferably one generated by a loan calculator, so that you can easily insert the specific amounts and due dates that make up your repayment.

Graduated. The following language describes a graduated repayment schedule for the same loan as described in the sample note ($10,000 at 12% interest for a three-year term). Notice that because it is a graduated loan, there are two steps (or increases) in the payment amount—with three "platforms" or "payment levels"—and that each step lasts for one year of 12 monthly payments, with the first and last date of that amount specified.

> Beginning on October 1, 2005 and continuing monthly on the first of each month through September 1, 2006, Borrower shall pay to Lender on the first of every month the sum of $238.89.
>
> Then, beginning on October 1, 2006 and continuing monthly on the first of each month through September 1, 2007, Borrower shall pay to Lender on the first of every month the sum of $361.11.
>
> Finally, beginning on October 1, 2007 and continuing monthly on the first of each month until September 1, 2008, Borrower shall pay to Lender on the first of every month the sum of $466.67.
>
> On September 1, 2008, (Final Due Date), Borrower shall pay all amounts remaining due under the terms of this Note.

Seasonal. For a seasonal repayment schedule, the amount you pay varies depending on the season. If, for example, the Amaranth Café was located on a college campus, it might be busy nine months out of the year but very slow during the summer months when students have vacated the campus. A customized seasonal repayment schedule for this kind of business could have nine months of high-season payments that correspond to the school schedule, and then switch to a low-season schedule of reduced payments for the summer months, when revenue is low or even zero if the business temporarily closes. Use language like the following:

Borrower shall make monthly payments as described below:

For the calendar months of September, October, November, December, January, February, March, April, and May of each year, Borrower shall pay on the first day of each month the sum of $429.52 to the Lender or Note Holder ("High Seasonal Monthly Payment"); and

For the calendar months of June, July, and August of each calendar year, Borrower shall pay on the first day of each month the sum of $159.95 to the Lender or Note Holder ("Low Seasonal Monthly Payment");

Finally, on September 1, 2008 ("Final Due Date"), Borrower shall pay all amounts remaining due under the terms of this Note.

Interest-only. If you are drafting a promissory note for an interest-only loan (one in which you will make payments of all interest and no principal for the life of the loan, then pay the entire principal back on the final due date), use language like the following:

Borrower will pay all interest that accrues during the term of the loan by making a payment every month. Borrower will make monthly payments on the first day of each month beginning on October 1, 2005. Borrower will make these payments every month until Borrower has paid all of the interest and any other charges described below that Borrower may owe under this Note. Each monthly payment will be applied as of its scheduled due date and will be applied to interest before principal. On September 1, 2008 ("Maturity Date"), Borrower will pay all remaining principal, interest, and any other amounts due to Lender under the terms of this Note.

As you can see, you can write the language in the promissory note to fit just about any repayment schedule you can come up with.

d. How the Note Addresses a Secured Loan

In our example, the promissory note was for an unsecured loan, so all the borrower needed to do was check off the unsecured loan box in paragraph 5. But if you're planning on securing your loan, this is the portion of the promissory note where you'll describe the asset and put your collateral on the line.

If you secure your note with collateral—in other words, if you promise to give up a business or personal asset to fulfill the debt obligation if you can't repay it in cash—you must of course check the other box in paragraph 5, for secured loans. Below that, there's space for you to add key identifying information describing the collateral you've offered, such as the type of property, the manufacturer, the model, the year, an ID number, and the color. Note that you don't need to include a dollar value. Cars, computers, and equipment are the most common items people list.

EXAMPLE: Your collateral descriptions might look like one of these:

> 2003 Dodge Durango, license number A2345678, Vehicle Identification Number JKLM1234567890.
>
> Three Acme natural gas-powered heat lamps, serial numbers: 1234567890; 2234567890; and 3234567890.

In addition to filling out this portion of the note, you'll separately need to do two things:

1. prepare a separate security agreement, and
2. file a Uniform Commercial Code (UCC) form.

The separate security agreement can be prepared without an attorney. Its purpose is simply to identify the collateral you wish to use and agree that it will become the property of the lender if you are unable to repay the loan. A blank form security agreement is provided in Appendix B and on the CD-ROM. If you need further assistance preparing the security agreement, you can find the same form, with an item-by-item explanation, in the latest edition of *101 Law Forms for Personal Use*, by Robin Leonard and Ralph Warner (Nolo).

⚠ **Do not use the agreement included in Appendix B and on the CD-ROM if the collateral is real estate or intellectual property (copyright, patent, trademark).** This form is intended only for tangible personal property. If you pledge your home or other real estate as security for a loan, a security agreement won't be adequate to protect the lender. A well-informed lender will ask you to sign a mortgage or a deed of trust, which can then be recorded (filed) with a designated county official to establish the lender's security interest in the real estate. Because title to real estate is a highly technical matter, you should seek the assistance of a real estate lawyer before signing a mortgage or deed of trust. For similar reasons, you should consult an intellectual property lawyer for help in pledging intangible personal property such as a copyright, trademark, or patent as security for a loan.

The Uniform Commercial Code (UCC) financing statement is a one-page form that you can obtain from the office of the secretary of state in the state where your business is located. The form happens to be identical from state to state, so you can also use the one in Appendix B and on the CD-ROM. The form is simple, requiring merely your name and contact information, your lender's name and contact information, and a description of the collateral.

After you've completed the UCC financing statement, all 50 states now require that you file it in the office of your secretary of state. This filing makes the statement available to any member of the public who wants to find out what liens are being held against your business's assets.

But which state is "yours," if your business operates in more than one? File your UCC form in the state in which (1) you are a resident, if your business is not incorporated, or (2) your business was incorporated (or formed, if it's another entity such as an LLC).

For example, if your business was incorporated in Delaware, but your office is in Massachusetts, you should file the UCC with the secretary of state in Delaware. In some states, you must also attach a copy of the security agreement. To find your state's requirements, contact the secretary of state's office directly, or check whether it has posted this information online at a state government website.

You probably won't be surprised to hear that most states charge a filing fee, ranging from $50 to $100.

e.   How the Note Penalizes Your Nonpayment

In paragraphs 6 through 9, the sample note travels into "may-not-happen" territory, intended to protect the lender in case you have trouble keeping up your end of the bargain. Even if you have every intention of making your payments, agreeing on what will happen if you can't make a payment (even within the grace period) is one of the best ways to forestall later disputes. The note describes nonpayment as a "default," which is a legal term meaning your failure to perform a legal duty. (In a more-complicated transaction, the promissory note might describe several types of default, but in this note, nonpayment is the only one.)

The penalty if you default on this note is that the entire unpaid amount comes due. This is often known as an "acceleration" clause. Although it sounds harsh, it's a traditional clause, and only fair to the lender—without it, he or she would end up having to separately sue you for each payment as it came due, regardless of the fact that you're clearly in default and probably not able to make these future payments.

> **EXAMPLE:** Arnold borrowed $15,000 from his brother to start a vitamin-drink business, to be paid back over three years. He made the first two payments, but then a slick new competitor grabbed away his growing customer base, and he missed the next three payments. With 31 payments to go, Arnold's business went bankrupt. The acceleration clause makes the remainder of the debt all come due so that Arnold's brother can, if he wishes, act to collect the full amount owed instead of having to wait out the term of the loan.

Fortunately, very few family and friend lenders would begin collections as early as a few days after you've missed your first payment. Most family and friend lenders think of default as the point at which the borrower finally tells the lender that he or she can't make any more payments, no matter what the note says.

Paragraph 6 also mentions that the lender can choose whether or not to exercise the acceleration clause—but can exercise it without giving the borrower a last chance to pay up.

> **Nothing in the sample note forces the lender to sue you over a default.** The note gives the lender discretion. That means that you can talk to your lender about the probability that you won't be able to make your upcoming payments and agree to a plan regarding those missed payments—which, legally, will then mean you are not in default.

f.   Protecting Your Right to Prepay

Though it contains only one short sentence, paragraph 7 is one that you should insist upon including. This is generally known as a "prepayment clause" and gives you the right to pay ahead or pay off the entire loan at once, with no "cost or penalty." The time may come when you've received a cash influx and can benefit financially from paying off this loan and perhaps later looking for more-advantageous financing elsewhere.

> **EXAMPLE:** Jerry had three years left on a loan he received from his uncle. However, Jerry's music store had been doing extremely well, thanks to a series of in-store events. By exercising his prepayment clause rights, he paid his uncle the unpaid balance of the loan and saved himself a number of future interest payments. Two years later, he was able to borrow a much larger amount from a bank, at a reasonable interest rate, for a deposit on a second store.

g.   Deciding Who Pays the Attorneys

Paragraph 8 of the sample promissory note could be called the "kick-you-when-you're-down" clause, though it's more officially known as the "attorneys' fees clause." It states that you will be responsible for any legal fees that the lender racks up in order to collect what you owe. This tool is a traditional form of protection for you to provide the lender.

h.   Easing the Collections Process for the Lender

Paragraph 9, known as the waiver clause, is a standard legal clause in the lending industry. It unfortunately does away with some of the borrower protections that banks traditionally had to comply with to collect on a bad loan. These protections were basically legal formalities, including a series of back-and-forth notices regarding the amount owed and the borrower's refusals to pay (called presentments and dishonors). The purpose of the clause is to speed up the process of collecting on the loan once it's clear that the borrower is unable or unwilling to make the scheduled payments.

If your lender is confused by the old-fashioned language in this clause, you can, in good conscience, reassure him or her that the clause is more to the lender's advantage than to yours! Nevertheless, there's no sense in trying to avoid this clause, because it is standard, and using it shows that you won't be trying to impede the lender's efforts to collect.

Paragraph 10, which we headed "Lender's Rights," is also sometimes known as a "Non-Waiver Clause" and offers an additional form of protection for your lender. This clause says that just because your lender may give you a break on one payment, perhaps by accepting a late payment without charging a late fee, that doesn't change the lender's overall rights, in this case to receive your payments on time and charge a late fee. In other words, the fact that in one instance your lender doesn't insist that you completely adhere to the terms of the note doesn't let you claim, "Since it was okay that one time, it must be okay all the time!"

i.   Sharing Your Liability With Coborrowers

Paragraph 11, the clause headed '"Liability of Individual Borrowers," means that if you sign the note with fellow borrowers, you are each liable individually for the full amount. If one borrower can't pay, the other owes the entire amount, not just a portion of it.

j.   Which State's Law Governs

Paragraph 12, the "governing law clause," is standard in promissory notes and many other contracts. It simply says that if any points of contention arise out of the agreement, the laws of the state named in the clause will be used to resolve the conflict.

k.   Signing the Promissory Note

The last portion of the sample note is called the "signature block." Whoever signs here becomes liable for the debt. If you are borrowing the money as an individual (as in the sample note), or if your business is a sole proprietorship, then you will sign the note and accept personal responsibility.

If your business is incorporated, is an LLC, or is a partnership, the business is the borrower and you must make sure to sign on behalf of the business. (See "Signing the Note for Your Business," below.) As long as you sign correctly, the business is liable for the debt, but you are not.

If loaning money to an incorporated business makes your lender anxious, you can offer to be a coborrower with your business. That way, if you fail to make payments, both the corporation and you can be held liable. This is a shorthand way of avoiding having you make a personal guarantee, an alternative requiring fairly complicated documentation.

Signing the Note for Your Business

If your business will be the borrower on the promissory note, you'll need to use a different signature block from the one on the sample note. Instead, you'll need to print the business name and then sign on behalf of the business. You do this by including your official title under your signature, as shown below:

Borrower:

  [*print business name*] _____

Dated: _____

By: _____ [*signature*] _____

Print name: _____

Title: _____

Since the promissory note represents your promise to pay, it requires only your signature to be legally binding. Sometimes lenders feel like they should be signing something, too. Actually, they shouldn't. By signing, the lender might call into question whether the document really is a note (representing an obligation owed) instead of some other type of legal document, such as a contract (which has a whole separate set of purposes and uses).

Finally, some lenders may want a notary public to witness your signing of the promissory note. If it makes your lender happy, do it, but it's not necessary to make the document legally binding. (All a notary public really does is confirm the identity of the person signing the document, and your lender should know who you are by now.) Add the following language to your note for the notary's use (available in Appendix B and on the CD-ROM).

Certificate of Acknowledgment of Notary Public

State of _____

County of _____

On _____, before me, _____
_____, a notary public in and for said state,
personally appeared _____, known
to me (or proved to me on the basis of satisfactory evidence) to be
the person whose name is subscribed to the within instrument,
and acknowledged to me that he or she executed the same in his
or her authorized capacity and that by his or her signature on the
instrument, the person, or the entity upon behalf of which the
person acted, executed the instrument.

WITNESS my hand and official seal.

_____

Notary Public for the State of _____

My commission expires _____

[NOTARY SEAL]

D. Participating in the Preparation of the Stock Purchase Agreement

Whether you're raising $20,000 in equity from four family investors
or $200,000 from a group of business angels, you and your attorney
need to do several things before you can seal the deal. First, you need
to figure out how much to say about the risks involved in making an
investment in your business—in other words, how much to disclose

(see Section 1, below)—and you'll need to make those disclosures in a way that satisfies securities laws (see Section 2, below). After that, to formalize the purchase of shares in your business, your attorney, or your investor's attorney, needs to prepare a stock purchase agreement, which you should carefully review before signing. (See Section 3, below.)

1.   Understanding Your Disclosure Obligations

Anyone who raises money for a business by selling shares in the business is subject to antifraud laws and regulations enforced by the Securities and Exchange Commission. One of the most important is Rule 10b-5, officially called "Employment of Manipulative and Deceptive Devices." This rule states that a person involved in the purchase or sale of a security may not make any material misstatements, or omit to make a statement that is material to the business. For you, this means that you must tell your investors things you know that could affect the course of your business. This is called disclosure.

For example, if for several years your largest contract has been from a defense contractor of the federal government, and—in the middle of a fundraising round—you find out suddenly that the program under which your contracts were awarded has been cut effective immediately, you can't just hope that a new star customer will come from somewhere else. Instead, you need to disclose the anticipated loss of that key customer and predict the impact it will have on your revenues and, thus, your ability to perform at the level the investor expects from your business projections.

Even if you don't know that something so specific will happen, you must also disclose potential risks, such as changes in weather if yours is a seasonal business, loss of key employees, increases in the price of energy, and shifts in the global market's taste for your product.

Perhaps you have already told your investors in person about these potential changes to the fortunes of your business. Unfortunately, that's not good enough. You also need to document your disclosures. Without a document, if your business tanks, your investors could deny the conversation took place and sue you for having misled them.

Another portion of the SEC rules relevant to you says that, to be allowed to raise funds from nonaccredited investors (which your friends and family may well be), you must supply all items on an SEC checklist of specific disclosure obligations (such as financial statements and resumes). (This rule appears under Section 502 of Regulation D.)

In general, as a sort of insurance policy against investor lawsuits and SEC investigations, most attorneys agree that entrepreneurs should put the key risks they know their business faces into writing and provide this to any potential investor.

2. Meeting Your Disclosure Obligation

The level and the character of the disclosures you make will be determined by which exemption your attorney decides best suits your fundraising effort (based on the amount of money to be raised, the number of people involved, whether the investors are accredited or not, and the cost of meeting the exemption requirements).

Your challenge is to figure out (with your attorney) the most inexpensive way to provide your prospective investors with the information that both federal and state laws say is needed for them to make an informed decision about whether to invest. While you of course want to spend as little as possible, you also want to avoid any liability brought on by not meeting your disclosure obligation.

The type and detail of legal documents and attachments that you give your prospective investor will be determined by the minimum level of disclosure required under the exemption you've selected. Three common types of documents are:

- a full-fledged "private placement memorandum"
- a simpler version of the private placement memorandum (PPM), or
- sections added to existing documents, such as your business plan or stock purchase agreement, disclosing risk factors.

If you're planning to rely on a small business exemption, you can't use advertising to "solicit" investors. All of the generally available exemptions that allow small businesses to raise equity without registering the securities require that there has been no "general solicitation" to potential investors. This includes distributing your PPM or any other offering document on the Internet.

Are Your Investors "Accredited"?

Who qualifies as an "accredited investor" is an important issue for a business wishing to become exempt from registering its offering of securities.

To qualify as an accredited investor, an investor must be either a financial institution (such as a bank or small business investment company), an affiliate of the issuer (such as a director or general partner), or an individual with a net worth of at least $1 million or an annual income of at least $200,000 (and the investment must not account for more than 20% of the investor's worth).

For the exact wording of the SEC's definition, see www.sec.gov/answers/accred.htm.

a.   Preview of the Private Placement Memorandum

The most common way that entrepreneurs meet their disclosure obligation is by creating a private placement memo (PPM). The PPM is a set of legal documents and attachments that typically describe the background of the company, the risks to the investor, and the terms of the securities. Note that the PPM is not only a disclosure document, it's also an offering document, because it sets forth the terms of the investment opportunity. For example, in addition to sections on risk factors, a PPM will include the terms of the offering, a description of the intended use of the capital being raised, and a description of the securities for sale.

A PPM for a private offering of several hundred thousand dollars by an established business can be so complex and daunting it might be mistaken for the prospectus the SEC requires of firms preparing their initial public offering. But it's possible to prepare a PPM for a smaller business with just a few years of operational history for a cost of $8,000–10,000. This needs to be done by an attorney familiar with your business.

b.   Preview of the Simple PPM

PPMs are not just for established businesses; your attorney may think that a PPM is the best way for your business to offer securities for sale. Fortunately, the younger your business, the fewer risks you ordinarily have to disclose, so the simpler your PPM can be. A simple PPM (one for a young business) shouldn't cost you more than $1,000–$3,000 in attorneys' fees. It can be patched together from material that already exists in your business plan, or that an attorney would create anyway for a stock purchase agreement. A simple PPM will normally include:
- a cover sheet outlining risks facing your company
- your latest business plan
- the section of your stock purchase agreement called "Representations and Warranties of the Company"
- historical financial statements (which may be few if you've only been in business a few months)
- reasonable financial projections for your business, and
- the sources of and planned uses for your financing.

c.   Preview of Adding Sections to Existing Documents

You and your attorney may decide you can do without a PPM and just expand or add new material to any existing discussions of risk in either your business plan or your stock purchase agreement (SPA). For example, using existing documents can be appropriate if your investor is a pro, has done thorough due diligence, and will be getting a full set of representations and warranties in the SPA.

Venture capital funds and structured angel groups don't often require PPMs, because they take on the task of documenting the riskiness of the investment to their own satisfaction. On the other end of the spectrum, if you're a young company doing a small deal with friends and family investors, you may be able to easily disclose the risks in your business plan or SPA. If, for example, you're raising only $5,000, it doesn't make any sense to pay $3,000 in attorneys' fees to prepare even a simple PPM.

⚠ **Each time you raise new money, reevaluate whether you need a PPM.** As the investment rounds get larger and the investors get more distant from you relationship-wise, you may decide it's time to do a PPM.

If you decide to forgo a PPM, the key is to make sure you've disclosed risks in writing somewhere. Your attorney can help you come up with a list and add it to your stock purchase agreement (SPA), your business plan, or both.

Within the stock purchase agreement, you'd want to mention these risks in the section where you make "representations and warranties" about your company. Some prefer to minimize the discussion of risk in the SPA, and instead discuss risk in the business plan. You can add a separate section near the end of the narrative where you outline specific risks. (However, some attorneys aren't comfortable with disclosing risks only in the business plan, preferring to cover them in the SPA and nowhere else.)

3.   Reviewing the Stock Purchase Agreement

If your investor is a friend or family member, it will be up to you to have an attorney prepare the stock purchase agreement. If, however, your investors are experienced with private business investing, they will almost always have their own attorneys draft the SPA as well as other legal documents. You and your attorney will, of course, have a chance to review and negotiate over the language in these documents before signing. Venture capital investors and angels, particularly the structured angel groups described in Chapter 7, increasingly prefer that their own attorney start the drafting process.

Because attorneys prepare their documents differently, there is no single, widely accepted format for an SPA. Some style it as a contract (most common when professional investors are involved), while other attorneys prefer to present the agreement in the form of a long letter from the investor to the company. If you've asked your attorney to draft an SPA for use with family and friend investors, don't be surprised if he or she comes back with the agreement styled as a letter, simply because it comes across as friendlier.

There are, however, standard subjects that you can expect to see covered in the SPA, including:

- purchase and sale of the stock
- representations and warranties of the company
- representations and warranties of the investor
- representations and warranties of the founders, and
- conditions at closing.

Below, you'll find the table of contents for a contract-style stock purchase agreement for series A preferred stock. (You don't want to see a full-length sample here—these documents can range from 20 to 50 pages with attachments!) The table of contents is from a model stock purchase agreement created by a team of attorneys at the National Venture Capital Association and is available in Appendix D and on the CD-ROM at the back of this book. In the following sections, you'll find an explanation of each part of the model stock purchase agreement, and a few highlights of key items within each part of the model document.

The exhibits are what make the paperwork so forbidding. Stock purchase agreements can come with anywhere from one to ten attachments, referred to as "exhibits," at the back of the document. You'll see ten included with the model NVCA agreement. Some of these may just be lists, like "Exhibit A: Schedule of Purchasers," which lists the names of the investors. Others may be long and complex documents that require their own drafting process, like "Exhibit B: Form of Amended and Restated Certificate of Incorporation." These exhibits will be referred to throughout the SPA by their shorthand, such as "Exhibit A" or "Exhibit B."

a.   Understanding the Purchase and Sale Paragraphs of the SPA

In the introductory sentences of an SPA, you'll normally find the name of your company and the state in which it was incorporated. If you'll have more than one investor, the agreement may refer to "the investors listed in Exhibit A attached to this agreement" (like the sample SPA does).

The model SPA then begins, "The parties hereby agree as follows," and goes on to discuss two important items: "Sale and Issuance of Series a Preferred Stock" and "Closing; Delivery."

Sample Stock Purchase Agreement Table of Contents

SERIES A PREFERRED STOCK PURCHASE AGREEMENT

TABLE OF CONTENTS

1.   Purchase and Sale of Preferred Stock

1.1   Sale and Issuance of Series A Preferred Stock

1.2   Closing; Delivery

1.3   Sale of Additional Shares of Preferred Stock

1.4   Defined Terms Used in this Agreement

2.   Representations and Warranties of the Company

2.1   Organization, Good Standing, Corporate Power and Qualification

2.2   Capitalization

2.3   Subsidiaries

2.4   Authorization

2.5   Valid Issuance of Shares

2.6   Governmental Consents and Filings

2.7   Litigation

2.8   Intellectual Property

2.9   Compliance with Other Instruments

2.10 Agreements; Actions

2.11 Conflicts of Interest

2.12 Rights of Registration and Voting Rights

2.13 Absence of Liens

2.14 Financial Statements

2.15 Changes

2.16 Employee Matters

2.17 Tax Returns and Payments

2.18 Insurance

2.19 Confidential Information and Invention Assignment Agreements

2.20 Permits

2.21 Corporate Documents

2.22 83(b) Elections

2.23 Real Property Holding Corporation

2.24 Environmental and Safety Laws

2.25 Qualified Small Business Stock

2.26   Disclosure

2.27   Small Business Concern

3.   Representations and Warranties of the Founders

3.1   Conflicting Agreements

3.2   Litigation

3.3   Stockholder Agreements

3.4   Representations and Warranties

3.5   Prior Legal Matters

4.   Representations and Warranties of the Purchasers

4.1   Authorization

4.2   Purchase Entirely for Own Account

4.3   Disclosure of Information

4.4   Restricted Securities

4.5   No Public Market

4.6   Legends

4.7   Accredited Investor

4.8   Foreign Investors

4.9   No General Solicitation

4.10   Exculpation Among Purchasers

4.11   Residence

5.   Conditions to the Purchasers' Obligations at Closing

5.1   Representations and Warranties

5.2   Performance

5.3   Compliance Certificate

5.4   Qualifications

5.5   Opinion of Company Counsel

5.6   Board of Directors

5.7   Indemnification Agreement

5.8   Investors' Rights Agreement

5.9   Right of First Refusal and Co Sale Agreement

5.10   Voting Agreement

5.11   Restated Certificate

5.12   Secretary's Certificate

5.13   Proceedings and Documents

5.14   Minimum Number of Shares at Initial Closing

5.15   SBA Matters

5.16   Management Rights

5.17   Preemptive Rights

6.   Conditions of the Company's Obligations at Closing

6.1   Representations and Warranties

6.2   Performance

6.3   Qualifications

6.4   Investors' Rights Agreement

6.5   Right of First Refusal and Co Sale Agreement

6.6   Voting Agreement

6.7   Minimum Number of Shares at Initial Closing

7.   Miscellaneous

7.1   Survival of Warranties

7.2   Transfer; Successors and Assigns

7.3   Governing Law

7.4   Counterparts

7.5   Titles and Subtitles

7.6   Notices

7.7   No Finder's Fees

7.8   Fees and Expenses

7.9   Attorney's Fees

7.10   Amendments and Waivers

7.11   Severability

7.12   Delays or Omissions

7.13   Entire Agreement

7.14   Corporate Securities Law

7.15   Dispute Resolution

Exhibit A   Schedule of Purchasers

Exhibit B   Form of Amended and Restated Certificate of Incorporation

Exhibit C   Disclosure Schedule

Exhibit D   Form of Indemnification Agreement

Exhibit E   Form of Investors' Rights Agreement

Exhibit F   Form of Management Rights Letter

Exhibit G   Form of Right of First Refusal and Co-Sale Agreement

Exhibit H   Form of Voting Agreement

Exhibit I   Form of Legal Opinion of [Company Counsel]

Exhibit J   Milestone Events

The "Sale and Issuance" paragraphs. Also often titled "subscription," this topic area states the agreed-on price per share in the company. This price will be based on a valuation of your company agreed to by you, your board of directors, and, of course, the investors who agree to purchase shares in your company. (See the discussion of valuation in Chapter 8.) Some SPAs will also mention the number of shares being purchased here; however, in the model document, you'll see that this information is included in "Exhibit A, Schedule of Purchasers."

The sample "Sale and Issuance" topic area also states that the company must file an amended or restated Certificate of Incorporation. You probably created this certificate (also sometimes known as the "Charter of the Company") when you formed your company. However, it needs to be revised every time you add new owners, because it details the rights and responsibilities of each new class of stock. (Your attorney will help you create this or create the related documents if you are organized as an LLC.)

The "Closing; Delivery" paragraphs. This topic area specifies the date of the closing and the manner of payment. The closing date clause contains important information and is mercifully easy to read. The bit about being able to change the closing date and time to "such other time and place as the Company and the Purchasers mutually agree upon, orally or in writing" is an important one. Including this language will save you the legal costs of redrafting the document if you have to reschedule the closing, perhaps to accommodate an investor.

The delivery clause is also fairly simple, just explaining that at the closing date specified, you will deliver a certificate representing the shares being purchased, and the purchaser will pay by check or wire transfer or by canceling a debt the company has to the purchaser. Typically, friend and family investors prefer paying by check (just don't insult them by insisting it be certified). Institutional investors tend to pay by wire transfer or certified check.

b.   Understanding the Representations and Warranties to Be Made by the Company

At paragraph 2 of the model SPA, you'll find a section headed "Representations and Warranties of the Company." The purpose of this topic area is to make sure that you tell your investors any relevant information about your company and its financial condition. "Representations and warranties" is a legal phrase that basically means, "I guarantee what I say is true." As you may recall from Chapter 8, your representations and warranties are likely to appear first in the term sheet. This part of the SPA is where they live in their final and complete form. The paragraph begins, "The Company hereby represents and warrants to each Purchaser that ...." It goes on to set forth a laundry list of items that you say are true (the list in the model agreement includes 27 items).

Typical representations and warranties include:

- that your company exists
- your company's capital structure
- that your offering of shares is legitimate and has been agreed to by existing investors and management
- that no outstanding litigation is pending against your company
- that the company has the intellectual property rights necessary to conduct its business (if applicable)
- that the company is not in violation of any other contracts or government filings of which it knows, nor has any outstanding taxes due
- that the company has disclosed any current or pending agreements or contracts that are material to the business (such as the proposed acquisition of another company)
- that the company has no conflicts of interest (such as informal financing arrangements with friends or family!)
- that the company is not required to register under the Securities Act
- that the company has provided purchasers with financial statements that have been prepared in accordance with generally accepted accounting principles
- a listing of employees, consultants, contractors, and the like, as well as various representations and warranties about the nature of their compensation, benefits, and related employee matters
- that the company is in compliance with environmental and safety laws, and
- that you have provided all information available to the purchasers related to their decision to acquire shares and have not lied about anything in the agreement.

Note that these representations and warranties are very specific, especially where they concern facts that may be pivotal to an investor's decision to invest. Additional representations and warranties may be necessary to cover the realities of your business. For example, if your business will utilize a new invention with a patent pending that will be the first of its kind on the market, your attorney may include a clause representing and warranting that the intellectual property contained in the invention is protected (from other businesses using it) by the pending patent. If in reality you never filed for the patent, but you sign the agreement anyway, you will be in immediate violation of the contract.

Although the list is seemingly endless, review your representations and warranties closely to make sure the statements your attorney makes about your business are true.

c. Understanding the Paragraphs Describing Representations and Warranties to Be Made by the Founders

In paragraph 3 of the model stock purchase agreement, you'll find a part called "Representations and Warranties to Be Made by the Founders." This is distinct from the earlier representations and warranties made by the company. It serves to reassure investors that you and your cofounders have not done anything separate from the company that would jeopardize the company or the investment. Representations and warranties of the founders tend to show up mostly in first-round agreements, not in documents for later rounds. After the first round, investors figure that the types of risks mentioned here are diminished.

This is usually a short section, which includes items to establish that:

- You have not signed any agreements that conflict with this SPA.
- No litigation or other legal or criminal proceedings are pending against you that would adversely affect the company.
- You have not entered into any agreements related to selling shares in the company that you have not disclosed.
- The representations and warranties of the company set forth in the previous part are "true and complete."

d.   Understanding the Representations and Warranties to Be Made by the Investor

The investor's representations serve to establish key facts about the investor—particularly facts to show that the investor meets the criteria allowing you to claim an exemption from registering your offering of securities. These might include that the investor:

- has the power and authority to enter into agreements related to the purchase of securities
- is making the purchase for his or her own accounts, and not for those of a third party
- has had the opportunity to review and discuss all matters related to the company and the investment
- understands that no public market exists for the shares, and that they are restricted for resale or transfer purposes until the company registers and makes a public offering, which the company is not obliged to do, and
- is an accredited investor as defined in Rule 501(a) of Regulation D of the federal Securities Act (see "Are Your Investors 'Accredited'?," above).

e.   Understanding the Conditions Required to Close the Deal

After all the representations and warranties have been spelled out (often in excruciating detail), the next two sets of numbered paragraphs detail the items that need to be in place, or events that need to occur, for the deal to proceed to a close. You and your investors can use this part of the SPA as a sort of checklist, showing each party what it needs to do.

The standard clauses usually say that the investor can't change his or her mind after signing the document; that the agreement can't be altered except by a newly signed, written document; that the investor can't give or sell his or her shares to someone else, although if the company changes hands, the agreement is still good; that if a dispute arises, it will be dealt with according to the laws of a chosen state; and that if any party to the agreement dies or ceases to exist, the agreement will carry on in the hands of the heirs or business successors.

f.   The End of the SPA: Final Items and Signatures

The last part is always a sort of catch-all for items that don't fit anywhere else in the agreement. It may be called "Miscellaneous" or "Other Matters" and usually includes a discussion of fees, waivers, and other standard investing fare.

Finally, the agreement ends with the signature block, a more elaborate one than for a promissory note. Both parties are required to sign, in accordance with the fact that each is making various statements and binding itself to various obligations within the agreement.

4.   Protecting Your Family-and-Friend Investors' Interests

If the equity investors with whom you're drafting this SPA are mostly friends and family, you take on a special responsibility to protect their interests in the future. In the best-case scenario, your business will really take off, and you'll later find yourself able to attract subsequent investments by professional venture capital investors. (A growing business uses a lot of capital, and these feedings of cash are most often organized into "financing rounds", so what we're really talking about is preparing for a whole new round of reaching out to various investors.)

Bringing in new capital, however, may create problems for your existing family and friend investors. There is a good chance that the later, professional investors will "cram them down." A "cram down" means that the later investors limit or reduce the value of the shares owned by earlier investors, in order to protect their own rights (and then some). It's completely unfair, but it happens all the time. Most of the savvy business angel investors have learned to avert this by making sure that they get preferred stock instead of common stock. But the reality remains that the founders, friends, and family investors agree to buy common stock, then find that the piece of the pie purchased with their initial investment is getting smaller and smaller.

You will need to look into your crystal ball and be as prescient as you can. If you don't expect to have future rounds of financing or professional equity investors, then the obvious choice is to issue common stock to your friends and family investors (for one thing, it's the least expensive and paperwork-intensive option). But if you hope to grow your business to the point where professional investors like venture capitalists are making investments, you must, even now, prepare for future rounds of financing. That means that, from the first round, you should issue preferred stock with terms that protect your early investors. There are three terms in particular (discussed in the previous chapter) that can help you do this.

Antidilution provisions. If your attorney is preparing an SPA for family and friend investors, ask that it address the threat of dilution. Dilution is when your early investors are "crammed down" as described above. An antidilution provision gives investors certain rights that protect their investment from such future threats. If you raise additional funds down the road from professional investors, but your current agreement doesn't contain antidilution provisions, there's a good chance that your family and friends who hold common stock will be reduced to an ownership stake less than their original investment.

Veto Rights. Another way to protect early investors is to give them veto rights over subsequent financing rounds. In other words, your agreement can specify that a certain percentage, say two-thirds, of existing investors must approve any subsequent rounds of financing. Although this ties your hands in terms of control over fundraising, it gives existing investors a say in what happens to their ownership stake in the business.

Right of First Refusal. A third tool is to give early investors the right of first refusal, also known as the "right of first offer" in the model NVCA "Investor Rights Agreement." (Experienced equity investors who come in at or near the beginning of your fundraising efforts often expect to be asked for additional money in subsequent rounds of financing. In fact, some will tell you that they're giving you only a part of what you need and are saving the rest for the next round.) The right of first refusal means you promise to offer your early investors shares in a new round before you open it up to new investors, thus giving the early ones the chance to retain their stake in the business.

Professional or business angel investors will probably know to ask for these provisions. Family and friends, however, may not. The best thing you can do to protect them is to issue preferred stock and include protective provisions in their stock purchase agreements, even if they haven't asked for them.

E. How to Close the Deal

At last, it's time for you to collect the loans or equity funding you've worked so hard to line up. If you have ever bought a home, you've probably experienced a "closing." It's traditionally a meeting where both parties (and their attorneys) sit together around a conference table to sign legal documents and exchange checks. Although bringing everyone together in this way is the ideal, it's not always realized with business loans and equity investments.

Especially if you have friends and family located in different parts of the country, doing the closing in person may be impossible. With the advent of fax machines, FedEx, and wire transfers, not to mention the cell phone, the business of signing documents and transferring funds can now be adequately accomplished from a distance. Don't worry if the signing of documents and the transfer of funds don't happen simultaneously; the important thing is that they all happen.

If your scheduling allows it, try to close the deal in person. It lends a professional air to the transaction. But don't force it: Do what's easiest and most comfortable for you, your lender, or your investor.

1. Closing a Private Business Loan

By now, if all has gone well, you've reached a verbal agreement with your lender, customized a loan request letter and sent it to the lender, and heard back that the lender is ready to make the loan. To close the deal, take the following steps:

- Draft a promissory note based on terms agreed to by the lender (see Section B, above) and send the draft note to the lender. Email is fine for drafts, and preferable if it speeds up the process.

- Have your lender review the draft promissory note and comment on any financial terms that do not appear as he or she expected or mention any other problems (like misspellings).
- Make agreed-upon changes and prepare the final copy of the promissory note—or share a second draft with your lender if the comments on the first draft were substantial.
- Sign the final promissory note (remember that typically only the borrower needs to sign), keep a copy for your records, and send the original back to the lender for safekeeping. Don't sign any additional copies—that will only confuse matters. In the future, remember that once the note has been repaid, you are entitled to get back the original, because the obligation no longer exists.
- Your lender disburses the funds. This is typically done using a personal check, cashier's check, or wire transfer. If you accept a personal check, note that the clearing period may be longer than usual due to the large amount.

Don't be surprised by last-minute changes of mind. I've known lenders to call shortly before a closing date and call the whole thing off because the lender has changed his or her mind, the lender's spouse has vetoed the deal, or the lender's tax bill was higher than expected. The only one I haven't heard yet is that the lender's dog ate the paperwork. Some lenders just get cold feet. If you really feel that the lender is someone you want associated with your business, don't give up. Of course, if the lender is a close friend or family member, or you sense you might hurt your relationship, don't exert too much pressure.

2. Closing an Equity Investment

Closing with your equity investors is typically a bigger deal (bigger amounts of money, bigger documents) than closing on a loan. Given that fact, you might expect your investors to want to meet in person. Rarely will they do so. An entrepreneur friend says he has *never* closed an equity investment from an angel in person; it always happens— successfully—from a distance.

In addition to being hard to track down, you may find that your family, friends, and angel investors don't have much respect for your deadlines. It's best to ignore the advice of "sophisticated" financing experts who tell you that closing dates should be firm. Now is not the time to teach your friends, family, or business associates a lesson in timeliness. The timing will depend entirely on the personalities and schedules of the folks involved. You will just have to persistently follow up by phone and email until you get the job done.

Closing your equity investment deal will involve the steps below:

- Make sure all the documents are in order. If exhibits will be attached to the agreement, those need to be ready as well, in their latest form.
- You and your investor both sign the stock purchase agreement, and possibly also sign additional documents within the exhibits.
- You and your investor each get a complete set of signed documents for your files.
- The investor transfers the funds, based on detailed instructions within the stock purchase agreement. Depending on your situation, your investor may arrive with a check or have it delivered. Alternatively, a wire transfer may be scheduled for the closing day. Let the investor call the shots on this; all you want is the money, regardless of the form it takes.

"Virtual" closings are harder to keep to a schedule. You may need to remind your investors several times to send the signed documentation and the check. One hint: It's much easier to get people to send signed documents than a check, so start with the documents and worry about the check later. Once the stock purchase agreement is signed, the investor is obliged to transfer the funds.

Chapter 10

Your Ongoing Relationship With the People Who Financed You

A. Communicating Your Progress 262

    1. Stay in Touch: Lenders Like It, Equity Investors Require It 263

    2. Informal Ways to Stay in Touch 264

    2. Formal Ways to Stay in Touch 265

B. If You Received Loan Capital 270

    1. Paying on Time 270

    2. Acting Responsibly When You Can't Make a Payment 279

    3. If You Have No Choice but to Default 283

C. If You Received Equity Investments 284

    1. Growing Your Business 284

    2. Managing Investor Expectations 286

    3. Creating a Board of Directors 287

Now that you've lined up your financing, your main task is to throw yourself into managing and growing your business, right? Well, yes and no. Unless you also keep a watchful eye on your obligations to the people who helped fund your business in the first place, they may think you just took the money and ran.

Regardless of the type of investment you received—gift, loan, or equity—maintaining open, honest, and regular communications with your investors is an important starting point. (See Section A, below.)

You may also, however, have agreed to more-specific duties. If you received a loan, you need to repay the money and otherwise comply with the terms of your promissory note. (See Section B, below.)

If you received an equity investment, your job is to grow the business, ideally to the point where the investor can "exit" and be paid for his or her stake in cash. (See Section C, below.)

A. Communicating Your Progress

You owe it to your investors to communicate with them regularly—whether or not you signed a legal agreement to that effect. Professionals call this "maintaining good investor relations," and it's simply good practice, whether your investors made you a gift, a loan, or an equity investment.

You've already convinced your investors that your business is the most exciting thing around—now let them know about the growth and new activities their money is helping to fuel. The more your investors feel like part of the action, the happier they'll be, and the more likely they'll be to either do you a favor in a crunch or to make future investments. Altruistic investors in particular, whose motivation for supporting you included sharing in your success or giving you a boost toward independence, will be happy to hear good news.

Good news is best, but some bad news should be shared, too. Don't feel like your investors only want to hear from you when business is booming and you've just landed a big new customer account. If, for example, a competitor has opened up across the street, your investors might appreciate knowing about this wrench in your plan and might even have constructive advice on dealing with it.

1.   Stay in Touch: Lenders Like It, Equity Investors Require It

There's a funny human tendency to think that, when you sign a legal agreement, you need not—or perhaps even should not—do anything outside of that agreement. And, indeed, the promissory note that you signed with your lender or the stock purchase agreement you signed with your investor will become central to your dealings with that person—you should read them more than once as time goes by. But when it comes to staying in touch, any obligations spelled out in the agreement are just a starting point. Try to get a sense of how much information each investor really wants, and give him or her just that amount—not more, and not less.

The promissory note you signed for your lender mostly talks about staying in touch when you're having difficulty with repayments. Without a doubt, that obligation is a crucial one. But imagine what your lender will think if you call only with plaintive cries for help. If you really want to keep the relationship strong, keep in touch during good times, as well.

If you signed a stock purchase agreement with an equity investor, it probably contains a clause spelling out what information (usually financial) you must provide and on what dates. Your family and friends and investors may not, however, have required this clause.

With or without such a clause, your equity investors, as co-owners in your company, will expect to be kept informed. Remember, they don't receive a monthly payment as evidence that things are humming along. Instead, it's up to you to develop a set of tools for showing them that all is going swimmingly. In fact, equity investors will probably get nervous if they don't hear from you regularly. Use the communications tools suggested in this section to keep a steady stream of news and updates headed their way. That way they'll stay out of your way for the most part but remain on deck in case you need to ask for greater involvement or more money.

⚠ **You may need to go back to these people in the future.** If dealing with touchy-feely communication issues feels like the last thing on your priority list, just remember, this round of financing won't last forever. Chances are your business will need money again later, to buy your next big piece of equipment or to hire your next salesperson. And if you're not yet profitable enough for institutional lenders and professional investors, the best people to ask are probably the people you've already asked, who know and trust you. By maintaining good relations with all your supporters, you'll keep the stage set for future fundraising.

2. Informal Ways to Stay in Touch

For some of your investors, keeping in touch in ways that simply acknowledge the person's support of your business will be enough. In particular, people who made gifts or loans won't expect you to provide detailed business information but would appreciate a friendly message once in a while.

Use any of the tools described below to make casual, but ideally regular, contact with these folks.

a. In-Person Updates

For people you see regularly, such as over the kitchen table or at a social event, you'll quite naturally want to tell them how your business is doing. For other people with whom you have a personal relationship, you might want to invite them to lunch or coffee. Don't turn your updates into a lecture—but think ahead about any fun facts or interesting stories you might share with this person. This is all some investors will need.

b. Holiday Cards

Businesses of all sizes use holiday cards as a way to cast a wide net of appreciation, once a year, to key customers, suppliers, business partners, and, yes, investors. If you haven't done so already, start a holiday mailing list and put every last one of your investors' names on it.

You can pick up a few boxes of cards at the store and fill them out by hand for friends and family. For other investors, you might want to go to websites that offer printed cards with a custom greeting and the name of your business.

c. Customer Mailings

If you hold a grand opening of your business, definitely make sure your investors get an invitation. As time goes on, some entrepreneurs also include their investors in mailings they make to customers, announcing new products, sales and other special events, and more. If, for example, you own a gallery, your lenders would probably be interested in announcements of your art openings. If you own a café that features live music, they might appreciate receiving a schedule.

d. Press Clippings

Whenever you receive coverage in the press—whether it's the local paper or *The New York Times*—make good-quality copies of the clipping and share it with your investors. Attach a simple, handwritten note saying that you thought the person might be interested in seeing that your business is getting some public recognition. Many press articles are now available online—if yours are, you might choose to send an email link rather than a printed version, to save time and money.

A favorable review of your new restaurant or bakery is, for example, a great piece of news to share. As you accumulate clippings, you'll soon share only the best ones, but you should keep track of the rest, anyway.

Most businesses dedicate a page on their website to press coverage. Also, favorable quotations from these sources look great added to your business plan, executive summary, or loan request letter.

2. Formal Ways to Stay in Touch

In addition to the tools described above, you'll need to use a more-formal set of tools, mostly for communicating with your equity investors. However, you'll find that some savvy lenders are eager to chew on quarterly reports and financial projections as well. Below are some of the most widely used tools for communicating business information to investors.

a.   The Business Letter

Quarterly or annually, write a letter for regular mail or email distribution to your investors. The letter should give them a sense of how things are going. Make the letter a serious discussion of your business's progress to date and your expectations for the quarter ahead.

Just the fact that you take the time to produce such a letter will be well received by your investors. They'll see it as a sign that you are managing your business responsibly and aren't drowning in other efforts to keep it afloat.

A standard business letter format is appropriate. The date should be the end of the quarter to which the letter refers. Begin with a salutation such as "Dear Supporter."

For the body of your letter or memo, open with a greeting paragraph that spells out the purpose of the letter. After that, I suggest including sections discussing:

- operating highlights
- a summary of recent financial performance, and
- a business update.

Operating highlights. This section—which, as with the coming sections, you might want to title just as we did here—should spell out a few key benchmarks or milestones achieved during the quarter that just ended. For example, "In this quarter we surpassed 1,000 lattes sold," or "In this quarter revenue exceeded $10,000 each month for the first time ever," or "We launched our first lawn care service specially designed for retirees."

Financial performance. This section should include a table with just three to five key financial indicators that tell the story of your business for the previous quarter. For most firms, the most important financial indicators include revenue, cost of goods, profit margin, operating expenses, and net income (or loss). You may want to offer additional columns for previous periods or even for the last fiscal year, so the user can compare the figures across periods. If your investors want additional or different information, they will no doubt let you know.

Business update. Now's your chance to give a narrative progress report. It should include a description of your current business strategy. If you've made any significant changes to that strategy since drafting your business plan, explain these and provide good reasons. Also use this section to offer insights into your industry that explain the prospects for the business (for example, how off-shoring has cut the costs of one of your major sources of raw materials). Describe events of the quarter, such as tradeshows attended, new employees hired, and equipment purchased.

Many entrepreneurs see bad news as merely a bump in the road or a new challenge to overcome. If you have bad news to report—like the loss of a major customer, a product recall, or the departure of a key employee—communicate not just the event, but also your solution for moving on and overcoming the problem. Leave the investor feeling confident that you've got the situation under control and it won't derail your business plan. Save your more-serious doubts for closed-door meetings with your closest advisers and investors and your board of directors. They can help you come up with both a solution and an appropriate message to communicate more widely.

Throughout the letter, include financial tables, pie charts that illustrate the growth of your product categories, representations of new brochures, snapshots of new Web pages, and favorable quotes from the media or satisfied customers. These are some of the nuggets that will really help your business come alive for the reader.

Conclude your letter with thanks for the person's support. Add your signature, printed name, and title. If you have company letterhead, use it to print the letter on.

b.   Quarterly Financial Statements

You or your accountant should be able to prepare a set of financial statements from your accounting system on a quarterly basis. The three key financial statements include the balance sheet, the income statement, and the cash flow statement. A longer discussion of the importance of these financial statements, as well as free templates to create them for your own business, is available in the forms library of the SBA website, www.sba.gov.

c.   Audited Annual Financial Statements

As soon as you can afford it, I recommend you pay for a set of audited financial statements. Expect them to cost anywhere from $5,000 to $20,000 the first time. The price will unfortunately increase each year, as your business grows into a more complex organization with bigger stacks of financial records. Businesses with an operating history of one to three years and that have reached an annual expense level exceeding $750,000 are normally at a point where they can justify the expense of an annual audit.

Few private businesses are legally required to provide audits (though the SEC requires them of all companies whose securities are publicly traded). Nevertheless, audits are a cornerstone to establishing credibility with professional investors.

To perform an audit, you would hire a certified public accountant (a CPA). CPAs are trained to understand and adhere to generally accepted accounting practices, known as GAAP. The CPA will probably set up camp in your office for several days. He or she will ask for every piece of financial information you've got, including payroll reports, invoices, and detailed reports from your accounting software. The CPA will review all this with the eye of a detective, one trained to find both honest mistakes and deliberate deceptions in your accounting practices.

At the end of the audit, the CPA will give a professional opinion about whether your numbers fairly represent the business. He or she will prepare a new set of the three major financial accounting statements— the balance sheet, the income statement, and the cash flow statement— accompanied by a cover letter summarizing the findings.

Most businesses will receive "an unqualified opinion," in which the auditor states that the accounting practices used by the business follow the rules and fairly present its true financial position. This assessment is also called "a clean opinion" and is what all companies hope for. CPAs may also issue a "qualified opinion," indicating concern about a piece of information or the lack of a piece of critical information. Finally, an auditor can issue an "adverse opinion." This indicates that even though the auditor has prepared financial statements, deviations in the business's accounting practices are serious enough to make the financial statements potentially misleading.

d.   Annual Report

The annual report is the ultimate of all business communications documents—typically a glossy document intended to show off the business at its best and costing many thousand dollars to produce. Luckily, you probably won't need to do your first annual report until you've been in operation for several years and have a large group of investors clamoring for it.

Although public companies are required to publish an annual report for shareholders, private businesses aren't. However, even without such a requirement, many private businesses will decide that the cost of writing, designing, and printing the document is worth the communications benefit.

Annual reports tend to include:

- a letter from the President or CEO
- a description of your business's products or services
- a description of your business's customers
- a breakdown of your business's activities over the course of the past year, usually by product category
- the audited financial statements for the year, and
- a list of board members and staff.

e.   An Investor Relations Page on Your Website

If you have a website, you might create a password-protected page where you post items of particular interest to your investors, including financial reports, business update letters, and your annual report. There's no need to create anything new just for this page. Simply use the materials you already send to investors or share with them in meetings. The point is to put all the material in one place in electronic form, so investors can go there and quickly get something they need.

Creating a special page for investors also allows you to refer them to it when they call and ask for something specific, rather than spending the time faxing or sending emails. CircleLending's investors requested such a page, and so I created it and update it regularly. They love to know that it's there, but I know from checking the electronic sign-in sheet that they rarely visit it!

B. If You Received Loan Capital

If you brought in loans as part of your business capital, your ongoing job as a borrower—at least, when it comes to basic legal or other requirements—is relatively straightforward. Know when your payments are due, and make them on time. (See Section 1, below.) If you happen to hit a stretch where you have difficulty repaying, talk to your lender about ways to adjust the repayment schedule until you get back on your feet. (See Section 2, below.)

1. Paying on Time

Of course, you have every intention of fulfilling your financial obligations to your lender by making your payments as promised. However, you wouldn't be the first busy entrepreneur to look at the calendar and realize in horror that the first of the month has come and gone. Strategies for avoiding such embarrassments or disasters are to:

- know your promissory note inside and out
- create a repayment schedule, and
- keep a loan log.

⚠️ **You and your lender should have already agreed on the logistics of making your payments.** Will you be mailing a check to your lender's home address? Making a direct deposit to a bank account? If this wasn't spelled out in your promissory note, you and your lender must agree to a procedure and arrange the details *before* the first payment comes due. The best time to do this is at the closing, when the promissory note and the money change hands (as described in the last section of Chapter 8).

a. Reading the Promissory Note

I am regularly surprised by how many borrowers (and lenders) never take the time to read their own promissory note. Maybe they're daunted by the legal language, or maybe they think that by signing the note, the rest will take care of itself. Hopefully, by using this book, you've already drafted a note that is written in plain English and understandable to the average reader. Now take the time to read your copy of the note again. Make sure there are no surprises and that you know how and when to fulfill the obligation it represents.

b.   Creating Your Repayment Schedule

Referring to the final version of your promissory note, use a loan calculator (like the ones on the CD-ROM at the back of this book) to generate a final repayment schedule. The schedule will tell you the due date for each payment and the total payment due. It will also break each payment down into its two components, principal and interest.

> **It's easy to mistakenly rely on a draft repayment schedule.** While you were still discussing options with your lender, you probably had a few draft repayment schedules fluttering around. And even if you thought you had a final schedule, but you and your lender made a last-minute adjustment to the loan start date, perhaps advancing it by a week, that would have thrown off the whole repayment schedule. Double check that you're using the latest version.

Print out the final schedule and keep it handy—tape it to your wall, write reminders into your calendar, and do whatever else you have to do to stay on top of your obligation. While an amortized schedule might be easy to remember (in which, for example, you owe $200 each month on the 1st of the month), other types of schedules might not be so obvious or unchanging.

To prepare yourself for reading your repayment schedule, look at the samples below. The first sample (generated using the loan calculators accessible from the enclosed CD-ROM) shows an amortized $10,000 loan with 8% interest due over a period of two years. As you'll see from the table, each monthly payment of $452.27 goes toward paying down both the principal and the interest on the loan.

Sample Repayment Schedule for Amortized Loan

Payment Schedule

Due date	Principal	Interest	Total
2/1/2006	$385.60	$66.67	$452.27
3/1/2006	388.17	64.10	452.27
4/1/2006	390.76	61.51	452.27
5/1/2006	393.37	58.90	452.27
6/1/2006	395.99	56.28	452.27
7/1/2006	398.63	53.64	452.27
8/1/2006	401.29	50.98	452.27
9/1/2006	403.96	48.31	452.27
10/1/2006	406.66	45.61	452.27
11/1/2006	409.37	42.90	452.27
12/1/2006	412.10	40.17	452.27
1/1/2007	414.84	37.43	452.27
2/1/2007	417.61	34.66	452.27
3/1/2007	420.39	31.88	452.27
4/1/2007	423.19	29.08	452.27
5/1/2007	426.02	26.25	452.27
6/1/2007	428.86	23.41	452.27
7/1/2007	431.72	20.55	452.27
8/1/2007	434.59	17.68	452.27
9/1/2007	437.49	14.78	452.27
10/1/2007	440.41	11.86	452.27
11/1/2007	443.34	8.93	452.27
12/1/2007	446.30	5.97	452.27
1/1/2008	449.34	3.00	452.34
Total	**$10,000.00**	**$854.55**	**$10,854.55**

The next sample repayment schedule is for a seasonal loan. It shows you how repayment amounts would vary on a two-year, $10,000 loan with 8% interest where monthly payments were set higher during the expected busy season, and lower during the slow season. If you've signed onto such a loan, you'll need to keep track of what month you're in and what amount is due.

Sample Repayment Schedule for Seasonal Loan

Payment Schedule

Due date	Principal	Interest	Total
2/1/2006	$250.00	$50.00	$300.00
3/1/2006	250.00	50.00	300.00
4/1/2006	250.00	50.00	300.00
5/1/2006	250.00	50.00	300.00
6/1/2006	750.00	50.00	800.00
7/1/2006	750.00	50.00	800.00
8/1/2006	750.00	50.00	800.00
9/1/2006	750.00	50.00	800.00
10/1/2006	250.00	50.00	300.00
11/1/2006	250.00	50.00	300.00
12/1/2006	250.00	50.00	300.00
1/1/2007	250.00	50.00	300.00
2/1/2007	250.00	50.00	300.00
3/1/2007	250.00	50.00	300.00
4/1/2007	250.00	50.00	300.00
5/1/2007	250.00	50.00	300.00
6/1/2007	750.00	50.00	800.00
7/1/2007	750.00	50.00	800.00
8/1/2007	750.00	50.00	800.00
9/1/2007	750.00	50.00	800.00
10/1/2007	250.00	50.00	300.00
11/1/2007	250.00	50.00	300.00
12/1/2007	250.00	50.00	300.00
1/1/2008	250.00	50.00	300.00
Total	**$10,000.00**	**$1,200.00**	**$11,200.00**

The next sample repayment table is for a graduated loan, which starts low and increases step by step over time. The following schedule shows a $10,000, two-year loan with a graduated repayment plan with two steps. The payments will change after the first year. Just when the borrower is getting used to one amount, it will to shift to a higher one. Again, you'll want to keep such a table someplace handy, so you don't lose track of those changing amounts.

Sample Repayment Schedule for a Graduated Loan

Payment Schedule

Due date	Principal	Interest	Total
2/1/2006	$277.78	$66.67	$344.44
3/1/2006	277.78	66.67	344.44
4/1/2006	277.78	66.67	344.44
5/1/2006	277.78	66.67	344.44
6/1/2006	277.78	66.67	344.44
7/1/2006	277.78	66.67	344.44
8/1/2006	277.78	66.67	344.44
9/1/2006	277.78	66.67	344.44
10/1/2006	277.78	66.67	344.44
11/1/2006	277.78	66.67	344.44
12/1/2006	277.78	66.67	344.44
1/1/2007	277.78	66.67	344.44
2/1/2007	555.56	44.44	600.00
3/1/2007	555.56	44.44	600.00
4/1/2007	555.56	44.44	600.00
5/1/2007	555.56	44.44	600.00
6/1/2007	555.56	44.44	600.00
7/1/2007	555.56	44.44	600.00
8/1/2007	555.56	44.44	600.00
9/1/2007	555.56	44.44	600.00
10/1/2007	555.56	44.44	600.00
11/1/2007	555.56	44.44	600.00
12/1/2007	555.56	44.44	600.00
1/1/2008	555.56	44.44	600.00
Total	**$10,000.00**	**$1,333.33**	**$11,333.33**

The last sample repayment schedule shows an interest-only loan, again for $10,000 over two years. You'll see that while monthly payments remain low, the last payment will include a much larger balloon payment—which you wouldn't want to forget is coming.

Sample Repayment Schedule for an Interest-Only Loan

Payment Schedule

Due date	Principal	Interest	Total
2/1/2006	$0.00	$66.67	$66.67
3/1/2006	0.00	66.67	66.67
4/1/2006	0.00	66.67	66.67
5/1/2006	0.00	66.67	66.67
6/1/2006	0.00	66.67	66.67
7/1/2006	0.00	66.67	66.67
8/1/2006	0.00	66.67	66.67
9/1/2006	0.00	66.67	66.67
10/1/2006	0.00	66.67	66.67
11/1/2006	0.00	66.67	66.67
12/1/2006	0.00	66.67	66.67
1/1/2007	0.00	66.67	66.67
2/1/2007	0.00	66.67	66.67
3/1/2007	0.00	66.67	66.67
4/1/2007	0.00	66.67	66.67
5/1/2007	0.00	66.67	66.67
6/1/2007	0.00	66.67	66.67
7/1/2007	0.00	66.67	66.67
8/1/2007	0.00	66.67	66.67
9/1/2007	0.00	66.67	66.67
10/1/2007	0.00	66.67	66.67
11/1/2007	0.00	66.67	66.67
12/1/2007	0.00	66.67	66.67
1/1/2008	10,000.00	66.67	10,066.67
Total	$10,000.00	$1,600.00	$11,600.00

c.   Keeping a Loan Log

At times, you may need to double check whether you actually made a previous payment (assuming you are managing your repayment yourself). For this purpose, you should create a record of your payments, often called a "loan log." While the repayment schedule tells you what you *should* do, the loan log is intended to document what you *actually* do.

Even if you've got a perfect memory, your lender may not. The loan log turns into an excellent tool for preserving the relationship between you and your lender, providing an immediate reference source if your lender believes you've missed a payment. The log also allows you to see how close you are to the finish line.

If others need to get involved in your affairs, a loan log will tell them the exact status of the loan. For example, if you or your lender were to die before the loan had been paid off, whoever was managing the estate would be pleased to find the loan log. It documents your progress in repaying the loan, allowing you, or your lender's estate administrator, to figure out the extent of the remaining obligation.

To create a loan log, set up a spreadsheet like the one below. A template is available in Appendix B, and on the CD-ROM at the back of this book.

Loan Log

Payment number	Payment due date	Total amount due	Payment paid date	Total amount paid	Principal paid	Interest paid	Date paid late	Evidence of payment	Other

Record the following information in your loan log each time you make a payment:

- **Payment number.** Give each payment a number, from "1" through your last payment (normally corresponding to the payment numbers on your repayment schedule).

- **Payment due date.** In most cases, payments are due on the first of the month. Check your promissory note or payment schedule to be sure.
- **Total amount due.** This is the total amount you owe on the payment.
- **Payment paid date.** Enter the date you actually send the check or make the payment.
- **Total amount paid.** This is the total amount for which you write the check or otherwise pay. If it isn't the amount listed on your repayment schedule, explain this in the far right column.
- **Principal paid.** This amount will probably come directly from your repayment schedule. However, sometimes borrowers like to pay ahead or pay down either interest or principal. If you do this, you'll probably need to recalculate the repayment schedule.
- **Interest paid.** See "Principal paid," above.
- **Date paid late.** If you pay late, indicate the date.
- **Late fee.** If your payment was late and you agreed to a late fee in your promissory note, note here how much you paid.
- **Evidence of payment.** If you paid with a check, write down the check number. If you're using a direct deposit system, examine your account and note the date the deposit went in. If, in the future, anyone questions whether or not you made a payment, this is the place where you should go to obtain that evidence.
- **Other.** If any other unusual circumstances arose, or you and your lender verbally agreed to any change related to this particular payment, note these here. For example, if the lender forgave the payment knowing that you had a difficult month, mention that here.

You might recommend that your lender keep a loan log as well. The only difference from yours should be that your lender's log has a column for the dates when he or she receives your payments, as opposed to the dates when you sent them.

Entrepreneur Finds the Limits of His Uncle's Flexibility

Dante had always wanted to take pictures for a living. After honing his photography skills and developing an impressive list of contacts, he finally put together a business plan and asked his Uncle Al to lend him $66,500.

Uncle Al agreed to a fairly generous loan: 0% interest, to be repaid on an amortized schedule (regular payments) over a term of five and a half years. Payments on the principal-only loan worked out to just over $1,000 a month, and Dante launched his venture.

Unfortunately, the 9/11 attacks occurred just months later. Not only was the business community in shock, but the World Trade Towers were among the very landmarks that Dante had planned to use in his work.

Dante described for Uncle Al the difficulties in signing new clients, and the two agreed to cut Dante's payments in half for six months. They hoped that the market would start moving by then. After the six months passed, the loan reverted to the original payment plan of about $1,000 due each month.

Before long, Dante realized that he just couldn't keep up with that full payment, and he asked his uncle for another break. Uncle Al agreed to another six months of half payments. Dante made those payments; $500 seemed an amount he could handle. When the six months were up, he once again asked Uncle Al to agree to a half-payment schedule.

Uncle Al said no. He'd decided he couldn't let the wrangling continue and wanted a repayment schedule to which Dante would adhere. After a difficult conversation in which Uncle Al expressed feeling taken advantage of, and Dante faced up to the painful economic realities of his struggling business, the two came up with a plan. Dante would keep his business but do it on the side, and would take a new job allowing him to repay the $1,000 per month he owed on the loan.

As it turns out, Dante's paycheck from his new job arrives the day his loan payment is due each month, so that his loan repayment check arrives at his uncle's home within the seven-day allotted grace period. This is by no means the happy ending Dante had envisioned. But the private loan gave Dante a chance to get started and gave the pair the flexibility to make adjustments to handle the vagaries of Dante's business.

2.   Acting Responsibly When You Can't Make a Payment

Cash flow crunches are not uncommon in the life of a small business. Perhaps a major customer cancels an order, the price of raw materials goes up dramatically, or you lose the day job that was helping you support your new venture. It's possible to weather both minor and major disasters—but not if you put your head in the sand and hope they go away.

Once you've recognized that a cash flow crunch is looming, check your repayment schedule to see if you'll have a problem making your payments in full, on time. Communication is key: Whether you need a short-term or a long-term change in your loan agreement, talk to your lender. While no agreement can completely soften the blow of a missed payment, most entrepreneurs find that their friends and family would rather find out about cash flow problems early on than have you keep them a secret until the business goes under. Family and friend lenders' first instincts are usually to want to help you, perhaps by modifying the repayment schedule, before the problem becomes a crisis.

Before talking to your lender, reread your promissory note. It will tell you how you agreed to handle late or missed payments.

Although you may feel embarrassed to admit to your difficulties, you'll only look worse if your lender has to figure out him- or herself that your payment is late—leading the lender to believe that you're an irresponsible borrower. In addition, it's only considerate to let your lender know that a payment will not arrive when expected. Your lender may be counting on your payment to pay his or her own bills from the same bank account.

Depending on the severity of your cash crunch, you can use one of the following strategies when you can't make a full payment by your due date:

- Make the most of the grace period.
- Offer an alternative, such as a partial payment.
- Restructure the entire schedule.

a.   Making the Most of Your Grace Period

Double check your promissory note to see whether it includes a grace period; that is, a preset number of days between when your loan payment is due and when it is considered overdue enough to charge you a late fee or put you in default. Family and friend lenders tend to use grace periods of ten to 15 days. A grace period of ten days, for example, means that although your payment may be due on the 1st of the month, you can't be penalized until after the 10th.

You can use your grace period to hold off making your loan payment until you have sufficient cash, if the timing is that close. Nevertheless, you should advise your lender that the payment won't be arriving on the due date.

⚠ Don't abuse your grace period. If you always make your payments on the last day of the grace period, you may give the impression that you are taking advantage of your lender. Make paying by your due date your habit, and use the grace period only when absolutely necessary.

b.   Offering Your Lender an Alternative

If you are unable to make a payment one month—but don't yet believe the situation is critical enough to restructure the entire loan agreement—you and your lender can agree to one of several options. For example, you might skip a payment but make it up later (extending the loan term by one additional payment period). Or, your lender can agree that you'll spread out the payment across several subsequent payments. You'll have to calculate this—for example, by dividing your payment by ten and adding that amount to each of your next ten payments. Finally, your lender could forgive the payment entirely (nothing forces your lender to pursue any remedies at all).

These solutions do not require any changes to the original loan documents. But you should write up a brief description of the solution to your missed payment problem, sign it and have your lender do the same, and keep it with your records.

If, however, you find yourself on the phone with your lender every month or two requesting an alternative payment method, it may be time to think about completely restructuring your loan agreement.

Is there no chance that you can catch up or keep up with the repayment schedule in your promissory note? Your best bet may be to hire a professional to help you completely restructure your loan with a realistic payment schedule.

c.   Changing Your Repayment Schedule

At a certain point, you may realize that your existing loan agreement just isn't realistic given the current state of your business or the market. For example, perhaps you're bringing in some revenue, but it's never quite enough to cover both your loan payments and your rent. Under such circumstances, you'll appreciate the flexibility of working with friends and family members. After all, their main goal is to help you succeed, not to tighten the screws and squeeze every dollar out of you by the due date.

If circumstances are causing you to regularly pay late or miss your payments altogether, perhaps a different payment schedule (lower payments, a longer interval between payments, or some similar change) might work better. Most private lenders will be only too happy to negotiate such a change in your payment schedule if it means you can resume making regular payments. Of course, I'm not recommending you take advantage of your lender's willingness to be flexible. The object here is to come to an arrangement that ultimately allows you to pay the debt in full, not to wiggle out of your payment obligations.

When it comes to restructuring the loan, your options include stretching out your payments over a longer term, selecting a lower interest rate, or switching to a different type of repayment plan (for example, one with different payments during busy and slow seasons). The loan calculators available on the enclosed CD-ROM will help you experiment with different types of payment schedules. Note that when you make changes to the terms of a loan that result in a new payment schedule, you need to draw up a new promissory note.

Changing the Loan Agreement When Profits Don't Meet Projections

Maria borrowed $10,000 from a friend to help launch her dream restaurant in Santa Fe, New Mexico. It was an upscale eatery featuring vegetarian Mexican food. Knowing that restaurants are expensive to start, and that it would take several months to earn enough to make significant loan payments, Maria and her friend negotiated a graduated loan with 5.5% interest, to be paid back over the course of three years. According to the schedule, in the first year Maria would make monthly payments of $184; in the second year her payments would increase to $316; and in the third and final year of the loan, she would pay $439 each month.

A few months into the second year, however, Maria realized that the restaurant's sales were not increasing as quickly as she had projected. Making the higher ($316) monthly payments was becoming a major problem.

Fortunately, Maria had been good about communicating with her friend/lender. She'd shared with her all the good news her first year of business had brought and felt comfortable talking with her about the loan. Maria sat down with her lender, showed her the numbers, and said that she feared that unless they restructured the loan she'd have to default. Her lender agreed with Maria's assessment, and the two calculated the remainder due on the loan, about $7,600, and set it up as a new loan.

The new agreement was for an amortized loan at a 7% interest rate for a term of nearly five years. (Maria chose the amortized structure because she specifically didn't want an increase in loan payments to sneak up on her.) This helped Maria by bringing the monthly payments down below $200. The higher interest rate, meanwhile, compensated the lender for the fact that she'd have to wait longer for the entire principal to be repaid.

This isn't the end of the story, however. Although Maria was doing well at making the monthly payments, she realized that the growing business needed new kitchen equipment—which would cost $40,000. Impressed at Maria's creativity in accessing flexible capital, her business partner, Ana, looked to her own circle of contacts. Ana didn't have to look far. Her father agreed to finance the purchase at 6% for three years. The restaurant now makes direct monthly payments of $1,216 into his bank account, as planned in their promissory note.

3.   If You Have No Choice but to Default

Chances are that you'll ultimately find some way to repay your loan, so long as you communicate with your lender about cash difficulties and restructure the agreement as necessary. Default on a private loan is extremely rare. But disaster can always strike—for example, if an irreplaceable business partner dies or your lender develops his or her own financial difficulties and can't be flexible about your loan.

A mediator can help you repair communications with your lender. If you are resorting to default because you and your lender have stopped communicating about your difficulties repaying the loan, consider hiring a mediation service. It's far more cost-effective to pay a neutral third party to help you negotiate a restructured payment plan than to face the penalties of not paying your lender back at all. Also see *Mediate, Don't Litigate: Strategies for Successful Mediation*, by Peter Lovenheim and Lisa Guerin (Nolo).

According to the promissory note, once you have missed a payment, your lender has the right to initiate a collections process. Your lender, an attorney, or another professional may begin sending you a series of sternly worded letters demanding repayment. The culmination of this process is usually a report of your default to the national credit agencies. This could seriously damage your future ability to borrow funds from any institutional lender for either business or personal use.

The only silver lining to your default is that your lender will probably be able to claim the unpaid amount on his or her taxes as a non-business bad debt. This is known as a short-term capital loss and is reported on the lender's Schedule D. All the lender will need to do is write a letter to you demanding repayment, then a memo for his or her file stating that the loan is uncollectible. You may be able to help your lender successfully get this past the IRS by providing a financial statement showing your inability to pay your debts.

Want more information on the rules and requirements for bad debt deductions? See IRS Publication 550, *Investment Income and Expenses*, specifically the subsection of Chapter 4 called "Nonbusiness Bad Debts." It's available at the IRS website, www.irs.gov.

Your lender has legal grounds on which to sue you if there is no other way to collect payment on the loan. Alternately, the lender can foreclose on the collateral you provided if the loan agreement included a security interest. Lawsuits and foreclosures are rare in private lending. Most family and friends would rather live with a bad-debt tax deduction than start litigation against someone they know. In fact, among CircleLending's clients, less than 0.25% actually end up in the courts.

C. If You Received Equity Investments

One of the most attractive benefits of equity capital is that you can spend the money on your business without worrying about monthly or quarterly payments. Of course, that doesn't let you off the hook completely. Your investors, especially the business angels, will be watching closely to make sure that you hit the revenue targets and other goals you set for yourself in your business plan. Chances are they invested in you because they saw the potential to make a buck and be a part of an exciting venture.

Your investors have an expectation of growth, and that's up to you to fulfill. (See Section 1, below.) At the same time, you'll need to manage your investors' expectations, to keep them in line with your plans. (See Section 2, below.) Finally, once you have investors, you'll soon need to assemble a board of directors. (See Section 3, below.)

1. Growing Your Business

The secret to growing your business is good planning—which means setting and reaching your goals. In a start-up business, things change so fast that you really need to set your goals on a quarterly basis. This keeps your focus on the short term, where it should be. Here's how to do it.

Set goals. Take the time to write down your business goals for the upcoming quarter. These will probably include broad goals set out in your business plan—which is where you should begin—but don't stop there. Spell out the quarterly goals required to meet the larger goals in your plan. Then, break each goal down into bite-size pieces, or tasks.

For each task, identify a "champion" (someone who will be accountable for getting the job done) and a deadline. Once you've taken these steps, those vague or lofty business goals should seem more achievable. Plus, once you've written down the tasks involved in reaching a goal, it's much easier to measure your progress in achieving them.

Communicate those goals. One entrepreneur I know believes so strongly in planning and setting quarterly goals that each quarter, he and his leadership team draft a memo setting forth everything that needs to be done (in the format described above). A revenue goal for each product line is stated up front, and then the rest of the memo spells out each and every task needed to meet the revenue goal. Employees get to view and comment on the draft. The draft document is reviewed one last time at a quarterly meeting.

When the meeting is over, the planning memo becomes a road map to everything that happens or should happen in the business in the coming quarter. Employees are held accountable to the tasks and deadlines to which they agreed. Communicating business goals with a simple tool like this planning memo ensures that the goals are concrete and meaningful and create a shared sense of purpose.

Sample Goal and Tasks Detail From a Quarterly Planning Memo

Goal: Increase sales of newest stunt kite model ZZZ.

> **Task 1:** Place ad in registration booklet for annual stunt kite competition.
> > *Champion: Sam Watt*
> > *Deadline: June 1, 2006*

> **Task 2:** Send sample to stunt kite association for new product review printed on their website and in monthly magazine.
> > *Champion: Bram Hollis*
> > *Deadline: June 15, 2006*

> **Task 3:** Hire amateur fliers to demonstrate kite at competition free fly.
> > *Champion: Margaret Ray*
> > *Deadline: July 15, 2006*

Meet those goals. If need be, motivate your employees to achieve their tasks. Sales staff nearly always has a "number to meet" and a bonus attached if they meet it. Sometimes a simple pep talk will do. If you receive a phone call or a letter from a satisfied customer, share it widely, particularly if you can congratulate one of your employees on a job well done.

Be willing to change the goals. Recognize that the best-laid plan is only a plan, and your ability to adapt your goals to reflect change is a sign of flexibility, not failure. Whether the unexpected force at work is the economy, customer preferences, or the reality of a task taking longer than expected, be alert and adjust or change your goals as needed. For example, the entrepreneur who owns the kite business portrayed in the sample memo above doesn't just draft the memo and then forget about it. He also holds a mid-quarter review session to check in with his employees. For each goal and task, the person designated as "champion" reports on tasks completed or proposes a new deadline and explains why the original deadline is now unworkable.

 Want more practical as well as legal information on growing a business that you'll enjoy being a part of? See:

- *Legal Guide for Starting & Running a Small Business*, by Fred S. Steingold (Nolo), which covers everything from negotiating with your landlord to dealing with customers to handling employees; and
- *How to Run a Thriving Business: Strategies for Success & Satisfaction*, by Ralph Warner (Nolo), which teaches you how to market creatively and keep your competitive edge, all while avoiding working long hours.

2. Managing Investor Expectations

You'll need to manage your investors' expectations after their investments are made. After all, each one has high hopes for you. Make sure that those high hopes both (a) stay in touch with your business reality and (b) don't become a burden.

The best tool for keeping investor expectations in line with your business reality is forthright and consistent communications, as described in the first section of this chapter. As long as you're sharing information, and the investor is reviewing it, there shouldn't be any surprises on either side. For example, an annual business letter gives you the chance each year to reset expectations to match what you think is reasonable for the upcoming year.

An investor with unmet expectations gets disappointed, and may even feel deceived. He or she is likely to get very involved in the life of the business, to try to fix whatever the perceived problem may be. Meet with the investor to try to adjust his or expectations to be more in line with your reality. If that doesn't work, you may even need to confront the investor and say that the extra involvement is becoming a burden to you and to the company. Ultimately, the investor's interest is the same as yours—to grow a successful company—so you should be able to reach a solution (such as a schedule for delivery of monthly financial statements) that will ease the investor's concern.

Sometimes investors need to touch base in person. If you have a high-touch investor like this, try scheduling regular update meetings, even when you have nothing major to discuss. The last thing you want with this type of investor is to hold meetings only after problems have arisen. Without having created a history of positive, calm meetings, every negative meeting will probably require two subsequent meetings in order to get back on track.

3. Creating a Board of Directors

If you've sold shares in your business, it's fairly safe to assume that, for legal reasons, you structured your business as a corporation or LLC.

If in fact you formed a corporation, your corporate bylaws will require you to designate one or more directors as decision makers for your company. Although some states allow for only one to three directors of a corporation, the more investors you bring on, the more will want to sit on your board and be involved in decision making. If you formed an LLC, you have the option of electing certain members of the LLC to become its managers, similar to a corporation's directors. But there is no requirement that an LLC have managers.

 Need more information on your legal obligations when running a corporation or LLC? See:

- *The Corporate Records Handbook: Meetings, Minutes, & Resolutions*, by Anthony Mancuso (Nolo), or
- *Your Limited Liability Company: An Operating Manual*, by Anthony Mancuso (Nolo).

Finding and Using Advisers

Running a business requires an amazing variety of skills. You've got to know about the product or service you're selling, manage a physical space, oversee people, crunch numbers, deal with paperwork, and much more. It probably wouldn't hurt to get some outside advice once in a while.

Fortunately, your group of equity investors provides a ready pool of advisers, perhaps even for help with difficult decisions. Even those who don't hold a decision-making role can be called upon for some informal input. Don't be concerned, however, if your equity investors' group doesn't supply all the expertise you need. Look for advisers in your own industry and through local business mentoring services.

Some businesses choose to form an advisory board. If you decide to go this route, you'll need to clearly set your expectations of the members in advance. Otherwise, you'll find that most advisory board members expect to be little more than figureheads, lending their impressive names to your publicity materials. Rarely do such folks actually roll up their sleeves and help you figure out how to balance paying your employees and paying the rent.

Follow these priorities when looking for advisers:

- Find someone with skills, information, or contacts you'll need in the short term. You'll need help leaping the hurdles you face in the next three months before you think about the next three years.
- Find someone well known in your field who can lend you credibility when you most need it to attract customers, good employees, and investors.
- Find an adviser who is content to receive a free lunch on the day of a meeting rather than one who insists on receiving shares in the company. As your company grows and takes more of the adviser's time, you should consider instituting both cash- and stock-compensation schemes.

Appendix A

How to Use the CD-ROM

A. Installing the Files Onto Your Computer 291

    1. Windows 9x, 2000, Me, and XP Users 291

    2. Macintosh Users 291

B. Using the Word Processing Files to Create Documents 291

    Step 1: Opening a File 292

    Step 2: Editing Your Document 293

    Step 3: Printing Out the Document 294

    Step 4: Saving Your Document 294

C. Using the UCC Financing Statement 295

    Step 1: Opening a Form 295

    Step 2: Filling in a Form 296

    Step 3: Printing a Form 296

D. Accessing the Online Resources 297

Τhe forms in Appendix B as well as links to useful online resources and loan calculators are included on a CD-ROM in the back of the book. This CD-ROM, which can be used with Windows computers, installs files that you use with software programs that are already installed on your computer. It is *not* a standalone software program. Please read this appendix and the README.TXT file included on the CD-ROM for instructions on using the Forms CD.

Note to Mac users: This CD-ROM and its files should also work on Macintosh computers. Please note, however, that Nolo cannot provide technical support for non-Windows users.

How to View the README File

If you do not know how to view the file README.TXT, insert the Forms CD-ROM into your computer's CD-ROM drive and follow these instructions:

- Windows 9x, 2000, Me, and XP: (1) On your PC's desktop, double click the My Computer icon; (2) double click the icon for the CD-ROM drive into which the Forms CD-ROM was inserted; (3) double click the file README.TXT.
- Macintosh: (1) On your Mac desktop, double click the icon for the CD-ROM that you inserted; (2) double click on the file README.TXT.

While the README file is open, print it out by using the Print command in the File menu.

Three different kinds of resources are contained on the CD-ROM:

- Word processing (RTF) forms that you can open, complete, print save with your word processing program (see Section B, below)
- A UCC Financing Statement from the International Association of Commercial Administrators that can be viewed only with Adobe Acrobat Reader 4.0 or higher. (See Section C, below.) This form has "fill-in" text fields and can be completed using your computer. You will not, however, be able to save the completed form with the filled-in data.
- Links to online resources and loan calculators that can be viewed through your web browser.

See Appendix B for a list of forms, their file names, and their file formats.

A. Installing the Files Onto Your Computer

Before you can do anything with the files on the CD-ROM, you need to install them onto your hard disk. In accordance with U.S. copyright laws, remember that copies of the CD-ROM and its files are for your personal use only.

Insert the Forms CD and do the following.

1. Windows 9x, 2000, Me, and XP Users

Follow the instructions that appear on the screen. (If nothing happens when you insert the Forms CD-ROM, then (1) double click the My Computer icon; (2) double click the icon for the CD-ROM drive into which the Forms CD-ROM was inserted; (3) double click the file WELCOME.EXE.)

By default, all the files are installed to the \Business Financing Resources folder in the \Program Files folder of your computer. A folder called "Business Financing Resources" is added to the "Programs" folder of the Start menu.

2. Macintosh Users

Step 1: If the "Business Financing CD" window is not open, open it by double clicking the "Business Financing CD" icon.
Step 2: Select the "Business Financing Resources" folder icon.
Step 3: Drag and drop the folder icon onto the icon of your hard disk.

B. Using the Word Processing Files to Create Documents

This section concerns the files for forms that can be opened and edited with your word processing program.

All word processing forms come in rich text format. These files have the extension ".RTF." For example, the form for the Best Bets List discussed in Chapter 4 is in the file BestBetsList.rtf. All forms, their file names, and their file formats are listed in Appendix B.

RTF files can be read by most recent word processing programs including all versions of MS Word for Windows and Macintosh, WordPad for Windows, and recent versions of WordPerfect for Windows and Macintosh.

To use a form from the CD to create your documents you must (1) open a file in your word processor or text editor; (2) edit the form by filling in the required information; (3) print it out; (4) rename and save your revised file.

The following are general instructions. However, each word processor uses different commands to open, format, save, and print documents. Please read your word processor's manual for specific instructions on performing these tasks.

Do not call Nolo's technical support if you have questions on how to use your word processor.

Step 1: Opening a File

There are three ways to open the word processing files included on the CD-ROM after you have installed them onto your computer.

- Windows users can open a file by selecting its "shortcut" as follows: (1) Click the Windows "Start" button; (2) open the "Programs" folder; (3) open the "Business Financing Resources" subfolder; (4) open the "Forms and Letters" subfolder; (5) click on the shortcut to the form you want to work with.
- Both Windows and Macintosh users can open a file directly by double clicking on it. Use My Computer or Windows Explorer (Windows 9x, 2000, Me, or XP) or the Finder (Macintosh) to go to the folder you installed or copied the CD-ROM's files to. Then, double click on the specific file you want to open.
- You can also open a file from within your word processor. To do this, you must first start your word processor. Then, go to the File menu and choose the Open command. This opens a dialog box where you will tell the program (1) the type of file you want to open (*.RTF) and (2) the location and name of the file (you will

need to navigate through the directory tree to get to the folder on your hard disk where the CD's files have been installed). If these directions are unclear you will need to look through the manual for your word processing program—Nolo's technical support department will *not* be able to help you with the use of your word processing program.

Where Are the Files Installed?

Windows users
- RTF files are installed by default to a folder named \Business Financing Resources\Forms and Letters in the \Program Files folder of your computer.

Macintosh users
- RTF files are located in the "Forms and Letters" folder within the "Business Financing Resources" folder.

Step 2: Editing Your Document

Fill in the appropriate information according to the instructions and sample agreements in the book. Underlines are used to indicate where you need to enter your information, frequently followed by instructions in brackets. Be sure to delete the underlines and instructions from your edited document. You will also want to make sure that any signature lines in your completed documents appear on a page with at least some text from the document itself. If you do not know how to use your word processor to edit a document, you will need to look through the manual for your word processing program—Nolo's technical support department will *not* be able to help you with the use of your word processing program.

Editing Forms That Have Optional or Alternative Text

Some of the forms have optional or alternate text:

- With optional text, you choose whether to include or exclude the given text.
- With alternative text, you select one alternative to include and exclude the other alternatives.

When editing these forms, we suggest you do the following.

Optional text

If you *don't want* to include optional text, just delete it from your document.

If you *do want* to include optional text, just leave it in your document.

In either case, delete the italicized instructions.

Alternative text

First delete all the alternatives that you do not want to include, then delete the italicized instructions.

Step 3: Printing Out the Document

Use your word processor's or text editor's "Print" command to print out your document. If you do not know how to use your word processor to print a document, you will need to look through the manual for your word processing program—Nolo's technical support department will *not* be able to help you with the use of your word processing program.

Step 4: Saving Your Document

After filling in the form, use the "Save As" command to save and rename the file. Because all the files are "read-only," you will not be able to use the "Save" command. This is for your protection. *If you save the file without renaming it, the underlines that indicate where you need to enter your information will be lost, and you will not be able to create a new document with this file without recopying the original file from the CD-ROM.*

If you do not know how to use your word processor to save a document, you will need to look through the manual for your word processing program—Nolo's technical support department will *not* be able to help you with the use of your word processing program.

C. Using the UCC Financing Statement

An electronic copy of a UCC Financing Statement from the International Association of Commercial Administrators is included on the CD-ROM in Adobe Acrobat PDF format. You must have Adobe Reader installed on your computer to use this form. Adobe Reader is available for all types of Windows and Macintosh systems. If you don't already have this software, you can download it for free at www.adobe.com.

All forms, their file names, and their file formats are listed in Appendix B. This form file was created by the International Association of Commercial Administrators, not by Nolo.

This form has fill-in text fields. To create your document using these file, you must: (1) open a file; (2) fill in the text fields using either your mouse or the tab key on your keyboard to navigate from field to field; and (3) print it out.

Step 1: Opening a Form

PDF files, like the word processing files, can be opened one of three ways.

- Windows users can open a file by selecting its "shortcut" as follows: (1) Click the Windows "Start" button; (2) open the "Programs" folder; (3) open the "Business Financing Resources" subfolder; (4) open the "Forms and Letters" folder; (5) click on the shortcut to the form you want to work with.
- Both Windows and Macintosh users can open a file directly by double clicking on it. Use My Computer or Windows Explorer (Windows 9x, 2000, Me, or XP) or the Finder (Macintosh) to go to the folder you created and copied the CD-ROM's files to. Then, double click on the specific file you want to open.

- You can also open a PDF file from within Adobe Reader. To do this, you must first start Reader. Then, go to the File menu and choose the Open command. This opens a dialog box where you will tell the program the location and name of the file. (You will need to navigate through the directory tree to get to the folder on your hard disk where the CD's files have been installed.) If these directions are unclear you will need to look through Adobe Reader's help—Nolo's technical support department will not be able to help you with the use of Adobe Reader.

Where Are the PDF Files Installed?

- **Windows users:** PDF files are installed by default to a folder named \Business Financing Resources\Forms and Letters in the \Program Files folder of your computer.
- **Macintosh users:** PDF files are located in the "Forms and Letters" folder within the "Business Financing Resources" folder.

Step 2: Filling in a Form

Use your mouse or the Tab key on your keyboard to navigate from field to field within these forms. Be sure to have all the information you will need to complete a form on hand, because you will not be able to save a copy of the filled-in form to disk. You can, however, print out a completed version.

Step 3: Printing a Form

Choose Print from the Acrobat Reader File menu. This will open the Print dialog box. In the "Print Range" section of the Print dialog box, select the appropriate print range, then click OK.

D. Accessing the Online Resources

Links to online resources and loan calculators are also included on the CD-ROM. These online resources are viewed as web pages and must be opened in a web browser. To access these online resources:

- Windows users should (1) click the Windows "Start" button; (2) open the "Programs" folder; (3) open the "Business Financing Resources" subfolder; (4) click on the shortcut for the appropriate link.
- Macintosh users should use Finder to go to the "Business Financing Resources" and open it. Then, double click on the online resources file you want to open.

Appendix B

Forms and Worksheets

Name of form	Discussed in	Disk file name
Best Bets List	Chapter 4	BestBetsList.rtf
Start-Up Costs Worksheet	Chapter 5	StartUpCosts.rtf
Recurring Costs Worksheet	Chapter 5	RecurringCost.rtf
Collateral List	Chapter 6	CollateralList.rtf
Loan Request Letter	Chapter 6	LoanRequest.rtf
Letter of Intent: Simple Version	Chapter 8	IntentSimple.rtf
Letter of Intent: Advanced Version	Chapter 8	IntentAdvanced.rtf
Gift Letter: Basic	Chapter 9	GiftBasic.rtf
Gift Letter: Loan Repayment Forgiveness	Chapter 9	ForgivenessLetter.rtf
Promissory Note (for an amortized loan)	Chapter 9	PromissoryAmortized.rtf
Promissory Note (for a graduated loan)	Chapter 9	PromissoryGraduated.rtf
Promissory Note (for a seasonal loan)	Chapter 9	PromissorySeasonal.rtf
Promissory Note (for an interest-only loan)	Chapter 9	PromissoryInterest.rtf
Promissory Note Modifications for a Loan to a Business	Chapter 9	ModBusiness.rtf
Promissory Note Modifications for Signature by Notary Public	Chapter 9	ModNotary.rtf
Security Agreement	Chapter 9	SecurityAgreement.rtf
UCC Financing Statement	Chapter 9	UCC1.pdf
Loan Log	Chapter 10	LoanLog.rtf

Best Bets List

Prospect Name	Prospect Description	Contact Information	Amount to Request

Start-Up Costs Worksheet

Description	Estimated cost
Legal fees	$
Rent (include deposit and 1st month)	$
Office equipment	$
Insurance (initial premium)	$
Business license	$
Stationery, logos, letterhead	$
Initial advertising	$
Other	$
Total start-up/expansion costs	$

Recurring Costs Worksheet

Description	Estimated monthly cost
Monthly rent	$
Payroll	$
Utilities	$
Insurance	$
Ongoing advertising	$
Association and other memberships	$
Other	$
Total monthly recurring costs	$

Collateral List

Item Description	Approximate Value
Business Assets	
	$
	$
	$
	$
	$
	$
	$
	$
	$
	$
	$
	$
Personal Assets	
	$
	$
	$
	$
	$
	$
	$
	$
	$
	$

Loan Request Letter

[*date*]

[*address line 1*]

[*address line 2*]

[*address line 3*]

Dear Friend and Supporter,

I am excited to tell you about a way for you to support [*business name*] and earn an attractive return. [*Business name*] is raising $[*total loan amount*] from relatives, friends, and business associates, and I thought you might be interested in participating. [*Optional:* Attached to this letter are [*number of*] loan options for you to consider; the loan amount and interest rate varies with each.]

[*Optional:* I've already raised $[*amount*] from family members and from [*awards or other sources*]. I thought you might be interested in providing a loan for the remaining $[*amount*].]

[*Write 1-2 paragraphs here describing the highlights of your business, for example, what you sell, who will buy it, why they'll buy it, and why now is the right time.*]

I offer you this opportunity because I believe it is good for my business and good for you. For me, it allows me to raise the money I need to grow my business from people I trust, and at an affordable rate. For you, the [*interest rate*]% I'm offering provides a competitive short-term return on your money. If you choose to make the loan, [*summarize repayment plan*].

[*Choose one of the next two options:*]

[*Option 1:*] In addition, my proposal offers you the protection of a legally binding loan agreement. If you agree to the loan terms set forth in this letter, I'll prepare a promissory note reflecting my promise to repay the loan at these terms. The loan will start on the day we transfer the funds.

I'll send a check from my business account to the address you specify, will maintain a loan log of my payments, and will have my accountant provide you year-end tax summary reports.

[*OR*]

[*Option 2:*] In addition, my proposal offers you the protection of a legally binding loan agreement and the convenience of a third party to manage the repayment. I have retained [*name and description of third party*] to handle our loan. [*Name of third party*] has created a promissory note for us and will manage the repayment of the loan. My repayments to you will be preauthorized to come out of the [*business name*] corporate account electronically, and the funds will be deposited into a bank account that you designate. [*Name of third party*] will also provide us access to information about payment status history, will maintain records, and will provide year-end tax summary reports.

I hope that you will consider this mutually beneficial opportunity. I truly believe that [*business name*] is poised for success and I look forward to your support in growing the business. Thank you for your consideration; I look forward to discussing this opportunity with you further.

Sincerely,

_____

[*your name*]

_____

[*business name*]

Letter of Intent: Simple Version

[*date*] _____

[*entrepreneur's name*] _____

[*business name*] _____

[*business address*] _____

Dear [*entrepreneur's first name*],

I am considering an investment of $_____ in the business known as [*business name*].

This is a letter of intent to invest, but it does not reflect a binding obligation.

Signature: [*investor's signature*] _____

Name: [*investor's name and address*] _____

Address: [*investor's address*] _____

_____

Date: [*date of signature*] _____

Letter of Intent: Advanced Version

[date] _____

[entrepreneur's name] _____

[business name] _____

[business address] _____

Dear [entrepreneur's name],

I am considering a purchase of [name of type of shares] in the amount of _____ units.

I understand that each unit comprises _____ Preferred Shares (a $ _____ investment at $ _____ per share).

Please forward investment documentation to me at the address below. This is a letter of intent to invest, but it does not reflect a binding obligation.)

Signature: [investor's signature]

Name: [investor's name and address] _____

Address: [investor's address] _____

_____

Date: [date of signature] _____

Gift Letter: Basic

[*recipient name*] _____

[*recipient address*] _____

[*recipient address*] _____

To [*recipient first name*]:

By my signature below, I hereby gift $_____ to you to use as you wish. I expect no repayment or services in return for this gift.

[*signature of giver*] _____

Date: _____

Gift Letter: Loan Repayment Forgiveness

[*borrower name*] _____

[*borrower address*] _____

[*borrower address*] _____

To [*recipient first name*]:

I made a loan of $[*total loan amount*] to you on [*loan date.*] This loan has an upcoming payment due from you to me on [*due date of payment to be forgiven*] in the amount of $_____ ("Loan Payment").

By my signature below, I hereby forgive all of this Loan Payment.

By signing this letter, I understand that I do not waive the right to choose to receive subsequent Loan Payments under the Promissory Note signed by the borrower on [*date note signed*].

[*signature of lender*] _____

Date: _____

Promissory Note (for an amortized loan)

1. **For Value Received,** [*borrower name*] ("Borrower") promises to pay to the order of [*lender name*], of [*city, state*] ("Lender"), the sum, in United States dollars, of [*amount of loan, spelled out*] ($_____) dollars, plus interest accruing at an annual rate of [*interest rate, spelled out*] percent (____%) on the unpaid principal amount beginning on [*loan start day/month/year*] (the "Debt").

2. **Transferability.** Borrower understands that the Lender may transfer this Note. The Lender or anyone who takes this Note by Transfer and who is entitled to receive payments under this Note is called the "Note Holder" and will have the same rights and remedies as the Lender under this Note.

3. **Payments.** Payment of the Debt shall be made in [*choose one: monthly/quarterly/annual*] payments, which include principal and interest, as follows:

   Beginning on [*loan start date*] and continuing [*choose one: monthly/ quarterly/annually*] on the [*for example, 1st or 15th*] day of each [*choose one: month/quarter/year*] (the "Due Date") until [*day/month/ year of last payment*] (the "Final Due Date"), Borrower shall pay to the Lender or Note Holder the sum of $_____ each [*choose one: month/quarter/year*] (the "[*choose one: Monthly/Quarterly/Annual*] Payment"). On the Final Due Date, Borrower shall pay all amounts remaining due under the terms of this Note.

4. **Grace Period and Late Fee.** If the Borrower fails to make any payment in the full amount and within [*number of days spelled out*] ([*number in figures*]) calendar days (the "Grace Period") after the date it is due, Borrower agrees to pay a late charge to the Lender or Note Holder in the amount of $_____ (the "Late Fee"). Borrower will pay this Late Fee promptly but only once on each late payment.

5. **Security.** [*choose one*]

   ☐ This is an unsecured note.

   ☐ Borrower agrees that until this Note is paid in full (including principal and interest, if any), this Note will be secured by a separate security agreement and, if applicable, a Uniform Commercial Code financing statement, giving Lender a security interest in the following property: _[describe asset]_

6. **Default and Acceleration.** If any installment payment due under this Note is not received by Lender within the Grace Period, the note will be in default and the entire amount of unpaid principal will become immediately due and payable at the option of Lender without prior notice of default to Borrower.

7. **Prepayment.** This Note may be prepaid in full at any time without cost or penalty to the Borrower.

8. **Attorneys' Fees.** If Lender prevails in a lawsuit to collect on this note, Borrower agrees to pay Lender's attorneys' fees in an amount the court finds to be just and reasonable.

9. **Waiver.** The undersigned and all other parties to this Note waive the following requirements:

    • presentment of the Note for payment by Lender

    • refusal of payment by Borrower after presentment of the Note by Lender, otherwise known as dishonor, and

    • Lender's notification to Borrower of Borrower's refusal to pay.

10. **Lender's Rights.** Lender's decision not to exercise a right or remedy under this Note at a given time does not waive the Lender's ability to exercise that right or remedy at a later date.

11. **Liability of Individual Borrowers.** The term "Borrower" may refer to one or more borrowers. If there is more than one borrower, they agree to be jointly and severally liable.

12. **Governing Law.** This agreement will be governed by and construed in accordance with the laws of the state of _____.

Borrower's signature: _____

Print name: _____

Date: _____

Promissory Note (for a graduated loan)

1. **For Value Received,** [*borrower name*] ("Borrower") promises to pay to the order of [*lender name*], of [*city, state*] ("Lender"), the sum, in United States dollars, of [*amount of loan, spelled out*] ($_____) dollars, plus interest accruing at an annual rate of [*interest rate, spelled out*] percent (_____%) on the unpaid principal amount beginning on [*loan start day/month/year*] (the "Debt").

2. **Transferability.** Borrower understands that the Lender may transfer this Note. The Lender or anyone who takes this Note by Transfer and who is entitled to receive payments under this Note is called the "Note Holder" and will have the same rights and remedies as the Lender under this Note.

3. **Payments.** Payment of the Debt shall be made in [*choose one: monthly/quarterly/annual*] payments, which include principal and interest, as follows:

   Beginning on [*repayment start day/month/year*] and continuing [*choose one: monthly/quarterly/annually*] on the [*for example, 1st or 15th*] day of each [*choose one: month/quarter/year*] through [*repayment end day/month/year (for first step)*] Borrower shall pay to lender the sum of
   $_____.

   Beginning on [*repayment start date of next step*] and continuing [*choose one: monthly/quarterly/annually*] on the [*for example, 1st or 15th*] day of each [*choose one: month/quarter/year*] through [*repayment end date of next step*], Borrower shall pay to lender the sum of $_____.

   Then, beginning on [*repayment start date of next step*] and continuing [*choose one: monthly/quarterly/annually*] on the [*for example, 1st or 15th*] day of each [*choose one: month/quarter/year*] through [*repayment end date of next step*], Borrower shall pay to lender the sum of $_____.

   [*insert additional sections as needed for additional steps of the loan*]

Finally, beginning on [*repayment start date of last step*] and continuing [*choose one: monthly/quarterly/annually*] on the [*for example, 1st or 15th*] day of each [*choose one: month/quarter/year*] until [*final payment date*], Borrower shall pay to lender the sum of $_____.

On [*final due date (day/month/year)*], Borrower shall pay all amounts remaining due under the terms of this Note.

4. **Grace Period and Late Fee.** If the Borrower fails to make any payment in the full amount and within [*number of days, spelled out*] ([*number in figures*]) calendar days (the "Grace Period") after the date it is due, Borrower agrees to pay a late charge to the Lender or Note Holder in the amount of $_____(the "Late Fee"). Borrower will pay this Late Fee promptly but only once on each late payment.

5. **Security.** [*choose one*]

   ☐ This is an unsecured note.

   ☐ Borrower agrees that until this Note is paid in full (including principal and interest, if any), this Note will be secured by a separate security agreement and, if applicable, a Uniform Commercial Code financing statement, giving Lender a security interest in the following property: [*describe asset*] _____

   _____

6. **Default and Acceleration.** If any installment payment due under this Note is not received by Lender within the Grace Period, the note will be in default and the entire amount of unpaid principal will become immediately due and payable at the option of Lender without prior notice of default to Borrower.

7. **Prepayment.** This Note may be prepaid in full at any time without cost or penalty to the Borrower.

8. **Attorneys' Fees.** If Lender prevails in a lawsuit to collect on this note, Borrower agrees to pay Lender's attorneys' fees in an amount the court finds to be just and reasonable.

9. **Waiver.** The undersigned and all other parties to this Note waive the following requirements:

   • presentment of the Note for payment by Lender

- refusal of payment by Borrower after presentment of the Note by Lender, otherwise known as dishonor, and

- Lender's notification to Borrower of Borrower's refusal to pay.

10. Lender's Rights. Lender's decision not to exercise a right or remedy under this Note at a given time does not waive the Lender's ability to exercise that right or remedy at a later date.

11. Liability of Individual Borrowers. The term "Borrower" may refer to one or more borrowers. If there is more than one borrower, they agree to be jointly and severally liable.

12. Governing Law. This agreement will be governed by and construed in accordance with the laws of the state of _____.

Borrower's signature: _____

Print name: _____

Date: _____

Promissory Note (for a seasonal loan)

1. **For Value Received,** [*borrower name*] ("Borrower") promises to pay to the order of [*lender name*], of [*city, state*] ("Lender"), the sum, in United States dollars, of [*amount of loan, spelled out*] ($_____) dollars, plus interest accruing at an annual rate of [*interest rate, spelled out*] percent (_____%) on the unpaid principal amount beginning on [*loan start day/month/year*] (the "Debt").

2. **Transferability.** Borrower understands that the Lender may transfer this Note. The Lender or anyone who takes this Note by Transfer and who is entitled to receive payments under this Note is called the "Note Holder" and will have the same rights and remedies as the Lender under this Note.

3. **Payments.** Payment of the Debt shall be made in monthly payments, which include principal and interest, as follows:

   Beginning on [*day/month/year repayment begins*] and continuing until [*day/month/year of final due date*], Borrower shall make monthly payments as described below:

   For the calendar months of [*list months of high season*] of each year, Borrower shall pay on the [*for example, 1st or 15th*] day of each month the sum of $ [*high-season payment amount*] to the Lender or Note Holder ("High Season Monthly Payment"); and

   For the calendar months of [*list months of low season*] of each year, Borrower shall pay on the [*for example, 1st or 15th*] day of each month the sum of $ [*low-season payment amount*] to the Lender or Note Holder ("Low-Season Monthly Payment");

   Finally, on [*day/month/year of final due date*], Borrower shall pay all amounts remaining due under the terms of this Note.

4. **Grace Period and Late Fee.** If the Borrower fails to make any payment in the full amount and within [*number of days, spelled out*] ([*number in figures*]) calendar days (the "Grace Period") after the date it is due, Borrower agrees to pay a late charge to the Lender or Note Holder in

the amount of $_____(the "Late Fee"). Borrower will pay this Late Fee promptly but only once on each late payment.

5. **Security.** [*choose one*]

☐ This is an unsecured note.

☐ Borrower agrees that until this Note is paid in full (including principal and interest, if any), this Note will be secured by a separate security agreement and, if applicable, a Uniform Commercial Code financing statement, giving Lender a security interest in the following property: [*describe asset*]_____

_____

6. **Default and Acceleration.** If any installment payment due under this Note is not received by Lender within the Grace Period, the note will be in default and the entire amount of unpaid principal will become immediately due and payable at the option of Lender without prior notice of default to Borrower.

7. **Prepayment.** This Note may be prepaid in full at any time without cost or penalty to the Borrower.

8. **Attorneys' Fees.** If Lender prevails in a lawsuit to collect on this note, Borrower agrees to pay Lender's attorneys' fees in an amount the court finds to be just and reasonable.

9. **Waiver.** The undersigned and all other parties to this Note waive the following requirements:

   • presentment of the Note for payment by Lender

   • refusal of payment by Borrower after presentment of the Note by Lender, otherwise known as dishonor, and

   • Lender's notification to Borrower of Borrower's refusal to pay.

10. **Lender's Rights.** Lender's decision not to exercise a right or remedy under this Note at a given time does not waive the Lender's ability to exercise that right or remedy at a later date.

11. **Liability of Individual Borrowers.** The term "Borrower" may refer to one or more borrowers. If there is more than one borrower, they agree to be jointly and severally liable.

12. Governing Law. This agreement will be governed by and construed in accordance with the laws of the state of _____.

Borrower's signature: _____

Print name: _____

Date: _____

Promissory Note (for an interest-only loan)

1. **For Value Received,** [*borrower name*] ("Borrower") promises to pay
   to the order of [*lender name*], of [*city, state*] ("Lender"), the sum, in
   United States dollars, of [*amount of loan, spelled out*] ($_____)
   dollars, plus interest accruing at an annual rate of [*interest rate,
   spelled out*] percent (_____%) on the unpaid principal amount
   beginning on [*loan start day/month/year*] (the "Debt").

2. **Transferability.** Borrower understands that the Lender may transfer
   this Note. The Lender or anyone who takes this Note by Transfer and
   who is entitled to receive payments under this Note is called the
   "Note Holder" and will have the same rights and remedies as the
   Lender under this Note.

3. **Payments.** Payment of the Debt shall be made as follows:

   Borrower will pay all interest that accrues during the term of the
   loan by making a payment every [*choose one: month/quarter/year*].
   Borrower will make [*choose one: monthly/quarterly/annual*]
   payments on the [*for example, 1st or 15th*] day of each [*choose one:
   month/quarter/year*] beginning on [*loan repayment start day/month/
   year*]. Borrower will make these payments every [*choose one: month/
   quarter/year*] until Borrower has paid all of the interest and any other
   charges described below that Borrower may owe under this Note.
   Each payment will be applied as of its scheduled due date and will
   be applied to interest before principal. On [*day/month/year of final
   due date*], Borrower will pay all remaining principal, interest, and any
   other amounts due to Lender under the terms of this Note.

4. **Grace Period and Late Fee.** If the Borrower fails to make any payment
   in the full amount and within [*number of days, spelled out*] ([*number
   in figures*]) calendar days (the "Grace Period") after the date it is due,
   Borrower agrees to pay a late charge to the Lender or Note Holder in
   the amount of $_____(the "Late Fee"). Borrower will pay this Late
   Fee promptly but only once on each late payment.

5. **Security.** [*choose one*]

   ☐ This is an unsecured note.

☐ Borrower agrees that until this Note is paid in full (including principal and interest, if any), this Note will be secured by a separate security agreement and, if applicable, a Uniform Commercial Code financing statement, giving Lender a security interest in the following property: _[describe asset]_ _____

_____

6. **Default and Acceleration.** If any installment payment due under this Note is not received by Lender within the Grace Period, the note will be in default and the entire amount of unpaid principal will become immediately due and payable at the option of Lender without prior notice of default to Borrower.

7. **Prepayment.** This Note may be prepaid in full at any time without cost or penalty to the Borrower.

8. **Attorneys' Fees.** If Lender prevails in a lawsuit to collect on this note, Borrower agrees to pay Lender's attorneys' fees in an amount the court finds to be just and reasonable.

9. **Waiver.** The undersigned and all other parties to this Note waive the following requirements:

   • presentment of the Note for payment by Lender

   • refusal of payment by Borrower after presentment of the Note by Lender, otherwise known as dishonor, and

   • Lender's notification to Borrower of Borrower's refusal to pay.

10. **Lender's Rights.** Lender's decision not to exercise a right or remedy under this Note at a given time does not waive the Lender's ability to exercise that right or remedy at a later date.

11. **Liability of Individual Borrowers.** The term "Borrower" may refer to one or more borrowers. If there is more than one borrower, they agree to be jointly and severally liable.

12. **Governing Law.** This agreement will be governed by and construed in accordance with the laws of the state of _____.

Borrower's signature: _____

Print name: _____

Date: _____

Promissory Note Modifications for a Loan to a Business

At the beginning, replace opening lines with the following:

1. **For Value Received,** [*name of your business*], a [*the U.S. state where your business was formed*] [*insert business structure, probably corporation/partnership/LLC*] with its principal place of business in [*city, state of business*] ("Borrower"), promises to pay ....

At the end, replace the signature block with the following:

Borrower: [*print business name*] _____

Dated: _____

By (signature): _____

Print name: _____

Title: _____

Promissory Note Modifications for Signature by Notary Public

Add the following to the end of your promissory note, after the signature block, if you plan to have a notary public witness the signing.

Certificate of Acknowledgment of Notary Public

State of _____

County of _____

On _____, before me, _____
_____, a notary public in and for said state, personally
appeared _____,
known to me (or proved to me on the basis of satisfactory evidence)
to be the person whose name is subscribed to the within instrument,
and acknowledged to me that he or she executed the same in his or her
authorized capacity and that by his or her signature on the instrument,
the person, or the entity upon behalf of which the person acted,
executed the instrument.

WITNESS my hand and official seal.

Notary Public for the State of _____

My commission expires _____

[NOTARY SEAL]

Security Agreement

Name of Borrower: _____

Name of Lender: _____

1. **Grant of Security Interest.** Borrower grants to Lender a continuing security interest in the following personal property: _____

   (the Secured Property). Borrower grants this security interest to secure performance of the promissory note dated _____ that Borrower executed in favor of Lender (the Note), which obligates Borrower to pay Lender $ _____ with interest at the rate of _____% per year, on the terms stated in the Note.

2. **Financing Statement.** Until the amount due under the Note is paid in full, the Note will be further secured by a Uniform Commercial Code (U.C.C.) Financing Statement. Borrower agrees to sign any other documents that Lender reasonably requests to protect Lender's security interest in the Secured Property.

3. **Use and Care of Secured Property.** Until the amount due under the Note is paid in full, Borrower agrees to:

   A. Maintain the Secured Property in good repair.

   B. Not sell, transfer, or release the Secured Property without Lender's prior written consent.

   C. Pay all taxes on the Secured Property as they become due.

   D. Allow Lender to inspect the Secured Property at any reasonable time.

4. **Borrower's Default.** If Borrower is more than _____ days late in making any payment due under the Note, or if Buyer fails to correct any violations of paragraph 3, within _____ days of receiving written notice from Lender, Borrower will be in default.

5. **Lender's Rights.** If Borrower is in default, Lender may exercise the remedies contained in the U.C.C. for the state of _____

and any other remedies legally available to Lender. Before exercising such remedies, Lender will provide at least ten days' advance notice, as provided in paragraph 6. Lender may, for example:

A. Remove the Secured Property from the place where it is then located.

B. Require Borrower to make the Secured Property available to Lender at a place designated by Lender that is reasonably convenient to Borrower and Lender.

C. Sell, lease, or otherwise dispose of the Secured Property.

6. **Notice.** Any notice may be delivered to a party at the address that follows a party's signature below, or to a new address that a party designates in writing. A notice may be delivered:

A. in person

B. by certified mail, or

C. by overnight courier.

7. **Entire Agreement.** This is the entire agreement between the parties. It replaces and supersedes any and all oral agreements between the parties, as well as any prior writings.

8. **Successors and Assigns.** This agreement binds and benefits the parties' heirs, successors, and assigns.

9. **Governing Law.** This agreement will be governed by and construed in accordance with the laws of the state of _____.

10. **Counterparts.** The parties may sign several identical counterparts of this agreement. Any fully signed counterpart shall be treated as an original.

11. **Modification.** This agreement may be modified only in writing.

12. **Waiver.** If one party waives any term or provision of this agreement at any time, that waiver will be effective only for the specific instance and specific purpose for which the waiver was given. If either party fails to exercise or delays exercising any of its rights or remedies under this agreement, that party retains the right to enforce that term or provision at a later time.

13. Severability. If any court determines that any provision of this agreement is invalid or unenforceable, any such invalidity or unenforceability will affect only that provision and will not make any other provision of this agreement invalid or unenforceable and such provision shall be modified, amended, or limited only to the extent necessary to render it valid and enforceable.

_____   _____
Lender's Signature   Date

_____
Print name

_____
Address

_____
Address

_____   _____
Borrower's Signature   Date

_____
Print name

_____
Address

_____
Address

UCC Financing Statement

UCC FINANCING STATEMENT
FOLLOW INSTRUCTIONS (front and back) CAREFULLY

A. NAME & PHONE OF CONTACT AT FILER [optional]

B. SEND ACKNOWLEDGMENT TO: (Name and Address)

THE ABOVE SPACE IS FOR FILING OFFICE USE ONLY

1. DEBTOR'S EXACT FULL LEGAL NAME - insert only one debtor name (1a or 1b) - do not abbreviate or combine names

1a. ORGANIZATION'S NAME			

OR	1b. INDIVIDUAL'S LAST NAME	FIRST NAME	MIDDLE NAME	SUFFIX

1c. MAILING ADDRESS	CITY	STATE	POSTAL CODE	COUNTRY

1d. TAX ID #: SSN OR EIN	ADD'L INFO RE ORGANIZATION DEBTOR	1e. TYPE OF ORGANIZATION	1f. JURISDICTION OF ORGANIZATION	1g. ORGANIZATIONAL ID #, if any	NONE

2. ADDITIONAL DEBTOR'S EXACT FULL LEGAL NAME - insert only one debtor name (2a or 2b) - do not abbreviate or combine names

2a. ORGANIZATION'S NAME			

OR	2b. INDIVIDUAL'S LAST NAME	FIRST NAME	MIDDLE NAME	SUFFIX

2c. MAILING ADDRESS	CITY	STATE	POSTAL CODE	COUNTRY

2d. TAX ID #: SSN OR EIN	ADD'L INFO RE ORGANIZATION DEBTOR	2e. TYPE OF ORGANIZATION	2f. JURISDICTION OF ORGANIZATION	2g. ORGANIZATIONAL ID #, if any	NONE

3. SECURED PARTY'S NAME (or NAME of TOTAL ASSIGNEE of ASSIGNOR S/P) - insert only one secured party name (3a or 3b)

3a. ORGANIZATION'S NAME			

OR	3b. INDIVIDUAL'S LAST NAME	FIRST NAME	MIDDLE NAME	SUFFIX

3c. MAILING ADDRESS	CITY	STATE	POSTAL CODE	COUNTRY

4. This FINANCING STATEMENT covers the following collateral:

5. ALTERNATIVE DESIGNATION [if applicable]:	LESSEE/LESSOR	CONSIGNEE/CONSIGNOR	BAILEE/BAILOR	SELLER/BUYER	AG. LIEN	NON-UCC FILING

6. This FINANCING STATEMENT is to be filed [for record] (or recorded) in the REAL ESTATE RECORDS. Attach Addendum [if applicable]	7. Check to REQUEST SEARCH REPORT(S) on Debtor(s) [ADDITIONAL FEE] [optional]	All Debtors	Debtor 1	Debtor 2

8. OPTIONAL FILER REFERENCE DATA

FILING OFFICE COPY — NATIONAL UCC FINANCING STATEMENT (FORM UCC1) (REV. 07/29/98)

UCC Financing Statement Instructions

Instructions for National UCC Financing Statement (Form UCC1)

Please type or laser-print this form. Be sure it is completely legible. Read all Instructions, especially Instruction 1; correct Debtor name is crucial. Follow Instructions completely.

Fill in form very carefully; mistakes may have important legal consequences. If you have questions, consult your attorney. Filing office cannot give legal advice.

Do not insert anything in the open space in the upper portion of this form; it is reserved for filing office use.

When properly completed, send Filing Office Copy, with required fee, to filing office. If you want an acknowledgment, complete item B and, if filing in a filing office that returns an acknowledgment copy furnished by filer, you may also send Acknowledgment Copy; otherwise detach. If you want to make a search request, complete item 7 (after reading Instruction 7 below) and send Search Report Copy, otherwise detach. Always detach Debtor and Secured Party Copies.

If you need to use attachments, use 8-1/2 X 11 inch sheets and put at the top of each sheet the name of the first Debtor, formatted exactly as it appears in item 1 of this form; you are encouraged to use Addendum (Form UCC1Ad).

A. To assist filing offices that might wish to communicate with filer, filer may provide information in item A. This item is optional.

B. Complete item B if you want an acknowledgment sent to you. If filing in a filing office that returns an acknowledgment copy furnished by filer, present simultaneously with this form a carbon or other copy of this form for use as an acknowledgment copy.

1. **Debtor name:** Enter only one Debtor name in item 1, an organization's name (1a) or an individual's name (1b). Enter Debtor's exact full legal name. Don't abbreviate.

1a. Organization Debtor. "Organization" means an entity having a legal identity separate from its owner. A partnership is an organization; a sole proprietorship is not an organization, even if it does business under a trade name. If Debtor is a partnership, enter exact full legal name of partnership; you need not enter names of partners as additional Debtors. If Debtor is a registered organization (e.g., corporation, limited partnership, limited liability company), it is advisable to examine Debtor's current filed charter documents to determine Debtor's correct name, organization type, and jurisdiction of organization.

1b. Individual Debtor. "Individual" means a natural person; this includes a sole proprietorship, whether or not operating under a trade name. Don't use prefixes (Mr., Mrs., Ms.). Use suffix box only for titles of lineage (Jr., Sr., III) and not for other suffixes or titles (e.g., M.D.). Use married woman's personal name (Mary Smith, not Mrs. John Smith). Enter individual Debtor's family name (surname) in Last Name box, first given name in First Name box, and all additional given names in Middle Name box.

For both organization and individual Debtors: Don't use Debtor's trade name, DBA, AKA, FKA, Division name, etc. in place of or combined with Debtor's legal name; you may add such other names as additional Debtors if you wish (but this is neither required nor recommended).

1c. An address is always required for the Debtor named in 1a or 1b.

1d. Debtor's taxpayer identification number (tax ID #) — social security number or employer identification number — may be required in some states.

1e,f,g. "Additional information re organization Debtor" is always required. Type of organization and jurisdiction of organization as well as Debtor's exact legal name can be determined from Debtor's current filed charter document. Organizational ID #, if any, is assigned by the agency where the charter document was filed; this is different from tax ID #; this should be entered preceded by the 2-character U.S. Postal identification of state of organization if one of the United States (e.g., CA12345, for a California corporation whose organizational ID # is 12345); if agency does not assign organizational ID #, check box in item 1g indicating "none."

Note: If Debtor is a trust or a trustee acting with respect to property held in trust, enter Debtor's name in item 1 and attach Addendum (Form UCC1Ad) and check appropriate box in item 17. If Debtor is a decedent's estate, enter name of deceased individual in item 1b and attach Addendum (Form UCC1Ad) and check appropriate box in item 17. If Debtor is a transmitting utility or this Financing Statement is filed in connection with a Manufactured-Home Transaction or a Public-Finance Transaction as defined in applicable Commercial Code, attach Addendum (Form UCC1Ad) and check appropriate box in item 18.

2. If an additional Debtor is included, complete item 2, determined and formatted per Instruction 1. To include further additional Debtors, or one or more additional Secured Parties, attach either Addendum (Form UCC1Ad) or other additional page(s), using correct name format. Follow Instruction 1 for determining and formatting additional names.

3. Enter information for Secured Party or Total Assignee, determined and formatted per Instruction 1. If there is more than one Secured Party, see Instruction 2. If there has been a total assignment of the Secured Party's interest prior to filing this form, you may either (1) enter Assignor S/P's name and address in item 3 and file an Amendment (Form UCC3) [see item 5 of that form]; or (2) enter Total Assignee's name and address in item 3 and, if you wish, also attaching Addendum (Form UCC1Ad) giving Assignor S/P's name and address in item 12.

4. Use item 4 to indicate the collateral covered by this Financing Statement. If space in item 4 is insufficient, put the entire collateral description or continuation of the collateral description on either Addendum (Form UCC1Ad) or other attached additional page(s).

5. If filer desires (at filer's option) to use titles of lessee and lessor, or consignee and consignor, or seller and buyer in the case of accounts or chattel paper), or bailee and bailor instead of Debtor and Secured Party, check the appropriate box in item 5. If this is an agricultural lien (as defined in applicable Commercial Code) filing or is otherwise not a UCC security interest filing (e.g., a tax lien, judgment lien, etc.), check the appropriate box in item 5, complete items 1-7 as applicable and attach any other items required under other law.

6. If this Financing Statement is filed as a fixture filing or if the collateral consists of timber to be cut or as-extracted collateral, complete items 1-5, check the box in item 6, and complete the required information (items 13, 14 and/or 15) on Addendum (Form UCC1Ad).

7. This item is optional. Check appropriate box in item 7 to request Search Report(s) on all or some of the Debtors named in this Financing Statement. The Report will list all Financing Statements on file against the designated Debtor on the date of the Report, including this Financing Statement. There is an additional fee for each Report. If you have checked a box in item 7, file Search Report Copy together with Filing Officer Copy (and Acknowledgment Copy). Note: Not all states do searches and not all states will honor a search request made via this form; some states require a separate request form.

8. This item is optional and is for filer's use only. For filer's convenience of reference, filer may enter in item 8 any identifying information (e.g., Secured Party's loan number, law firm file number, Debtor's name or other identification, state in which form is being filed, etc.) that filer may find useful.

Loan Log

Payment number	Payment due date	Total amount due	Payment paid date	Total amount paid	Principal paid	Interest paid	Date paid late	Evidence of payment	Other

Appendix C

Online Small-Business Resources

A. Business Planning Resources 330

B. Loan Resources 334

C. Equity Resources 336

The wealth of information that the Internet puts at our fingertips can be overwhelming—it's hard to know where to start and whom to believe. The small business finance field in particular is swarmed by websites promising quick, easy, cheap solutions to your problems.

Presented here are some of the best Internet resources we've found designed to help entrepreneurs raise capital for their small businesses. When you're ready to start surfing, the Resource List available via the CD-ROM has the same links—and they are "live," so with just a click you can go directly to each of the sites listed.

Most of these sites have been mentioned in the text of the book—although a few are new. They're organized alphabetically into three areas:

- General Resources
- Loan Capital Resources
- Equity Investing Resources.

A. Business Resources

This section contains links to free online business planning resources such as articles, forms, templates, and calculators as well as links to companies that sell key start-up business services, like software. If you're looking for free assistance from a real person on your business plan, make sure you use the SBA and SCORE links.

AnnualCreditReport.com

www.annualcreditreport.com

AnnualCreditReport.com is a centralized service for consumers to request annual credit reports. Consumers can request and obtain a free credit report once every 12 months from each of the three nationwide consumer credit reporting companies, Equifax, Experian, and TransUnion.

Bankrate

www.bankrate.com

Bankrate, Inc. is the Web's leading aggregator of financial rate information. Use this site to look up the yields on any number of financial investment options.

Bplans.com

www.bplans.com

Palo Alto Software makes one of the most popular business planning software packages available and offers hundreds of sample business plans online.

The Company Corporation

www.corporate.com

This is a great site to visit if you're seeking information on how to form a corporation or a limited liability company.

The Global Entrepreneurship Monitor (GEM)

www.gemconsortium.org

GEM is a research program conducted by several leading institutions of entrepreneurship that completes annual assessments of U.S. entrepreneurial activity.

Internal Revenue Service (IRS)

www.irs.gov

Visiting the website of the Internal Revenue Service is useful for more information on the tax implications of your capital choice. Following is a list of IRS items mentioned in this book that are available on the IRS website. You can look up any of these items by typing the title into the search box provided at the IRS home page or by clicking "Forms and Publications" and going to the scroll-down lists.

- Publication 950, *Introduction to Estate and Gift Taxes*
- Publication 550, *Investment Income and Expenses*
- Publication 535, *Business Expenses*
- Form 1065, *Partnership Return of Income*
- Form 1120S, *Income Tax Return for S Corporations*
- Form 8832, *Entity Classification Election*
- Schedule D, *Capital Gains and Losses*
- Index of Applicable Federal Rates

The Kaufman Foundation

www.entreworld.org

The Kaufman Foundation Entreworld site contains a collection of links to articles for entrepreneurs, gathered into topic areas. Click on the tab titled "Starting Your Business" to access the articles.

Lemonade Stories

www.lemonadestories.com

This website for the award-winning film of the same name tells the compelling stories of how mothers have contributed to the entrepreneurial spirit of a few famous entrepreneurs.

LogoYes.com

www.logoyes.com

If you don't already have a business logo or the money to hire a graphics designer, you can create your business logo online using LogoYes.

MicroMentor

www.micromentor.org

If you and your business are located in a distressed community (a low-income or otherwise disadvantaged area), the MicroMentor website can help you locate a mentor who will share business experience and fundraising networks.

Nolo

www.nolo.com

Nolo, the nation's leading provider of do-it-yourself legal solutions for consumers and small businesses (and publisher of this book), offers a wide variety of free information as well as books, forms, and software products at its site.

Pensco Trust Company

www.pensco.com

At Pensco you can learn more about self-directed IRAs, which allow you or your prospect to invest retirement assets in your business.

SCORE

www.score.org

> The SCORE Association, headquartered in Washington, DC, is a nonprofit association with over 10,000 retired and working business executive volunteers who provide free business counseling and advice as a public service. The website allows you to find a local SCORE counselor and access a variety of articles and other Internet resources. Also check out their "template gallery"—a collection of financial spreadsheets and related financial planning tools at www.score.org/template_gallery.html.

U.S. Census Bureau

www.census.gov

> If you're looking for data as you prepare your business plan, the first place you'll want to visit is the Census Bureau website. Look in the "Business" section for economic statistics on a variety of topics, including the income levels of the people in your area and the number of businesses in your sector and industry.

U.S. Chamber of Commerce

www.uschamber.com

> The Chamber of Commerce is the voice of small business in Washington, DC, representing the interests of over three million businesses. Its website includes a comprehensive small business planning toolkit at www.uschamber.com/sb/learn/sbtoolkit, which includes articles and sample forms, documents, and worksheets. Some of these resources are free, some require membership to access.

U.S. Small Business Administration (SBA)

www.sba.gov

> The SBA is the primary government resource for small businesses. Visit its website for articles on starting, financing, and managing a business as well as descriptions of SBA financial and technical assistance programs. Don't miss these portions of the website:
>
> - a free online course in entrepreneurship at www.sba.gov/starting_business/index.html
> - a startup cost calculator at www.sba.gov/financing/basics/estimating.html

- template forms for building financial statements at www.sba.gov/library/forms.html, and
- free electronic newsletters, with links to business planning tips and resources, at http://web.sba.gov/list.

Wall Street Journal

www.startupjournal.com

The popular Wall Street Journal Center for Entrepreneurs provides free articles and links related to small business news and resources.

Websites for popular business magazines:

- Entrepreneur: www.entrepreneur.com
- Inc: www.inc.com
- Fortune: www.fortune.com

B. Loan Resources

If you type the term "small business loan" into any Internet search engine, a long list of websites will come up, many credible and some questionable. The websites below are your shortcut to information about banks and other financial institutions, like credit unions and nonprofit organizations, with a reputation for lending to small businesses.

Association for Enterprise Opportunity (AEO)

www.microenterpriseworks.org

AEO provides a national website for microenterprise programs that assist entrepreneurs in starting, stabilizing, and expanding businesses. Go to the page called "Microenterprise Organizations Near You" to see a state-by-state listing of these nonprofit financial intermediaries: www.microenterpriseworks.org/nearyou/bystate.asp. You can also find a report on microenterprise called "Opening Opportunities, Building Ownership: Fulfilling the Promise of Microenterprise in the United States" at http://fieldus.org/li/sof.htm.

CircleLending

www.circlelending.com

> CircleLending has pioneered the market for managing loans between relatives, friends, and other private parties. The company has helped thousands of individuals to raise capital in an affordable and flexible manner, from within their circle of relatives and friends. For business owners, CircleLending offers a range of services to help entrepreneurs manage private loans including loan documentation, customized repayment schedules, payment processing, tax statements, record keeping, and credit reporting.

Community Development Financial Institutions (CDFI) Fund

www.cdfifund.gov

> The CDFI Fund is an agency within the U.S. Department of Treasury that provides capital to CDFIs and banks interested in financing community development. There's a state-by-state listing of who makes these loans available to borrowers at www.cdfifund.gov/docs/certification/cdfi/CDFI-state.pdf.

National Congress for Community Economic Development (NCCED)

www.ncced.org

> NCCED is the trade association for the community economic development (CED) industry and provides a list of its members at www.ncced.org/resources. (Although unfortunately the list is not organized by state, many of the organizations mention their state, city, or county in their name.)

"Top Commercial Lenders to Small Businesses"

www.fortune.com

> The *Fortune* magazine website lists the ten top large national banks for small business loans. Each link takes you to a "bank locator" page where you can search for a local branch or representative: www.fortune.com/fortune/smallbusiness/articles/0,15114,361160,00.html.

U.S. Small Business Administration (SBA)

www.sba.gov

> The SBA's popular 7(a) Loan Guaranty Program and the 7(m) Micro-loan Program help banks, credit unions, and nonprofit financial

intermediaries lend to small businesses unable to secure financing on reasonable terms elsewhere. To look up the 7(a) and microloan lenders in your state, go to www.sba.gov/regions/states.html and click on your state. A page designed for your state should appear, from which you can click on "financing," then click on the links to lists of preferred/certified lenders, microlenders, and other SBA resources in your state. You can also call 1-800-8-ASK-SBA to locate a small-business friendly lender near you.

C. Equity Resources

If you were to type the term "equity capital" or, better yet, "angel" or "venture capital" into an Internet search engine, you'd get a long and unwieldy list of websites to visit. Instead, start with the list of sites collected below.

Active Capital
www.activecapital.org
> Originally created by the SBA, Active Capital is a way for entrepreneurs to list their securities for sale in an Internet database used by angel investors nationwide. From the home page, click on the "Entrepreneurs" tab to enroll in their database or to access other investing resources, news, and events.

The Angel Capital Association
www.angelcapitalassociation.org
> This website for the peer organization of angel investing groups in North America includes a variety of resources designed mostly for angel investors. However, entrepreneurs will be interested in the directory of angel groups available on the site.

Angel Investor News.com
www.angel-investor-news.com
> The Angel Investor News website provides a collection of online articles and resources both for entrepreneurs trying to raise equity from angels and for angels trying to learn more about angel investing.

The Center for Venture Research (CVR)

www.unh.edu/cvr

> The CVR is an online resource for early-stage equity investment resources and contacts. In addition to research and analysis on the angel investing industry, CVR maintains a list of early-stage venture capital groups, organized by state. Currently, access to the list can be purchased for $40.

Community Development Venture Capital Alliance (CDVCA)

www.cdvca.org

> CDVCA is a trade association of community development venture capital funds. CDVCA's membership includes over 100 organizations that invest in businesses that advance the livelihoods of low-income people and the economies of distressed communities. For a list of community development venture capital funds serving your area, visit www.cdvca .org/index.cfm?fuseaction=Page.viewPage&pageId=197.

Every Business Needs an Angel

www.everybusinessneedsanangel.com

> The "Every Business Needs an Angel" website is based on a book of the same name, one of the most popular and widely read books for entrepreneurs about raising money from angel investors.

The National Venture Capital Association (NVCA)

www.nvca.org

> NVCA is a trade association representing the U.S. venture capital industry. Its members consist of venture capital firms that manage pools of risk equity capital designated to be invested in high-growth companies. The site includes a list of regional venture capital groups at www.nvca.org/resources/regintvo.html.

U.S. Small Business Administration

www.sba.gov

> The SBA administers an equity investment program geared to larger venture-style investing though a network of Small Business Investment Companies (SBICs). You can access the program directly at www.sba .gov/INV or the links for SBICs on the SBA state pages found at www .sba.gov/regions/states.html.

Securities and Exchange Commission (SEC)

www.sec.gov

If you're planning on selling shares in your company, you'll need to make sure you comply with federal securities laws, enforced by the SEC. In the box titled "Information for," click on the link for "Small Business."

■

Sample Equity Investing Documents

Term Sheet..340

Series A Preferred Stock Purchase Agreement...360

T his appendix contains the two sample equity investing documents discussed in Chapter 8; the term sheet and the stock purchase agreement. These documents were created by the National Venture Capital Association (NVCA). Because they are intended primarily for your reference, they are not included on the enclosed CD-ROM. However, they can also be found online at the NVCA website at www.nvca.org (under "Industry Information," click "Model Legal Documents").

Note from the NVCA: *These sample documents are the work product of a coalition of attorneys who specialize in venture capital financings, working under the auspices of the NVCA. See the NVCA website for a list of the Working Group members. These documents are intended to serve as a starting point only and should be tailored to meet your specific requirements. These documents should not be construed as legal advice for any particular facts or circumstances. Note that these sample documents present an array of (often mutually exclusive) options with respect to particular deal provisions.*

Term Sheet

Preliminary Notes

This Term Sheet maps to the NVCA model documents, and for convenience the provisions are grouped according to the particular model document in which they may be found. Although this Term Sheet is perhaps somewhat longer than a "typical" VC Term Sheet, the aim is to provide a level of detail that makes the Term Sheet useful as both a road map for the document drafters and as a reference source for the business people to quickly find deal terms without the necessity of having to consult the legal documents (assuming of course there have been no changes to the material deal terms prior to execution of the final documents).

TERM SHEET
FOR SERIES A PREFERRED STOCK FINANCING OF
[Insert Company Name], INC.
[_____ _____, 200____]

     This Term Sheet summarizes the principal terms of the Series A Preferred Stock Financing of [_____], Inc., a [Delaware] corporation (the "**Company**"). In consideration of the time and expense devoted and to be devoted by the Investors with respect to this investment, the No Shop/ Confidentiality and Counsel and Expenses provisions of this Term Sheet shall be binding obligations of the Company whether or not the financing is consummated. No other legally binding obligations will be created until definitive agreements are executed and delivered by all parties. This Term Sheet is not a commitment to invest, and is conditioned on the completion of due diligence, legal review and documentation that is satisfactory to the Investors. This Term Sheet shall be governed in all respects by the laws of the [State of Delaware].

Offering Terms

Closing Date:	As soon as practicable following the Company's acceptance of this Term Sheet and satisfaction of the Conditions to Closing (the "**Closing**"). [*provide for multiple closings if applicable*]
Investors:	Investor No. 1: [_____] shares ([__]%), $[_____]
	Investor No. 2: [_____] shares ([__]%), $[_____]
	[as well other investors mutually agreed upon by Investors and the Company]
Amount Raised:	$[_____], [including $[_____] from the conversion of principal [and interest] on bridge notes].[1]
Price Per Share:	$[_____] per share (based on the capitalization of the Company set forth below) (the "**Original Purchase Price**").

---

[1]   Modify this provision to account for staged investments or investments dependent on the achievement of milestones by the Company.

Pre-Money Valuation:	The Original Purchase Price is based upon a fully-diluted pre-money valuation of $[_____] and a fully-diluted post-money valuation of $[_____] (including an employee pool representing [___]% of the fully-diluted post-money capitalization).
Capitalization:	The Company's capital structure before and after the Closing is set forth below:

	Pre-Financing		Post-Financing	
Security	# of Shares	%	# of Shares	%
Common – Founders				
Common – Employee Stock Pool				
Issued				
Unissued				
[Common – Warrants]				
Series A Preferred				
Total				

CHARTER[2]

Dividends:	[*Alternative 1:* Dividends will be paid on the Series A Preferred on an as-converted basis when, as, and if paid on the Common Stock]
	[*Alternative 2*: Non-cumulative dividends will be paid on the Series A Preferred in an amount equal to $[_____] per share of Series A Preferred when and if declared by the Board.]
	[*Alternative 3:* The Series A Preferred will carry an annual [___]% cumulative dividend

---

[2] The Charter is a public document, filed with the [Delaware] Secretary of State, that establishes all of the rights, preferences, privileges and restrictions of the Preferred Stock. Note that if the Preferred Stock does not have rights, preferences, and privileges materially superior to the Common Stock, then (after Closing) the Company cannot defensibly grant Common Stock options priced at a discount to the Preferred Stock.

[compounded annually], payable upon a liquidation or redemption. For any other dividends or distributions, participation with Common Stock on an as-converted basis.] [3]

Liquidation Preference: In the event of any liquidation, dissolution or winding up of the Company, the proceeds shall be paid as follows:

[*Alternative 1 (non-participating Preferred Stock)*: First pay [one] times the Original Purchase Price [plus accrued dividends] [plus declared and unpaid dividends] on each share of Series A Preferred. The balance of any proceeds shall be distributed to holders of Common Stock.]

[*Alternative 2 (full participating Preferred Stock)*: First pay [one] times the Original Purchase Price [plus accrued dividends] [plus declared and unpaid dividends] on each share of Series A Preferred. Thereafter, the Series A Preferred participates with the Common Stock on an as-converted basis.]

[*Alternative 3 (cap on Preferred Stock participation rights)*: First pay [one] times the Original Purchase Price [plus accrued dividends] [plus declared and unpaid dividends] on each share of Series A Preferred. Thereafter, Series A Preferred participates with Common Stock on an as-converted basis until the holders of Series A Preferred receive an aggregate of [___] times the Original Purchase Price.]

A merger or consolidation (other than one in which stockholders of the Company own a majority by voting power of the outstanding shares

---

[3]   In some cases, accrued and unpaid dividends are payable on conversion as well as upon a liquidation event. Most typically, however, dividends are not paid if the preferred is converted. Another alternative is to give the Company the option to pay accrued and unpaid dividends in cash or in common shares valued at fair market value. The latter are referred to as "PIK" (payment-in-kind) dividends.

of the surviving or acquiring corporation) and a sale, lease, transfer or other disposition of all or substantially all of the assets of the Company will be treated as a liquidation event (a "**Deemed Liquidation Event**"), thereby triggering payment of the liquidation preferences described above [unless the holders of [___]% of the Series A Preferred elect otherwise].

Voting Rights: The Series A Preferred Stock shall vote together with the Common Stock on an as-converted basis, and not as a separate class, except (i) the Series A Preferred as a class shall be entitled to elect [_____] [(___)] members of the Board (the "Series A Directors"), (ii) as provided under "Protective Provisions" below or (iii) as required by law. The Company's Certificate of Incorporation will provide that the number of authorized shares of Common Stock may be increased or decreased with the approval of a majority of the Preferred and Common Stock, voting together as a single class, and without a separate class vote by the Common Stock.[4]

Protective Provisions: So long as [insert fixed number, or %, or "any"] shares of Series A Preferred are outstanding, the Company will not, without the written consent of the holders of at least [___]% of the Company's Series A Preferred, either directly or by amendment, merger, consolidation, or otherwise:

(i) liquidate, dissolve or wind-up the affairs of the Company, or effect any Deemed Liquidation Event; (ii) amend, alter, or repeal any provision of the Certificate of Incorporation or Bylaws [in

---

[4] For California corporations, one cannot "opt out" of the statutory requirement of a separate class vote by Common Stockholders to authorize shares of Common Stock.

a manner adverse to the Series A Preferred];[5]
(iii) create or authorize the creation of or
issue any other security convertible into or
exercisable for any equity security, having
rights, preferences or privileges senior to or on
parity with the Series A Preferred, or increase
the authorized number of shares of Series A
Preferred; (iv) purchase or redeem or pay any
dividend on any capital stock prior to the Series
A Preferred, [other than stock repurchased from
former employees or consultants in connection
with the cessation of their employment/services,
at the lower of fair market value or cost;] [other
than as approved by the Board, including the
approval of [_____] Series A Director(s)];
or (___) create or authorize the creation of
any debt security [if the Company's aggregate
indebtedness would exceed $[_____] [other
than equipment leases or bank lines of credit]
[other than debt with no equity feature][unless
such debt security has received the prior
approval of the Board of Directors, including
the approval of [   ] Series A Director(s)];
(vi) increase or decrease the size of the Board
of Directors.

Optional Conversion: The Series A Preferred initially converts 1:1 to
Common Stock at any time at option of holder,
subject to adjustments for stock dividends, splits,
combinations and similar events and as described
below under "Anti-dilution Provisions."

---

[5]   Note that as a matter of background law, Section 242(b)(2) of the Delaware
General Corporation Law provides that if any proposed charter amendment
would adversely alter the rights, preferences and powers of one series of
Preferred Stock, but not similarly adversely alter the entire class of all Preferred
Stock, then the holders of that series are entitled to a separate series vote on
the amendment.

Anti-dilution Provisions: In the event that the Company issues additional securities at a purchase price less than the current Series A Preferred conversion price, such conversion shall be adjusted in accordance with the following formula:

[*Alternative 1:* "Typical" weighted average:

$$CP_2 = CP_1 * (A+B) / (A+C)$$

CP_2 = New Series A Conversion Price

CP_1 = Series A Conversion Price in effect immediately prior to new issue

A = Number of shares of Common Stock deemed to be outstanding immediately prior to new issue (includes all shares of outstanding common stock, all shares of outstanding preferred stock on an as-converted basis, and all outstanding options on an as-exercised basis; and does not include any convertible securities converting into this round of financing)

B = Aggregate consideration received by the Corporation with respect to the new issue divided by CP_1

C = Number of shares of stock issued in the subject transaction]

[Alternative 2: Full-ratchet – the conversion price will be reduced to the price at which the new shares are issued.]

[Alternative 3: No price-based anti-dilution protection.]

The following issuances shall not trigger anti-dilution adjustment:[6]

---

[6] Note that additional exclusions are frequently negotiated, such as issuances in connection with equipment leasing and commercial borrowing.

(i) securities issuable upon conversion of any of the Series A Preferred, or as a dividend or distribution on the Series A Preferred; (ii) securities issued upon the conversion of any debenture, warrant, option, or other convertible security; (iii) Common Stock issuable upon a stock split, stock dividend, or any subdivision of shares of Common Stock; and (iv) shares of Common Stock (or options to purchase such shares of Common Stock) issued or issuable to employees or directors of, or consultants to, the Company pursuant to any plan approved by the Company's Board of Directors [including at least [_____] Series A Director(s)] [(____) shares of Common Stock issued or issuable to banks, equipment lessors pursuant to a debt financing, equipment leasing or real property leasing transaction approved by the Board of Directors of the Corporation [, including at least [_____] Series A Director(s)]

Mandatory Conversion: Each share of Series A Preferred will automatically be converted into Common Stock at the then applicable conversion rate in the event of the closing of a [firm commitment] underwritten public offering with a price of [____] times the Original Purchase Price (subject to adjustments for stock dividends, splits, combinations and similar events) and [net/gross] proceeds to the Company of not less than $[_____] (a "**QPO**"), or (ii) upon the written consent of the holders of [_____]% of the Series A Preferred.[7]

---

[7]   The per share test ensures that the investor achieves a significant return on investment before the Company can go public. Also consider allowing a non-QPO to become a QPO if an adjustment is made to the Conversion Price for the benefit of the investor, so that the investor does not have the power to block a public offering.

[Pay-to-Play: [Unless the holders of [____]% of the Series A elect
                       otherwise,] on any subsequent down round all
                       [Major] Investors are required to participate to the
                       full extent of their participation rights (as described
                       below under "Investor Rights Agreement – Right
                       to Participate Pro Rata in Future Rounds"), unless
                       the participation requirement is waived for all
                       [Major] Investors by the Board [(including vote of
                       [a majority of] the Series A Director[s])]. All shares
                       of Series A Preferred[8] of any [Major] Investor failing
                       to do so will automatically [lose anti-dilution rights]
                       [lose right to participate in future rounds] [convert
                       to Common Stock and lose the right to a Board
                       seat if applicable].[9]

Redemption Rights:[10]   The Series A Preferred shall be redeemable
                       from funds legally available for distribution at
                       the option of holders of at least [____]% of the
                       Series A Preferred commencing any time after the
                       fifth anniversary of the Closing at a price equal to

---

8   Alternatively, this provision could apply on a proportionate basis (e.g., if
    Investor plays for ½ of pro rata share, receives ½ of anti-dilution adjustment).

9   If the punishment for failure to participate is losing some but not all rights
    of the Preferred (e.g., anything other than a forced conversion to common),
    the Charter will need to have so-called "blank check preferred" provisions at
    least to the extent necessary to enable the Board to issue a "shadow" class of
    preferred with diminished rights in the event an investor fails to participate.
    Note that as a drafting matter it is far easier to simply have (some or all of) the
    preferred convert to common.

10 Redemption rights allow Investors to force the Company to redeem their shares
    at cost [plus a small guaranteed rate of return (e.g., dividends)]. In practice,
    redemption rights are not often used; however, they do provide a form of exit
    and some possible leverage over the Company. While it is possible that the
    right to receive dividends on redemption could give rise to a Code Section 305
    "deemed dividend" problem, many tax practitioners take the view that if the
    liquidation preference provisions in the Charter are drafted to provide that,
    on conversion, the holder receives the greater of its liquidation preference
    or its as-converted amount (as provided in the NVCA model Certificate of
    Incorporation), then there is no Section 305 issue.

the Original Purchase Price [plus all accrued but unpaid dividends]. Redemption shall occur in three equal annual portions. Upon a redemption request from the holders of the required percentage of the Series A Preferred, all Series A Preferred shares shall be redeemed [(except for any Series A holders who affirmatively opt-out)].[11]

STOCK PURCHASE AGREEMENT

Representations and Warranties:	Standard representations and warranties by the Company. [Representations and warranties by Founders regarding [technology ownership, etc.].[12]
Conditions to Closing:	Standard conditions to Closing, which shall include, among other things, satisfactory completion of financial and legal due diligence, qualification of the shares under applicable Blue Sky laws, the filing of a Certificate of Incorporation establishing the rights and preferences of the Series A Preferred, and an opinion of counsel to the Company.
Counsel and Expenses:	[Investor/Company] counsel to draft closing documents. Company to pay all legal and administrative costs of the financing [at Closing], including reason-

---

[11] Due to statutory restrictions, it is unlikely that the Company will be legally permitted to redeem in the very circumstances where investors most want it (the so-called "sideways situation"), investors will sometimes request that certain penalty provisions take effect where redemption has been requested but the Company's available cash flow does not permit such redemption - - e.g., the redemption amount shall be paid in the form of a one-year note to each unredeemed holder of Series A Preferred, and the holders of a majority of the Series A Preferred shall be entitled to elect a majority of the Company's Board of Directors until such amounts are paid in full.

[12] Note that while it is not at all uncommon in east coast deals to require the Founders to personally rep and warrant (at least as to certain key matters, and usually only in the Series A round), such Founders reps are rarely found in west coast deals.

able fees (not to exceed $[_____])and expenses of Investor counsel[, unless the transaction is not completed because the Investors withdraw their commitment without cause][13].

Company Counsel: [_____

_____

_____]

Investor Counsel: [_____

_____

_____]

INVESTOR RIGHTS AGREEMENT

Registration Rights:

Registrable Securities: All shares of Common Stock issuable upon conversion of the Series A Preferred and [any other Common Stock held by the Investors] will be deemed "**Registrable Securities**."[14]

Demand Registration: Upon earliest of (i) [three-five] years after the Closing; or (ii) [six] months following an initial public offering ("IPO"), persons holding [____]% of the Registrable Securities may request [one] [two] (consummated) registrations by the Company of their shares. The aggregate offering price for such registration may not be less than $[5-10] million. A registration will count for this purpose only if (i) all Registrable Securities requested to be registered are registered and (ii) it is closed, or withdrawn at the request of the Investors (other

---

[13] The bracketed text should be deleted if this section is not designated in the introductory paragraph as one of the sections that is binding upon the Company regardless of whether the financing is consummated.

[14] Note that Founders/management sometimes also seek registration rights.

than as a result of a material adverse change to the Company).

Registration on Form S-3: The holders of [10-30]% of the Registrable Securities will have the right to require the Company to register on Form S-3, if available for use by the Company, Registrable Securities for an aggregate offering price of at least $[1-5 million]. There will be no limit on the aggregate number of such Form S-3 registrations, provided that there are no more than [two] per year.

Piggyback Registration: The holders of Registrable Securities will be entitled to "piggyback" registration rights on all registration statements of the Company, subject to the right, however, of the Company and its underwriters to reduce the number of shares proposed to be registered to a minimum of [30]% on a pro rata basis and to complete reduction on an IPO at the underwriter's discretion. In all events, the shares to be registered by holders of Registrable Securities will be reduced only after all other stockholders' shares are reduced.

Expenses: The registration expenses (exclusive of stock transfer taxes, underwriting discounts and commissions will be borne by the Company. The Company will also pay the reasonable fees and expenses [, not to exceed _____,] of one special counsel to represent all the participating stockholders.

Lock-up: Investors shall agree in connection with the IPO, if requested by the managing underwriter, not to sell or transfer any shares of Common Stock of the Company [(excluding shares acquired in or following the IPO)] for a period of up to 180 days following the IPO (provided all directors and officers of the Company and [1 – 5]% stockholders agree to the same lock-up). Such lock-up agreement shall provide that any discretionary

11

waiver or termination of the restrictions of such agreements by the Company or representatives of the underwriters shall apply to [Major] Investors, pro rata, based on the number of shares held. A "**Major Investor**" means any Investor who purchases at least $[_____] of Series A Preferred.

Termination:

Earlier of [5] years after IPO, upon a Deemed Liquidation Event, or when all shares of an Investor are eligible to be sold without restriction under Rule 144(k) within any 90-day period.

No future registration rights may be granted without consent of the holders of a [majority] of the Registrable Securities unless subordinate to the Investor's rights.

Management and Information Rights:

A Management Rights letter from the Company, in a form reasonably acceptable to the Investors, will be delivered prior to Closing to each Investor that requests one.[15]

Any Major Investor [(who is not a competitor)] will be granted access to Company facilities and personnel during normal business hours and with reasonable advance notification. The Company will deliver to such Major Investor (i) annual, quarterly, [and monthly] financial statements, and other information as determined by the Board; (ii) thirty days prior to the end of each fiscal year, a comprehensive operating budget forecasting the Company's revenues, expenses, and cash position on a month-to-month basis for the upcoming fiscal year; and (iii) promptly following the end of each quarter an up-to-date capitalization table, certified by the CFO.

---

[15] See commentary in introduction to NVCA model Managements Rights Letter, explaining purpose of such letter.

Right to Participate Pro *Rata in Future Rounds:*	All [Major] Investors shall have a pro rata right, based on their percentage equity ownership in the Company (assuming the conversion of all outstanding Preferred Stock into Common Stock and the exercise of all options outstanding under the Company's stock plans), to participate in subsequent issuances of equity securities of the Company (excluding those issuances listed at the end of the "Anti-dilution Provisions" section of this Term Sheet and issuances in connection with acquisitions by the Company). In addition, should any [Major] Investor choose not to purchase its full pro rata share, the remaining [Major] Investors shall have the right to purchase the remaining pro rata shares.
Matters Requiring *Investor Director* *Approval:*	[So long as [____]% of the originally issued Series A Preferred remains outstanding] the Company will not, without Board approval, which approval must include the affirmative vote of [____] of the Series A Director(s):

> (i) make any loan or advance to, or own any stock or other securities of, any subsidiary or other corporation, partnership, or other entity unless it is wholly owned by the Company;
> (ii) make any loan or advance to any person, including, any employee or director, except advances and similar expenditures in the ordinary course of business or under the terms of a employee stock or option plan approved by the Board of Directors; (iii) guarantee, any indebtedness except for trade accounts of the Company or any subsidiary arising in the ordinary course of business; (iv) make any investment other than investments in prime

commercial paper, money market funds, certificates of deposit in any United States bank having a net worth in excess of $100,000,000 or obligations issued or guaranteed by the United States of America, in each case having a maturity not in excess of [two years]; (v) incur any aggregate indebtedness in excess of $[_____] that is not already included in a Board-approved budget, other than trade credit incurred in the ordinary course of business; (vi) enter into or be a party to any transaction with any director, officer or employee of the Company or any "associate" (as defined in Rule 12b-2 promulgated under the Exchange Act) of any such person [except transactions resulting in payments to or by the Company in an amount less than $[60,000] per year], [or transactions made in the ordinary course of business and pursuant to reasonable requirements of the Company's business and upon fair and reasonable terms that are approved by a majority of the Board of Directors];[16] (vii) hire, fire, or change the compensation of the executive officers, including approving any option plans; (viii) change the principal business of the Company, enter new lines of business, or exit the current line of business; or (ix) sell, transfer, license, pledge or encumber technology or intellectual property, other than licenses granted in the ordinary course of business.

---

[16] Note that Section 402 of the Sarbanes-Oxley Act of 2003 would require repayment of any loans in full prior to the Company filing a registration statement for an IPO.

Non-Competition and Non-Solicitation and Agreements:[17]	Each Founder and key employee will enter into a [one] year non-competition and non-solicitation agreement in a form reasonably acceptable to the Investors.
Non-Disclosure and Developments Agreement:	Each current and former Founder, employee and consultant with access to Company confidential information/trade secrets will enter into a non-disclosure and proprietary rights assignment agreement in a form reasonably acceptable to the Investors.
Board Matters:	Each Board Committee shall include at least one Series A Director.
	The Board of Directors shall meet at least [monthly][quarterly], unless otherwise agreed by a vote of the majority of Directors.
	The Company will bind D&O insurance with a carrier and in an amount satisfactory to the Board of Directors. In the event the Company merges with another entity and is not the surviving corporation, or transfers all of its assets, proper provisions shall be made so that successors of the Company assume Company's obligations with respect to indemnification of Directors.

---

[17] Note that non-compete restrictions (other than in connection with the sale of a business) are prohibited in California, and may not be enforceable in other jurisdictions, as well. In addition, some investors do not require such agreements for fear that employees will request additional consideration in exchange for signing a Non-Compete/Non-Solicit (and indeed the agreement may arguably be invalid absent such additional consideration - - although having an employee sign a non-compete contemporaneous with hiring constitutes adequate consideration). Others take the view that it should be up to the Board on a case-by-case basis to determine whether any particular key employee is required to sign such an agreement. Non-competes typically have a one year duration, although state law may permit up to two years.

Employee Stock Options:	All employee options to vest as follows: [25% after one year, with remaining vesting monthly over next 36 months].
	[Immediately prior to the Series A Preferred Stock investment, [_____] shares will be added to the option pool creating an unallocated option pool of [_____] shares.]
Key Person Insurance:	Company to acquire life insurance on Founders [name each Founder] in an amount satisfactory to the Board. Proceeds payable to the Company.
[IPO Directed Shares:[18]	To the extent permitted by applicable law and SEC policy, upon an IPO consummated one year after Closing, Company to use reasonable best efforts to cause underwriters to designate [10]% of the offering as directed shares, 50% of which shall be allocated by Major Investors.]
[QSB Stock:	Company shall use reasonable best efforts to cause its capital stock to constitute Qualified Small Business Stock unless the Board determines that such qualification is inconsistent with the best interests of the Company.]
Termination:	All rights under the Investor Rights Agreement, other than registration rights, shall terminate upon the earlier of an IPO, a Deemed Liquidation Event or a transfer of more than 50% of Company's voting power.

---

[18] SEC Staff examiners have taken position that, if contractual right to friends and family shares was granted less than 12 months prior to filing of registration statement, this will be considered an "offer" made prematurely before filing of IPO prospectus. So, investors need to agree to drop shares from offering if that would hold up the IPO. While some documents provide for alternative parallel private placement where the IPO does occur within 12 months, such a parallel private placement could raise integration issues and negatively impact the IPO. Hence, such an alternative is not provided for here.

RIGHT OF FIRST REFUSAL/CO-SALE AGREEMENT AND VOTING AGREEMENT

Right of first Refusal/ Right of Co-Sale (Take-me-Along):	Company first and Investors second (to the extent assigned by the Board of Directors,) have a right of first refusal with respect to any shares of capital stock of the Company proposed to be sold by Founders [and employees holding greater than [1]% of Company Common Stock (assuming conversion of Preferred Stock)], with a right of oversubscription for Investors of shares unsubscribed by the other Investors. Before any such person may sell Common Stock, he will give the Investors an opportunity to participate in such sale on a basis proportionate to the amount of securities held by the seller and those held by the participating Investors.[19]
Board of Directors:	At the initial Closing, the Board shall consist of [_____] members comprised of (i) [Name] as [the representative designated by [____], as the lead Investor, (ii) [Name] as the representative designated by the remaining Investors, (iii) [Name] as the representative designated by the Founders, (iv) the person then serving as the Chief Executive Officer of the Company, and (v) [_____] person(s) who are not employed by the Company and who are mutually acceptable [to the Founders and Investors][to the other directors].
[Drag Along:	Holders of Preferred Stock and the Founders [and all current and future holders of greater than [1]% of Common Stock (assuming conversion of Preferred Stock and whether then held or subject to the exercise of options)] shall be required to enter into an agreement with the Investors that

---

[19] Certain exceptions are typically negotiated, e.g., estate planning or *de minimis* transfers

provides that such stockholders will vote their shares in favor of a Deemed Liquidation Event or transaction in which 50% or more of the voting power of the Company is transferred, approved by [the Board of Directors] [and the holders of a [majority][super majority] of the outstanding shares of Preferred Stock, on an as-converted basis].

Termination: All rights under the Right of First Refusal/Co-Sale and Voting Agreements shall terminate upon an IPO, a Deemed Liquidation Event or a transfer of more than 50% of Company's voting power.

OTHER MATTERS

Founders' Stock: All Founders to own stock outright subject to Company right to buyback at cost. Buyback right for [____]% for first [12 months] after Closing; thereafter, right lapses in equal [monthly] increments over following [____] months.

[Existing Preferred Stock:[20] The terms set forth below for the Series [____] Stock are subject to a review of the rights, preferences and restrictions for the existing Preferred Stock. Any changes necessary to conform the existing Preferred Stock to this term sheet will be made at the Closing.]

No Shop/Confidentiality: The Company agrees to work in good faith expeditiously towards a closing. The Company and the Founders agree that they will not, for a period of [six] weeks from the date these terms are accepted, take any action to solicit, initiate, encourage or assist the submission of any proposal, negotiation or offer from any person or entity other than the Investors relating to the sale or issuance,

---

[20] Necessary only if this is a later round of financing, and not the initial Series A round.

of any of the capital stock of the Company [or the acquisition, sale, lease, license or other disposition of the Company or any material part of the stock or assets of the Company] and shall notify the Investors promptly of any inquiries by any third parties in regards to the foregoing. [In the event that the Company breaches this no-shop obligation and, prior to [_____], closes any of the above-referenced transactions [without providing the Investors the opportunity to invest on the same terms as the other parties to such transaction], then the Company shall pay to the Investors $[_____] upon the closing of any such transaction as liquidated damages.][21] The Company will not disclose the terms of this Term Sheet to any person other than officers, members of the Board of Directors and the Company's accountants and attorneys and other potential Investors acceptable to [_____], as lead Investor, without the written consent of the Investors.

Expiration: This Term Sheet expires on [_____ ___, _____] if not accepted by the Company by that date.

EXECUTED THIS [_____] DAY OF [_____], 200[____   ].

[SIGNATURE BLOCKS]

---

[21] It is unusual to provide for such "break-up" fees in connection with a venture capital financing, but might be something to consider where there is a substantial possibility the Company may be sold prior to consummation of the financing (e.g., a later stage deal).

Series A Preferred Stock Purchase Agreement

Preliminary Note

The Stock Purchase Agreement sets forth the basic terms of the purchase and sale of the preferred stock to the investors (such as the purchase price, closing date, conditions to closing) and identifies the other financing documents. Generally this agreement does <u>not</u> set forth either (1) the characteristics of the stock being sold (which are defined in the Certificate of Incorporation) or (2) the relationship among the parties after the closing, such as registration rights, rights of first refusal and co-sale, voting arrangements (these matters often implicate other persons than just the Company and the investors in this round of financing, and are usually embodied in separate agreements to which those others persons are parties, or in some cases by the Certificate of Incorporation). The main items of negotiation in the Stock Purchase Agreement are therefore the price and number of shares being sold, and the representations and warranties that the Company, and sometimes the Founders as well, must make to the investors.

TABLE OF CONTENTS

Page

1. Purchase and Sale of Preferred Stock.. 1
   1.1   Sale and Issuance of Series A Preferred Stock................................. 1
   1.2   Closing; Delivery.. 1
   1.3   Sale of Additional Shares of Preferred Stock................................... 2
   [1.4   Use of Proceeds] 3
   1.5   Defined Terms Used in this Agreement 3

2. Representations and Warranties of the Company.............................. 6
   2.1   Organization, Good Standing, Corporate Power and Qualification......7
   2.2   Capitalization... 7
   2.3   Subsidiaries... 9
   2.4   Authorization... 9
   2.5   Valid Issuance of Shares...10
   2.6   Governmental Consents and Filings..11
   2.7   Litigation..11
   2.8   Intellectual Property 12
   2.9   Compliance with Other Instruments 13
   2.10 Agreements; Actions...14
   2.11 Certain Transactions 15
   2.12 Rights of Registration and Voting Rights......................................16
   2.13 Absence of Liens...16
   2.14 Financial Statements 17
   2.15 Changes 18
   2.16 Employee Matters..19
   2.17 Tax Returns and Payments.. 22
   2.18 Insurance.. 22
   2.19 Confidential Information and Invention Assignment Agreements... 22
   2.20 Permits.. 22

TABLE OF CONTENTS
(continued)

2.21   Corporate Documents 23

[2.22   83(b) Elections].. 23

[2.23   Real Property Holding Corporation]........................ 23

2.24   Environmental and Safety Laws.............................. 23

[2.25   Qualified Small Business Stock]............................. 24

2.26   Disclosure... 25

[2.27   Small Business Concern] 26

[3.   Representations and Warranties of the Founders 26

3.1   Conflicting Agreements 27

3.2   Litigation 27

3.3   Stockholder Agreements... 27

3.4   Representations and Warranties............................. 27

3.5   Prior Legal Matters 37

4.   Representations and Warranties of the Purchasers................... 28

4.1   Authorization.. 28

4.2   Purchase Entirely for Own Account 28

4.3   Disclosure of Information 29

4.4   Restricted Securities.. 29

4.5   No Public Market 30

4.6   Legends.. 30

4.7   Accredited Investor 30

4.8   Foreign Investors.. 30

4.9   No General Solicitation..31

4.10   Exculpation Among Purchasers 31

4.11   Residence...31

TABLE OF CONTENTS
(continued)

5.   Conditions to the Purchasers' Obligations at Closing...............32
    5.1   Representations and Warranties........................32
    5.2   Performance 32
    5.3   Compliance Certificate 33
    5.4   Qualifications 33
    5.5   Opinion of Company Counsel 33
    5.6   Board of Directors 33
    5.7   Indemnification Agreement............................33
    5.8   Investors' Rights Agreement..........................33
    5.9   Right of First Refusal and Co-Sale Agreement 33
    5.10   Voting Agreement 33
    5.11   Restated Certificate 33
    5.12   Secretary's Certificate...............................34
    5.13   Proceedings and Documents 34
    5.14   Minimum Number of Shares at Initial Closing.............34
    5.15   Management Rights................................34
    [5.16 SBA Matters]...................................34
    [5.17 Preemptive Rights].................................34

6.   Conditions of the Company's Obligations at Closing 35
    6.1   Representations and Warranties........................35
    6.2   Performance 35
    6.3   Qualifications 35
    6.4   Investors' Rights Agreement..........................35
    6.5   Right of First Refusal and Co-Sale Agreement 35
    6.6   Voting Agreement 35
    [6.7   Minimum Number of Shares at Initial Closing].............35

TABLE OF CONTENTS
(continued)

7.   Miscellaneous...35

    7.1   Survival of Warranties...35

    7.2   Successors and Assigns.. 36

    7.3   Governing Law.. 36

    7.4   Counterparts; Facsimile 36

    7.5   Titles and Subtitles.. 36

    7.6   Notices... 36

    7.7   No Finder's Fees..37

    7.8   Fees and Expenses 37

    7.9   Attorney's Fees...37

    7.10   Amendments and Waivers...37

    7.11   Severability... 38

    7.12   Delays or Omissions.. 38

    7.13   Entire Agreement.. 38

    [7.14 Corporate Securities Law]... 38

    7.15   Dispute Resolution... 39

    [7.16 No Commitment for Additional Financing]..................... 40

Exhibit A   Schedule of Purchasers
Exhibit B   Form of Amended and Restated Certificate of Incorporation
Exhibit C   Disclosure Schedule
Exhibit D   Form of Indemnification Agreement
Exhibit E   Form of Investors' Rights Agreement
Exhibit F   Form of Management Rights Letter
Exhibit G   Form of Right of First Refusal and Co-Sale Agreement
Exhibit H   Form of Voting Agreement
Exhibit I   Form of Legal Opinion of [Company Counsel]
[Exhibit J   Milestone Events]

SERIES A PREFERRED STOCK
PURCHASE AGREEMENT

THIS SERIES A PREFERRED STOCK PURCHASE AGREEMENT (the "Agreement") is made as of the [___] day of [_____ ___, 200_] by and among [___], a Delaware corporation (the "**Company**"), the investors listed on <u>Exhibit A</u> attached to this Agreement (each a "**Purchaser**" and together the "**Purchasers**") [and the persons listed as "Founders" on the signature pages to this Agreement (each a "**Founder**" and together the "**Founders**")].

The parties hereby agree as follows:

1.   <u>Purchase and Sale of Preferred Stock.</u>

    1.1.   <u>Sale and Issuance of Series A Preferred Stock.</u>

        (a)   The Company shall adopt and file with the Secretary of State of the State of Delaware on or before the Initial Closing[1] (as defined below) the Amended and Restated Certificate of Incorporation in the form of <u>Exhibit B</u> attached to this Agreement (the "**Restated Certificate**").[2]

        (b)   Subject to the terms and conditions of this Agreement, each Purchaser agrees to purchase at the Closing and the Company agrees to sell and issue to each Purchaser at the Closing that number of shares of Series A Preferred Stock set forth opposite each Purchaser's name on <u>Exhibit A</u>, at a purchase price of $[_____] per share. The shares of Series A Preferred Stock issued to the Purchasers pursuant to this Agreement (including any shares issued at the Initial Closing and any [Milestone Shares or] Additional Shares, as defined below) shall be referred to in this Agreement as the "**Shares**."

    1.2.   <u>Closing; Delivery.</u>

        (a)   The initial purchase and sale of the Shares shall take place remotely via the exchange of documents and signatures, at [_____]

---

[1]   If only one closing is contemplated, references to "Initial Closing," "each Closing," "such Closing" etc. should be modified.

[2]   Sometimes only a Certificate of Amendments is required.

[___].m., on [_____ ____, 200__], or at such other time and place as the Company and the Purchasers mutually agree upon, orally or in writing (which time and place are designated as the "**Initial Closing**").[3] In the event there is more than one closing, the term "**Closing**" shall apply to each such closing unless otherwise specified.

(b)   At each Closing, the Company shall deliver to each Purchaser a certificate representing the Shares being purchased by such Purchaser at such Closing against payment of the purchase price therefor by check payable to the Company, by wire transfer to a bank account designated by the Company, by cancellation or conversion of indebtedness of the Company to Purchaser [, including interest[4]], or by any combination of such methods.

1.3.   <u>Sale of Additional Shares of Preferred Stock.</u>

(a)   After the Initial Closing, the Company may sell, on the same terms and conditions as those contained in this Agreement[5], up to [___] additional shares of Series A Preferred Stock (the "**Additional Shares**"), to one or more purchasers (the "**Additional Purchasers**") [reasonably acceptable to Purchasers holding a *[specify percentage]* of the then

---

[3]   If the Agreement is signed prior to the Closing, this provision gives the parties flexibility to change the closing date as contingencies arise. As a practical matter, however, the Agreement is usually signed on the date of the Closing. This means that, until the Closing, everyone has an opportunity to back out of the deal.

[4]   If some or all of the Purchasers will be converting previously issued notes to Shares, consider paying the interest in cash, if the terms of the notes permit this, to avoid last-minute recomputations if the closing is delayed. Note that cancellation of interest in return for stock may be a taxable event in the amount of the interest cancelled. Accordingly, some of the Purchasers may require payment of interest in cash to avoid imputation of income without the corresponding payment of cash to pay the tax.

[5]   The Company will often try to negotiate a "cushion" in the negotiated limit of the number of preferred shares in order to permit it to issue additional shares of preferred stock in transactions outside the financing, e.g., warrants for preferred stock issued in connection with an equipment financing. The language "on the same terms and conditions as those contained in this Agreement" is flexible enough to permit this. If the investors want to limit the number of preferred shares to be issued to those preferred shares issued in the financing, the language "pursuant to this Agreement" should be substituted.

outstanding Shares[6]], provided that (i) such subsequent sale is consummated prior to [90] days after the Initial Closing, (ii) each Additional Purchaser shall become a party to the Transaction Agreements, (as defined below) (other than the Management Rights Letter), by executing and delivering a counterpart signature page to each of the Transaction Agreements[, and (iii) [____], counsel for the Company, provides an opinion dated as of the date of such Closing that the offer, issuance, sale and delivery of the Additional Shares to the Additional Purchasers do not require registration under the Securities Act of 1933, as amended, or applicable state securities laws.] Exhibit A to this Agreement shall be updated to reflect the number of Additional Shares purchased at each such Closing and the parties purchasing such Additional Shares.

[(b) After the Initial Closing, the Company shall sell, and the Purchasers shall purchase, on the same terms and conditions as those contained in this Agreement, up to [____] additional shares of Series A Preferred Stock (the "**Milestone Shares**"), *pro rata* in accordance with the number of Shares being purchased by each such Purchaser at all prior Closings, on the certification by the [Board] [Purchasers] that the events specified in Exhibit J attached to this Agreement have occurred (the "**Milestone Events**"). The date of the purchase and sale of the Milestone Shares are referred to in this Agreement as the "**Milestone Closing**."[7]]

[1.4.   Use of Proceeds. In accordance with the directions of the Company's Board of Directors, as it shall be constituted in accordance with the Voting Agreement, the Company will use the proceeds from the sale of the Shares for product development and other general corporate purposes.]

1.5.   Defined Terms Used in this Agreement. In addition to the terms defined above, the following terms used in this Agreement shall be construed to have the meanings set forth or referenced below.

"**Affiliate**" means, with respect to any specified Person, any

---

[6] The Company may want to limit this approval right to the larger Purchasers. As an alternative, the Agreement may specify that Additional Purchasers must be approved by the Board of Directors, including the directors elected by the Series A Preferred Stockholders.

[7] Consider whether the obligations of each Purchaser at a Milestone Closing are conditioned on (i) the representations and warranties remaining true (or materially so) as of such Milestone Closing, (ii) each other Purchaser purchasing shares at the Milestone Closing (i.e., if one Purchaser breaches then no others are obligated), and (iii) any other conditions.

other Person who or which, directly or indirectly, controls, is controlled by, or is under common control with such specified Person, including, without limitation, any partner, officer, director, member or employee of such Person and any venture capital fund now or hereafter existing that is controlled by or under common control with one or more general partners or managing members of, or shares the same management company with, such Person.

"**Code**" means the Internal Revenue Code of 1986, as amended.

"**Company Intellectual Property**" means all patents, patent applications, trademarks, trademark applications, service marks, tradenames, copyrights, trade secrets, licenses, domain names, mask works, information and proprietary rights and processes as are necessary to the conduct of the Company's business as now conducted and as presently proposed to be conducted.

"**Indemnification Agreement**" means the agreement among the Company and a representative of any Purchaser entitled to designate a member of the Board of Directors pursuant to the Voting Agreement, dated as of the date of the Initial Closing, in the form of <u>Exhibit D</u> attached to this Agreement.

"**Investors' Rights Agreement**" means the agreement between the Company and the Purchasers[8] dated as of the date of the Initial Closing, in the form of <u>Exhibit E</u> attached to this Agreement.

"**Key Employee**" means any executive-level employee (including division director and vice president-level positions) as well as any employee or consultant who either alone or in concert with others develops, invents, programs or designs any Company Intellectual Property.[9]

---

[8] In Series A Preferred Stock financings, the Investors' Rights Agreement will normally be signed by all the Series A Purchasers. In subsequent financing rounds, the standard practice is to amend and restate the Investor Rights Agreement, which will then be signed by the Company as well as the subsequent and prior round purchasers.

[9] In a Series A round at a high-tech start-up, it is likely that the only key employees in addition to management, if any, are those who are responsible for developing the Company's key intellectual property assets. It may be simpler for these early-stage companies to list the Key Employees by name. In later rounds, it may be appropriate to include others, e.g., important salespeople or consultants and define Key Employees by function (e.g., division director).

"Knowledge," including the phrase **"to the Company's knowledge,"** shall mean the actual knowledge [after reasonable investigation] of the following officers: [specify names].[10]

"**Management Rights Letter**" means the agreement between the Company and [Purchaser], dated as of the date of the Initial Closing, in the form of Exhibit F attached to this Agreement.

"**Material Adverse Effect**" means a material adverse effect on the business, assets (including intangible assets), liabilities, financial condition, property, prospects[11] or results of operations of the Company.

"**Person**" means any individual, corporation, partnership, trust, limited liability company, association or other entity.

"**Purchaser**" means each of the Purchasers who is initially a party to this Agreement and any Additional Purchaser who becomes a party to this Agreement at a subsequent Closing under Section 1.3.

"**Right of First Refusal and Co-Sale Agreement**" means the agreement among the Company, the Purchasers, and certain other stockholders of the Company, dated as of the date of the Initial Closing, in the form of Exhibit G attached to this Agreement.

"**Securities Act**" means the Securities Act of 1933, as amended, and the rules and regulations promulgated thereunder.

"**Shares**" means the shares of Series A Preferred Stock issued at the Initial Closing and any [Milestone Shares or] Additional Shares issued at a subsequent Closing under Section 1.3.

"**Transaction Agreements**" means this Agreement, the

---

[10] An important point of negotiation is often whether the Company will represent that a given fact (a) is true or (b) is true to the Company's knowledge. Alternative (a) requires the Company to bear the entire risk of the truth or falsity of the represented fact, regardless whether the Company knew (or could have known) at the time of the representation whether or not the fact was true. Alternative (b) is preferable from the Company's standpoint, since it holds the Company responsible only for facts of which it is actually aware.

[11] Since the prospects of high-tech start-up companies are by definition highly uncertain, the Company may resist the inclusion of the word "prospects" on the grounds that investors in a Series A financing are in the business of shouldering that risk.

Investors' Rights Agreement, the Management Rights Letter, the Right of First Refusal and Co-Sale Agreement, the Voting Agreement and [list any other agreements, instruments or documents entered into in connection with this Agreement].

"Voting Agreement" means the agreement among the Company, the Purchasers and certain other stockholders of the Company, dated as of the date of the Initial Closing, in the form of <u>Exhibit H</u> attached to this Agreement.

2. <u>Representations and Warranties of the Company</u>. The Company hereby represents and warrants to each Purchaser that, except as set forth on the Disclosure Schedule attached as Exhibit C to this Agreement which exceptions shall be deemed to be part of the representations and warranties made hereunder, the following representations are true and complete as of the date of the Initial Closing, except as otherwise indicated. The Disclosure Schedule shall be arranged in sections corresponding to the numbered and lettered sections and subsections contained in this Section 2, and the disclosures in any section or subsection of the Disclosure Schedule shall qualify other sections and subsections in this Section 2 only to the extent it is readily apparent from a reading of the disclosure that such disclosure is applicable to such other sections and subsections.[12]

---

[12] The purpose of the Company's representations is primarily to create a mechanism to ensure full disclosure about the Company's organization, financial condition and business to the investors. The Company is required to list any deviations from the representations on a Disclosure Schedule, the preparation and review of which drives the due diligence process on both sides of the deal. For subsequent closings, changes to the Disclosure Schedule are sometimes simply referenced on the Compliance Certificate. The introductory paragraph to this <u>Section 2</u> may be modified to permit an update to the Disclosure Schedule that would be reasonably acceptable to each of the Purchasers. If this modification is made, a closing condition should be added to indicate that the updated Disclosure Schedule will be delivered and that each of the Purchasers may refuse to close if the updated Disclosure Schedule is reasonably unacceptable to that Purchaser. If there is to be a Milestone Closing, specific representations and warranties to be true as of the Milestone Closing date may need to be negotiated. Some practitioners prefer to deliver the Disclosure Schedule separately, instead of as an exhibit to the Stock Purchase Agreement, so that the Disclosure Schedule will not have to be publicly filed in the event the Stock Purchase Agreement is filed as an exhibit to a public offering registration statement.

For purposes of these representations and warranties (other than those in Sections 2.2, 2.3, 2.4, 2.5 and 2.6), the term "the Company" shall include any subsidiaries of the Company, unless otherwise noted herein.

2.1.   Organization, Good Standing, Corporate Power and Qualification.[13] The Company is a corporation duly organized, validly existing and in good standing under the laws of the State of Delaware and has all requisite corporate power and authority to carry on its business as presently conducted and as proposed to be conducted. The Company is duly qualified to transact business and is in good standing in each jurisdiction in which the failure to so qualify would have a Material Adverse Effect.

2.2.   Capitalization.[14] The authorized capital of the Company consists, immediately prior to the Initial Closing, of:

(a)   [____] shares of Common Stock, [____] shares of which are issued and outstanding immediately prior to the Initial Closing. All of the outstanding shares of Common Stock have been duly authorized, are fully paid and nonassessable and were issued in compliance with all applicable federal and state securities laws. [The Company holds no treasury stock and no shares of Series A Preferred Stock in its treasury.]

---

[13] The purpose of this representation is to ensure that basic corporate maintenance has been properly carried out by the Company. Note that the Company is required to disclose failure to qualify in other jurisdictions where it does business only if failure to do so could have a "material adverse effect;" the purpose of this language is to eliminate the time and expense of doing a state-by-state analysis to determine whether the Company should technically be qualified. If the Company has material connections to states in which it is not qualified, these states must be investigated by counsel to determine whether qualification is necessary and whether there are potential adverse effects of having failed to qualify.

[14] Section 2.2 describes the Company's capital structure and can be stated either immediately prior to or upon the Initial Closing of the financing. This description details any outstanding rights or privileges with respect to the Company's securities. In later round financings, this description would also list any co-sale rights and rights of first refusal granted to investors in prior rounds. In later round financings, consider adding representations that there have been no conversions of previously-issued preferred stock to common stock, the number of shares that would be outstanding on an as-converted-to-common stock basis and the current conversion ratios of each series of preferred stock.

(b)   [____] shares of Preferred Stock, of which [____] shares have been designated Series A Preferred Stock, none of which are issued and outstanding immediately prior to the Initial Closing. The rights, privileges and preferences of the Preferred Stock are as stated in the Restated Certificate and as provided by the general corporation law of the jurisdiction of the Company's incorporation.

(c)   The Company has reserved [____] shares of Common Stock for issuance to officers, directors, employees and consultants of the Company pursuant to its [*Plan Year*] Stock [Option] Plan duly adopted by the Board of Directors and approved by the Company stockholders (the "**Stock Plan**"). Of such reserved shares of Common Stock, [____] shares have been issued pursuant to restricted stock purchase agreements, options to purchase [____] shares have been granted and are currently outstanding, and [____] shares of Common Stock remain available for issuance to officers, directors, employees and consultants pursuant to the Stock Plan. The Company has furnished to the Purchasers complete and accurate copies of the Stock Plan and forms of agreements used thereunder.

(d)   Section 2.2(d) of the Disclosure Schedule sets forth the capitalization of the Company immediately following the Initial Closing including the number of shares of the following: (i) issued and outstanding Common Stock, including, with respect to restricted Common Stock, vesting schedule and repurchase price; (ii) issued stock options; (iii) stock options not yet issued but reserved for issuance, including vesting schedule and exercise price; (iv) each series of Preferred Stock; and (v) warrants or stock purchase rights, if any.[15] Except for (A) the conversion privileges of the Shares to be issued under this Agreement, (B) the rights provided in Section 4 of the Investors' Rights Agreement, and (C) the securities and rights described in Section 2.2(c) of this Agreement and Section 2.2(d) of the Disclosure Schedule, there are no outstanding options, warrants, rights (including conversion or preemptive rights and rights of first refusal or similar rights) or agreements, orally or in writing, to purchase or acquire from the Company any shares of Common Stock or Series A Preferred Stock, or any securities convertible into or exchangeable for shares of Common Stock or Series A Preferred Stock. All outstanding shares of the Company's Common Stock and

---

[15] Some practitioners prefer to delete this representation, provided the capitalization table is a separate document.

all shares of the Company's Common Stock underlying outstanding options are subject to (i) a right of first refusal in favor of the Company upon any proposed transfer (other than transfers for estate planning purposes); and (ii) a lock-up or market standoff agreement of not less than 180 days following the Company's initial public offering pursuant to a registration statement filed with the Securities and Exchange Commission under the Securities Act.

(e)   None of the Company's stock purchase agreements or stock option documents contains a provision for acceleration of vesting (or lapse of a repurchase right) or other changes in the vesting provisions or other terms of such agreement or understanding upon the occurrence of any event or combination of events. The Company has never adjusted or amended the exercise price of any stock options previously awarded, whether through amendment, cancellation, replacement grant, repricing, or any other means. No stock options, stock appreciation rights or other equity-based awards issued or granted by the Company are subject to the requirements of Section 409A of the Code. Except as set forth in the Restated Certificate, the Company has no obligation (contingent or otherwise) to purchase or redeem any of its capital stock.

2.3   Subsidiaries.[16] The Company does not currently own or control, directly or indirectly, any interest in any other corporation, partnership, trust, joint venture, limited liability company, association, or other business entity. The Company is not a participant in any joint venture, partnership or similar arrangement.

2.4.   Authorization.[17] All corporate action required to be taken by the Company's Board of Directors and stockholders in order to authorize the Company to enter into the Transaction Agreements, and to issue the Shares at the Closing and the Common Stock issuable upon conversion of

---

[16] The purpose of this representation is to require the Company to fully disclose its structure, including other corporations, if any, that it controls. If the Company does have subsidiaries, you should add to Section 2.3 a representation with respect to the subsidiaries of the Company modeled after Section 2.1 regarding the organization, good standing and qualification of each such subsidiary.

[17] In certain jurisdictions, ancillary agreements executed in connection with the financing, such as noncompetition provisions or voting agreements, may be subject to some question regarding their enforceability, and the representation should be modified accordingly.

the Shares, has been taken or will be taken prior to the Closing. All action on the part of the officers of the Company necessary for the execution and delivery of the Transaction Agreements, the performance of all obligations of the Company under the Transaction Agreements to be performed as of the Closing, and the issuance and delivery of the Shares has been taken or will be taken prior to the Closing. The Transaction Agreements, when executed and delivered by the Company, shall constitute valid and legally binding obligations of the Company, enforceable against the Company in accordance with their respective terms except (i) as limited by applicable bankruptcy, insolvency, reorganization, moratorium, fraudulent conveyance, or other laws of general application relating to or affecting the enforcement of creditors' rights generally, (ii) as limited by laws relating to the availability of specific performance, injunctive relief, or other equitable remedies, or (iii) to the extent the indemnification provisions contained in the Investors' Rights Agreement and the Indemnification Agreement may be limited by applicable federal or state securities laws.

2.5. Valid Issuance of Shares.[18] The Shares, when issued, sold and delivered in accordance with the terms and for the consideration set forth in this Agreement, will be validly issued, fully paid and nonassessable and free of restrictions on transfer other than restrictions on transfer under the Transaction Agreements, applicable state and federal securities laws and liens or encumbrances created by or imposed by a Purchaser. Assuming the accuracy of the representations of the Purchasers in Section [3/4] of this Agreement and subject to the filings described in Section 2.6(ii) below, the Shares will be issued in compliance with all applicable federal and state securities laws. The Common Stock issuable upon conversion of the Shares

---

[18] The representations in Sections 2.4 and 2.5 are intended to ensure that the Company has taken all steps necessary to issue the preferred stock in accordance with applicable corporate law. This means that, before the closing, the Company must (A) obtain the requisite stockholder and board approvals to amend the Certificate of Incorporation and issue the stock; (B) file the Restated Certificate and (C) obtain any other stockholder consents or waivers required pursuant to the Restated Certificate, Bylaws, and existing agreements with securityholders (most importantly, waivers to any existing rights of first offer or refusal). Section 2.5 also requires the Company to disclose any restrictions on transfer other than those contained in the Transaction Agreements (such as any contained in the Restated Certificate and Bylaws, or any preemptive rights contained in agreements with other securityholders).

has been duly reserved for issuance, and upon issuance in accordance with the terms of the Restated Certificate, will be validly issued, fully paid and nonassessable and free of restrictions on transfer other than restrictions on transfer under the Transaction Agreements, applicable federal and state securities laws and liens or encumbrances created by or imposed by a Purchaser. Based in part upon the representations of the Purchasers in Section [3/4] of this Agreement, and subject to Section 2.6 below, the Common Stock issuable upon conversion of the Shares will be issued in compliance with all applicable federal and state securities laws.

2.6. <u>Governmental Consents and Filings</u>. Assuming the accuracy of the representations made by the Purchasers in Section [3/4] of this Agreement, no consent, approval, order or authorization of, or registration, qualification, designation, declaration or filing with, any federal, state or local governmental authority is required on the part of the Company in connection with the consummation of the transactions contemplated by this Agreement, except for (i) the filing of the Restated Certificate, which will have been filed as of the Initial Closing, and (ii) filings pursuant to Regulation D of the Securities Act, and applicable state securities laws, which have been made or will be made in a timely manner.

2.7. <u>Litigation</u>.[19] There is no claim, action, suit, proceeding, arbitration, complaint, charge or investigation[20] pending or to the Company's knowledge, currently threatened [in writing] (i) against the Company or any officer, director or Key Employee of the Company; [or] (ii) [to the Company's knowledge,] that questions the validity of the Transaction Agreements or the right of the Company to enter into them, or to consummate the transactions contemplated by the Transaction Agreements; [or (iii) to the Company's knowledge, that would reasonably be expected to have, either individually or in the aggregate, a Material Adverse Effect.] Neither the Company nor, to the

---

[19] The litigation representation will often be unqualified in Series A financings. The bracketed materiality qualifiers are more common in later rounds of financings. In subsequent rounds it is no longer appropriate to have the Company make representations regarding directors (as opposed to employees), since directors will include investor representatives.

[20] It may be appropriate to include a knowledge qualifier as to investigations since it would be difficult for the Company to know of an investigation unless it had been notified. Some investors nevertheless feel the risk is appropriately borne by the Company.

Company's knowledge, any of its officers or directors, is a party or is named as subject to the provisions of any order, writ, injunction, judgment or decree of any court or government agency or instrumentality (in the case of officers or directors, such as would affect the Company) There is no action, suit, proceeding or investigation by the Company pending or which the Company intends to initiate. The foregoing includes, without limitation, actions, suits, proceedings or investigations pending or threatened in writing (or any basis therefor known to the Company) involving the prior employment of any of the Company's employees, their services provided in connection with the Company's business, or any information or techniques allegedly proprietary to any of their former employers, or their obligations under any agreements with prior employers.

      2.8.   *Intellectual Property*.[21] [The Company owns or possesses or [believes it] can acquire on commercially reasonable terms sufficient legal rights to all Company Intellectual Property without any known conflict with, or infringement of, the rights of others.] To the Company's knowledge, no product or service marketed or sold (or proposed to be marketed or sold) by the Company violates or will violate any license or infringes or will infringe any intellectual property rights of any other party. Other than with respect to commercially available software products under standard end-user object code license agreements, there are no outstanding options, licenses, agreements, claims, encumbrances or shared ownership interests of any kind relating to the Company Intellectual Property, nor is the Company bound by or a party to any options, licenses or agreements of any kind with respect to the patents, trademarks, service marks, trade names, copyrights, trade secrets, licenses, information, proprietary rights and processes of any other Person. The Company has not received any communications alleging that the Company has violated or, by conducting its business, would violate

---

[21] Section 2.8 gives the Purchasers assurances that the Company has the intellectual property rights necessary to conduct its business, or has disclosed its need to acquire further rights. Although Purchasers prefer an unqualified representation, this provision is often heavily negotiated, and may be impossible for the Company to make with certainty for a product in a very early stage of development. Under a common compromise, the Company provides an unqualified representation with respect to everything but patents, on the theory that potential patent conflicts cannot always be uncovered even after reasonable investigation, and that patent conflicts therefore represent an unknown risk that is fairly borne by both parties.

any of the patents, trademarks, service marks, tradenames, copyrights, trade secrets, mask works or other proprietary rights or processes of any other Person. The Company has obtained and possesses valid licenses to use all of the software programs present on the computers and other software-enabled electronic devices that it owns or leases or that it has otherwise provided to its employees for their use in connection with the Company's business. To the Company's knowledge, it will not be necessary to use any inventions of any of its employees or consultants (or Persons it currently intends to hire) made prior to their employment by the Company. Each employee and consultant has assigned to the Company all intellectual property rights he or she owns that are related to the Company's business as now conducted and as presently proposed to be conducted. Section 2.8 of the Disclosure Schedule lists all Company Intellectual Property. The Company has not embedded any open source, copyleft or community source code in any of its products generally available or in development, including but not limited to any libraries or code licensed under any General Public License, Lesser General Public License or similar license arrangement. For purposes of this Section 2.8, the Company shall be deemed to have knowledge of a patent right if the Company has actual knowledge of the patent right or would be found to be on notice of such patent right as determined by reference to United States patent laws.

2.9.   Compliance with Other Instruments. The Company is not in violation or default (i) of any provisions of its Restated Certificate or Bylaws, (ii) of any instrument, judgment, order, writ or decree, (iii) under any note, indenture or mortgage, or (iv) under any lease, agreement, contract or purchase order to which it is a party or by which it is bound that is required to be listed on the Disclosure Schedule, or, [to its knowledge], of any provision of federal or state statute, rule or regulation applicable to the Company, the violation of which would have a Material Adverse Effect. The execution, delivery and performance of the Transaction Agreements and the consummation of the transactions contemplated by the Transaction Agreements will not result in any such violation or be in conflict with or constitute, with or without the passage of time and giving of notice, either (i) a default under any such provision, instrument, judgment, order, writ, decree, contract or agreement or (ii) an event which results in the creation of any lien, charge or encumbrance upon any assets of the Company or the suspension, revocation, forfeiture, or nonrenewal of any material permit or license applicable to the Company.

2.10. Agreements; Action.[22]

(a) Except for the Transaction Agreements, there are no agreements, understandings, instruments, contracts or proposed transactions to which the Company is a party or by which it is bound that involve (i) obligations (contingent or otherwise) of, or payments to, the Company in excess of [_____], (ii) the license of any patent, copyright, trademark, trade secret or other proprietary right to or from the Company, (iii) the grant of rights to manufacture, produce, assemble, license, market, or sell its products to any other Person that limit the Company's exclusive right to develop, manufacture, assemble, distribute, market or sell its products, or (iv) indemnification by the Company with respect to infringements of proprietary rights.

(b) The Company has not (i) declared or paid any dividends, or authorized or made any distribution upon or with respect to any class or series of its capital stock, (ii) incurred any indebtedness for money borrowed or incurred any other liabilities individually in excess of [_____] or in excess of [_____] in the aggregate, (iii) made any loans or advances to any Person, other than ordinary advances for travel expenses, or (iv) sold, exchanged or otherwise disposed of any of its assets or rights, other than the sale of its inventory in the ordinary course of business. For the purposes of subsections (b) and (c) of this Section 2.10, all indebtedness, liabilities, agreements, understandings, instruments, contracts and proposed transactions involving the same Person (including Persons the Company has reason to believe are affiliated with each other) shall be aggregated for the purpose of meeting the individual minimum dollar amounts of such subsection.

(c) The Company is not a guarantor or indemnitor of any indebtedness of any other Person.

[(d) The Company has not engaged in the past [three (3) months] in any discussion with any representative of any Person regarding (i) a sale or exclusive license of all or substantially all of the Company's assets, or (ii) any merger, consolidation or other business combination transaction of the

---

[22] Sections 2.10(a) and (b) require the Company to disclose material contracts as well as other agreements or arrangements that might be important from a due diligence standpoint regardless of dollar amount (such as intellectual property licenses or a proposed acquisition of the Company). The disclosure thresholds are negotiable.

Company with or into another Person.][23]

    2.11.   <u>Certain Transactions.</u>[24]

      (a)   Other than (i) standard employee benefits generally made available to all employees, (ii) standard director and officer indemnification agreements approved by the Board of Directors, and (iii) the purchase of shares of the Company's capital stock and the issuance of options to purchase shares of the Company's Common Stock, in each instance, approved in the written minutes of the Board of Directors (previously provided to the Purchasers or their counsel), there are no agreements, understandings or proposed transactions between the Company and any of its officers, directors, consultants or Key Employees, or any Affiliate thereof.

      (b)   The Company is not indebted, directly or indirectly, to any of its directors, officers or employees or to their respective spouses or children or to any Affiliate of any of the foregoing, other than in connection with expenses or advances of expenses incurred in the ordinary course of business or employee relocation expenses and for other customary employee benefits made generally available to all employees. None of the Company's directors, officers or employees, or any members of their immediate families, or any Affiliate of the foregoing (i) are, directly or indirectly, indebted to the Company or, (ii) to the Company's knowledge, have any direct or indirect ownership interest in any firm or corporation with which the Company is affiliated or with which the Company has a business relationship, or any firm or corporation which competes with the Company except that directors, officers or employees or stockholders of the Company may own stock in (but not exceeding two percent (2%) of the outstanding capital stock of) publicly traded companies that may compete with the Company. [To the Company's knowledge,] none of the Company's Key Employees or directors or any members of their immediate families or any Affiliate of any of the

---

[23] This representation is not standard, but is sometimes requested by investors concerned that the Company might be considering a business combination transaction.

[24] This representation requires disclosure of situations which could create a conflict of interest. This is an item of particular concern in the first round of venture capital financing, since loans among the Company and its founders and their families (which may not be well documented) are especially common prior to the first infusion of outside capital.

foregoing are, directly or indirectly, interested in any [material] contract with the Company. None of the directors or officers, or any members of their immediate families, has any material commercial, industrial, banking, consulting, legal, accounting, charitable or familial relationship with any of the Company's customers, suppliers, service providers, joint venture partners, licensees and competitors.[25]

2.12. <u>Rights of Registration and Voting Rights</u>.[26] Except as provided in the Investors' Rights Agreement, the Company is not under any obligation to register under the Securities Act any of its currently outstanding securities or any securities issuable upon exercise or conversion of its currently outstanding securities. To the Company's knowledge, except as contemplated in the Voting Agreement, no stockholder of the Company has entered into any agreements with respect to the voting of capital shares of the Company.

2.13. <u>Absence of Liens</u>. The property and assets that the Company owns are free and clear of all mortgages, deeds of trust, liens, loans and encumbrances, except for statutory liens for the payment of current taxes that are not yet delinquent and encumbrances and liens that arise in the ordinary course of business and do not materially impair the Company's ownership or use of such property or assets. With respect to the property and assets it leases, the Company is in compliance with such leases and, to its knowledge, holds a valid leasehold interest free of any liens, claims or encumbrances other than those of the lessors of such property or assets.

---

[25] Here, too, it is appropriate to include directors in this representation only at the first financing round. In subsequent rounds the directors will include investor representatives, and it should not be incumbent on the Company to make disclosures as to them.

[26] Prior registration rights may conflict with those currently being negotiated among the investors and the Company. Therefore, any such rights must be carefully reviewed and any conflicts resolved. It is common to have any previous registration rights agreement amended to include the new investors, or replaced by a new agreement including the old and new investors and clarifying their rights relative to each other as well as the Company. It is preferable to have all registration rights relating to the Company's securities set forth in one document. Having several different sets of rights outstanding can be a significant (and confusing) complication when the Company goes public.

2.14.   Financial Statements.[27] The Company has delivered to each Purchaser its [unaudited] [audited] financial statements as of [_____ ____, 200__] and for the fiscal year ended [_____ ____, 200__] [and its unaudited financial statements (including balance sheet, income statement and statement of cash flows) as of [_____ ____, 200__] and for the [___]-month period ended [_____ ____, 200__]] (collectively, the "**Financial Statements**"). The Financial Statements have been prepared in accordance with generally accepted accounting principles applied on a consistent basis throughout the periods indicated, [except that the unaudited Financial Statements may not contain all footnotes required by generally accepted accounting principles]. The Financial Statements fairly present in all material respects the financial condition and operating results of the Company as of the dates, and for the periods, indicated therein, subject in the case of the unaudited Financial Statements to normal year-end audit adjustments. Except as set forth in the Financial Statements, the Company has no material liabilities or obligations, contingent or otherwise, other than (i) liabilities incurred in the ordinary course of business subsequent to [_____] (ii) obligations under contracts and commitments incurred in the ordinary course of business and (iii) liabilities and obligations of a type or nature not required under generally accepted accounting principles to be reflected in the Financial Statements, which, in all such cases, individually and in the aggregate would not have a Material Adverse Effect. The Company maintains and will continue to maintain a standard system of accounting established and administered in accordance with generally accepted accounting principles.

---

[27] For early stage companies without financial statements, it may be appropriate to have an alternative provision, such as the following:

Material Liabilities. The Company has no liability or obligation, absolute or contingent (individually or in the aggregate), except (i) obligations and liabilities incurred after the date of incorporation in the ordinary course of business that are not material, individually or in the aggregate, and (ii) obligations under contracts made in the ordinary course of business that would not be required to be reflected in financial statements prepared in accordance with generally accepted accounting principles.

2.15.   Changes.[28] Since [date of most recent financial statements/ date of incorporation if no financial statements] there has not been:

(a)   any change in the assets, liabilities, financial condition or operating results of the Company from that reflected in the Financial Statements, except changes in the ordinary course of business that have not caused, in the aggregate, a Material Adverse Effect;

(b)   any damage, destruction or loss, whether or not covered by insurance, that would have a Material Adverse Effect;

(c)   any waiver or compromise by the Company of a valuable right or of a material debt owed to it;

(d)   any satisfaction or discharge of any lien, claim, or encumbrance or payment of any obligation by the Company, except in the ordinary course of business and the satisfaction or discharge of which would not have a Material Adverse Effect;

(e)   any material change to a material contract or agreement by which the Company or any of its assets is bound or subject;

(f)   any material change in any compensation arrangement or agreement with any employee, officer, director or stockholder;

(g)   any resignation or termination of employment of any officer or Key Employee of the Company;

(h)   any mortgage, pledge, transfer of a security interest in, or lien, created by the Company, with respect to any of its material properties or assets, except liens for taxes not yet due or payable and liens that arise in the ordinary course of business and do not materially impair the Company's ownership or use of such property or assets;

---

[28] The purpose of this representation is to "bring down" the financial statements from the period covered thereby. Therefore, the blank in Section 2.15 should be filled with the last date covered by the financial statements provided to the investors, and any of the changes listed in this section must be disclosed on the Disclosure Schedule. While the itemization in this section serves as a useful due diligence checklist, this section can be replaced by a much shorter section reading simply, "[To the Company's knowledge], since [_____,] there have been no events or circumstances of any kind that have had or could reasonably be expected to result in a Material Adverse Effect."

(i) any loans or guarantees made by the Company to or for the benefit of its employees, officers or directors, or any members of their immediate families, other than travel advances and other advances made in the ordinary course of its business;

(j) any declaration, setting aside or payment or other distribution in respect of any of the Company's capital stock, or any direct or indirect redemption, purchase, or other acquisition of any of such stock by the Company;

(k) any sale, assignment or transfer of any Company Intellectual Property that could reasonably be expected to result in a Material Adverse Effect;

(l) receipt of notice that there has been a loss of, or material order cancellation by, any major customer of the Company;

(m) to the Company's knowledge, any other event or condition of any character, other than events affecting the economy or the Company's industry generally, that could reasonably be expected to result in a Material Adverse Effect; or

(n) any arrangement or commitment by the Company to do any of the things described in this Section 2.15.

2.16. Employee Matters.

(a) As of the date hereof, the Company employs [____] full-time employees and [____] part-time employees and engages [____] consultants or independent contractors. [Section 2.16 of] the Disclosure Schedule sets forth a detailed description of all compensation, including salary, bonus, severance obligations and deferred compensation paid or payable for each officer, employee, consultant and independent contractor of the Company who received compensation in excess of $[   ] for the fiscal year ended [_____ ____, 200_] or is anticipated to receive compensation in excess of $[___] for the fiscal year ending [_____ ____, 200_].[29]

---

[29] Many practitioners prefer not to list employee compensation in the Disclosure Schedule, particularly if employees are participating in the round. Even if there is no employee participation, however, employee compensation is a sensitive matter for many companies, and there is always a risk of the Disclosure Schedule inadvertently winding up in the wrong hands.

(b)   To the Company's knowledge, none of its employees is obligated under any contract (including licenses, covenants or commitments of any nature) or other agreement, or subject to any judgment, decree or order of any court or administrative agency, that would materially interfere with such employee's ability to promote the interest of the Company or that would conflict with the Company's business. Neither the execution or delivery of the Transaction Agreements, nor the carrying on of the Company's business by the employees of the Company, nor the conduct of the Company's business as now conducted and as presently proposed to be conducted, will, to the Company's knowledge, conflict with or result in a breach of the terms, conditions, or provisions of, or constitute a default under, any contract, covenant or instrument under which any such employee is now obligated.

(c)   The Company is not delinquent in payments to any of its employees, consultants, or independent contractors for any wages, salaries, commissions, bonuses, or other direct compensation for any service performed for it to the date hereof or amounts required to be reimbursed to such employees, consultants, or independent contractors. The Company has complied in all material respects with all applicable state and federal equal employment opportunity laws and with other laws related to employment, including those related to wages, hours, worker classification, and collective bargaining. The Company has withheld and paid to the appropriate governmental entity or is holding for payment not yet due to such governmental entity all amounts required to be withheld from employees of the Company and is not liable for any arrears of wages, taxes, penalties, or other sums for failure to comply with any of the foregoing.

(d)   To the Company's knowledge, no Key Employee intends to terminate employment with the Company or is otherwise likely to become unavailable to continue as a Key Employee, nor does the Company have a present intention to terminate the employment of any of the foregoing. The employment of each employee of the Company is terminable at the will of the Company. Except as set forth in <u>Section 2.16</u> of the Disclosure Schedule or as required by law, upon termination of the employment of any such employees, no severance or other payments will become due. Except as set forth in <u>Section 2.16</u> of the Disclosure Schedule, the Company has no policy, practice, plan, or program of paying severance pay or any form of severance compensation in connection with the termination of employment services.

(e)   The Company has not made any representations

regarding equity incentives to any officer, employees, director or consultant that are inconsistent with the share amounts and terms set forth in the Company's board minutes.

(f)   Each former Key Employee whose employment was terminated by the Company has entered into an agreement with the Company providing for the full release of any claims against the Company or any related party arising out of such employment.

(g)   Section 2.16 of the Disclosure Schedule sets forth each employee benefit plan maintained, established or sponsored by the Company, or which the Company participates in or contributes to, which is subject to the Employee Retirement Income Security Act of 1974, as amended ("**ERISA**"). The Company has made all required contributions and has no liability to any such employee benefit plan, other than liability for health plan continuation coverage described in Part 6 of Title I(B) of ERISA, and has complied in all material respects with all applicable laws for any such employee benefit plan.

[(h)   The Company is not bound by or subject to (and none of its assets or properties is bound by or subject to) any written or oral, express or implied, contract, commitment or arrangement with any labor union, and no labor union has requested or, to the knowledge of the Company, has sought to represent any of the employees, representatives or agents of the Company. There is no strike or other labor dispute involving the Company pending, or to the Company's knowledge, threatened, which could have a Material Adverse Effect, nor is the Company aware of any labor organization activity involving its employees.]

[(i)   To the Company's knowledge, none of the Key Employees or directors[30] of the Company has been (a) subject to voluntary or involuntary petition under the federal bankruptcy laws or any state insolvency law or the appointment of a receiver, fiscal agent or similar officer by a court for his business or property; (b) convicted in a criminal proceeding or named as a subject of a pending criminal proceeding (excluding traffic violations and other minor offenses); (c) subject to any order, judgment, or decree (not subsequently reversed, suspended, or vacated) of any court of competent jurisdiction permanently or temporarily enjoining him from engaging, or otherwise imposing limits or conditions on his engagement in any securities, investment advisory, banking, insurance, or other type of business or acting

---

[30] See Footnote 24 – same point.

as an officer or director of a public company; or (d) found by a court of competent jurisdiction in a civil action or by the Securities and Exchange Commission or the Commodity Futures Trading Commission to have violated any federal or state securities, commodities, or unfair trade practices law, which such judgment or finding has not been subsequently reversed, suspended, or vacated.]

2.17. <u>Tax Returns and Payments</u>. There are no federal, state, county, local or foreign taxes dues and payable by the Company which have not been timely paid. There are no accrued and unpaid federal, state, country, local or foreign taxes of the Company which are due, whether or not assessed or disputed. There have been no examinations or audits of any tax returns or reports by any applicable federal, state, local or foreign governmental agency. The Company has duly and timely filed all federal, state, county, local and foreign tax returns required to have been filed by it and there are in effect no waivers of applicable statutes of limitations with respect to taxes for any year.

2.18. <u>Insurance</u>.[31] The Company has in full force and effect fire and casualty insurance policies with extended coverage, sufficient in amount (subject to reasonable deductions) to allow it to replace any of its properties that might be damaged or destroyed.

2.19. <u>Confidential Information and Invention Assignment Agreements</u>.[32] Each current and former employee, consultant and officer of the Company has executed an agreement with the Company regarding confidentiality and proprietary information substantially in the form or forms delivered to the counsel for the Purchasers (the "**Confidential Information Agreements**"). No current or former Key Employee has excluded works or inventions from his or her assignment of inventions pursuant to such Key Employee's Confidential Information Agreement. The Company is not aware that any of its Key Employees is in violation thereof.

2.20. <u>Permits</u>. The Company and each of its subsidiaries has all franchises, permits, licenses and any similar authority necessary for the

---

[31] The investors may negotiate life insurance coverage in favor of the Company for certain founders or other key employees. If such coverage is in effect prior to the closing, it may be appropriate to add to this representation a statement of the covered individuals and amount of coverage for each.

[32] Consider expanding this representation to include non-competition agreements, perhaps limited to Key Employees.

conduct of its business, the lack of which could reasonably be expected to have a Material Adverse Effect. The Company is not in default in any material respect under any of such franchises, permits, licenses or other similar authority.

      2.21.   <u>Corporate Documents</u>. The Restated Certificate and Bylaws of the Company are in the form provided to the Purchasers. The copy of the minute books of the Company provided to the Purchasers contains minutes of all meetings of directors and stockholders and all actions by written consent without a meeting by the directors and stockholders since the date of incorporation and accurately reflects in all material respects all actions by the directors (and any committee of directors) and stockholders with respect to all transactions referred to in such minutes.

      [2.22   <u>83(b) Elections</u>. To the Company's knowledge, all elections and notices under Section 83(b) of the Code have been or will be timely filed by all individuals who have acquired unvested shares of the Company's Common Stock.][33]

      [2.23   <u>Real Property Holding Corporation</u>.[34] The Company is not now and has never been a "United States real property holding corporation" as defined in the Code and any applicable regulations promulgated thereunder. The Company has filed with the Internal Revenue Service all statements, if any, with its United States income tax returns which are required under such regulations.]

      2.24.   <u>Environmental and Safety Laws</u>. Except as could not reasonably be expected to have a Material Adverse Effect [to the best of its knowl-

---

[33] This representation is fairly standard in West Coast venture financing transactions; it is much less common in financings originating on the East Coast.

[34] This representation is appropriate if there are foreign investors (<u>i.e.</u>, nonresident aliens) involved in the financing, since they are subject to the Foreign Investment Real Property Tax Act of 1980 ("<u>FIRPTA</u>"). Under FIRPTA, a transfer of an interest in a U.S. Real Property Holding Corporation (a "<u>USRPHC</u>") by a foreign investor is subject to tax withholding, notwithstanding the general rule that sales of stock by foreigners are not subject to U.S. taxation. A corporation is USRPHC if more than 50% of its assets consist of U.S. real property. While very few, if any, venture capital investors are USRPHC's, it is customary to provide this representation in order to ensure that any foreign investors will not be subject to tax withholding. Regardless of FIRPTA, if a foreign person or entity is, directly or indirectly, acquiring an 10% or greater voting interest in the Company, it must file Form BE-13 with the U.S. Department of Commerce unless an exemption applies.

edge] (a) the Company is and has been in compliance with all Environmental Laws; (b) there has been no release or [to the Company's knowledge] threatened release of any pollutant, contaminant or toxic or hazardous material, substance or waste, or petroleum or any fraction thereof, (each a "**Hazardous Substance**") on, upon, into or from any site currently or heretofore owned, leased or otherwise used by the Company; (c) there have been no Hazardous Substances generated by the Company that have been disposed of or come to rest at any site that has been included in any published U.S. federal, state or local "superfund" site list or any other similar list of hazardous or toxic waste sites published by any governmental authority in the United States; and (d) there are no underground storage tanks located on, no polychlorinated biphenyls ("**PCBs**") or PCB-containing equipment used or stored on, and no hazardous waste as defined by the Resource Conservation and Recovery Act, as amended, stored on, any site owned or operated by the Company, except for the storage of hazardous waste in compliance with Environmental Laws. The Company has made available to the Purchasers true and complete copies of all material environmental records, reports, notifications, certificates of need, permits, pending permit applications, correspondence, engineering studies, and environmental studies or assessments.

For purposes of this Section 2.24, "**Environmental Laws**" means any law, regulation, or other applicable requirement relating to (a) releases or threatened release of Hazardous Substance; (b) pollution or protection of employee health or safety, public health or the environment; or (c) the manufacture, handling, transport, use, treatment, storage, or disposal of Hazardous Substances.

[2.25   Qualified Small Business Stock.[35] As of and immediately following the Closing: (i) the Company will be an eligible corporation as defined in Section 1202(e)(4) of the Code, (ii) the Company will not have made

---

[35] Section 1202 of the Internal Revenue Code provides for a 50% exclusion (subject to certain limitations) from taxable income of gains recognized on the disposition of certain stock in qualifying corporations that has been held for at least five years. Although investors may ask for such a representation, companies may resist on the theory that the analysis regarding current compliance is complex, and that many elements of the test are outside the Company's control. In any event, compliance with numerous other requirements during the time the investor holds the stock is needed for the investor to qualify for the benefits of Section 1202.

purchases of its own stock described in Code Section 1202(c)(3)(B) during the one-year period preceding the Initial Closing, except for purchases that are disregarded for such purposes under Treasury Regulation Section 1.1202-2 and (iii) the Company's aggregate gross assets, as defined by Code Section 1202(d)(2), at no time between its incorporation and through the Initial Closing have exceeded $50 million, taking into account the assets of any corporations required to be aggregated with the Company in accordance with Code Section 1202(d)(3); <u>provided, however</u>, that in no event shall the Company be liable to the Purchasers or any other party for any damages arising from any subsequently proven or identified error in the Company's determination with respect to the applicability or interpretation of Code Section 1202, unless such determination shall have been given by the Company in a manner either grossly negligent or fraudulent.]

2.26   <u>Disclosure</u>.[36] The Company has made available to the Purchasers all the information reasonably available to the Company that the Purchasers have requested for deciding whether to acquire the Shares, including certain of the Company's projections describing its proposed business plan (the "**Business Plan**"). [To the Company's knowledge,] no representation or warranty of the Company contained in this Agreement, as qualified by the Disclosure Schedule, and no certificate furnished or to be furnished to Purchasers at the Closing contains any untrue statement of a material fact or omits to state a material fact necessary in order to make the statements contained herein or therein not misleading in light of the circumstances under which they were made. The Business Plan was prepared in good faith; however, the Company does not warrant that it will

---

[36] There is no consensus position on what should be included in the "Disclosure" representation. Purchasers will generally try to obtain an unqualified representation that none of the written information and business plan information provided to them by the Company contains a material misstatement or a materially misleading omission. The Company will generally try to resist such a broad representation, on the basis that a 10b-5 type representation, commonly found in an IPO prospectus, is inappropriate for a private financing in which a prospectus-type due diligence process has not occurred. The language shown represents a compromise position. It is important to note that the investors' right of recovery for a breach of this rep may be broader than under Rule SEC 10b-5, because in order to prevail in a Rule 10b-5 securities fraud action, the purchaser must establish that the seller acted with scienter. That is, a purely innocent misrepresentation normally does not give rise to civil liability under 10b-5.

achieve any results projected in the Business Plan. It is understood that this representation is qualified by the fact that the Company has not delivered to the Purchasers, and has not been requested to deliver, a private placement or similar memorandum or any written disclosure of the types of information customarily furnished to purchasers of securities.

[2.27 Small Business Concern.[37] The Company together with its "affiliates" (as that term is defined in Section 121.103 of Title 13 of the Code of Federal Regulations ("**CFR**"), is a ["small business concern"]["smaller business"] within the meaning of the Small Business Investment Act of 1958, as amended (the "**Small Business Act**"), and the regulations promulgated thereunder, including [Section 121.301 of Title 13 of the CFR] [Section 107.710 of Title 13 of the CFR]. The information delivered to each Purchaser that is a licensed Small Business Investment Company (an "**SBIC Purchaser**") on SBA Forms 480, 652 and 1031 delivered in connection herewith is true and complete. The Company is not ineligible for financing by any SBIC Purchaser pursuant to Section 107.720 of the CFR. The Company acknowledges that each SBIC Purchaser is a Federal licensee under the Small Business Act.]

[3. Representations and Warranties of the Founders.[38] Except as set forth on the Disclosure Schedule, each of the Founders, severally and not jointly, represents and warrants to each Purchaser as of the date of the Closing at which such Purchaser is purchasing Shares as follows [(it being understood and agreed that any Founder's liability for breaches of any provisions of this Section 3 shall be limited to the then current fair market value of the shares of Common Stock of the Company currently owned by such Founder and such Founder may in his sole discretion, discharge such liability by the surrender of such shares or the payment of cash and will terminate on the earlier of (i)

---

[37] The Small Business Concern representation is only necessary if one or more Purchasers is an SBIC.

[38] Founders' representations are controversial and may elicit significant resistance. They are more common in the Northeast and counsel should be warned that they may not be well received elsewhere. They are more likely to appear if Founders are receiving liquidity from the transaction or if there is heightened concern over intellectual property (e.g., the Company is a spin-out from an academic institution or the Founder was formerly with another Company whose business could be deemed competitive with the Company). Founders' representations are not common in subsequent rounds, even in the Northeast, where risk is viewed as significantly diminished and fairly shared by the investors rather than being disproportionately borne by the Founders.

[one year/two years] after the date of this Agreement, or (ii) the completion of an initial public offering of the Company's Common Stock)]:

3.1   Conflicting Agreements. Such Founder is not, as a result of the nature of the business conducted or currently proposed to be conducted by the Company or for any other reason, in violation of (i) any fiduciary or confidential relationship, (ii) any term of any contract or covenant (either with the Company or with another entity) relating to employment, patents, assignment of inventions, confidentiality, proprietary information disclosure, non-competition or non-solicitation, or (iii) any other contract or agreement, or any judgment, decree or order of any court or administrative agency binding on the Founder and relating to or affecting the right of such Founder to be employed by or serve as a director or consultant to the Company. No such relationship, term, contact, agreement, judgment, decree or order conflict with such Founder's obligations to use his best efforts to promote the interests of the Company nor does the execution and delivery of this Agreement, nor such Founder's carrying on the Company's business as a director, officer, consultant or Key Employee of the Company, conflict with any such relationship, term, contract, agreement, judgment, decree or order.

3.2   Litigation. There is no action, suit or proceeding, or governmental inquiry or investigation, pending or, to such Founder's knowledge, threatened against such Founder, and, to such Founder's knowledge, there is no basis for any such action, suit, proceeding, or governmental inquiry or investigation that would result in a Material Adverse Effect.

3.3   Stockholder Agreements. Except as contemplated by or disclosed in the Transaction Agreements, such Founder is not a party to and has no knowledge of any agreements, written or oral, relating to the acquisition, disposition, registration under the Securities Act, or voting of the securities of the Company.

3.4   Representations and Warranties. [To such Founder's knowledge,] all of the representations and warranties of the Company set forth in Section 2 are true and complete.

3.5   Prior Legal Matters. Such Founder has not been (a) subject to voluntary or involuntary petition under the federal bankruptcy laws or any state insolvency law or the appointment of a receiver, fiscal agent or similar officer by a court for his business or property; (b) convicted in a criminal proceeding or named as a subject of a pending criminal proceeding

27

(excluding traffic violations and other minor offenses); (c) subject to any order, judgment, or decree (not subsequently reversed, suspended, or vacated) of any court of competent jurisdiction permanently or temporarily enjoining him from engaging, or otherwise imposing limits or conditions on his engagement in any securities, investment advisory, banking, insurance, or other type of business or acting as an officer or director of a public company; or (d) found by a court of competent jurisdiction in a civil action or by the Securities and Exchange Commission or the Commodity Futures Trading Commission to have violated any federal or state securities, commodities or unfair trade practices law, which such judgment or finding has not been subsequently reversed, suspended, or vacated.]

4.   Representations and Warranties of the Purchasers.[39] Each Purchaser hereby represents and warrants to the Company, severally and not jointly, that:

4.1.   Authorization. The Purchaser has full power and authority to enter into the Transaction Agreements. The Transaction Agreements to which such Purchaser is a party, when executed and delivered by the Purchaser, will constitute valid and legally binding obligations of the Purchaser, enforceable in accordance with their terms, except (a) as limited by applicable bankruptcy, insolvency, reorganization, moratorium, fraudulent conveyance, and any other laws of general application affecting enforcement of creditors' rights generally, and as limited by laws relating to the availability of specific performance, injunctive relief, or other equitable remedies, or (b) to the extent the indemnification provisions contained in the Investors' Rights Agreement or the Indemnification Agreement may be limited by applicable federal or state securities laws.

4.2.   Purchase Entirely for Own Account.[40] This Agreement is made with the Purchaser in reliance upon the Purchaser's representation to

---

[39] The main purpose of the Purchasers' representations and warranties in Section 4 are to ensure that the investors meet the criteria for private placement exceptions under applicable state and federal securities laws.

[40] Occasionally, a venture capital fund will allow its employees and principals to co-invest through a special entity as nominee. Assuming these employees and principals meet the accreditation or sophistication standards necessary for the private placement exemption being relied on, and assuming the special purpose entity is not formed solely for the purpose of this investment, the language of this provision can be tailored to carve out that special entity.

the Company, which by the Purchaser's execution of this Agreement, the Purchaser hereby confirms, that the Shares to be acquired by the Purchaser will be acquired for investment for the Purchaser's own account, not as a nominee or agent, and not with a view to the resale or distribution of any part thereof, and that the Purchaser has no present intention of selling, granting any participation in, or otherwise distributing the same. By executing this Agreement, the Purchaser further represents that the Purchaser does not presently have any contract, undertaking, agreement or arrangement with any Person to sell, transfer or grant participations to such Person or to any third Person, with respect to any of the Shares. The Purchaser has not been formed for the specific purpose of acquiring the Shares.

4.3.   Disclosure of Information. The Purchaser has had an opportunity to discuss the Company's business, management, financial affairs and the terms and conditions of the offering of the Shares with the Company's management and has had an opportunity to review the Company's facilities. The foregoing, however, does not limit or modify the representations and warranties of the Company in Section 2 of this Agreement or the right of the Purchasers to rely thereon.

4.4   Restricted Securities. The Purchaser understands that the Shares have not been, and will not be, registered under the Securities Act, by reason of a specific exemption from the registration provisions of the Securities Act which depends upon, among other things, the bona fide nature of the investment intent and the accuracy of the Purchaser's representations as expressed herein. The Purchaser understands that the Shares are "restricted securities" under applicable U.S. federal and state securities laws and that, pursuant to these laws, the Purchaser must hold the Shares indefinitely unless they are registered with the Securities and Exchange Commission and qualified by state authorities, or an exemption from such registration and qualification requirements is available. The Purchaser acknowledges that the Company has no obligation to register or qualify the Shares, or the Common Stock into which it may be converted, for resale except as set forth in the Investors' Rights Agreement. The Purchaser further acknowledges that if an exemption from registration or qualification is available, it may be conditioned on various requirements including, but not limited to, the time and manner of sale, the holding period for the Shares, and on requirements relating to the Company which are outside of the Purchaser's control, and which the

Company is under no obligation and may not be able to satisfy. [Purchaser acknowledges that the Company filed a registration statement for a public offering of its Common Stock, which was withdrawn effective [_____ ____, 200_]. Purchaser understands that this offering is not intended to be part of the public offering, and that Purchaser will not be able to rely on the protection of Section 11 of the Securities Act.[41]]

4.5.   <u>No Public Market</u>. The Purchaser understands that no public market now exists for the Shares, and that the Company has made no assurances that a public market will ever exist for the Shares.

4.6.   <u>Legends</u>. The Purchaser understands that the Shares and any securities issued in respect of or exchange for the Shares, may bear one or all of the following legends:

(a)   "THE SHARES REPRESENTED BY THIS CERTIFICATE HAVE NOT BEEN REGISTERED UNDER THE SECURITIES ACT OF 1933, AND HAVE BEEN ACQUIRED FOR INVESTMENT AND NOT WITH A VIEW TO, OR IN CONNECTION WITH, THE SALE OR DISTRIBUTION THEREOF. NO SUCH TRANSFER MAY BE EFFECTED WITHOUT AN EFFECTIVE REGISTRATION STATEMENT RELATED THERETO OR AN OPINION OF COUNSEL IN A FORM SATISFACTORY TO THE COMPANY THAT SUCH REGISTRATION IS NOT REQUIRED UNDER THE SECURITIES ACT OF 1933."

(b)   Any legend set forth in, or required by, the other Transaction Agreements.

(c)   Any legend required by the securities laws of any state to the extent such laws are applicable to the Shares represented by the certificate so legended.

4.7.   <u>Accredited Investor</u>. The Purchaser is an accredited investor as defined in Rule 501(a) of Regulation D promulgated under the Securities Act.

4.8.   <u>Foreign Investors</u>. If the Purchaser is not a United States person (as defined by Section 7701(a)(30) of the Code), such Purchaser hereby represents that it has satisfied itself as to the full observance of the

---

[41] Include the bracketed language if the private placement exemption is based on the safe harbor in Rule 155(c) under the Securities Act for private offerings following an abandoned public offering.

laws of its jurisdiction in connection with any invitation to subscribe for the Shares or any use of this Agreement, including (i) the legal requirements within its jurisdiction for the purchase of the Shares, (ii) any foreign exchange restrictions applicable to such purchase, (iii) any governmental or other consents that may need to be obtained, and (iv) the income tax and other tax consequences, if any, that may be relevant to the purchase, holding, redemption, sale, or transfer of the Shares. Such Purchaser's subscription and payment for and continued beneficial ownership of the Shares will not violate any applicable securities or other laws of the Purchaser's jurisdiction.

4.9   No General Solicitation. Neither the Purchaser, nor any of its officers, directors, employees, agents, stockholders or partners has either directly or indirectly, including through a broker or finder (a) engaged in any general solicitation, or (b) published any advertisement in connection with the offer and sale of the Shares.

4.10.   Exculpation Among Purchasers. Each Purchaser acknowledges that it is not relying upon any Person, other than the Company and its officers and directors, in making its investment or decision to invest in the Company. [Each Purchaser agrees that no Purchaser nor the respective controlling Persons, officers, directors, partners, agents, or employees of any Purchaser shall be liable to any other Purchaser for any action heretofore or hereafter taken or omitted to be taken by any of them in connection with the purchase of the Shares.][42]

4.11.   Residence. If the Purchaser is an individual, then the Purchaser resides in the state or province identified in the address of the Purchaser set forth on Exhibit A; if the Purchaser is a partnership, corporation, limited liability company or other entity, then the office or offices of the Purchaser in which its principal place of business is identified in the address or addresses of the Purchaser set forth on Exhibit A.

---

[42] This provision is intended to protect the lead investor from claims of reliance by other investors.

5.   Conditions to the Purchasers' Obligations at Closing.[43] The obligations of each Purchaser to purchase Shares at the Initial Closing [or any subsequent Closing] are subject to the fulfillment, on or before such Closing, of each of the following conditions, unless otherwise waived:

5.1.   Representations and Warranties. The representations and warranties of the Company contained in Section 2 [and the representations and warranties of the Founders in Section 3] shall be true and correct in all material respects as of such Closing, except that any such representations and warranties shall be true and correct in all respects where such representation and warranty is qualified with respect to materiality.

5.2.   Performance. The Company shall have performed and complied with all covenants, agreements, obligations and conditions contained in this Agreement that are required to be performed or complied with by the Company on or before such Closing.

---

[43] Section 5 contains the conditions which the Company must satisfy (or which must be waived) prior to closing in order to trigger the investors' obligation to purchase the shares; Section 6 contains the conditions the investors must satisfy to trigger the Company's obligation to sell the shares. With respect to each side, the essential requirements are (A) that all of the representations and warranties each makes in the Agreement are still true at the closing and (B) that the other parties have entered into the other Transaction Agreements.

Sections 5.3 and 5.5 specifically require the Company to deliver at the Closing a Compliance Certificate and opinion of Company Counsel. In addition, it is generally necessary to deliver at the Closing (A) a Secretary's certificate certifying the Company's bylaws, board resolutions approving the transaction, and stockholder resolutions approving the Restated Certificate (B) good standing certificates from the Secretary of State (C) the certified Restated Certificate, and (D) waivers of any rights of first refusal triggered by the financing. These documents are therefore listed as "Closing Documents" on transaction checklists even though they are not specifically required to be delivered by the Agreement and are technically covered by the Compliance Certificate and the opinion of the Company's counsel. If the transaction is structured as a simultaneous signing and closing, the closing conditions serve as a convenient closing checklist, but are significantly diminished in importance.

If there are to be subsequent closings, consider whether all of the closing conditions applicable to the Initial Closing should be applicable to the subsequent closing. It may be appropriate to include a separate, more limited set of closing conditions for a subsequent closing.

5.3.   <u>Compliance Certificate</u>. The President of the Company shall deliver to the Purchasers at such Closing a certificate certifying that the conditions specified in <u>Sections 5.1 and 5.2</u> have been fulfilled.

5.4.   <u>Qualifications</u>. All authorizations, approvals or permits, if any, of any governmental authority or regulatory body of the United States or of any state that are required in connection with the lawful issuance and sale of the Shares pursuant to this Agreement shall be obtained and effective as of such Closing.

5.5.   <u>Opinion of Company Counsel</u>. The Purchasers shall have received from [____], counsel for the Company, an opinion, dated as of the Initial Closing, in substantially the form of <u>Exhibit I</u> attached to this Agreement.

5.6.   <u>Board of Directors</u>. As of the Initial Closing, the authorized size of the Board shall be [____], and the Board shall be comprised of [____].[44]

5.7   <u>Indemnification Agreement</u>. The Company and each Purchaser (other than the Purchaser relying upon this condition to excuse such Purchaser's performance hereunder) shall have executed and delivered the Indemnification Agreement.

5.8.   <u>Investors' Rights Agreement</u>. The Company and each Purchaser (other than the Purchaser relying upon this condition to excuse such Purchaser's performance hereunder) and the other stockholders of the Company named as parties thereto shall have executed and delivered the Investors' Rights Agreement.

5.9.   <u>Right of First Refusal and Co-Sale Agreement</u>. The Company, each Purchaser (other than the Purchaser relying upon this condition to excuse such Purchaser's performance hereunder), and the other stockholders of the Company named as parties thereto shall have executed and delivered the Right of First Refusal and Co-Sale Agreement.

5.10.   <u>Voting Agreement</u>. The Company, each Purchaser (other than the Purchaser relying upon this condition to excuse such Purchaser's performance hereunder), and the other stockholders of the Company named as parties thereto shall have executed and delivered the Voting Agreement.

5.11.   <u>Restated Certificate</u>. The Company shall have filed the

---

[44] If this section is used, the Company must take the actions necessary to elect the agreed-upon Board of Directors.

Restated Certificate with the Secretary of State of Delaware on or prior to the Closing, which shall continue to be in full force and effect as of the Closing.

5.12. Secretary's Certificate. The Secretary of the Company shall have delivered to the Purchasers at the Closing a certificate certifying (i) the Bylaws of the Company, (ii) resolutions of the Board of Directors of the Company approving the Transaction Agreements and the transactions contemplated under the Transaction Agreements, and (iii) resolutions of the stockholders of the Company approving the Restated Certificate.

5.13. Proceedings and Documents. All corporate and other proceedings in connection with the transactions contemplated at the Closing and all documents incident thereto shall be reasonably satisfactory in form and substance to each Purchaser, and each Purchaser (or its counsel) shall have received all such counterpart original and certified or other copies of such documents as reasonably requested. Such documents may include good standing certificates.

5.14 Minimum Number of Shares at Initial Closing. A minimum of [____] Shares must be sold at the Initial Closing.[45]

5.15 Management Rights.[46] A Management Rights Letter shall have been executed by the Company and delivered to each Purchaser to whom it is addressed.

[5.16 SBA Matters. The Company shall have executed and delivered to each SBIC Purchaser a Size Status Declaration on SBA Form 280 and an Assurance of Compliance on SBA Form 652, and shall have provided to each such Purchaser information necessary for the preparation of a Portfolio Financing Report on SBA Form 1031.]

[5.17 Preemptive Rights. The Company shall have fully satisfied (including with respect to rights of timely notification) or obtained enforceable waivers in respect of any preemptive or similar rights directly or indirectly affecting any of its securities.[47]]

---

[45] Sometimes the term sheet will specify that a minimum number of Shares must be sold at the Initial Closing.

[46] See explanatory commentary in introduction to model Management Rights Letter.

[47] Usually only necessary at a later round of financing, when there are existing preemptive rights holders.

6.   <u>Conditions of the Company's Obligations at Closing</u>. The obligations of the Company to sell Shares to the Purchasers at the Initial Closing [or any subsequent Closing] are subject to the fulfillment, on or before the Closing, of each of the following conditions, unless otherwise waived:

     6.1.   <u>Representations and Warranties</u>**.** The representations and warranties of each Purchaser contained in <u>Section [3/4]</u> shall be true and correct in all material respects as of such Closing.

     6.2.   <u>Performance</u>. The Purchasers shall have performed and complied with all covenants, agreements, obligations and conditions contained in this Agreement that are required to be performed or complied with by them on or before such Closing.

     6.3.   <u>Qualifications</u>. All authorizations, approvals or permits, if any, of any governmental authority or regulatory body of the United States or of any state that are required in connection with the lawful issuance and sale of the Share pursuant to this Agreement shall be obtained and effective as of the Closing.

     6.4.   <u>Investors' Rights Agreement</u>. Each Purchaser shall have executed and delivered the Investors' Rights Agreement.

     6.5.   <u>Right of First Refusal and Co-Sale Agreement</u>. Each Purchaser and the other stockholders of the Company named as parties thereto shall have executed and delivered the Right of First Refusal and Co-Sale Agreement.

     6.6.   <u>Voting Agreement</u>. Each Purchaser and the other stockholders of the Company named as parties thereto shall have executed and delivered the Voting Agreement.

     [6.7   <u>Minimum Number of Shares at Initial Closing</u>. A minimum of [____] Shares must be sold at the Initial Closing.]

7.   <u>Miscellaneous</u>.

     7.1.   <u>Survival of Warranties</u>. Unless otherwise set forth in this Agreement, the representations and warranties of the Company [, the Founders] and the Purchasers contained in or made pursuant to this Agreement shall survive the execution and delivery of this Agreement and the Closing and shall in no way be affected by any investigation or knowledge of the subject matter thereof made by or on behalf of the Purchasers or the

Company.[48]

   7.2. <u>Successors and Assigns</u>. The terms and conditions of this Agreement shall inure to the benefit of and be binding upon the respective successors and assigns of the parties. Nothing in this Agreement, express or implied, is intended to confer upon any party other than the parties hereto or their respective successors and assigns any rights, remedies, obligations, or liabilities under or by reason of this Agreement, except as expressly provided in this Agreement.

   7.3. <u>Governing Law</u>. This Agreement shall be governed by and construed in accordance with the General Corporation Law of the State of [Delaware] as to matters within the scope thereof, and as to all other matters shall be governed by and construed in accordance with the internal laws of [state of principal place of business], without regard to its principles of conflicts of laws.

   7.4. <u>Counterparts; Facsimile</u>. This Agreement may be executed and delivered by facsimile signature and in two or more counterparts, each of which shall be deemed an original, but all of which together shall constitute one and the same instrument.

   7.5. <u>Titles and Subtitles</u>. The titles and subtitles used in this Agreement are used for convenience only and are not to be considered in construing or interpreting this Agreement.

   7.6. <u>Notices</u>. All notices and other communications given or made pursuant to this Agreement shall be in writing and shall be deemed effectively given: (a) upon personal delivery to the party to be notified, (b) when sent by confirmed electronic mail or facsimile if sent during normal business hours of the recipient, and if not so confirmed, then on the next business day, (c) five (5) days after having been sent by registered or certified mail, return receipt requested, postage prepaid, or (d) one (1) day after deposit with a nationally recognized overnight courier, specifying next day delivery, with written verification of receipt. All communications shall be sent to the respective parties at their address as set forth on the signature page or <u>Exhibit A</u>, or to such e-mail address, facsimile number or address as subsequently modified by written notice given in accordance with this <u>Section 7.6</u>. If notice is given to the Company, a copy shall also be sent to [*Company*

---

[48] Sometimes a limited survival period is negotiated.

Counsel Name and Address] and if notice is given to the Purchasers, a copy shall also be given to [*Purchaser Counsel Name and Address].*

    7.7.   <u>No Finder's Fees</u>[49]. Each party represents that it neither is nor will be obligated for any finder's fee or commission in connection with this transaction. Each Purchaser agrees to indemnify and to hold harmless the Company from any liability for any commission or compensation in the nature of a finder's or broker's fee arising out of this transaction (and the costs and expenses of defending against such liability or asserted liability) for which each Purchaser or any of its officers, employees, or representatives is responsible. The Company agrees to indemnify and hold harmless each Purchaser from any liability for any commission or compensation in the nature of a finder's or broker's fee arising out of this transaction (and the costs and expenses of defending against such liability or asserted liability) for which the Company or any of its officers, employees or representatives is responsible.

    7.8.   <u>Fees and Expenses</u>. At the Closing, the Company shall pay the reasonable fees and expenses of [____], the counsel for [name of lead Purchaser[50]], in an amount not to exceed, in the aggregate, $[____].

    [7.9.   <u>Attorney's Fees</u>. If any action at law or in equity (including arbitration) is necessary to enforce or interpret the terms of any of the Transaction Agreements, the prevailing party shall be entitled to reasonable attorney's fees, costs and necessary disbursements in addition to any other relief to which such party may be entitled.]

    7.10   <u>Amendments and Waivers</u>.[51] Except as set forth in Section 1.3 of this Agreement, any term of this Agreement may be amended, terminated or waived only with the written consent of the Company and (i)

---

[49] This provision may need to be modified to fit the facts of a particular transaction.

[50] Typically, only the lead Purchaser is actually represented by counsel, with the other Purchasers relying on the lead Purchaser's having conducted due diligence and hired legal counsel. Occasionally, counsel will represent the Purchasers as a group, or one or more of the other Purchasers will have separate counsel, in which case this provision will need to be tailored accordingly.

[51] This provision may need to be tailored if there are to be Milestone Closings to permit or prevent, as appropriate, a majority from waiving or changing the agreed-upon milestones and related conditions. In addition, if Founder's representations are included, this provision may need to give the Founder protection against adverse amendments.

the holders of at least [*specify percentage*] of the then-outstanding Shares
or (ii) for an amendment, termination or waiver effected prior to the Initial
Closing, Purchasers obligated to purchase [*specify percentage*] of the Shares
to be issued at the Initial Closing. Any amendment or waiver effected in
accordance with this Section 7.10 shall be binding upon the Purchasers and
each transferee of the Shares (or the Common Stock issuable upon conversion
thereof), each future holder of all such securities, and the Company.

7.11.   Severability. The invalidity or unenforceability of any
provision hereof shall in no way affect the validity or enforceability of any
other provision.

7.12.   Delays or Omissions. No delay or omission to exercise any
right, power or remedy accruing to any party under this Agreement, upon
any breach or default of any other party under this Agreement, shall impair
any such right, power or remedy of such non-breaching or non-defaulting
party nor shall it be construed to be a waiver of any such breach or default,
or an acquiescence therein, or of or in any similar breach or default thereafter
occurring; nor shall any waiver of any single breach or default be deemed
a waiver of any other breach or default theretofore or thereafter occurring.
Any waiver, permit, consent or approval of any kind or character on the part
of any party of any breach or default under this Agreement, or any waiver
on the part of any party of any provisions or conditions of this Agreement,
must be in writing and shall be effective only to the extent specifically set
forth in such writing. All remedies, either under this Agreement or by law or
otherwise afforded to any party, shall be cumulative and not alternative.

7.13.   Entire Agreement. This Agreement (including the Exhibits
hereto), the Restated Certificate and the other Transaction Agreements
constitute the full and entire understanding and agreement between the
parties with respect to the subject matter hereof, and any other written or oral
agreement relating to the subject matter hereof existing between the parties
are expressly canceled.

[7.14   Corporate Securities Law.[52] THE SALE OF THE SECURITIES
WHICH ARE THE SUBJECT OF THIS AGREEMENT HAS NOT BEEN QUALIFIED
WITH THE COMMISSIONER OF CORPORATIONS OF THE STATE OF
CALIFORNIA AND THE ISSUANCE OF THE SECURITIES OR THE PAYMENT

---

[52] Section 7.14 is to be used for transactions governed by California law that are
not relying on NSMIA for a state securities law exemption.

OR RECEIPT OF ANY PART OF THE CONSIDERATION THEREFOR PRIOR
TO THE QUALIFICATION IS UNLAWFUL, UNLESS THE SALE OF SECURITIES
IS EXEMPT FROM THE QUALIFICATION BY SECTION 25100, 25102 OR
25105 OF THE CALIFORNIA CORPORATIONS CODE. THE RIGHTS OF ALL
PARTIES TO THIS AGREEMENT ARE EXPRESSLY CONDITIONED UPON THE
QUALIFICATION BEING OBTAINED UNLESS THE SALE IS SO EXEMPT.]

    7.15   <u>Dispute Resolution</u>.[53] The parties (a) hereby irrevocably
and unconditionally submit to the jurisdiction of the state courts of [state] and
to the jurisdiction of the United States District Court for the District of [judicial
district] for the purpose of any suit, action or other proceeding arising out of
or based upon this Agreement, (b) agree not to commence any suit, action
or other proceeding arising out of or based upon this Agreement except in
the state courts of [state[or the United States District Court for the District
of [judicial district], and (c) hereby waive, and agree not to assert, by way of
motion, as a defense, or otherwise, in any such suit, action or proceeding,
any claim that it is not subject personally to the jurisdiction of the above-
named courts, that its property is exempt or immune from attachment or
execution, that the suit, action or proceeding is brought in an inconvenient
forum, that the venue of the suit, action or proceeding is improper or that
this Agreement or the subject matter hereof may not be enforced in or by
such court. [*Alternative*: Any unresolved controversy or claim arising out
of or relating to this Agreement, except as (i) otherwise provided in this
Agreement, or (ii) any such controversies or claims arising out of either party's
intellectual property rights for which a provisional remedy or equitable relief
is sought, shall be submitted to arbitration by one arbitrator mutually agreed
upon by the parties, and if no agreement can be reached within thirty (30)
days after names of potential arbitrators have been proposed by the American
Arbitration Association (the "**AAA**"), then by one arbitrator having reasonable
experience in corporate finance transactions of the type provided for in this
Agreement and who is chosen by the AAA. The arbitration shall take place
in [location], in accordance with the AAA rules then in effect, and judgment
upon any award rendered in such arbitration will be binding and may be
entered in any court having jurisdiction thereof. There shall be limited

---

[53] Although the evidence is only anecdotal, many members of the Model
Documents Working Group expressed a preference for litigation rather than
arbitration. In the experience of some, contrary to its reputation, arbitration can
be even slower and more expensive than litigation.

discovery prior to the arbitration hearing as follows: (a) exchange of witness lists and copies of documentary evidence and documents relating to or arising out of the issues to be arbitrated, (b) depositions of all party witnesses and (c) such other depositions as may be allowed by the arbitrators upon a showing of good cause. Depositions shall be conducted in accordance with the [*State*] Code of Civil Procedure, the arbitrator shall be required to provide in writing to the parties the basis for the award or order of such arbitrator, and a court reporter shall record all hearings, with such record constituting the official transcript of such proceedings. [Each party will bear its own costs in respect of any disputes arising under this Agreement.] [The prevailing party shall be entitled to reasonable attorney's fees, costs, and necessary disbursements in addition to any other relief to which such party may be entitled.] Each of the parties to this Agreement consents to personal jurisdiction for any equitable action sought in the U.S. District Court for the District of [____] or any court of the [State][Commonwealth] of [*State] having subject matter jurisdiction.]*

[7.16   No Commitment for Additional Financing. The Company acknowledges and agrees that no Purchaser has made any representation, undertaking, commitment or agreement to provide or assist the Company in obtaining any financing, investment or other assistance, other than the purchase of the Shares as set forth herein and subject to the conditions set forth herein. In addition, the Company acknowledges and agrees that (i) no statements, whether written or oral, made by any Purchaser or its representatives on or after the date of this Agreement shall create an obligation, commitment or agreement to provide or assist the Company in obtaining any financing or investment, (ii) the Company shall not rely on any such statement by any Purchaser or its representatives and (iii) an obligation, commitment or agreement to provide or assist the Company in obtaining any financing or investment may only be created by a written agreement, signed by such Purchaser and the Company, setting forth the terms and conditions of such financing or investment and stating that the parties intend for such writing to be a binding obligation or agreement. Each Purchaser shall have the right, in it sole and absolute discretion, to refuse or decline to participate in any other financing of or investment in the Company, and shall have no obligation to assist or cooperate with the Company in obtaining any financing, investment or other assistance.]

[Remainder of Page Intentionally Left Blank]

IN WITNESS WHEREOF, the parties have executed this Series A Preferred Stock Purchase Agreement as of the date first written above.

COMPANY:

By: _____

Name: _____
(print)

Title: _____

Address: _____

[FOUNDERS:

By: _____

Name: _____
(print)

Title: _____

Address: _____

_____]

PURCHASERS:

_____
(Print Name of Purchaser)

By: _____

Name: _____
(print)

Title: _____

Address: _____

SIGNATURE PAGE TO PURCHASE AGREEMENT

EXHIBITS

Exhibit A -   Schedule of Purchasers

Exhibit B -   Form of Amended and Restated Certificate of Incorporation

Exhibit C -   Disclosure Schedule

Exhibit D -   Form of Indemnification Agreement

Exhibit E -   Form of Investors' Rights Agreement

Exhibit F -   Form of Management Rights Letter

Exhibit G -   Form of Right of First Refusal and Co-Sale Agreement

Exhibit H -   Form of Voting Agreement

Exhibit I -   Form of Legal Opinion of [Company Counsel]

[Exhibit J -   Milestone Events]

EXHIBIT A

SCHEDULE OF PURCHASERS

EXHIBIT B

FORM OF AMENDED AND RESTATED
CERTIFICATE OF INCORPORATION

EXHIBIT C

DISCLOSURE SCHEDULE

EXHIBIT D

FORM OF INDEMNIFICATION AGREEMENT

EXHIBIT E

FORM OF INVESTORS' RIGHTS AGREEMENT

<u>EXHIBIT F</u>

FORM OF MANAGEMENT RIGHTS LETTER

FORM OF RIGHT OF FIRST REFUSAL
AND CO-SALE AGREEMENT

EXHIBIT H

FORM OF VOTING AGREEMENT

EXHIBIT I

FORM OF LEGAL OPINION
OF
[COMPANY COUNSEL]

[EXHIBIT J]

MILESTONE EVENTS]

Index

A

Acceleration clause, in promissory note, 236–37
Accountants, importance of, 103
Accounts receivable, factoring of, 19
Accredited investor
  equity investment and, 175
  qualifying as, 244
Active Capital, 336
Adjustable interest rates, 164
Adobe Acrobat PDF files, 295–96
Advisors and mentors, 25
Affirmative covenants, 211
AFR (Applicable Federal Rate), 71–72, 123
Altruistic motives of investors, 43–44
Amortized loan, 129, 134
  promissory note for, 227–28
  repayment schedule for, 271–72
Amount of loan payment, 133–35
Amount of loan request
  calculating, 107–11
  dividing request among prospects, 111–13
  recurring cost estimates, 109–10
  start-up cost estimates, 108–9
  total funds needed, 110–11
  See also Loans
Angel Capital Association, 180, 336
Angels. See Business angels
Annual financial statements, 268
Annual report, 269
Antidilution provisions, 64, 210, 256
Applicable Federal Rate (AFR), 71–72, 123
Aspen Institute, 24
Association for Enterprise Opportunity, 183, 334
Attorneys, for equity investment, 66–67
Attorney's fees
  clause in promissory note, 238
  equity investments and, 213
Audited annual financial statements, 268

B

Bad-debt deduction, 73–75, 283
Balance sheet, 105
Balloon payments, 131

Bank financing, 20–25
  criteria used by, 21–22
  interest rates, 124
  rejection by bank, 37
Bankrate, 330
Behavior patterns of prospects
  analyzing, 91–95
  appealing to, 161–63
Best bets list of investors, 87–88
Blank forms. *See* Forms and
  worksheets
Board of directors, creating, 287–88
Bonus payment to investor, 164
Borrower, defined, 8
Break-even analysis, 105–6
Break-up fee in Term Sheet, 205
Business advisors and mentors, 25
Business angels, 26
  equity capital from, 177–78
  establishing a relationship with,
   188–89
  investment proposals and, 204
  locating, 178–80
  structured groups of, 180–82
  See also Equity investment
Business investing experience
  analyzing, 91–95
  of prospective investors, 89–90
Business letter to investors, 266–67
Business opportunity statement, 101
Business plan
  cover letter for, 107
  danger of not having one, 99
  equity investors and, 190
  executive summary, 107
  financial description, 103–6
  narrative description, 101–3
  preparing, 100–107
  resources for, 100
  supporting documents, 106

C

Cash flow statement, 105
C-Cap, 180
C corporation, 30–31
CDFI Fund, 335
CD-ROM
  forms and worksheets listed, 299
  installing files from, 291
  online resources, 297
  UCC Financing Statement file,
   295–96
  word processing files for
   documents, 291–95
Census Bureau, 333
Center for Venture Research, 337
Certified public accounts and audits,
  268
Chamber of Commerce, 333
Charter, 209–10
CircleLending, 3–4, 335
"Closing; Delivery" paragraphs, 251
Closing the deal
  conditions required in the SPA, 254
  equity investment, 258–59
  private business loans, 257–58
Collateral for loans, 60–61, 118–23
  depreciation of asset and, 121
  family loans and, 119
  what to offer, 120–23
Common stock, 206
Communicating with lenders and
  investors
  formal communication, 265–69

importance of, 262–64
informal communication, 264–65
Community Development Financial
  Institutions Fund, 335
Community Development Venture
  Capital Alliance, 337
Company Corporation, 331
Competition, statement about in
  business plan, 102
Confidentiality provision, 207
Convertible note, 165
Convertible stock, 206
Corporate business structure, 30–31
CPAs and audits, 268
Credit card interest rates, 124
Credit rating, improving with private
  loans, 13, 41
Credit report
  AnnualCreditReport.com, 330
  obtaining, 160
Customer mailings, 265

D

Defaulting on a loan, 283–84
Demand option in loan agreement,
  163–65
Demographic information, in
  business plan, 102
Depreciation of asset used for
  collateral, 121
Dilution protection, 64, 210, 256
Disclosure obligations
  private placement memorandum
    (PPM), 244–46
  risk discussions added to existing
    documents, 245–46
  understanding, 242–43

Documentation
  averting misunderstandings with,
    221–22
  clarification of expectations, 217–20
  equity investment requirements,
    221
  importance of, 216–17
Due diligence, equity investors and,
  203, 207, 208

E

Editing document files, 293–94
Employees, statement about in
  business plan, 103
Equity investment
  advantages and disadvantages, 68
  attorney must document, 66–67
  closing the deal, 258–59
  compensating investors, 186
  establishing a relationship, 184–88
  growth of business and, 284–86
  hybrid forms of, 165
  indecisive investors, 197–98
  investment proposal, drafting,
    201–3
  investor expectations, managing,
    286–87
  letter of intent, 193–99
  locating investors, 172, 174–83
  online resources, 336–38
  participation levels of investors, 187
  pitch meeting, 189–93
  protections for, 64–65
  reluctant investors, 199
  rewards of, 62–64
  securities laws compliance, 65–66,
    173

setting up, 61–67

shared ownership, 65

term sheet, 200–201

written agreement requirement, 221

Equity investor, defined, 8

Executive summary, in business plan, 107

F

Family bank approach to loans, 86

Financial description, in business plan, 103–6

Financial statements for investors, 267–69

Financing options

bank financing, 20–25

existing business resources and, 18–19

family and friends, 19–20

features of, 54

legal structure of business and, 27–34

minimizing the amount needed, 15–16

primary sources, 14

by stage of business, 15

tax implications of options, 67–76

venture capital investors, 25–26

your personal money, 16–18

See also Business angels; Equity investment; Gifts; Loans

Forms and worksheets

blank forms, 300–327

listed, 299

Friends-and-family loans. *See* Private party loans

G

GAAP (generally accepted accounting practices), 268

GEM Study, 3

Generally accepted accounting practices (GAAP), 268

Gift giver, defined, 8

Gifts

gift letter, 223–25

setting up, 55–56

Gift tax exemptions

IRS limits on, 69–70

private loans to maximize, 48

Global Entrepreneurship Monitor

GEM Study, 3

website of, 331

Governing law clause, in promissory note, 239

Grace period, for loan payment, 280

Graduated loan, 130

promissory note language, 232

repayment schedule for, 273–74

H

Holiday cards, 264–65

I

Income statement, 105

Inc. survey of start-up capital, 2

Individual retirement accounts, self-directed and private loans, 156–57

Inexperienced and analytical prospect, 94–95

Inexperienced and worried prospect, 93–94

Informal loans. *See* Private party loans

Installing the CD-ROM files, 291
Interest-only loan, 130–31, 134
   promissory note language, 233–34
   repayment schedule for, 274–75
Interest rates
   adjustable interest rates, 164
   Applicable Federal Rate, 71–72, 123
   for loans, 58, 59, 123–26
   private financing and, 38, 45
   SBA 7(a) loan program, 38, 39, 124
   state limits on, 125–26
   tax liability for paying too little,
      71–72
Internal rate of return (IRR), 64
Internal Revenue Service. *See* IRS
Interpersonal loans. *See* Private party
   loans
Investment proposal, drafting, 201–3
Investor relations page for website,
   269
Investors
   advantages of private financing by,
      42–49
   behavior patterns of prospects,
      91–95
   best bets list, 87–88
   defined, 8
   developing a list of prospects, 78–88
   evaluating the prospects, 89–95
   family bank approach, 86
   most promising type of, 85
   narrowing the list of prospects,
      81–87
   who makes investments, 79
   See also "Kitchen table pitch"
IRAs, self-directed and private loans,
   156–57

IRR (internal rate of return), 64
IRS
   Applicable Federal Rate, 71–72, 123
   website resources of, 331
   See also Tax issues

K

Kaufman Foundation, 332
Key employees, statement about in
   business plan, 103
"Kitchen table pitch"
   cultivating prospects over time, 153
   follow-up meetings, 155
   hesitancies and concerns of
      prospect, 156–60
   make the pitch compelling, 149–55
   planning for, 144–49
   prospect says "No," what to do
      next, 167–69
   prospect says "Yes," what to do
      next, 160–67
   what to bring along, 148
   where to meet, 146–47
   See also Investors

L

Lease-backs, 19
Legal structure of business
   advantages and drawbacks of,
      32–33
   C corporation, 30–31
   fundraising possibilities and, 27–28
   limited liability company (LLC), 32
   partnership, 29–30
   resources for choosing, 34
   S corporation, 31
   sole proprietorship, 28–29

tax issues, 75–76

Lemonade Stories, 42, 43, 332

Lender, defined, 8

Letter of intent
 consideration of equity investment,
  193–99
 term sheet compared to, 204

Limited liability company (LLC), 32

Liquidation preference, 64, 210

LLC (limited liability company), 32

Loan repayment forgiveness letter, 69,
 224–25

Loans
 administration by third party,
  135–36
 advantages and disadvantages, 68
 closing the deal, 257–58
 collateral for, 60–61, 118–23
 defaulting on, 283–84
 grace period, 280
 interest rates, 58, 59, 123–26
 interest rates, paying too little,
  71–72
 log for payments, 275–77
 management of, 61
 online resources for, 334–36
 paying on time, 270–78
 payment terms, 126–36
 repayment schedule, 271–75
 repayment schedule, changing,
  281–82
 request letter, 136–37
 sample letter, 137–42
 setting up, 57–61
 tax deductions for, 72–73
 tax deductions for lender, 73–75
 tax liability, 70–72

 terms of, 117–18
 trouble making payments, 279–82
 written agreement and repayment
  schedule, 57–58
 See also Amount of loan request;
  Private party loans

Log for loan payments, 275–77

Logo for your business, 148

M

Market analysis, 102

Microenterprise assistance, 24, 183

MicroMentor, 332

Mixing money and relationships
 comfort level of prospective
  investor, 90
 private party loans, 49–52

Motown Records start-up financing, 6

N

Narrative description, in business
 plan, 101–3

National Congress for Community
 Economic Development, 335

National Venture Capital Association,
 337
 sample Preferred Stock Purchase
  Agreement, 360–416
 sample Term Sheet, 340–59

Negative covenants, 211

Non-waiver clause, in promissory
 note, 238

No-shop provision, 207

Notarizing, the signing of a
 promissory note, 240–41

NVCA. See National Venture Capital
 Association

O

Offering Terms, 208–9
Online resources
  accessing on the CD-ROM, 297
  equity investing resources, 336–38
  general business resources, 330–34
  loan capital resources, 334–36
Opening document files, 292–93
Operating plan, 101–2

P

Partnership, 29–30
Payment terms for a loan, 126–36
  amortized loan, 129, 134
  amount of payment, 133–35
  balloon payments, 131
  frequency of payments, 128
  graduated loan, 130
  interest-only loan, 130–31, 134
  seasonal payments, 132
PDF files, 295–96
Pensco Trust Company, 332
Personality types. *See* Behavior
  patterns of prospects
Personnel, statement about in
  business plan, 103
Pitching your business idea. *See*
  "Kitchen table pitch"
Post-money valuation, 209
PPM (private placement
  memorandum), 244–46
Preferred stock, 206
Pre-money valuation, 209
Prepayment clause, in promissory
  note, 237
Press clippings, 265

Printing
  document files, 294
  PDF form, 296
Private party loans
  advantages for entrepreneur, 36–42
  advantages for investor, 42–49
  defined, 8
  family and friends, 19–20
  mixing money and relationships,
    49–52
  overcoming poor credit rating with,
    13, 41
  primary sources of, 14
  See also Loans
Private placement memorandum
  (PPM), 244–46
Pro forma financials, 105–6
Projections in business plans, 105–6
Promissory note
  preparing, 225–41
  secured interest provision, 122–23,
    234–36
  signing, 239–41
Prospective investors. *See* Investors

Q

Quarterly financial statements, 267

R

README file, 290
Recurring cost estimates, 109–10
Regulation D exemption, 173, 243
Representations and warranties
  made by company, 251–53
  made by founders, 253
  made by investor, 254

in Term Sheet, 210–11
Return on investment (ROI), 64
Revenue-linked loan, 165
Right of first refusal
  subsequent financing rounds,
    256–57
  term sheet provision for, 211–12
Risk disclosure. *See* Disclosure
  obligations
ROI (return on investment), 64
Royalty-based financing, 165
RTF (word processing) files for
  documents, 291–95

S

"Sale and Issuance" paragraphs, 251
Sale-backs, 19
Saving document files, 294–95
Savvy and analytical prospect, 92–93
Savvy and worried prospect, 92
SBA. *See* Small Business
  Administration
SBICs (Small Business Investment
  Companies), 337
SCORE (Service Corps of Retired
  Executives), 25, 333
S corporation, 31
Seasonal loan, 132
  promissory note language, 232–33
  repayment schedule for, 272–73
SEC. *See* Securities and Exchange
  Commission
Secured interest provision, in
  promissory note, 122–23, 234–36
Securities and Exchange Commission
  disclosure rules for selling shares,
    242–43

registration exemptions, 66, 173
  website resources, 338
Securities laws compliance, 65–66,
  173
Self-directed IRAs, private loans and,
  156–57
Self-interested motives of investors,
  44–47
Service Corps of Retired Executives
  (SCORE), 25, 333
Signing, promissory note, 239–41
Small Business Administration (SBA)
  equity investment program of, 337
  MicroLoan Program, 24
  7(a) loan program, 22–23
  7(a) loan program interest rates, 38,
    39, 124
  Small Business Development
    Centers, 25
  Small Business Investment
    Companies, 337
  website resources, 333–34, 335–36
Small business exemption
  prohibition against soliciting
    investors, 243
  See also Securities and Exchange
    Commission
Small Business Investment
  Companies (SBICs), 337
Sole proprietorship, 28–29
Sources and Uses of Funds Table, 104
SPA. *See* Stock purchase agreement
Start-up costs
  estimating, 108–9
  primary sources of financing, 14
Start-up loan, 130
  See also Graduated loan

State limits on interest rates, 125–26
Stock
   protection and privileges for
    investors, 209–10
   types of for term sheet, 205–6
Stock purchase agreement
   "Closing; Delivery" paragraphs, 251
   disclosure obligations, 242–46
   exhibits for, 247
   private placement memorandum
    (PPM), 244–46
   protections for family-and-friend
    investors, 255–57
   representations and warranties
    made by company, 251–53
   representations and warranties
    made by founders, 253
   representations and warranties
    made by investor, 254
   "Sale and Issuance" paragraphs, 251
   sample NVCA Preferred Stock
    Purchase Agreement, 360–416
   sample table of contents, 248–50
   See also Term Sheet
Subway start-up financing, 5
Supporting documents, for business
   plan, 106

T

Tax issues
   bad-debt deduction, 73–75, 283
   gifts and, 48, 69–70
   legal structure of business and,
    75–76
   loans and, 70–75
   See also IRS

Term Sheet, 200–201
   amount of investment, 208–9
   backing out after signing, 205
   binding nature of, 205
   investor's offer in, 203–5
   no-shop provision, 207
   representations and warranties,
    210–11
   right of first refusal, 211–12
   sample NVCA Term Sheet, 340–59
   stock protection and privileges,
    209–10
   stock types in, 205–6
   See also Stock purchase agreement
The Limited start-up financing, 7
Total funds needed, 110–11
Trade credit, 19

U

UCC Financing Statement, 234–36
   CD-ROM file, 295–96
Unsecured private loans, 119–20
UPS start-up financing, 3
U.S. Census Bureau, 333
U.S. Chamber of Commerce, 333
Uses of Funds Table, 104
U.S. Small Business Administration.
   See Small Business Administration
Usury laws, 125–26

V

Valuation of the business, 209
Venture capital investors, 25–26,
   182–83
Veto rights over financing, 256
Virgin Records, 43

W

Waiver clause, in promissory note, 238

Wall Street Journal Center for Entrepreneurs, 334

Wal-Mart start-up financing, 4

Warranties. *See* Representations and warranties

Websites
 Angel Investor News website, 179, 180, 336
 AnnualCreditReport.com, 330
 Bplans.com, 331
 www.everybusinessneedsanangel .com, 337
 Fortune magazine website, 335
 LogoYes.com, 148, 332
 Nolo website resources, 332

Word processing files for documents, 291–95

Worksheets. *See* Forms and worksheets

Written agreement. *See* Documentation

Advertisement

Quicken Legal Business Pro 2006
Windows CD-ROM
Software
SBQB6
$109.99

When starting and running a business, most of the legal work involved simply requires proper forms and reliable information—and with *Quicken Legal Business Pro*, you'll get everything you need to get the job done and save money on legal fees.

The software provides over 140 legal, business, tax and marketing documents—many of which you can complete onscreen with a simple step-by-step interview!

Powered with the contents of five Nolo business books, *Quicken Legal Business Pro* also provides a robust business library. Find answers quickly and easily to your business questions! Books in the program include:
- *Legal Guide for Starting & Running a Small Business*
- *Tax Savvy for Small Business*
- *Everyday Employment Law: The Basics*
- *Leasing Space for Your Small Business*
- *Marketing Without Advertising*

Completely searchable, *Quicken Legal Business Pro* is the all-in-one legal resource that every businessperson needs. Give your business the advantage it needs to succeed—get it today!

Want a big discount on *Quicken Legal Business Pro*?
ORDER IT ONLINE AT NOLO.COM

more from

NOLO
Law for All

Tax Savvy for Small Business
by Attorney Frederick W. Daily

Nearly every decision a business makes has tax consequences that affect its bottom line, and the IRS is always watching. Fortunately, it's possible to run an honest business, minimize taxes and stay out of trouble—and this book shows you how.

$36.99/SAVVY

Deduct It!
Lower Your Small Business Taxes
by Attorney Stephen Fishman

The fastest way for any small business to make more money is to pay less to the IRS. Let *Deduct It!* show you how to maximize the business deductions you're entitled to—quickly, easily and legally. Covers start-up costs, operating expenses, meals, travel, vehicles, inventory, entertainment, equipment and more!

$34.99/DEDU

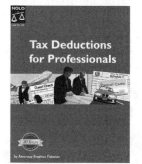

Tax Deductions for Professionals
by Attorney Stephen Fishman

What do architects, lawyers, dentists, chiropractors, doctors and other licensed professionals have in common? Answer: Special tax considerations. If you're ready to hold on to more of your hard-earned money, turn to *Tax Deductions for Professionals*.

$34.99/DEPO

CATALOG

...more from nolo

CONSUMER

	PRICE	CODE
How to Win Your Personal Injury Claim	$29.99	PICL
Nolo's Encyclopedia of Everyday Law	$29.99	EVL
Nolo's Guide to California Law	$24.99	CLAW

ESTATE PLANNING & PROBATE

	PRICE	CODE
8 Ways to Avoid Probate	$19.99	PRAV
Estate Planning Basics	$21.99	ESPN
The Executor's Guide: Settling a Loved One's Estate or Trust	$34.99	EXEC
How to Probate an Estate in California	$49.99	PAE
Make Your Own Living Trust (Book w/CD-ROM)	$39.99	LITR
Nolo's Simple Will Book (Book w/CD-ROM)	$36.99	SWIL
Plan Your Estate	$44.99	NEST
Quick & Legal Will Book	$16.99	QUIC
Quicken Willmaker: Estate Planning Essentials (Book w/ Interactive CD-ROM)	$49.99	QWMB
Special Needs Trust: Protect Your Child's Financial Future	$34.99	SPNT

FAMILY MATTERS

	PRICE	CODE
Building a Parenting Agreement That Works	$24.99	CUST
The Complete IEP Guide	$34.99	IEP
Divorce & Money: How to Make the Best Financial Decisions During Divorce	$34.99	DIMO
Do Your Own California Adoption: Nolo's Guide for Stepparents and Domestic Partners (Book w/CD-ROM)	$34.99	ADOP
Every Dog's Legal Guide: A Must-Have for Your Owner	$19.99	DOG
Get a Life: You Don't Need a Million to Retire Well	$24.99	LIFE
The Guardianship Book for California	$39.99	GB
A Legal Guide for Lesbian and Gay Couples	$34.99	LG
Living Together: A Legal Guide (Book w/CD-ROM)	$34.99	LTK
Living Wills and Powers of Attorney in California (Book w/CD-ROM)	$21.99	CPOA
Nolo's IEP Guide: Learning Disabilities	$29.99	IELD
Prenuptial Agreements: How to Write a Fair & Lasting Contract (Book w/CD-ROM)	$34.99	PNUP
Using Divorce Mediation: Save Your Money & Your Sanity	$29.99	UDMD

GOING TO COURT

	PRICE	CODE
Beat Your Ticket: Go To Court and Win! (National Edition)	$21.99	BEYT
The Criminal Law Handbook: Know Your Rights, Survive the System	$34.99	KYR
Evrybody's Guide to Small Claims Court (National Edition)	$26.99	NSCC
Everybody's Guide to Small Claims Court in California	$29.99	CSCC
Fight Your Ticket and Win in California	$29.99	FYT
How to Change Your Name in California	$34.99	NAME
How to Collect When You Win a Lawsuit (California Edition)	$29.99	JUDG
The Lawsuit Survival Guide	$29.99	UNCL
Nolo's Deposition Handbook	$29.99	DEP
Represent Yourself in Court: How to Prepare & Try a Winning Case	$34.99	RYC
Win Your Lawsuit: A Judge's Guide to Representing Yourself in CA Superior Court	$29.99	SLWY

HOMEOWNERS, LANDLORDS & TENANTS

	PRICE	CODE
California Tenants' Rights	$27.99	CTEN
Deeds for California Real Estate	$24.99	DEED
Every Landlord's Legal Guide (National Edition, Book w/CD-ROM)	$44.99	ELLI
Every Landlord's Tax Deduction Guide	$34.99	DELL
Every Tenant's Legal Guide	$29.99	EVTEN
For Sale by Owner in California	$29.99	FSBO
How to Buy a House in California	$34.99	BHCA
The California Landlord's Law Book: Rights & Responsibilities (Book w/CD-ROM)	$44.99	LBRT
The California Landlord's Law Book: Evictions (Book w/CD-ROM)	$44.99	LBEV
Leases & Rental Agreements	$29.99	LEAR
Neighbor Law: Fences, Trees, Boundaries & Noise	$26.99	NEI
The New York Landlord's Law Book (Book w/CD-ROM)	$39.99	NYLL
New York Tenants' Rights	$29.99	NYTEN
Renters' Rights (National Edition)	$24.99	RENT

IMMIGRATION	PRICE	CODE
Becoming a U.S. Citizen: A Guide to the Law, Exam and Interview	$24.99	USCIT
Fiancé & Marriage Visas (Book w/ CD-ROM)	$44.99	IMAR
How to Get a Green Card	$29.99	GRN
Student & Tourist Visas	$29.99	ISTU
U.S. Immigration Made Easy	$44.99	IMEZ

MONEY MATTERS

	PRICE	CODE
101 Law Forms for Personal Use (Book w/CD-ROM)	$29.99	SPOT
Bankruptcy: Is It the Right Solution to Your Debt Problems?	$21.99	BRS
Chapter 13 Bankruptcy: Repay Your Debts	$36.99	CHB
Credit Repair (Book w/CD-ROM)	$24.99	CREP
Getting Paid: How to Collect from Bankrupt Debtors	$29.99	CRBNK
How to File for Chapter 7 Bankruptcy	$29.99	HFB
IRAs, 401(k)s & Other Retirement Plans: Taking Your Money Out	$34.99	RET
Solve Your Money Troubles	$29.99	MT
Stand Up to the IRS	$29.99	SIRS
Surviving an IRS Tax Audit	$24.95	SAUD
Take Control of Your Student Loan Debt	$26.95	SLOAN

PATENTS AND COPYRIGHTS

	PRICE	CODE
All I Need is Money: How to Finance Your Invention	$19.99	FINA
The Copyright Handbook: How to Protect and Use Written Works (Book w/CD-ROM)	$39.99	COHA
Copyright Your Software (Book w/CD-ROM)	$34.95	CYS
Getting Permission: How to License and Clear Copyrighted Materials Online and Off (Book w/CD-ROM)	$34.99	RIPER
How to Make Patent Drawings Yourself	$29.99	DRAW
The Inventor's Notebook	$24.99	INOT
License Your Invention (Book w/CD-ROM)	$39.99	LICE
Nolo's Patents for Beginners	$29.99	QPAT
Patent, Copyright & Trademark	$39.99	PCTM
Patent It Yourself	$49.99	PAT
Patent Pending in 24 Hours	$29.99	PEND
The Public Domain	$34.99	PUBL
Trademark: Legal Care for Your Business and Product Name	$39.99	TRD
Web and Software Development: A Legal Guide (Book w/ CD-ROM)	$44.99	SFT
What Every Inventor Needs to Know About Business and Taxes (Book w/ CD-ROM)	$34.99	ILAX

RESEARCH & REFERENCE

	PRICE	CODE
Legal Research: How to Find & Understand the Law	$39.99	LRES

SENIORS

	PRICE	CODE
Long-Term Care: How to Plan & Pay for It	$21.99	ELD
Social Security, Medicare & Goverment Pensions	$29.99	SOA

SOFTWARE

Call or check our website at www.nolo.com for special discounts on Software!

	PRICE	CODE
Incorporator Pro	$89.99	STNC1
LLC Maker—Windows	$89.95	LLP1
Patent Pending Now!	$19.99	PP1
PatentEase—Windows	$349.00	PEAS
Personal RecordKeeper 5.0 CD—Windows	$59.95	RKD5
Quicken Legal Business Pro 2006—Windows	$109.99	SBQB6
Quicken WillMaker Plus 2006—Windows	$79.99	WQP6

SPECIAL UPGRADE OFFER—Get 35% off the latest edition of your Nolo book

It's important to have the most current legal information. Because laws and legal procedures change often, we update our books regularly. To help keep you up-to-date we are extending this special upgrade offer. Cut out and mail the title portion of the cover of your old Nolo book and we'll give you 35% off the retail price of the NEW EDITION of that book when you purchase directly from us. For more information call us at 1-800-728-3555. This offer is to individuals only.

Order Form

Name _____

Address _____

City _____

State, Zip _____

Daytime Phone _____

E-mail _____

Item Code	Quantity	Item	Unit Price	Total Price

Method of payment

☐ Check   ☐ VISA   ☐ MasterCard
☐ Discover Card   ☐ American Express

Subtotal	
Add your local sales tax (California only)	
Shipping: RUSH $12, Basic $9 (See below)	
"I bought 3, ship it to me FREE!"(Ground shipping only)	
TOTAL	

Account Number _____

Expiration Date _____

Signature _____

Shipping and Handling

Rush Delivery—Only $12

We'll ship any order to any street address in the U.S. by UPS 2nd Day Air* for only $12!

* Order by noon Pacific Time and get your order in 2 business days. Orders placed after noon Pacific Time will arrive in 3 business days. P.O. boxes and S.F. Bay Area use basic shipping. Alaska and Hawaii use 2nd Day Air or Priority Mail.

Basic Shipping—$9

Use for P.O. Boxes, Northern California and Ground Service.

Allow 1-2 weeks for delivery. U.S. addresses only.

For faster service, use your credit card and our toll-free numbers

**Call our customer service group
Monday thru Friday 7am to 7pm PST**

Phone	1-800-728-3555
Fax	1-800-645-0895
Mail	Nolo
950 Parker St.
Berkeley, CA 94710

Order 24 hours a day @
www.nolo.com

Remember:

Little publishers have big ears.
We really listen to you.

Take 2 Minutes & Give Us Your 2 cents

Your comments make a big difference in the development and revision of Nolo books and software. Please take a few minutes and register your Nolo product—and your comments—with us. Not only will your input make a difference, you'll receive special offers available only to registered owners of Nolo products on our newest books and software. Register now by:

PHONE
1-800-728-3555

FAX
1-800-645-0895

EMAIL
cs@nolo.com

or **MAIL** us
this registration card

fold here

Registration Card

NAME _____ DATE _____

ADDRESS _____

CITY _____ STATE _____ ZIP _____

PHONE _____ EMAIL _____

WHERE DID YOU HEAR ABOUT THIS PRODUCT? _____

WHERE DID YOU PURCHASE THIS PRODUCT? _____

DID YOU CONSULT A LAWYER? (PLEASE CIRCLE ONE)   YES   NO   NOT APPLICABLE

DID YOU FIND THIS BOOK HELPFUL?   (VERY)   5   4   3   2   1   (NOT AT ALL)

COMMENTS _____
_____
_____

WAS IT EASY TO USE?   (VERY EASY)   5   4   3   2   1   (VERY DIFFICULT)

We occasionally make our mailing list available to carefully selected companies whose products may be of interest to you.
❑ If you do not wish to receive mailings from these companies, please check this box.
❑ You can quote me in future Nolo promotional materials.
   Daytime phone number _____ .

FINBUS 1.0

fold here

- -

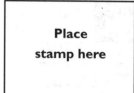

Place
stamp here

Nolo
950 Parker Street
Berkeley, CA 94710-9867

Attn: FINBUS 1.0